RITUALIZING ON THE BOUNDARIES

Studies in Comparative Religion
Frederick M. Denny, Series Editor

RITUALIZING ON THE BOUNDARIES

Continuity and Innovation in the Tamil Diaspora

FRED W. CLOTHEY

The University of South Carolina Press

Published by the University of South Carolina Press
Columbia, South Carolina 29208

www.sc.edu/uscpress

Manufactured in the United States of America

15 14 13 12 11 10 09 08 07 06 10 9 8 7 6 5 4 3 2 1
Clothey, Fred W.
Ritualizing on the boundaries : continuity and innovation in the Tamil diaspora / Fred W. Clothey.
p. cm. — (Studies in comparative religion)
Includes bibliographical references and index.
ISBN-13: 978-1-57003-647-7 (cloth : alk. paper)
ISBN-10: 1-57003-647-0 (cloth : alk. paper)
1. Tamil (Indic people)—India—Bombay—Rites and ceremonies. 2. Tamil (Indic people)—Malaysia—Rites and ceremonies. 3. Tamil (Indic people)—Singapore—Rites and ceremonies. 4. Tamil (Indic people)—Ethnic identity. 5. Hindu diaspora. I. Title. II. Series: Studies in comparative religion (Columbia, S.C.)
BL2032.T3C56 2006
305.89'4811—dc22
2006016890

This book was printed on Glatfelter Natures, a recycled paper with 50 percent postconsumer waste content.

CONTENTS

ILLUSTRATIONS

Figures

Maps

Tables

SERIES EDITOR'S PREFACE

An earlier book in this series that also addresses Tamil Hindu beliefs and practices is *The Vernacular Veda: Revelation, Recitation, and Ritual* by Vasudha Narayanan (1994). The focus of that book is the *Tiruvaymoli,* a tenth-century Tamil-language poem that became—and continues to be—an essential part of the Tamil devotional canon. Following extensive field research within Tamil communities and temples of South India, the author reported on contemporary ritual piety based on the *Tiruvaymoli.*

Fred W. Clothey has gone beyond native South Asian Tamil locations to investigate quite diverse diasporic Tamil communities. The importance of his idea of "ritualizing on the boundaries" is considerable, as it provides the context for a detailed, historically and culturally well-informed survey of people's lives, beliefs, and practices in Tamil populations in Singapore; Kuala Lumpur, Malaysia; Pittsburgh, Pennsylvania; and the Indian port-city of Mumbai.

Ritualizing on the Boundaries: Continuity and Innovation in the Tamil Diaspora is broad and ambitious in scope and treatment, combining the fruits of the author's many years of field observation as well as textually based research. Now we have an opportunity to read and reflect on the considerable accumulation of Clothey's findings within the contemporary contexts of globalization (and "glolocalization," as coined by Roland Robertson) and of the increasingly diasporic dispersion of Tamil peoples (not limited to Hindus, but also including "Tamil Muslims" as well as "Muslim Tamils" of differing orientations and socioeconomic classes in Mumbai). Of particular interest in the project is how Clothey addresses the ways in which Tamil people re-create and reinterpret, in new cultural and national contexts, their familiar and beloved religio-cultural surroundings through ritual, linguistic, architectural, and artistic practices stemming from their ethnic and cultural origins in South India. Thus, the project treats, in considerable detail, how Tamils are engaged in influencing and controlling (to some degree) the continuities—and the challenging transitions and transformations—of their customs and traditions in diverse regions. This process is of central importance in Tamil identity preservation as well as to how Tamil people invent ways of surviving and prospering in alien environments. But, as Clothey's book also demonstrates, Tamil folk have been doing precisely that, in creative and courageous ways, for over a thousand years. *Ritualizing on the Boundaries* is not only a penetrating comparative study of Tamil Hindus and Muslims, but also an innovative discourse that will be of value to scholars and students of other diasporic communities in today's religious worlds.

Frederick M. Denny

PREFACE

This volume has been taking shape for longer than I like to admit. In a certain sense it started in my youth, when I spent years in Tamil Nadu, befriended by its people and shaped by its culture. Yet from the time I lived in a relatively isolated, largely American boarding school in the hills of South India until my late college years, I struggled to come to terms with my bicultural identity. In retrospect, only as an adult did I learn to be comfortable as a "global nomad" who lived, worked, and thought on the boundaries between cultures, religions, and academic disciplines.

In many ways, therefore, I identify with the people described in this book, especially in their struggle to define and redefine themselves while living away from their ancestral home. At the same time, however, I am painfully aware of my being an outsider to them, humbled that I cannot fully enter into the world of expatriated Tamils and thus fully grasp every nuance of their experience. As a result, my research is always collaborative, always indebted to partners and colleagues who have been generous in sharing their time and emic insights.

I also share a certain discomfort with my American identity, not least of all with the assumptions of the American academy and especially with its disciplinary fiefdoms and their reliance on paradigms and theories that are all too Euro-American. One result of this dialogue between emic and etic, field and academy, in my work, and especially in this volume, is my tendency to offer modest theoretical suggestions only after consideration of the view of "insiders" rather than imposing grand theories on the data at the outset.

The studies that compose this volume have been done over more than two decades, starting with the months when I first joined the faculty of the University of Pittsburgh. Serendipitously, the community of Indian immigrants in the city was in the early stages of constructing a temple, and I was intrigued by the process and privileged to observe it throughout. A grant from the Pennsylvania Committee for the Humanities enabled me and my assistants to do a comprehensive survey of the growing Indian community in the Pittsburgh area. If I am not mistaken, it was the first formal study of Indian Americans in the United States. The same grant enabled us to film the ceremonies associated with the dedication of the new Śrī Veṅkaṭeśvara Temple. The experience piqued my interest in the way South Indians, and especially Tamils, were using ritual to negotiate their adjustments to life outside their ancestral homes. My essay summarizing this process first appeared in the volume *Rhythm and Intent,* published in 1983 by Blackie and Son of Chennai, India. That volume is now out of print, but the essay has been modified and updated and appears in this volume as chapter 2 with the permission of the publishers.

Much of the subsequent ethnography for this volume was done in 1991–92. Thanks to a fellowship from the American Institute of Indian Studies, I was able to spend several months in Mumbai, mentored by Professor K. K. A. Venkatacharya, then director of the Anantacarya Indological Institute. During that period I familiarized myself with the overall religious landscape of Mumbai; then, especially with the help of colleagues in the institute, I spent considerable time in conversations with a wide range of Tamils—from scholars to street vendors. Most of my time was spent in Matunga, the center of the Tamil establishment; in Chembur, a growing subdivision in the north-central portion of the city; in Dharavi, said to be Asia's largest slum; and in Cheetah Camp, a recently created subdivision along the inner harbor, populated almost entirely by lower- and middle-class Tamils. Many of the discussions that follow in this book were gathered and stimulated during these months of research, especially those on the Smārta brahmin establishments in Mumbai (chapter 5), on the Nadars of Dharavi (chapter 4), on the Navarāttiri festival (chapter 8), and some portions of the material on the Aruṇakiri singers (chapter 10).

The Mumbai research was followed in 1992 by several months of research in Malaysia and Singapore while I was a Fulbright Southeast Asia Regional Fellow. I was hosted in Kuala Lumpur by the Department of Indian Studies of the University of Malaya, where Professors P. Rajoo and Singaravelu and Professor Raymond Lee of the Department of Anthropology were especially generous with their time. In Singapore I was hosted by the Southeast Asian Institute on the campus of the Singapore National University. During these months much of the research was done on the Tai Pūcam festival (chapter 9), the Kuala Lumpur variations of the libations with 1,008 pots (chapter 7), and the brahmins of the Malaysian Peninsula (chapter 5), as well as the fieldwork on the Singapore temples (chapter 3).

I was able to spend an additional summer in Mumbai in 1994, funded again by the American Institute of Indian Studies and hosted again by the Anantacarya Indological Institute. During that period I could not only revisit and supplement my understandings from previous study but also collect most of my findings on the Tamil Muslims of Dharavi and Cheetah Camp (chapter 6). Dr. V. Parthasarathy of Anantacarya Institute and my research assistant, Ms. Tasqeen Macchiawalla, were especially helpful during that period.

I spent several subsequent summers in Hyderabad, India (1999–2001), accompanying students engaged in a study program at the University of Hyderabad. During these months I engaged in some research on the ways Tamils were participating in a popular Hyderabad festival known as Bonalu. This research does not appear in this volume, but I had occasion to discuss ideas and exchange notes, especially with members of the

History Department and Department of Folk Studies. These conversations have proven helpful in giving me perspective on the studies included in this volume.

Each of the chapters included in this volume is a study in and of itself, each a portrait of an institution, a group of people, or an event that illustrates in some way how a resilient, diverse, and fascinating people have acted out who they are in their ritual life. These studies clearly do not tell the whole story—a great deal more work could be done in Mumbai or Kuala Lumpur, for example. But I hope they will invite the reader to catch glimpses of how various groups of people who share a common language even while living on the boundaries recycle and innovate ritual patterns in expressing their heritage.

In addition to chapter 2, two other segments in this volume have been published earlier and are reused here with permission. Chapter 10 is condensed and adapted from the introduction to my book *Quiescence and Passion: The Vision of Aruṇakiri, Tamil Mystic,* published in 1996 by Austin and Winfield. The brief descriptions found in chapter 3 of the Paṅkuṉi Uttiram festival observed in Singapore first appeared in the essay "Rituals and Reinterpretation: South Indians in Southeast Asia," published in the volume *A Sacred Thread,* edited by Raymond Williams. It is reprinted here with the permission of Bochasanwasi Swaminarayanan Sanstha Inc. (Flushing, N.Y.), which currently holds the copyright to that volume. I am grateful to these agencies for permission to reuse this material. In addition, the map of Singapore accompanying chapter 3 is reprinted from one produced with the permission of the publisher, Lonely Planet, and the map of Mumbai accompanying chapter 4 is reprinted with the permission of www.mapsofindia.com.

I am especially grateful to Elspeth Wissner, who has shepherded this manuscript through its various incarnations to its final form and has managed to keep her sanity and gracious spirit throughout.

Finally, a word on diacritical marks is appropriate. I have followed the Tamil lexicon in transliterating Tamil terms. Most of the technical terms used in ritual were expressed in Tamil (rather than Sanskrit); hence, I have transliterated them in their Tamil form. One exception was the rituals used in Pittsburgh's Śrī Veṅkaṭeśvara Temple, which have been transliterated from their Sanskrit form. Some terms that have become anglicized, such as places, caste names, and languages, I have reproduced in their anglicized forms.

RITUALIZING ON THE BOUNDARIES

CHAPTER I

Introduction

Boundaries and the Tamil Diaspora

Circumstances over the last half century have created a planet of people who live on boundaries. These boundaries are of various kinds. They often have to do with shifting senses of identity as individuals and ethnic groups interact more intensively with persons of alternate backgrounds and assume multiple personae. The boundaries often elicit a longing for a sense of community and for being connected in the face of increased mobility and depersonalization. Boundaries can be territorial (e.g., what space is "ours"?); more often they are boundaries of mind and spirit as people struggle for a sense of self between and within cultures, between generations, between the world of work and that of home, between the metaphors of their youth and those of their children.

More specifically, the boundaries of the contemporary period reflect changes and transitions of various kinds and engender a search for more-satisfying orientations in the face of perceived threats to old verities. The loss of a sense of one's personhood, for example, may make one want to rediscover what it is to be human. Loneliness and the concomitant sense of separation or isolation can catalyze a search for community. Mobility engenders a search for "roots." The loss of trust in authority is often accompanied by a longing for some trustworthy "authentic" human, someone deemed to be wise, a "magus." Lack of intellectual compass evokes a need for myth, whether eclectic or orthodox, that offers a contemporary worldview, rooted in some legitimating past.

The boundaries may also span the scope of a lifetime. While the ancients marked major transitions in life with rites of passage, contemporaries often find themselves without rituals to mark crisis moments. We inherit few, if any, rituals, for example, for moments such as when our children leave home, our divorces, changes in jobs, midlife crises, or financial or medical losses. Many of our passages have become perfunctory or dehumanized, whether it be birth, retirement, or the process of dying. And even the rituals we have inherited may seem increasingly inadequate—they can become ceremonial vestiges whose intentions are outdated or too narrow, provincial, ingrown, or sexist.

The experience of living on the boundaries can be exhilarating for some who recognize it as a time of change, growth, and rethinking of values; for others it is lonely and traumatic. Persons who spend extended periods of time—or immerse themselves intellectually—in more than one culture know what it is to live on the boundaries. So also do many who are the products of multireligious or multiracial homes. Among those who live on the boundaries in today's world are émigrés and expatriates, people who have set up domiciles in places removed from their homeland.

The studies that follow in this volume are focused on a particular set of people who are living on such boundaries. They share a single language—Tamil—and a common ancestral homeland in South India. But the Tamils described in this volume are in diaspora, seeking to make themselves at home in cities considerably removed from the home of their ancestors. Tamils are by no means a monolithic bloc of people. Indeed, they are enormously diverse—brahmin, merchant, *dalit;* Hindu, Muslim, Christian. By no means are they unanimous as to what it means to be Tamil or how to juggle their various identities.

One of the strategies, nevertheless, these communities have used in negotiating their boundaries is the performance of various kinds of rituals: festivals, domestic rituals, the building of shrines, and so on. The present studies, in fact, focus on the ritual life of particular groups of Tamils who have settled in four cities: Kuala Lumpur, Malaysia; Singapore; Mumbai, India; and Pittsburgh, Pennsylvania. Each study is like a single cell in a moving picture—it tries to capture a particular ritual occasion or a particular group of people as they engage in ritual activity, and explore what each such portrait tells us about the dynamics by which participants negotiate passages and express their sense of who they are. The studies have been collected over a period of two decades, each such study reflecting in various ways the complexities of that community. In this chapter I will introduce these Tamil communities briefly and sketch out some of the boundaries on which they live.

The Tamil Diaspora

Some Historical Notes

It is not my intention here to provide a detailed history of the role Tamil peoples and cultures have played outside of South India. Suffice it to say that in the early years of what is generally called "Greater India," Tamils have had a rather significant impact. From at least the time that Greek and Roman traders discovered the trade winds in the first century B.C.E. and became frequent visitors to the southern coast of the Indian subcontinent, Tamil merchants exported spices, pearls, peacocks, and presumably other products to the Mediterranean world. Herodotus (7.70) had spoken of Dravidians (the cultural matrix of which Tamils are a part) as "Ethiopians," and Homer before him referred to them as "Eastern Ethiopians" *(Odyssey* 1.23).[1] Ktesias in his *Indikā* (a source that proved to be unreliable) refers to certain imported products by their Tamil name, especially cinnamon (Tamil, *karppu;* Greek, *karpion*) and the sweet wine of the palm, toddy, as *tādī.*[2] Beyond that, it becomes purely speculative as to whether Tamils were among those Indians who settled and/or traded in cosmopolitan Mediterranean ports such as Alexandria and Antioch.

By contrast, the early Tamil impact in Sri Lanka and Southeast Asia is beyond dispute. The Pāṇṭiyaṉs of Maturai controlled the pearl trade in the Palk Straits separating

South India from Sri Lanka's Jaffna Peninsula, and there are hints in early Ceylonese records that Tamils were migrating onto the island before the common era.[3] Rule by Pāṇṭiyaṉ chieftains in Sri Lanka was sporadic but included reigns in the first century B.C.E. and the third century C.E.[4] From the fifth to the tenth centuries, the Cōḻa clan, headquartered in the Kāvēri delta of South India, was exerting considerable influence in Sri Lanka. The Cōḻas captured Anuradhapura, the Sinhalese capital, in 993 and retained control in the northeast portion of the island until the resurgence of the Sinhalese under Parakrama Boku (1153–86).[5] During the Cōḻa years there was a significant influx of *vāṇiyar*s (a caste of peasants and cultivators). At least three Śiva temples were built and Tamil brahmins brought in to serve in them. In 1325 Tamils established Jaffna as a separate kingdom, and it thrived as such until the sixteenth century.[6] With the ascendancy to power of the Vijayanagar Dynasty in South India in the fourteenth through sixteenth centuries and the Muslim sultanates that succeeded it, a new influx of Tamils into Sri Lanka was stimulated—many of them *vēḷāḷa*s, a well-placed caste of landowners who had served as tax collectors and military chiefs in the Maturai and Tanjavur districts in the Cōḻa era. The *vēḷāḷa*-brahmin alliances that had flourished in Tamil country were reconstructed in Sri Lanka as the *vēḷāḷa*s became the dominant Tamil community there, in time numbering almost half the Sri Lankan Tamil population.[7] The *vēḷāḷa*s became the keepers of the conservative practices associated with Sri Lankan Tamil culture and religion. They maintained the rules for marriage, dowry, and inheritance and guarded the traditions associated with Tamil Śaivism, including the principles of Śaiva Siddhānta and temple worship. Other castes, while present, often became part of the *vēḷāḷa* orbit, including those depressed castes (such as those once known as *paḷḷar* and *paṟaiyar*) who were retained as virtual slaves.

In Southeast Asia, Tamil influence in the medieval period was visible in Myanmar, Sumatra, and the Malay Straits, but especially in Cambodia during the heyday of the Khmers. By the time the city that came to be known as Pagan in Myanmar was built around the year 849, there was evidence of Tamil settlers. For example, a Tamil merchant community had built a Vaiṣṇava temple, called the Nānādēsi Viṇṇagar Āḻvār (literally, the Viṣṇu temple of those coming from various countries).[8] Yet another temple to Viṣṇu along with Lakṣmī was built within the walls of Pagan. In addition, the Buddhist kings of Pagan, following the lead of King Kalancascā, found ways to emulate Indian models of kingship. Kalancascā, for example, constructed an edifice in honor of Nārāyaṇa (avatar of Viṣṇu) and referred to himself as an avatar of Viṣṇu; that is, the king became homologized to Viṣṇu, and the earthly palace and/or temple were homologized to Nārāyaṇa's celestial abode.[9] In subsequent courts, brahmins were at the service of the king and conducted rituals of libation (a*bhiṣeka*s) at the time of a coronation. While some of the patterns that were emulated had their sources in Bengal and were apparently a product of the Pala period, the major models for the Buddhist kings of Burma were South Indian in origin—most particularly the royal cult and architecture of the Pallavas and/or Cōḻas and the canonical traditions of the *Śaivāgamas* brought into Southeast Asia by Tamil brahmins in these southern courts.[10]

The impact of Tamil culture on the area now known as Indonesia and the Malay Straits and on the Khmer Dynasty is even more abundantly documented. Inscriptions, architectural remnants, and sources in Tamil literature refer to several kinds of influence from Tamil country into this part of Greater India. One of these was the visiting and eventual settling of adventurers or merchants. Some of these adventurers claimed to be of royal stock, distributed goods purporting to offer cures, married daughters of local chiefs, then began to introduce Indian ideas or customs. This was apparently the case in fifth-century Java.[11] The founding of the Funan Dynasty in the Indochina peninsula may have been the result of a similar circumstance, as the myth of founding (later emulated by the Khmers) was virtually identical to founding myths associated with the Pallavas. In this case a "brahmin" marries a (indigenous) daughter of the Nāgas (snake people) to establish a dynastic line.[12] Similarly, King Mutavarman of Borneo had a grandfather Kundunga, whose name may be Tamil.[13] A millennium later, certain Tamil Muslims used a similar strategy; most particularly, Raja Kasim, son of a concubine who was the daughter of a Tamil Muslim merchant, assumed the throne of Malacca in 1437.[14] The Śrīvijaya Dynasty, which assumed power in Java after the collapse of the Funan Dynasty in the late sixth century, was Śaivite, only to be followed by a Buddhist sovereign by the mid–eighth century who retained certain ties with Śaivism and the South Indian Cōḻas.[15] That there were also settlements in the Indonesian islands of merchants from Tamil country is attested by certain inscriptions and temples. In addition to the reference near Pagan already cited, one finds a Tamil inscription in Baros, Sumatra (1088), the apparent product of a Tamil merchant guild.[16] Another settlement of Tamil merchants was attested by a ninth-century inscription and accompanying Vaiṣṇava statuaries at Tahnapo on the Malay Peninsula. One of the models for the statuaries is Pallava. Such influences as these were making their way into the peninsula primarily from the ports of Nagapattinam and Mahabalipuram, the latter the Pallava seaport.[17]

Quite apart from the role of adventurers and merchants, there is considerable evidence that both Pallava and Cōḻa dynasties had measurable contact in the area. During the reign of the Cōḻa king Rājarāja I, for example, the king offered large revenues at a Buddhist temple built at Nagapattana by a Śrīvijaya king.[18] Two years later, however, Rājarāja I claimed to have conquered twelve thousand islands, and by 1025 his son Rajendira Cōḻa had conquered some territory from the Śrīvijayas, ranging from Sumatra to the Malay Peninsula. Kulottunga I sent an embassy to China in 1077 (he had apparently held a similar office in the Śrīvijaya court before assuming the Cōḻa throne).[19] Javanese inscriptions mention several South Indian communities known to the area. These include Cōḻika (Cōḻas), Pāṇṭikāra (Pāṇṭiyaṉs), and Dravida (Tamils).[20] Interestingly, inscriptions also refer to Klings (apparently people from Kalinga in northeast India), but the term is used derogatorily in Malaysia for Tamils even today.

That Tamil brahmins were part of this Indianized landscape is also evident. Kings, both Hindu and Buddhist in Southeast Asia, employed brahmins in their courts. These brahmins played a major role in the construction of temples, cities, and palaces and in sacralizing the role of king. Nowhere, perhaps, was this role more evident than at Angkor in Cambodia. Indeed, the Khmers had assumed a Hindu aura from the reign of Jeyavarman II (crowned in 802). The king shared something of the nature (*āmśa*) of Śiva; he would be crowned in a manner consistent with that of Indian kings. This cult of the sacred king (*dēvarāja*) was maintained by a hereditary line of priests, right down to Dīvakarapandita (b. 1050), who was the major adviser to Sūryavarman, the king who started the building of Angkorwat, as well as his two successors.[21] As a result, the temples of Angkorwat bear striking resemblances to those of the Pallavas. The Hindu borrowings are too numerous to identify, but they include frequent depictions of stories from the *Rāmāyaṇa;* a fondness for the myth of the creation of the world by the churning of milk; sculptural depictions of Śiva, Lakṣmī, and Viṣṇu; and *apsaras* in various expressions of Bharata Nātyam dance. Not least striking is the depiction of cosmological and chronometric themes that mirror Indian cosmology: the use of the numbers 33, 5, and 108 and the replication of the mythic cosmography of Mt. Meru and of the formulations of the homology between ritual space and the human torso (the *vāstupuruṣamaṇḍala*).[22] The cities, temples, and palaces throughout Southeast Asia from Pagan to Ayuthia, Thailand, shared many of these cosmological and numerical symbols.

Ironically, with the exception of Java and Sri Lanka, this Hindu/Tamil influence was not lasting. Few Tamilized communities persisted intact into the present era. Further, the impact was felt, for the most part, at the level of the royal court and seldom among the common people. Be that as it may, certain patterns are apparent in these medieval Tamil incursions into Southeast Asia that prefigure today's diaspora. Among other things these patterns include the following:

1. The propensity to mingle forms and motifs with those of indigenous peoples as well as with those of other Indians so that the resulting architecture and ethos reflected the indigenous landscape as well as the intra-Indian reciprocities forged abroad.
2. The will to build temples that make a new homeland seem like home. This was thoroughly consistent with Tamil tradition, which thinks of no place as home unless it is centered by a temple.
3. The practice of carrying a fundamental cosmology with them, articulated in the mind and body. This included a sense of mythic cosmology as understood and expressed in temple and dance, but also a sense of the world as represented in the social and political alliances of home, nonetheless reconfigured in the alliances of the new landscape. This is what Vasudha Narayanan has called the "embodied cosmology" of diasporic Indian communities.[23]
4. The propensity to express in ritual form the agendas associated with retention of lineage and resettlement outside the homeland. More than in any single text

(though portions of some texts were retained by priests with prodigious memories), it was in practice and enactment that "tradition" was expressed. Catherine Bell has suggested that "ritualization" has a way of embedding "cultural schemes" in people's bodies.[24] At the least, certain customary ways of acting seem to have been a part of the mindset of many of these medieval migrants.

The Modern Diaspora

The story of the more recent emigration of Tamils into other societies starts, as much as at any point, in the 1830s. With the Act of Emancipation in 1834, slavery was abolished throughout the British Empire. Immediately owners of sugar and tea and other plantations sought cheap labor. Arrangements were made with British colonial authorities to set up a system of indentured servitude, headquartered in Calcutta and Madras, from which Indian émigrés could be employed. French and Dutch plantation owners reached similar agreements in 1846 and 1873, respectively. Recruiters sought potential emigrants, who would sign contracts of indenture for at least five years; during the period of employment, indentured workers would receive basic pay, shelter, food rations, medical facilities, and partial or full return passage to India. During the period from approximately 1834 to 1912, 1.2 million persons emigrated, only about one-third of whom returned to their homeland.[25] As a result, 453,063 Indian immigrants were sent to Mauritius between 1834 and 1912; 238,909 to British Guyana from 1838 to 1917; 152,184 to Natal in South Africa between 1860 and 1911; 143,949 to Trinidad from 1845 to 1917; and 118,000 to Réunion between 1829 and 1924.[26]

Most of these emigrants were from Bengal or Tamil Nadu. Indeed, the number of indentured servants leaving Tamil Nadu for other colonies between 1842 and 1879 was said to be 533,595, of whom 112,178 returned once their contract had expired.[27] However, this Tamil emigration was enhanced by a system known as the *kaṅkāṇi* system: a recruiter, known as a *kaṅkāṇi,* or foreman, whose language was Tamil, would secure workers from rural areas of Tamil Nadu when there had been crop failures or other problems. These recruits were to work on rubber plantations in Malaysia and to pick tea in the central highlands of Sri Lanka. Estimates as to the number of Tamils so recruited vary for the Malay Straits, but one official figure (itself an estimate) suggests the number of indentured servants recruited from India to work in Malaysia had totaled 181,132 by the year 1938, when large-scale "assisted" migration ceased. Added to this figure was an estimated 1,186,717 who had been recruited by *kaṅkāṇi*s by the same year.[28] The vast majority of these were Tamils.

Following the great famine of 1876–78, emigration from Tamil Nadu grew significantly, especially to the Malay Straits and Sri Lanka as well as to cities in northern India. During the decade 1875–84, for example, gross emigration from Tamil Nadu was said to be 92,335 a year by one estimate, though most such émigrés eventually returned, usually after their three- or five-year contract expired. Net emigration during each of these years, as a result, was 21,873 or 23.6 percent.[29] Most of the recruits were young men experiencing the vicissitudes of unemployment or underemployment. That there was considerable "push" or incentive to seek employment elsewhere is also suggested by the agrarian system that some critics have called "agrestic slavery." A Methodist missionary named William Goudie described the system, albeit with some rhetorical excess, in a paper published in 1894:

> Labour is so miserably underpaid that the first law of life in the *parchery* is that for every mouth that eats there must be two hands earning. From the child of four upwards they must all be breadwinners or they cannot be bread-eaters. It is a common thing to see the owner of a few acres seated at the head of a field commanding the labour of ten or twelve poor pariah women who are engaged in planting out or weeding or reaping for him. The caste man is the only member of his family engaged on his farm and this is the extent of his labour. The Pariah woman has brought her baby with her, laying it under the shelter of a bush, or slinging it in a cloth over the branch of a tree; her husband is treading the beam of some water lift, balancing himself in mid air. Her little five-year old is watching the baby, or seeking crabs and shell fish in the water channels to add to the evening meal. The older children are herding sheep, tending village cattle or following the plough. Life is almost literally from hand to mouth, and a few days without work or a sick person in the house means hunger. With all this, in the busy seasons of a prosperous year there is labour enough and no great lack of food; but between these seasons there are whole months, and in years of drought there are much longer periods, when the life of the labourer is one long battle with the ghastly presence of hunger.[30]

Upon arrival in the plantations, the Tamil workers were provided certain amenities. In Malaysia these became known pejoratively as the three Ts. First was the provision of Tamil schools. Unfortunately, these schools, which only went up to the fifth grade, were operated by undertrained teachers. Tamil was the only language used; neither English nor Malay was taught. The schools' effect was to inhibit mobility and the capacity to communicate with any but fellow Tamils. The result was to keep Tamil workers "down on the farm" for generations. The second "T" was the temple. Shrines were constructed to the deities brought from home, on land made available to the *kaṅkāṇi,* or foreman. One of the most popular deities on the Malaysian plantations was the goddess Māriyammaṉ, the goddess of smallpox and rains and preferred by those who tilled the soil. Those who came not to farm but to clear land, break rocks, or tend animals preferred the goddess Kāḷiyammaṉ, who had been a part of the rural Tamil pantheon since the thirteenth century at least. Shrines to protector deities, such as Maṉmathaṉ and Maturai Vīraṉ, deities worshipped by lower-class workers, were also to be found. The third "T" was the toddy shop or "tavern," one of the few forms of entertainment available to the plantation worker.

These indentured Tamils were joined by other Indians, including Tamils who came on a more voluntary basis; one such group was composed of those who accepted clerical positions under British administrators whether on the plantations, in the railroad system, or within the governmental structure. Colonial administrators wanted people who could use English but also communicate with Tamil workers. Both *kaṅkāṇis* (foremen) and *kirāṇis* (clerks) on the plantations had to be persons who could mediate between administrator and worker. Tamil *vēḷāḷas* (members of the landowning communities, such as *piḷḷais* and *muṭaliyārs*) tended to fill these roles.

Similarly, Sri Lankan Tamils of *vēḷāḷa* background benefited from the English-medium education provided on the Jaffna Peninsula primarily by various missionary groups. As early as 1826 in Sri Lanka a regulation was passed that ruled that even a good village headman should be able to read and write English. British colonial funds had been funneled into the construction of mission schools that taught both English and Tamil. By 1830, as a result, American missionaries had established some ninety-three schools in Jaffna alone, and by 1834 Jaffna Central College had been founded.[31]

As Jaffna's population increased and Tamils from all walks of life sought English-medium education, the competition for jobs in Sri Lanka's civil service became more intense. Indeed, Tamils had come to outnumber or equal their Sinhalese counterparts in getting access to governmental or professional jobs. For example, in 1911 nearly half of the medical practitioners in Sri Lanka were Tamils.[32] Applicants for government jobs soon exceeded available positions. In 1912, 276 candidates sat for the clerical service exam to qualify for one of forty vacancies.

Meanwhile, in the Malay Straits, the need for clerks increased in the railway system, in the development of telegraphic communication, sanitary boards, public works, and various other colonially administered agencies. Because indigenous Malays tended to prefer education in the vernacular, the engagement of English-speaking Tamils from both India and Sri Lanka proceeded apace. Indeed, despite attempts dating from at least 1904 by governmental officials in Malaysia to educate Malays in English and provide jobs at least at the lower levels of the bureaucracy, as late as 1920, of the "1001 clerks of all grades in the General Clerical Service of the Federated Malay States, only 10.5% were Malays."[33] The rest were Indian and Sri Lankan Tamils, along with some Chinese.

While some 10 percent of the upper-class Sri Lankan Tamils had converted to Christianity (some 85 percent of these to Roman Catholicism) as a result of the education afforded by missionaries,[34] most of these Ceylon Tamils had remained devout Śaivites. As such, whether in Jaffna or in the Malay Straits, they were watchdogs of the theological traditions associated with Śaiva Siddhānta, a school of thought indigenous to Tamil Nadu. As the number of Jaffna Tamils grew in the Malay Straits, they built and retained hegemony over at least one temple in virtually every town in which they settled, including at least four in Kuala Lumpur (KL) alone.

The migration of Tamils from Sri Lanka during the colonial period has been enlarged by those who left as refugees since the civil war erupted in Sri Lanka in the 1970s. Those refugees who have been able to settle in Malaysia and Singapore, often thanks to connections with extended family members, have been relatively few as compared with those who have been dispersed worldwide. One estimate has it that five hundred thousand to seven hundred thousand Tamils have migrated out of northern and eastern Sri Lanka in the last three decades, almost a third of the total prewar population.[35] The largest settlements of these Sri Lankan Tamils are to be found in Canada, England, Germany, and Switzerland, but they have been scattered from Japan to Botswana, Panama, Finland, and Norway.[36]

Another group of Tamil entrepreneurs who made their way into Southeast Asia in the colonial period were the capitalists known as Ceṭṭiyārs (anglicized as Chettiyars). Traditionally moneylenders and traders in salt and other commodities, Chettiyars, especially that branch known as Nattukottai Chettiyars, came to be known for their capitalistic initiative and their considerable wealth. As British banks came to monopolize the servicing of British credit, the Nattukottai Chettiyars looked to Sri Lanka, Burma, and the Malay Straits for business opportunities. In the Malay Straits, for example, by the 1870s and 1880s these Chettiyars financed most of the opium trade in Singapore and Penang and monopolized a position as intermediaries between British banks and Chinese traders.[37] Through investments in tin and rubber plantations and/or lending money to mine and plantation owners, they increased their wealth; indeed, by 1938 Chettiyars had come to own most of the 87,795 acres owned by Indians in Malaysia.[38]

For decades Chettiyar males usually came to these Southeast Asian outposts without their wives, a pattern they had followed in their trading for much of the preceding two centuries. At first they usually stayed for three years at a stretch, only to be succeeded by other Chettiyars. They brought with them their devotion to the deity Taṇṭāyutapāṉi, the form of Murukaṉ, enshrined at Paḻaṉi, where the Chettiyars had established trading and ritual relationships in the seventeenth century.[39] Their shrines were simple at first, characterized by the implanting of a *vēl* (lance), the portable insignia of the deity. As their families eventually settled in the straits, much of their wealth went into the construction and maintenance of significant temples and the patronage of elaborate festivals.

These voluntary arrivals were joined by other Indian communities, Tamil and otherwise; Sindhis and Gujaratis, for example, had come as entrepreneurs, setting up businesses in the cities of the straits. Sikhs came, often finding work as security personnel. Tamil Muslim merchants came, often marrying local women and setting up retail shops. In short, it is a diverse Indian population that now constitutes about 10.5 percent of the population of Malaysia. As late as 1980, 59 percent of the Indian population in Malaysia was still concentrated in the plantations of western Malaysia,[40] though subsequently, as cheaper Javanese and Filipino labor was hired in the plantations, workers filtered into the cities to find jobs. As of that same year, 89 percent of the Indian population were "manual laborers" (though their unemployment rate was at 11 percent), while 4 percent were clerks and 6.5 percent held technical, professional, managerial, and administrative posts.[41] As a result of this background, the Indian population in

Malaysia today owns 1.2 percent of Malaysia's wealth, and 90 percent of that is owned by some 10 percent of the Indian population.[42] A more recent breakdown of the demographic makeup of this population is not available, but as of 1970, 80 percent of the Indian population was Indian Tamil, 8.1 percent other South Indian (i.e., Telugu and Malayali), 2.7 percent Ceylon Tamil, and 7.7 percent other Indians.[43] According to the same census, 81.2 percent of the total Indian population was Hindu, 8.4 percent Christian, 6.7 percent Muslim, and 3.7 percent all others.[44]

In Singapore 6.8 percent of the population is Indian, the vast majority of these Tamil. As in Malaysia, the Tamil population is heterogeneous. Working-class persons, many of them descended from "outcastes" or low-caste indentured servants, compose the vast majority, many of whom still struggle to find work and get their children through the high-pressure public school system. Chettiyars, Ceylon Tamils, Indian *vēḷāḷas*, and, to a greater extent than in Malaysia, brahmins, constitute the elite of Singaporean society. In subsequent chapters I shall explore more fully how the communities in Malaysia and Singapore interact and/or express their varying identities in their shrines and in their ritual life.

Migrants from the full spectrum of Tamil society have made their way into the cities of northern India over the past one and a half centuries. Something of that pattern will be discussed as it relates to Mumbai in a subsequent chapter. For now, it may be useful to focus briefly on Tamil brahmins who made their way to Singapore (as well as a trickle into Malaysia) and especially to northern Indian cities and to the United States.

Not only was there a "pull" of opportunities that attracted well-educated brahmins to a variety of cities, but also a "push" from Tamil Nadu, especially after the 1920s. Brahmins had been among the elites of Tamil Nadu, forging alliances with royalty and landowners for centuries and exercising a power far in excess of their numbers. They also took advantage of British presence, learning English and finding positions in the colonial structure. Less than one-third of the brahmin workforce derived its income from the land early in the twentieth century. But in those jobs that demanded literacy skills, especially in English, brahmins were ubiquitous. According to the 1921 census, Tamil brahmin males had a literacy rate in Tamil of 71.5 percent and an English literacy rate of 28.21 percent, greatly exceeding other groups. The closest nonbrahmin group with literacy in English, for example, was Indian Christian males at 5.47 percent and in Tamil, Chettiyars at 39.5 percent.[45] And though in 1912 brahmins represented only 3.2 percent of the male population of Tamil Nadu, they held 83.3 percent of the subjudgeships (immediately under British personnel), 55 percent of the deputy collectorships, and 72.6 percent of the district administrative posts.[46] Sixty-seven percent of those receiving baccalaureate degrees from Madras University in 1918 were brahmins. Of those receiving law degrees, brahmins outnumbered all nonbrahmin Hindus 3.5 to 1, while brahmins receiving teaching licentiates outnumbered all nonbrahmin Hindus by more than 6.5 to 1.[47] These realities created resentment, not only among the British administrators who saw brahmins as something of a threat to their hegemony but also among nonbrahmin Hindus of all stripes. Antibrahmin sentiment became organized in the formation of the Justice Party in late 1916. This party composed of upper-class nonbrahmins was committed to enhancing the opportunities for nonbrahmins. The Justice Party was succeeded in 1944 by the Dravida Kaḻakam, founded by Ramaswami Naicker (commonly known as Periyār or "great one"). The party was committed to the goals for which Naicker had been fighting for almost a decade—namely, the glorification of Tamil culture and diminishing the role of the "brahmin infection" (Irschick's term), and of religion as a whole, as well as resisting British hegemony and any attempts to make Hindi a compulsory subject in the schools of Tamil Nadu.[48] In 1967 a successor party to the DK, namely, the Dravida Muṉṉetra Kaḻakam (DMK, party for the advancement of Dravida), which had broken off from the DK in 1949, was elected to power in the state government, and some form of that party or a spin-off has been in control of the state ever since. Brahmins found it increasingly uncomfortable to affirm their caste identities publicly and to find the kinds of positions that had been so accessible earlier in the century. Many welcomed the opportunity to find professional opportunities outside the state and/or to have their children educated elsewhere. It is not surprising then, when large-scale emigration to the United States started after 1965, that brahmins of all ethnic backgrounds were a significant presence among the early settlers. Indeed, a survey taken of Pittsburgh's Indian immigrants in 1978 found that 40 percent of the settlers claimed to be brahmin. Of the Tamils who were part of that migration, a similarly disproportionate number were brahmins.

Immigration into the United States from India increased sharply after 1965, when Lyndon Johnson signed a new immigration law into effect. The new law discarded the older national quota system for potential American citizens and opened up allocations so that half would come from the Old World and half from the New. The change led to significant shifts in the flow of immigrants. For example, from 1931 to 1960 only 5 percent of all legal immigrants came from Asia, and 15 percent came from Latin America, while 58 percent came from Europe and 21 percent from Canada.[49] In the 1970s three-quarters of all immigrants came from Latin America (41 percent) and Asia (34 percent), and between 1980 and 1984 nearly half of all immigrants came from Asia.[50] At first, the number of Indians in this flow remained relatively modest. As of 1970 Asian Indians numbered only 75,000.[51] However, according to the 2000 census, the Asian Indian population has reached 1,678,765, an increase of 106 percent over the 1990 census. It is the fastest-growing Asian American population and the third largest (after the Chinese and Filipino communities).

The early post-1965 Indian immigrants to the United States were largely professional. According to the 1980 census, 52 percent of Asian Indians in the United States were college graduates (as compared to 35 percent of all Asian Americans and 17 percent of white Americans).[52] They were also relatively affluent, as according to the 1980 census, they had the highest per capita income of any ethnic group in the United States. Because extended families have joined these early settlers and more younger semiprofessional workers have arrived—those working in software technology, for example—the relative educational and income levels have decreased. Nonetheless, the Indian American population has become a significant part of the U.S. landscape.

How many of these Indian Americans are Taṃils? There appears to be no precise statistical measurement. However, inasmuch as Tamils constitute 6 percent of the total population of India (or roughly 60 million), it would be reasonable to estimate that 6 percent of the Indian American population is Tamil. That would suggest a figure of more than 100,725 Tamils. This Tamil population, unlike that of Malaysia, is virtually all middle- or upper-class level. Their agendas and identities, as a result, are negotiated quite differently. I turn to that story momentarily.

To summarize this discussion of the modern Tamil diaspora, I identify three broad categories of Tamil émigrés:

1. At one level, one finds those who tend to be professionally, educationally, and economically well placed and have been so for several generations. These are almost always English-trained Tamils. In the Malaysian Straits certain castes or subgroups could traditionally have been found in this group: brahmins, Chettiyars, Ceylon Tamils, and a few South Indian *vēḷāḷa*s (e.g., *piḷḷais* and *muṭaliyārs*). Certain non-Tamils would also fit into this category: some Malayalis, Sindhis, Gujaratis, and Panjabis, for example, most of whose ancestors migrated to the straits voluntarily for purposes of economic betterment. The early leadership of Indian communities in the straits was drawn from this group, especially brahmins, Chettiyars, and Ceylon Tamils, though members of this group now often distance themselves from other Tamils and seek to be more visible in the national polity of Malaysia and Singapore. Brahmins were also among the South Indian elites of Mumbai and Pittsburgh. In Mumbai they found their place in many professional contexts, from atomic scientists to writers and performers; in Pittsburgh, during the early years of systematic immigration (the 1970s), 85 percent of the émigrés were professionals with graduate degrees, of whom 40 percent claimed to be brahmin.
2. A second category is composed of a middle-class group of persons, many of whom have worked their way up from lower-status positions. They have become shop proprietors, clerks, accountants. In Mumbai this configuration has been derived largely from groups such as *nāṭar*s (anglicized as nadars) and the Saurashtra Tamils (these are Tamil speakers who descended from communities of weavers brought from Saurashtra, Gujarat, into Tamil Nadu by medieval rulers such as the Cōḻas); in Malaysia and Singapore, people who were historically *tēvar*s, *kauṇṭar*s, and *kaḷḷar*s are often middle class. Within this group there have often been significant distinctions of caste and intercaste rivalry until as recently as a generation ago and which may still prevail in marriage and temple politics, for example. Many of those in this category are the descendants of ancestors who migrated only semivoluntarily to work in relatively menial jobs.

3. A third category is composed of the working-class communities; these are generally the descendants of those who migrated as indentured servants or as part of the *kaṅkāṇi* system. Even today most of them remain in relatively low-paying jobs in the estates or the city. In Malaysia some 90 percent of the Tamil population continues to live in economically marginal circumstances, and in Singapore their children struggle to find a place in a closed society. Their parents seldom knew English, but increasingly their spokespersons and younger generation are assuming places of leadership in the overall Indian (or Tamil) population. Now known as *dalit*s, *adidravida*s, or "subaltern" people, many persons in this category of émigrés are descended from low-caste or outcaste groups such as those once known as *paḷḷar*s, *paṟaiyar*s, and *ambutiyar*s. In Mumbai these working-class Tamils remain some 80 percent of the city's Tamil population, where very few dare to aspire to emigrate to the United States, Great Britain, or Australia (though some aspire to work in the Persian Gulf). Needless to say, this group of Tamils is far less likely to perpetuate or act out caste identities, though some will espouse the genetic nomenclature of the *dalit*s as a form of empowerment. Further, the ways in which this group acts out ethnic, subethnic, or supraethnic identities vary widely.

Ritualizing as a Strategy

Tamils settling outside their ancestral homes have used a variety of strategies by which they negotiate their identities and transmit their heritage in not always hospitable cities. One of these strategies is ritualization in its various forms. In fact, even the casual observer cannot but notice the proliferation of ritual events, especially in the temples of overseas South Indian Hindus. Everywhere temple dedications (*kumbhābhiṣeka*) are being held as temples are built in North America or renovated in Southeast Asia. These temples are becoming the venues for more elaborate rituals as the sponsoring communities become more affluent. Relatively recently, for example, libations with 1,008 pots (*sahasrakalaśābhiṣeka*) were held in North America for the first time (Pittsburgh, 1987, and again in 2002) and in Malaysia for the first time (Kuala Lumpur, December 1990, and again in April 1991, in a different venue). The same ritual took place in Singapore for the first time in the mid-1980s at a temple administered by the Hindu Endowments Board. Libations with shells (*caṅkābhiṣeka*), whether 108 or 1,008, are done almost routinely now in Southeast Asia, but only for the first time with 1,008 shells in Singapore in the early 1980s. Patrons are signed up months in advance for the privilege of sponsoring shell libations held daily at the Piḷḷaiyār temple in Pudu, KL. Fire sacrifices (*homa*s) of various kinds have become commonplace. Not least elaborate of these fire sacrifices are those done for the goddess; in these sacrifices, offerings deemed especially pleasing to the goddess, often including jewelry and silk garments, are offered by means of fire.

At one level, to be sure, these kinds of rituals are sponsored by temples seeking to demonstrate that they are large and wealthy enough to warrant the support of devotees. Often they are explicitly intended to raise funds from the faithful. But these events are part of a larger strategy by which temples become cultural spaces and the venues for a pragmatic ritualism. Rituals have become so visible for many reasons in the mushrooming temples of South Indian Hindus living outside their ancestral homes—visible even when participants themselves may not be able to express the meanings of specific ritual events. For one thing, ritual expresses and purveys the essence of Hindu (or for that matter, Muslim or Christian) identity. For most South Indians (and probably most Indians), religion is expressed primordially as performance. Ritual is prediscursive, supratextual, experiential, visceral. In ritual one hears, albeit not propositionally, but also senses, sees, even smells the tradition. In theory at least, ritual invites the engagement of the entire person. Ritual acts out aesthetically and dramatically that which is the tradition. It links one to one's community and to one's lineage symbolically. It affords in its expressiveness the opportunity to reflect on its meanings, insofar as one wishes to do so.

These rituals are pragmatic in other respects, however. People engage in them to seek redress for the mundane concerns with which they are engaged in their urban lives: academic hurdles, financial crunches, domestic uncertainties, loss of a sense of community or personhood. It is no accident that ritual is the recourse for persons at all those stages of life that are boundaries—transitions to adolescence, parenthood, retirement—and at those geographic and societal interstices in which people live. Rituals also serve to maintain and restate historical identities at the same time that they are expected to ease transitions into new situations. Rituals re-present one's image of India even as they act out the reciprocities and social landscape of one's new home.

In short, ritualizing consists of symbolic expressions enacted in ways that serve to define, orient, or transform persons or communities. Responding to globalization, the traumas of urbanization, and the exigencies of raising children in multicultural settings, Tamils (along with other South Indians) have experimented with a variety of ways to act out who they are and enable their children to claim some sense of that heritage. Tradition for them is enacted; it is a constantly fluid process, less a noun than a verb. Ritualizations often reflect the boundaries on which people in diaspora live and, in some cases, enable participants to straddle, integrate, or transcend boundaries. Here I suggest something of these boundary situations and the role of ritual in them.

Ethnic, Transnational, and Subethnic Boundaries

One set of boundaries that these émigrés straddle is that associated with their ethnic, superethnic, and subethnic identities. Here the term "ethnic" is used in its simplest sense—those who share a common language, in this case Tamil, and claim a common ancestral homeland in that southeastern part of India known as Tamil Nadu. Yet, as I have observed, these Tamil speakers are by no means a monolithic group, and their "identity" is not some essential core of truth or culture. Rather, Tamils in diaspora have many identities—each of them a created definition of self always in relationship to others. Indeed, as many social scientists have pointed out—such as Barth andBerreman—these identities are fluid and contextual, negotiated on the boundaries with persons of other linguistic or cultural orientations.

Yet there is a certain shared sense of the desirability to preserve Tamil identity. Most of those interviewed in my four cities expressed their being Tamil as the first identifying marker, often more important than their being Indian or American or Malaysian. This was especially true in the United States with first-generation immigrants (but also true of other Indian linguistic groups). In general, Tamils have great pride in their language, its presumed antiquity, its mellifluous oral character, and its rich literary tradition. In fact, in the early years of Indian independence, Tamil Nadu was the scene of riots fueled by a pride in Tamil language and "Dravidian" culture and the unwillingness to have Hindi imposed as a national language. Immigrants commonly express pride that in "Tamil country," the classical traditions of India have been preserved in relatively pure form. This is derived in part because of the presence of a language, literature, and culture prior to the significant influence of Sanskrit and because Islamic incursions and concomitant influence were much less pronounced in the deep south than in northern India. Hence, Carnatic music, the classical dance form of Bharata Nātyam, and the rich classical traditions of temple architecture, iconography, and ritual have been preserved, perhaps more carefully than in any other part of India. In any case, there persists a myth, especially among nonbrahmin elite, of a glorious Tamil past that has been preserved into the present. In a certain sense, then, the performance of public ritual, like that of dance or music, to use Milton Singer's term, is a "cultural performance" that encapsulates within a confined space and time a sense of what a community wants to demonstrate of itself to its children as well as to outsiders.[53]

But in addition to being Tamil, these diasporic communities have other agendas and identities. Many are transnational, having become a part of a globalized landscape, shaped by the internationalization of entertainment, commerce, media presentations, and communication systems. Yet this global impact varies from city to city and from elites to those on the lower echelons of society. In Kuala Lumpur, for example, the global economy has brought more than two hundred companies from the United States; it means ordering a McDonalds meal in English, Bahasa Malay, Chinese, or Tamil. It means walking through mall after mall where Japanese, Taiwanese, European, and American goods are displayed, or watching CNN news on television only to have it interrupted at sunset by state-sponsored prayers. Similarly, Singapore seeks to be self-consciously global, having one of the two busiest harbors in the world (along with Rotterdam) and the world's most efficient airport and wherein virtually anything can be purchased on Orchard Road. Yet in Singapore, to an even greater extent than in KL, the global impact is constrained by government control as news programs and social engineering reflect Singapore values and seek to construct a nation that is identifiably Singaporean; hence, migrations into the city are limited and foreign films heavily censored. Further, in both Singapore and KL, the working-class

Tamil scarcely has the opportunity to make use of the global market save in a most derivative way.

Mumbai, where about one-third of India's tax revenues are generated, and where businesses of foreign origin were permitted to compete only after 1989, has experienced its own forms of globalization. The city's elites, in addition to having access to e-mail, the Internet, and satellite television, frequently travel abroad and may have children or aspire to have children studying in the United States, the United Kingdom, or Australia. Yet in urban slums or in rural areas, the impact of global currents is less self-consciously evident. The poor came to know of globalization only through their pocketbooks. For example, in the early 1990s, during the first Gulf War and in the wake of the opening of commerce to foreign competition, prices skyrocketed; fuel oil was virtually impossible to purchase; the price of vegetables doubled and tripled, making it necessary for the poor to spend more than half of their budgets on food alone.

"Global culture," in sum, has not yet affected every city to the same degree, let alone every person within a given city. One may speak, therefore, of at least three levels of globalization. At one level is accessibility, the availability of the global marketplace, systems, and culture despite the various constraints in a given city. This global culture is more accessible in Singapore, for example, than in Mumbai, more in urban areas than in rural settings, more to elites than to the poor. At another level, there is the matter of appropriation, where persons within a particular city adopt, usually selectively, elements of that global culture. Yet at the same time as there is a selective appropriation of a perceived global culture, there may be a selective reappropriation of what is perceived to be local or traditional. This phenomenon is what Roland Robertson has called "glolocalization."[54] This suggests a third level of global consciousness: interiorization. This connotes the degree to which one's attitudes and fundamental orientations are significantly influenced by a global network. Generally speaking, persons who have traveled abroad; have frequent, even daily, contact with foreigners; develop friendships with persons of alternative cultural orientations; or have reason to study such persons or cultures are more likely to think globally.

A part of this global landscape is the impact of transnational civilizational and religious streams. Virtually all middle-class Indians (and not only Tamils), for example, have been influenced by the forces of colonialism, Marxism, or feminism. And in the various cities where émigré Tamils have settled, transnational religious streams are at work. Today Hinduism is transnational, and there are many forms of it abroad, whether disseminated through movements such as the Vishwa Hindu Parisad (VHP) or sects such as the Satya Sai Baba movement or ISKCON or by various gurus purporting to offer particular interpretations of the tradition. It is not uncommon, therefore, for Hindus in KL to look not only to India but also to the Hindus in Singapore for a sense of how to be Hindu. Similarly, those in Amsterdam will look to Hindus in London. And, of course, the Internet, with Web sites representing varying Hindu movements, becomes a basic source for the homogenization of Hindu practice. In addition to various forms of transnational Hinduism, Tamil Hindus are reinterpreting their tradition in the face of other transnational religious movements or subsects thereof. In Malaysia, for example, Tamil Malaysians redefine themselves in the face of a resurgent Islam, of Pentecostal Christianity, or of various forms of Chinese popular religion. In Singapore, one lives in the context of an implicit Confucian ethic and in juxtaposition with an evangelizing Christianity. In the United States, Tamil Hindus worry about their children marrying Christians or into a post-Christian secular culture.

These transnational identities are usually factored into the ritual life of émigrés. The geographical landscape of the new homeland, for example, especially its rivers and hills, becomes homologized to those of the ancestral home—rivers become the Ganges or Jumna, and even the Kāvēri, a river with a long-standing sacral tradition in Tamil Nadu. Penn Hills, Pennsylvania, where the Śrī Veṅkaṭeśvara Temple stands, is homologized to the hills associated with the mother temple at Tirupati. Cosmologies derived from the classical mythography of India or Tamil Nadu are grafted into the new homeland. Deities associated with specific places in the homeland are reinstalled in new settings, thus legitimating the immigrant experience by making the deity itself an immigrant. As myths were told and songs sung by poetic bards of famous shrines in Tamil country, myths emerge and songs are sung at the newly established shrines. The gods, now in the United States or Malaysia, are ascribed the full powers of those to be found "back home."

In addition to these superethnic identities by which Tamils, to varying degrees, define themselves, there are subethnic identities—that is, differences among Tamils—that become compelling at times. One of these factors is caste. Generally speaking, consciousness of caste identity among expatriate Tamils increases in direct proportion to several factors: the number of persons of that caste available in the immediate geographic area, the higher one perceives oneself to be in the caste hierarchy, and the closer in time and/or space one is to one's ancestral home. Even those persons who claim not to be self-conscious about caste may well continue to exercise some authority to see that their children marry within the "community," or at least refrain from marrying persons of castes perceived to be widely disparate. In addition to certain rituals associated with marriage, caste distinctions may become evident in other contexts. One of these is the kinds of food one eats. Orthoprax Tamil brahmins are likely to retain a "sattvic" diet—that which eschews meat and garlic; and Nattukottai Chettiyars retain their own culinary traditions. Occasionally, shrines are built by and for particular caste groups—for example, the Smārta brahmins of Mumbai who patronize the Śrī Śaṅkara Maṭam or the Chettiyars of KL or Singapore who maintain their own temples. Occasionally, the roles of various castes are negotiated in various shrines or festivals, just as they are in India.

But for some expatriates, particularly by the third generation and those whose ancestors were from lower or outcaste groups, the notion of caste per se is replaced by considerations such as economic or professional standing. In Malaysia and Singapore especially, where many Tamils are descended from lower-class immigrants, the term *ubayam* (sometimes translated "classte") has come to designate groups who share a certain profession or workplace—for example, those who work for the railroad, the airlines, and so on. These *ubayams* functioned unofficially since the mid-eighteenth century and officially since the 1930s, when they were sanctioned by the court in KL as having appropriate authority within the temple life.[55] These *ubayams* have taken responsibility for temple management or for particular ritual events within the life of a temple or festival. It was no coincidence that *ubayams* were often found living in enclaves in the 1900s inasmuch as the British East India Company policy was to settle Indian railroad workers or road builders (usually drawn from the same geographical districts and castes back home) in specific parts of the city, almost always as far as possible from the European core of the city, while Chinese and Malay workers were placed closer to the core.

In more recent years geographical proximity plays a larger role in determining subethnic configurations. Those Indians who live in a certain neighborhood may not be of a common caste, especially in Singapore, Malaysia, or the United States, but may nevertheless form bonds and attend the neighborhood temple. Even in Mumbai, where the most conservative patterns of retaining subethnic alliances are retained, those who share a common housing unit will form their own social connectedness; as a result, nonbrahmins may be invited to a Navarāttiri celebration in a brahmin house because the invitee "works with my husband" or "lives in our building." Yet, while linguistic ties remain profoundly important for most Tamils, caste groupings remain important for many of these Tamil communities, especially brahmins, nadars, and Saurashtra Tamils in Mumbai; Chettiyars, brahmins, and Sri Lankan Tamils in KL and Singapore; and, in more subtle ways, brahmins, naidus, Chettiyars, and other groups in the United States.

There is, in addition to ethnicity and caste, the identity provided by one's geographic district or even village of ancestry. Val Daniel has argued that persons of Tamil Nadu share a certain character (*kuṇam*) with the very soil of the hometown (*ūr*).[56] Some remnants of that persist in certain first-generation immigrants. In Pittsburgh, for example, one finds the occasional immigrant who can think of certain qualities he or she believes are shared with people of his or her hometown. More commonly, however, many first-generation Tamil immigrants in the United States have been away from their ancestral home for most of their lives (that is, they may have been born in Mumbai or Delhi) and have little sense of a specific hometown in Tamil Nadu. Many Mumbai Tamils, however, maintain ties with a Tamil village or town (for example, Saurashtra Tamils who have come from Salem; nadars who have come from specific locales in Tirunelveli District; Muslims who retain ties to towns such as Melapalaiyam or Paṭṭampaṭṭi). Such people keep in touch with relatives there, occasionally sending money home, visiting it, or seeking spouses there for their children. In Malaysia and Singapore, Ceylon Tamils have had strong ties to the Jaffna area, though their children, born in the Malay Straits, have seldom or never visited Jaffna, have no conscious memory of it, and think of themselves as Singaporeans or Malaysians. Chettiyars, more than any other Tamil group in Southeast Asia, maintain strong ties to their ancestral home, specifically to the area surrounding the town of Karaikkuti in Ramnad District. There the nine temples emblematic of the nine exogamous subgroups of Chettiyars keep track of Chettiyar genealogy, and it is that spot to which many Chettiyars (at least those over forty) still want to return.

More common than specific towns, nonetheless, is a sense of ancestry from a particular district. Third-generation Tamil Malaysians, for example, may be able to report that their ancestors came from Tanjavur District, though they themselves have never visited or have no sense of loyalty there. Such district configurations, however, did play a significant role in the migratory process. For example, nadars from Tirunelveli District heard from relatives of jobs available in Mumbai and often came to live with or were afforded jobs in Mumbai by other Tirunelveli nadars. The same was true of Ceylon Tamils who came to the straits from the Jaffna Peninsula and of many *dalit*s from Tanjavur or Arcot districts who went as plantation or construction workers to the straits in the nineteenth century. Those historical connections, however, have become largely vestigial in the consciousness of second- and third-generation immigrants, but they have influenced the housing and temple attendance patterns of people in Singapore and Malaysia, and (to some extent) Mumbai, insofar as where they came to live, work, and worship was often a function of their coming to an area where "people from back home" could take care of them in the early years of migration. Such settlements occurred at Serangoon Road in Singapore (largely lower-class municipal workers from Tanjavur District); Chulia and Market streets in Singapore (Chettiyars and Tamil Muslim merchants); Brickfields in Kuala Lumpur (Ceylon Tamils from Jaffna Peninsula and laborers from Tanjavur and other districts working in the railway system of the Malay Peninsula); Matunga in Mumbai (brahmins from eastern Tamil Nadu and from Palghat); Dharavi in Mumbai (nadars, Muslims, and others largely from Tirunelveli District). Of course, these historical enclaves have changed over the years as families have become affluent and moved out or other ethnic groups have moved in (for example, natives of Maharashtra in Matunga or Dharavi, Mumbai; Chinese in Brickfields and Serangoon Road in Singapore). In subsequent chapters I shall examine how some of these ancestral ties are retained in the ritual life. For now it is enough to note that Ceylon Tamils build and maintain temples to Subrahmaṇiam (or Murukaṉ) patterned after those remembered in the Jaffna area; Chettiyars maintain temples to Taṇṭāyutapāṇi (Murukaṉ), especially as embodied in his lance and as enshrined in Paḻaṉi, Tamil Nadu, where the Chettiyars had alliances at least since the seventeenth century; and various *dalit* and low-caste communities brought with them the veneration of Maturai Vīraṉ or Maṉmathaṉ, protector deities in villages "back home."

Space

As noted, one of the most visible ways in which émigré Tamils seek to maintain their identities is through the reconstruction of spaces that embody the psycho-cultural-religious landscapes of their lineage. This concern for space is implied in the term "diaspora," which connotes a sense of "being out of place."[57] That religion should be one of the responses to the diaspora experience is consistent with the sense that religion, and especially ritual, is, as Jonathan Z. Smith has noted, a matter of "emplacement," being placed in the context of the entire, of mapping one's place in life and cosmos.[58] Spatial reconfigurations (often done in the name of religion) can take many forms, from literal construction of sacred structures (the favored way of many Tamilians) to the reimaging of new configurations in ways that are congruent to old ones. Thus, segments of subdivisions in Mumbai (*chawls*) become imagined replicas of ancestral villages, and shanties become the venues for housing joint or extended families.

More specifically, one may identify at least two approaches to the ordering of meaningful space among Tamil émigrés: the first is in the ascribing of meaning to given space—to body, home, or neighborhood—so that these are reimagined as sacred or socially significant worlds; the second is in constructing with considerable care literal sacred edifices that symbolize and provide a centering for their psychosocial universe in a new homeland. I reflect briefly on these two options.

For some South Indian émigrés, remembered places have been replaced by "virtual spaces"[59]—that is, imagined space that embodies one's sense of the world and one's place in it. These virtual spaces replicate, at least mythically, something of one's lineage and identity and embody both one's connections to a past and to the realities of the present living circumstances. Hindus settling down in the United States prior to the 1970s, for example, often alone and isolated, acted out their Hindu identities and rituals within their own skins—cosmicized bodies served as temples; flesh and bone became the symbols of one's continuities with the past. The home could also serve as such a microcosm where things from the homeland—art, music, and so on—could be celebrated in private. Dress and culinary principles (*pūjās*) could be acted out in ways that negotiated a family's attempt to express selective continuations of heritage and adaptations to change.

For Tamil Muslim women, similarly, especially that majority who did not have access to the public *masjid,* the body, home, and neighborhood have become the arenas for embodying who they are; the body, even when it is not enshrouded in the burqa (and most Tamil Muslim women do not wear these outer garments), nonetheless becomes a metaphor of the community's values and tastes, the gateway, as Mary Douglas reminds us, that opens or shuts to other persons,[60] thereby embodying the endogamous network maintained by Tamil Muslim communities. Similarly, the home, even a modest hovel in a Mumbai slum, retains the dignity of Islamic identity—here the women's prayer (*namāz*) is said; here the ethnic and subethnic foods are prepared, and appropriate guests given hospitality.

In a still larger concentric circle, the chawl or lane of a Mumbai subdivision or a small neighborhood in a U.S. city may reflect a carefully gathered minicommunity of people with connections to one's roots.[61] The ethnic circles can be drawn even larger. It is not uncommon to find small portions of cities in North India or Southeast Asia, for example, that have become enclaves and/or cultural centers for Tamilians—"little India" along Serangoon Road, Singapore; Brickfields in Kuala Lumpur; and Matunga in Mumbai are cases in point. On occasion, finally, Tamils and other South Indians, by virtue of their being Muslim or Hindu, may be drawn into the struggle to negotiate or define a body politic or state that expresses their understanding of divine purpose. For Muslims, this may take the form of a dar-ul-Islām, a transnational identity, centered in Mecca, wherein sacred and political laws are thought to be consistent with the injunctions of the sharī'a; for Hindus, the call for "Hindutva" has attempted to "recover" an imagined, mythical state believed consistent with Hindu dharma. Even the struggles of Tamils in Sri Lanka included at times this concern for hegemony, for establishing space where a Tamil, even Hindu, sense of political identity is possible.

In an even less physical sense, "space" for the uprooted may be replaced by subtler measures of identity maintenance. The experience is not unlike what it was for ancient Jews who were dispersed, whose principles of temple ritual, no longer literally enactable because of their temple's destruction, became metaphorically reexpressed in the Mishnah as principles for living ethically in a larger world.[62] In a similar way, in the brahmanic tradition the Laws of Manu, whatever else they intended, appear to have been an attempt at continuity from the more nearly rural forms of the sacrificial system, dependent on highly symbolic sacrificial huts, into a system for maintaining ritual purity and identity fulfillment through appropriate behavior in an urban setting.[63] To put it differently, a certain way of acting, of living out one's identity became a substitute for literal space. For some Hindus, the world itself can be seen as the playground (*līlā*) of the divine; hence, all life itself is touched by the sacred.[64] Traditionally, instructions for the construction of a city were often juxtaposed in classical Sanskrit texts to a full retelling of the myth of the world's creation; further, texts frequently reminded the believer that the world itself is permeated by the divine brahmanic essence. Occasionally, this kind of imagined space is self-consciously expressed by expatriated South Indians. One will sometimes find a South Indian, usually a scientist or an engineer, actively involved in the process of "reclaiming" the environment or renewing cities, in part because they are perceived to be microcosms or because one is engaged in an "ecological ethic" for keeping the planet habitable. However, the imagined environment for which one is ritually responsible is more commonly the prescribed world of self, family, and those structures literally enclosed by walls.

A more common approach to the sacralization of space for South Indians (and especially Tamils) is the construction of physical edifices, especially designated as sacred centers.[65] These shrines serve to center one's life-space, as in Tamil Nadu, where the temple centers the village and makes it habitable. These shrines embody the nature of their builders, reflecting remembered elements from the ancestral home at the same time that they express the rapprochement and social reciprocities of the builders' new circumstances. The construction of a shrine attempts to reimplant a people's perception of their history just as the people themselves have become reimplanted; the deity for whom the shrine has been built is a migrant, like its builders, present in all his or her power. Living in any place becomes legitimated and sacrally sanctioned by the dedication of a shrine to the deity of choice. The construction of such a sacred space illustrates the construction of tradition itself, insofar as tradition itself is a construction, a pastiche or collage selectively appropriated from a remembered past, mixed with elements modified and adapted from the new surroundings.

It is ritual that creates or reorients these spaces, and it is myth that links them to the past. Myth reads the present into the past; it is constructed of the bits of memory of "home" mingled with the bricolage of present circumstances. Myth rearticulates the cosmology that has been reinvented and expressed in newly constructed spaces; it attests that the sociopsychic ambience of new spaces is indeed like those "back home." Rituals are used to create homey spaces and provide some continuity in the process.

Transitions in the Life Process

Another one of the boundaries so evident in these diaspora communities is that between generations and those through which persons pass in their life journeys. Various stages of life bring about varying degrees of pressure regarding whether to continue certain patterns of identity or to distance oneself from them.

In traditional Indian society, rites of passage (*saṁskāras*) have been one of the most important and persistent ways of expressing and maintaining identity and socializing persons into their appropriate place in the kinship group and negotiating transitional moments.[66] Mobility and migration, however, have forced changes in older patterns. Migrants have generally been separated from the extended family, whose members are no longer present to declare what rituals should be done when. Details of sacred rituals are often forgotten by all but the most orthoprax of these émigrés—indeed, freedom from the in-laws sometimes becomes license to ignore such details. Moreover, émigré women (the traditional "keepers" of the ritual flame) are often working and have less time for maintaining classical *pūjā* at home. The result is an ambivalent one. On the one hand, women sometimes speak of the freedom from "legalistic" practices that would have been done back home out of custom (*parakkam*). On the other hand, there is a crisis of identity for those persons as well as for their children, at least from the point of view of parents of first-, second-, or third-generation émigrés. Parents generally believe it necessary to enable their young as well as themselves to find ways (sometimes other than through rites of passage) to provide a nest for the nurture of their own heritage and access to the cultural roots that have shaped their lineage.

I sketch here some junctures in the life cycle at which these identities are most likely to be negotiated, and some of the ways in which it is done. I look less at the details of rites of passage retained or alternative strategies developed than at the principles of selectivity, the push and pull, the functions that determine whether and why persons seek some sort of continuity with their past or accommodate change. Continuity, it must be stressed, is a term used advisedly, for it is most unlikely that rituals used or created by one generation of immigrants will be the exact replicas of those used in earlier generations. In fact, rituals are virtually never identical the second time used. Tradition is usually constructed from a pastiche of remembered and borrowed elements. The past is selectively remembered and appropriated. It is frequently mythologized from the collage of perceptions nursed by the nostalgic.

Infancy and Childhood

Few processes are more likely to cause a person to reflect on one's values and fundamental identity than the birth and growth of one's child. Who is this person to be? What does it mean to be a person? For virtually all Tamils (as for people in most "traditional" cultures) of whatever religion, a child becomes a social person when he or she is fully connected to the social network.

But there is already a negotiation of multiple concerns, some of which serve as impetuses for change and accommodation and some of which stimulate the desire for maintenance of specificity in identity. On the one hand, even in families with orthoprax backgrounds (such as most brahmin couples in Mumbai), there are elements of pragmatism: the perceived need to get children into English-language schools, to have access to international opportunities and successful careers. In Singapore the pressures are especially strong to affirm a national Singaporean identity and to socialize youngsters for careers in high-tech society. In Malaysia the movement to Malay-medium national schools (especially after grade six) and the push for rapid economic growth and urbanization serve as an impetus for young parents to provide their children the best possible education. Across the board and especially among elites in all these cities, parenthood affords the opportunity to reflect on ethnic and religious priorities, and to deselect more traditional rituals that are little understood or for which there is little time (especially in dual-career homes, such as are especially common in Pittsburgh and Singapore). An increasingly common result of these pressures is that the home is less apt to be used for ritual occasions, except perhaps in Mumbai, and fewer traditional rites of passage are performed, and those usually in a temple.

On the other hand, young parents struggle to find ways to instill their values and the sense of lineage that are crucial in forming personhood. The home becomes a womb where music, art, and literature from the homeland nurture the young in a sense of the tradition. Virtually all parents see to it that the children learn to speak and understand the written tongue, though it is increasingly difficult to find systematic ways to help them learn to read and write it. There is some selective performance of *saṁskāras*, especially those of naming, tonsure, and initiation, but these are often done in the precincts of a temple, under the guidance of a resident priest rather than the traditional household priest or *purohita;* often without the participation of familial elders (though these may be present); and at times selected more for their convenience for participants than for their astrological precision (though inauspicious times are still avoided by the orthoprax). The tendency toward orthopraxy in maintenance of those childhood rituals remains stringent among Tamil brahmins in Pittsburgh and Mumbai and among brahmins, Chettiyars, and Ceylon Tamils in Malaysia and Singapore. But in the Malay Straits, those once considered untouchables or lower caste are increasingly seeing to it that their children are provided some rites of passage, in part to assume a sense of participation and upward mobility. Performance of these rituals serves many functions: humanizing the passages of life in the face of urban depersonalization; affirming family and kinship ties; socialization of the infant or child into his or her appropriate place in the lineage; and keeping religious commitments and vows to senior members of the family, some of whom may not be able to attend.

It is worth observing that it is young parents who have often been providing the leadership within the expatriated South Indian communities. In Singapore it is often this age group in the middle classes who have assumed leadership of the Indian community and affiliate with one or more ethnically oriented organizations. Today in Malaysia it is often the younger *dalit* parents who are assuming leadership roles within the Indian community; in Pittsburgh it has been young parents, with children reaching the age of accountability, who were most active in constructing the now-famed Śrī Veṅkaṭeśvara Temple.

The temple or cultural center by and large has become the extension of the domestic sphere for these émigré couples,[67] and major religious events such as festivals and the occasional rite of passage have remained one means by which children are socialized. Where once a young Tamil mother was socialized into her role as "bearer of the tradition" by her grandmother and mother-in-law, with whom she lived, as an expatriate, she is much more apt to depend on her Indian peer group for advice and on the public religious and cultural sphere to provide the ambience and maintenance for her children once done at home. Parenting, for the South Indian expatriate, presents the most rewarding of times and the most trying of times.

Youth and Young Adulthood

Adolescence is in any setting a difficult passage—not least of all because of the need to sort out one's sense of self. The passage is no less problematic for the Tamilian in diaspora.[68] Indeed, an entire book could be written on the experience of young South Indian expatriates in these various cities, but in this context it will suffice to note but a few salient features.

On the one hand, there are a number of stimuli inviting the adolescent to distance oneself from one's parents' forms of self-expression. While outright rebellion may be relatively rare in these settings, there is the inevitable sense of need for "personal space" and a sense of self one can claim irrespective of parents' perceptions. Further, children of immigrants are likely to have much more interaction with non-Indian peers than may have been the case with their parents.

From the first year of school through college, the teenager is rubbing shoulders with classmates of differing ethnic and religious orientations. Clearly this can lead in either direction: to a questioning of the values with which one grew up and an engaging in a pilgrimage to discover more satisfying values, or to a return to the relative safety of a supportive family and religious network. The pressure to succeed in a career that is deemed prestigious or highly paid is one that can lead to a pragmatic "yuppieism," but not necessarily to orthopraxy. The attraction of popular culture (especially in the United States), materialistic opportunities, and the lure of the larger world (whether it be the increased Islamization of Malaysia, the particular form of multiculturalism found in Singapore, or the post-Christian secularity of the United States) are all a part of the matrix in which identities are formed. Occasionally, one even finds a thoughtful second-generation Indian (for example, in Pittsburgh) who seeks to distance himself or herself from the perceived attitudes, insularity, or "arrogance" of the Indian peer group, or who chafes at the orthopraxy of his or her elders (as with some Ceylon Tamils of Kuala Lumpur). All of these factors can discourage continuities in religious practice.

On the other hand, it is tempting to suggest that it is during these years that many expatriated Indians show the most inclination toward being religious—at least this is the case in KL and Singapore. In the context of the high-pressure school system of Singapore, many young adolescents can be seen in animated conversation with religious recruits. Youngsters from working-class families, in particular, are attracted to nonestablishment forms of religious expression—for example, consulting with mediums, dancing on the fringes of festival processions, or becoming possessed. Indian Malaysian college students in KL, more than at any other time in their lives, are interacting with Chinese and Malay peers and, as a result, engage in religious activities as a form of ethnic marking. Such students seek out meditation and study groups, engage in vow taking during the annual Tai Pūcam festival, and in other ways deepen their awareness of Tamil/Indian/Hindu/subethnic orientations.

The factors working in favor of this youthful turning to religious expressions are many. There is the need for a sense of rootedness in the context of transition and urbanization. There is the longing for community and peer support (and community is often shaped along ethnic and subethnic lines). Further, younger Indians, like their Chinese counterparts, are socialized to respect parents and authority; thus, breaking with tradition can become especially traumatic. As the age of marriageability approaches, there is the perceived need to be visible to prospective partners and to be seen as apt embodiments of the tradition from which a partner is presumably being sought. This form of "religion for courtship purposes" is most likely to be found among the elites of Mumbai or Singapore, where remnants of the traditional forms of arranged marriage are still likely to prevail.

But it is marriage itself that becomes the single most significant symbol of the generational differences in self-expression. Some Indian émigré parents, especially of elite caste subgroups, prefer to arrange marriages for their children (with varying degrees of input from the candidates), preferably with partners from the same linguistic group, caste, and economic and educational status on the grounds that compatibility is more important than love (or perhaps will lead to love) in making a marriage work. The younger generation is much more likely than their parents were to at least want a say in whom they marry (and preferably to pick such a partner). In the United States, pressures to date like their majority American counterparts increase the likelihood that a marriage will not be quite as the parents would have arranged. But even in the other cities studied, there is an increased acceptance of "love marriage" (though it remains more painful for upper-class parents). In fact, in Singapore 3 to 5 percent of marriages by Indian Singaporeans are interethnic.

All of these factors have led to considerable discussion and experimentation among expatriates of ways to maintain "family values" in the next generation. The institutions available (temples, culture centers, and so on) have organized a wide range of activities to increase the chances that the young will retain their ethnic and religious ties. These activities include camps (Pittsburgh), academies of music and dance (all the cities), language classes (Pittsburgh) or schools (the other cities), and contests in oratory and religious or historical knowledge (all the cities). It is as if rites of passage have been replaced with quasi-religious forms of achievement. An especially apt illustration of this phenomenon, perhaps, is the *aṅgetra,* that occasion when a young woman performs the minimum repertoire of the "graduated" dancer for the first time. This can be done in the environs of a temple, cultural center, or school in front of her affirming community of friends and family, but also for the larger body of acquaintances to whom she can affirm who she is and what she has achieved. In the dance, the young woman embodies the values and cosmology of the culture she inherits.

The Mature Years

As these South Indian expatriates mature and age, principles of selectivity shift somewhat. Careers, especially in dual-career households, have forced the juggling of time and preclude excessive commitments for religious activity. For males especially, the tendency to measure fulfillment in terms of one's career—of what one "does"—catalyzes a tendency toward religious compromises and pragmatism, toward finding avenues of ritual neutrality where one can interact with nonethnic professional peers in contexts where strict religious rules may be temporarily suspended. In such families, there may be a propensity to grope for the "bottom line" of religion, a search for what is deemed to be its essence in spirit rather than the form or letter. At the same time, in cities such as Singapore, Kuala Lumpur, and Mumbai, elites are likely, during their professional years, to express their leadership outside the Indian landscape, either within their professions or within civil associations that transcend ethnicity.

By contrast, the professional years can also provide an impetus for maintaining traditional activities. There are those women, for example, who are not working outside the home; men and women whose careers are not fulfilling; first-generation émigrés with a strong sense of nostalgia for the homeland; lower-class communities that find in religion a way to attain upward mobility; and others who seek fulfillment in communally oriented activities such as song groups (*bhajan̲*), study or discussion groups (*sabhas*), and leadership in temples and cultural centers. In Kuala Lumpur especially, persons from the once "lower classes" are emerging into positions of leadership among the Indian community at large—as public speakers, committee members in religious groups, even in the spawning and maintenance of distinct religious organizations (there were approximately forty of these in the 1990s) under the general umbrella of the Malaysian Hindu Organization. Meanwhile, those elites (for example, Ceylon Tamils and Chettiyars) who are active in religious organizations tend to do so within the subethnic groups that serve as the self-proclaimed "watchdogs of orthodoxy."

As children marry and increasingly set up their own households, there is a tendency even among orthodox families in Mumbai or Singapore toward an increased willingness to accommodate or negotiate the sense of what is important in the religious tradition. Yet as grandchildren arrive, grandparents usually resume the role of "bearers of the torch" and find themselves often in the role of exemplars (if not the propagators) of the tradition.

Retirement offers its own challenges. For some it provides a time for reflection and occasionally a more thoughtful and self-consciously selective participation in the tradition. For others it is a time for "rest" and leaving the leadership for the young. Yet for many (and this is especially notable among the Tamil brahmins of Mumbai), there is a propensity to engage even more intensely in the religious opportunities afforded. It is as if, for some retired men especially, this is the period of life for assuming the role of the seeker-mendicant, and possibly for redressing the guilt felt for the compromises of the working years, and to address the fundamental question, "What must I do, at last, to be 'saved'?"

These remarks, though general, nonetheless illustrate the factors in the life course that have a push-you, pull-you effect within these communities. At almost every stage are impetuses that invite greater participation in the perpetuation of the more narrowly focused markers of identity as well as impetuses for participating in supraethnic patterns. The pressures toward a more religious lifestyle seem greatest in early adolescence in Singapore, the college years in Kuala Lumpur, early parenthood in Pittsburgh, and the retirement years in Mumbai. But even in those phases of life, there is great diversity in the ways people pattern their responses and in degrees of intensity in that response.

Other Boundaries

In addition to those boundaries already discussed, there are still others. Not least important are those between "us" and "them." However seriously a Tamil émigré may take his or her Tamil-ness or caste, invariably that is enacted only in a selective way.

Émigrés have almost always found that they forge reciprocities with neighbors, especially other Indians, in their public ritual life. Tamils associated with the Śrī

Veṅkaṭeśvara Temple in Pittsburgh, for example, share governance, priests, and facilities with Telugus and Kannadas. Gujaratis and other North Indians participate in festivals such as the Navarāttiri, the festival of nine nights dedicated to the goddess in September or October. Shrines in Kuala Lumpur and Singapore, once intended for a founding group, add icons and festivals representing the identities of other Indian communities who become part of the neighborhood. Just as in the era of kingship in Tamil Nadu, when temple ritual reflected the reciprocities of brahmin, king, and landowner, so now temples and their rituals reflect the broader coalition of their neighborhoods. Hence, the temple and its ritual are both "ours" in a narrow sense, and "ours" in a variety of broader senses, even while it is not "theirs"—that is, it remains Hindu (or Muslim) and often significantly South Indian and even incorporates the ambience of its diasporic geography without ceasing to be what it is, a statement about "us."

One of the other more subtle boundaries reflected in the ritualizing of these communities is the rather blurred line between religion on the one hand and everything else on the other. No one can deny that temples and their rituals are religious, but they are seldom constructed as the result of an epiphany from above. The religious/ritual life is a human, even a political construction. People make decisions (whether in response to a dream, or nostalgia, or the perceived needs of their children) about where a shrine should be built and which rituals should be performed. People decide whether and when brahmin priests should be employed and when a degree of authority should be vested in them as agents of the sacred. Artists who paint and sculpt depictions of mythological figures on temple walls also serve as agents of the sacred, as do those boards that manage the institution and its activities. Religious persons are mapmakers who place themselves as they deem necessary within their cosmic and social worlds.

At the same time, these religious expressions have many apparently areligious functions. Temples are sociocultural centers where mother tongues are taught, family and ethnic events are enacted, and friendships are affirmed. Rituals, similarly, are often pragmatic ways of raising money, establishing hegemony over rival institutions, enhancing status, expressing identities, and seeking the enrichment of one's personal life. Where religion leaves off and everything else begins is often difficult to determine.

Explicit in many of these dichotomies that invite the negotiation of identity is yet another boundary, that between past and future. Most Tamils are proud of their collective past—the ancient and rich literary and cultural heritage; the notion that Tamil is, after Sanskrit, the oldest continuous classical language of India; the fact that from the eighth to the fourteenth centuries C.E., Tamil country was home to a flourishing Hindu civilization and, indeed, among the richest civilizations in the world of that era. Looking back and owning one's heritage are important elements in defining who one is. Yet, at the same time, the opportunities of the modern moment invite rapid social change with its concomitant invitations to consumerism. Traditions are therefore often constructed in the modern moment and are collections of selected appropriations from a perceived past. Myth reinterprets this past to make it a reservoir for the present. Ritual is a reflection of this continuum of time. Elements that are thought to be ancient—and the older the better—but are nonetheless given a modern "reading" are recycled in contemporary idiom. The ancient sages who created the rituals are understood to have been wise enough to know the scientific and medical efficacy of such performances. The "ancient" rituals can be interpreted in ways befitting the perception of the modern viewer. In at least this respect, Caroline Humphrey and James Laidlaw are correct: meaning is often ascribed post facto to rituals by those who participate in them.[69]

Rituals similarly reflect the propensity of émigrés to bridge the difference between orthopraxy and hybridization. Tamil brahmins, in particular, want their rituals to be orthoprax, following as carefully as possible the prescriptions laid down by their ancestors. Yet ritual performances of the ancients were already hybridizations, borrowing from various schools and families of performances, reflecting the will of various *yajamānas* (ritual patrons), and mingling "classical" practices with folk or indigenous practice. There is no such thing as a pure primordial "correct" form of ritual. Textual descriptions are not consistent with the varieties of practice done even at the time of writing, let alone today. That rituals performed on behalf of Tamils today are hybridizations is hardly surprising. They do mingle, as they always have, the worlds of their various patrons, the social reciprocities of their participants, and the changes that time and circumstance demand.

In sum, the ritual life of the Tamil communities examined in this volume serves to reflect and/or negotiate various boundaries. A shrine or temple can, at one and the same time, embody Tamil values in its architecture or iconography, as well as transnational influences by its maintenance of a Web site, for example, and its mingling of imageries, both Indian and non-Indian. Such shrines can also accommodate subethnic values by virtue of including an icon or a festival representing a particular caste or geographical region in the homeland. Rituals, similarly, can accommodate the various agendas of participants, mingling archaic and contemporary idiom, classical cosmography, and local geography. Because ritualizing is always a process and lends itself to varying interpretations, it becomes both a mirror and a template of the people who engage in it and of the boundaries on which they live. In subsequent chapters I explore some of the ways these things are expressed in the lives of some Tamils living outside their ancestral homes.

CHAPTER 2

The Construction of a Temple in an American City and the Acculturation Process

The Śrī Veṅkaṭeśvara Temple in Penn Hills, Pennsylvania, a suburb of Pittsburgh, has become a prototypical illustration of the role of religion in the life of South Indians living in the United States. By the time of its twenty-fifth anniversary, celebrated in 2001–2, it had become one of the most prosperous Hindu temples in the world outside of India. It has served as the focus of pilgrimage and visitation by South Indian Americans on the eastern seaboard; the venue of choice for performing of rites of passage for such visitors; and the model that has been followed by most temple builders across North America. Nestled in about fourteen acres on the side of a hill, the temple complex has become host to classes in language, music, and dance; celebrations of various ethnic and family milestones; and a full range of rituals consistent with the Pāñcarātra traditions of Śrī Vaiṣṇavism. It has attained a level of renown and sacrality such that visitors from South India try to make sure they receive *darśan* (a viewing) of Penn Hills' Veṅkaṭeśvara.

For purposes of this volume, of particular interest is the way the ritual life of the temple reflects the processes by which Indian Americans settled into the United States, interacted with their neighbors, and developed reciprocities with fellow South Indians. Tamil, Telugu, and Kannada speakers had to find ways to work together in the temple's development and use it to express their various agendas. The rituals associated with the temple's construction in the late 1970s serve as an apt paradigm of some of those processes. It is worthwhile, therefore, to reconstruct that process in this context.

Pittsburgh, like so many American cities, was settled by immigrants, many of them from eastern Europe. Throughout the 1800s, Croatians, Slavs, Serbs, Poles, Ukrainians, and others mingled with Scotch and Irish settlers, seeking new opportunities and work in steel mills and other industries. They were Catholic (of both Latin and Byzantine rites), Eastern Orthodox, Jewish, Presbyterian. Many of these ethnic groups built churches and synagogues not only as institutions for worship but also as cultural centers where their national heritage and identities could be preserved. These Caucasian groups were joined by African Americans, who now constitute 13 percent of Pittsburgh's population, and more recently by a growing minority of people of Hispanic backgrounds, who number less than 5 percent of the total population of this area. In this ethnic mix one finds an increasing number of Asian Americans, especially Chinese, Japanese, Koreans, Vietnamese, and Indians.

In some respects, the Indian settlers in Pittsburgh expressed their self-identities in ways consistent with those of earlier migrants into the city. Orthodox Christians from eastern Europe, for example, became a particularly visible part of the region. They built churches embodying their ethnic and religious identities, complete with mini domes and icon screens; cathedrals built by Ukrainian, Carpatho-Russian, Serbian, or Greek communities still dot the landscape. For one or two generations, clergy in these churches used their specific historical languages in liturgy—in the Serbian churches, for example, Old Church Slavonic. By the third and fourth generation, however, English had become the dominant language of liturgy; more and more women were participating in the politics of the churches; some majority Americans were marrying or converting into the once totally ethnic churches; and certain forms of hybridization and accommodation to the American landscape occurred. Yet the clergy remained the primary purveyors of specific ethnic traditions. These churches remain centers for instructing the young about their ethnic heritage—for example, on the walls of many of the Sunday school rooms in Serbian churches are maps of Serbia. Rituals specific to the ethnic traditions are still performed—in Serbian orthodox churches and homes, for example, the Slava ritual marking the ancestral tribal identities of a family is performed each year, and at Easter time eggs are painted red, harking back to a pre-Christian Serbian tradition of honoring the dead.

The Indian immigrant population in the Pittsburgh area proved to be a particularly enterprising group. Though their arrival in southwestern Pennsylvania had started as a trickle in the mid-1960s, by the time the Śrī Veṅkaṭeśvara Temple was under construction, many of these immigrants had become quite visible in the area's professional life—its hospitals, universities, and industries. It seemed appropriate to make a formal study of the community. Accordingly, thanks to funding from the Public Committee for the Humanities in Pennsylvania in 1978, the author directed one of the first such studies to be done in the United States. Over two hundred Indian immigrants in the Pittsburgh area were interviewed. The results helped the researchers get a sense of the character of these early immigrants and the factors underlying their interest in building a temple.

Virtually all the Indian settlers in southwestern Pennsylvania were first-generation immigrants. Indeed, 66 percent of them had arrived in the United States since 1968, following the revision of the Immigration and Nationality Act of 1965, a law that tended to liberalize to some extent the quota system for non-European immigrants. The Pittsburgh Indians were clearly a mobile group: 52 percent had been in the Pittsburgh area less than five years, while less than 12 percent had been in the area more than ten years.[1] They were attracted to Pittsburgh by the city's academic and industrial opportunities (at the time, Pittsburgh was the headquarters for more than a dozen multinational corporations, making the city fourth in that category after New York, Chicago, and Los Angeles). Yet there was also an active kinship system at work that helped place Indian immigrants. For example, 71.3 percent of the Indian immigrants surveyed had relatives in the United States; in fact, more than 17 percent had relatives in the Pittsburgh area. This was also a rather young community: the mean age of all adults sampled was thirty-four; 42 percent of them were between the ages of twenty-four and thirty-four; 41.8 percent were thirty-five to forty-four years of age. More than 84 percent of them were married. Families tended to consist of 1.5 children, of whom the oldest had a mean age of eight. The second child—in those families where one existed—had a mean age of 6.2. These early Indian immigrants perhaps more than any immigrant group before them were highly educated, professional people. Of the entire adult population sampled, 75.2 percent had a graduate degree (including 86.3 percent of the men and 54.9 percent of the women). Some 23.3 percent of the interviewed population were currently studying, 87.2 percent of these at a graduate level.[2]

The statistics on the educational level of that generation of Indian immigrants suggest several things. It is clear, for example, that these immigrants were in many ways eminently qualified to contribute to American life professionally. Virtually all of them—with only an occasional exception—used the English language well. Most of them had mastered aspects of Western education and technology even before they came to the United States. That is not to say, of course, that all of them were comfortable with the Western values or mind-set (on which more later). Similarly, the highly professional character of this immigrant population belied some of the stereotypes Americans had of India as a whole—that India, for example, was simply an economically deprived, poverty-stricken nation. In point of fact, the educated professional population of India—those holding postgraduate degrees—is larger than the entire population of France, and its number is among the largest in the world.

Yet the study confirmed that the American response to the Indian presence, at least in the Pittsburgh area, was not always enlightened, and the perceptions of Indian immigrants themselves of that American response were mixed. It is true that the largest single perception Indians registered during interviews was that Americans were "friendly" and "respectful" toward them; 47 percent of all respondents made such an assertion (incidentally, 60 percent of the women, but only 44 percent of the men). All other perceptions, however, tended to be negative: 13.9 percent (including 12.3 percent of the women and 15.7 percent of the men) felt Americans were misinformed and ignorant about India and Indian culture; 11.4 percent (15.1 percent of the men and 6.2 percent of the women) felt that the American majority accepted them on a professional level, but not on a personal or social level. Not surprisingly, 6.4 percent (7.7 percent of the women) reported they had experienced outright discrimination. Another 5.4 percent felt Americans were disinterested or apathetic toward them (see figure 1). Women, in particular, were having difficulty finding work commensurate with their education and training. They were more frequently apt to be at home without access to transportation, while husbands had the family car at work. These may be some of the reasons why 62.3 percent of the women (as compared with 40.2 percent of the men) expressed the desire to live close to other Indian families.

Figure 1. Perceptions Indian immigrants have of American attitudes toward them

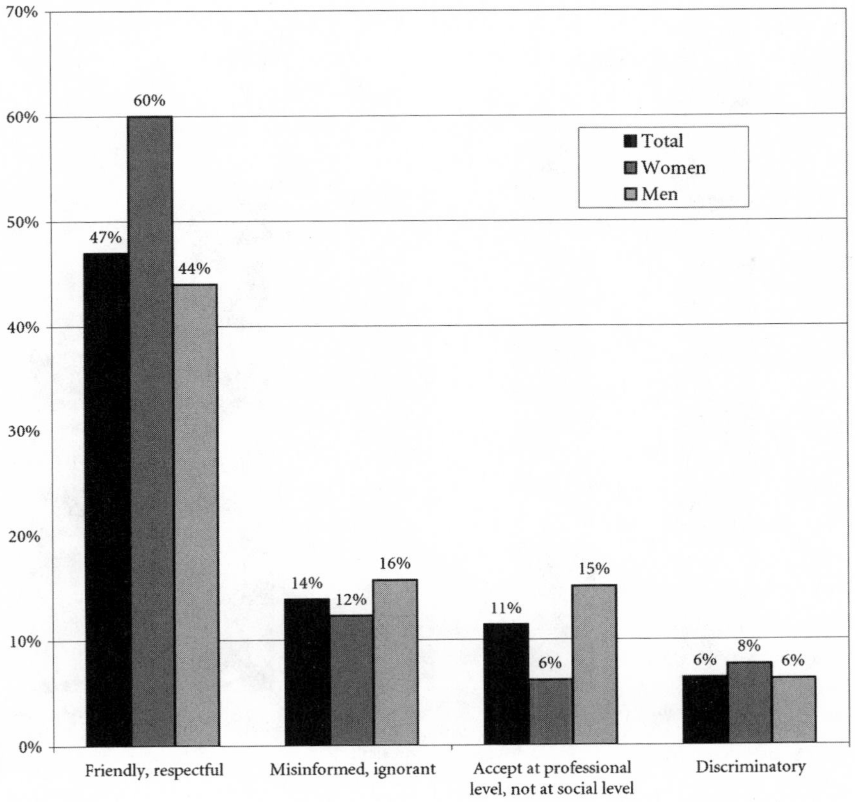

A considerable proportion of these Indian immigrants, in sum, did not feel themselves a fully accepted part of the American landscape. At best, they felt accepted insofar as they were professionally competent or industrious or insofar as they behaved like the American majority. But it was precisely when they seemed different—that is, when they were *Indian*—that they sensed a lack of acceptance. As a result, disillusionment was evident on the part of some Indian immigrants with respect to the American response to them. This disillusionment seemed greater on the part of those Indians who had thought of themselves as substantially Westernized before they arrived (and, therefore, more like Americans). Indians more comfortable with their "Indianness" and therefore only selectively Westernized—in profession, for example, though not necessarily in lifestyle or values—seemed more able to live with the American attitudes toward them. That is to say, members of the latter group apparently accepted themselves as Indians more easily and expected less

Figure 2. Ways of affirming cultural identity

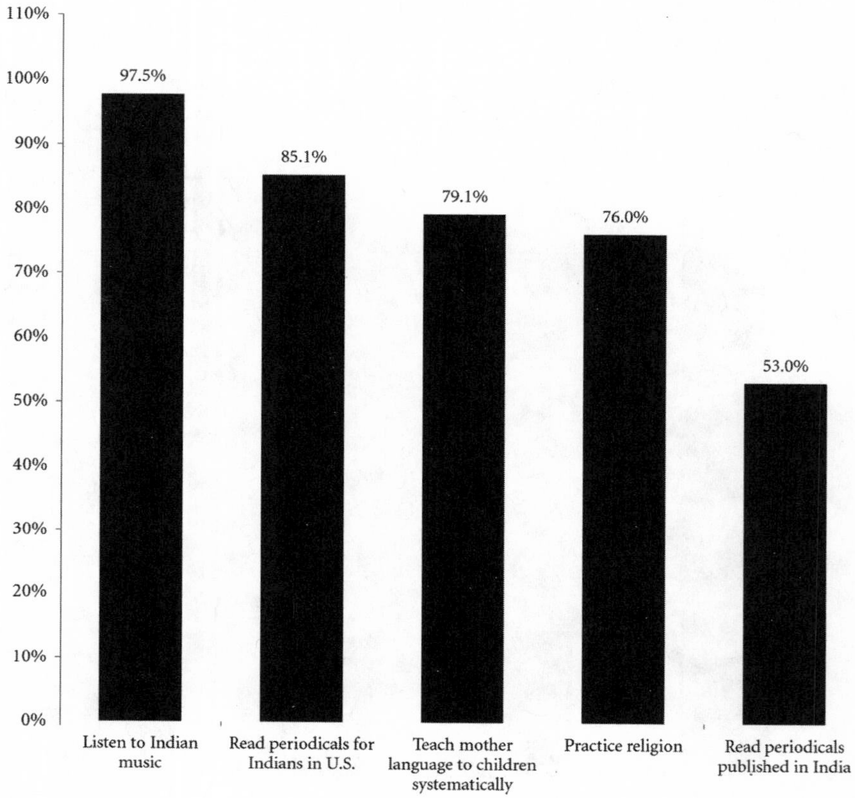

of Americans, and hence they experienced less disillusionment with American attitudes toward them.

First-generation Indian immigrants focused on several questions: To what extent were they American? To what extent Indian? The questions became especially crucial when one's children grew to the age of accountability: In what ways did they want their children to be American? In what ways Indian? What Indian values did they wish their children to retain? What image did they wish their children to have of their heritage?

It is in the context of this concern for cultural identity, the perpetuation of cultural heritage, and the enhancement of self-image that the practice of religion and, especially, the building of a temple, came in to focus. The practice of religion, however selectively, became, at the least, one way to maintain one's cultural heritage, affirm one's ethnoreligious identity, and assure one's children of familiarity with their spiritual-cultural lineage. The construction of a temple was thought to make that identity public and visible.

Figure 3. Ways of practicing religion

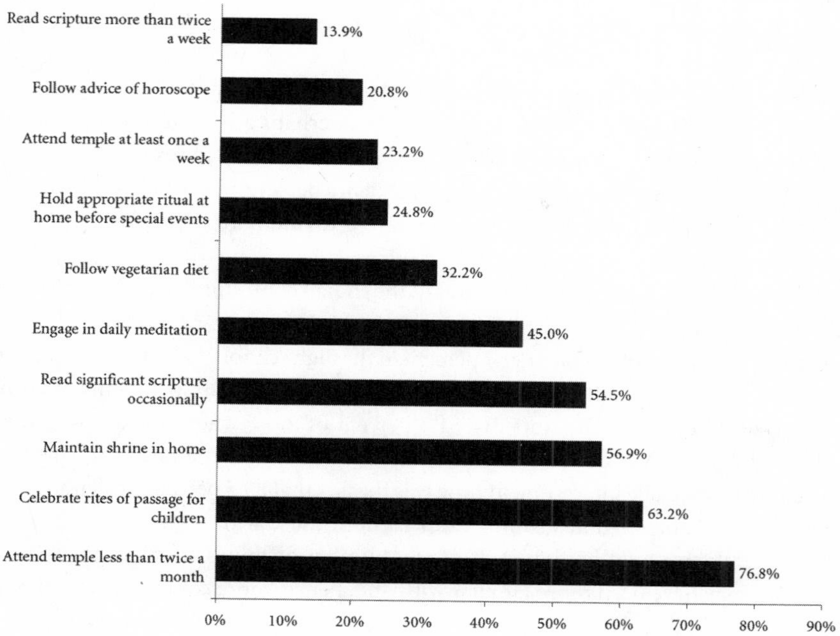

But for Hindu immigrants, generally, the practice of religion was only *one* way of maintaining cultural identity, and the building and attending of a temple was *one* way of being religious.[3] To illustrate, 76 percent of the Indian immigrants in the Pittsburgh study claimed to be religious, yet a larger percentage than that found other ways of expressing their Indian identities. For example, 97.5 percent said they listened to Indian music either through their own recording system or by way of one of the weekly programs of Indian music carried on local radio; 85.1 percent read periodicals published in the United States expressly for Indians; 79.7 percent taught the mother language to their children systematically. At the same time, 53 percent read periodicals published in India (see figure 2).

Similarly, even though more than three-quarters claimed to be religious, only 23.2 percent of the population were attending a temple or religious institution at least once a week, and 76.8 percent were attending less than twice a month. To be sure, some nonreligious factors were involved in this pattern of attendance, not the least of which was geographic—a family living twenty miles from a temple was apt to attend less often than one within five miles, for example. It was also clear, however, that for many Hindus some aspects of religion continued to be practiced not only in a temple but also internally or in the home. For example, 63.2 percent of the Hindus said that they observed rites of passage for their children (though these were often done in the temple); 56.9 percent maintained a shrine in their homes; 54.5 percent read some significant scripture at least occasionally (although only 13.9 percent did so more than twice a week); 45 percent said they engaged in daily meditation; 32.2 percent claimed to be vegetarian; 24.8 percent said they would hold appropriate rituals at home prior to special events; 20.8 percent said they continued to follow the advice of a horoscope or astrologer (see figure 3). Perhaps as significant, a considerable retention of beliefs was recognizably Hindu: 91.6 percent, for example, believed that "there is one God who has many names"; 88.1 percent believed "family duty is sacred"; 75.2 percent believed "all people have a divine nature"; and 49.5 percent believed in "reincarnation."

It is also interesting that certain groups of the Indian community tended to be more religious than others—for example, 84.3 percent of the women respondents as compared to 74.2 percent of the men; 91.7 percent of the high school graduates as compared to 75.8 percent of graduate degree holders; 78 percent of the nonstudents as compared to 69.4 percent of the students; 81.3 percent of those who came to the United States as immigrants as compared to 71.1 percent of those who came as students (see figure 4). An especially interesting finding was the fact that 83.5 percent of all nonbrahmins claimed to be religious, while 71.6 percent of those with brahmin background did. This statistic could be the result of any number of things—for example, some brahmins may have been more familiar with and, hence, more contemptuous of religion; they may have felt freer from the social constraints they would have felt back home to transcend external religious forms; as for nonbrahmins, some may have viewed religion as a form of social mobility, insomuch as they could participate in temple activities in ways their ancestors may not have been able to.

There is no doubt that the construction of a temple had obvious religious as well as cultural significance for Hindu Indian immigrants. Yet this study did suggest at least two words of caution that qualify the discussion that follows:

1. Some religious attrition seemed to have occurred in this community since its arrival in the United States, and that attrition had been more evident in the area of religious *practice* than in the area of religious *belief.* For example, while 57.9 percent said that there had been no substantive change in their religious practice since having come to the United States, 61.4 percent did say that they attended a temple less here than they had in India. (No less than 94.1 percent had attended a temple at least occasionally in India.) Similarly, while 52 percent claimed their concept of religion was not different from that of their parents, 58.9 percent believed they were less religious in practice. However, even though some Hindus were less rigorous in their observance of ritual practice since having immigrated, at least two groups tended to remain relatively orthoprax: women and families of brahmin background. For example, 70 percent of the women said they visited the temple at least once a month, while 46.9 percent of the men claimed to do so (see figure 5). This should not be surprising, not only in terms of the woman's role in

Figure 4. Identification of who is religious

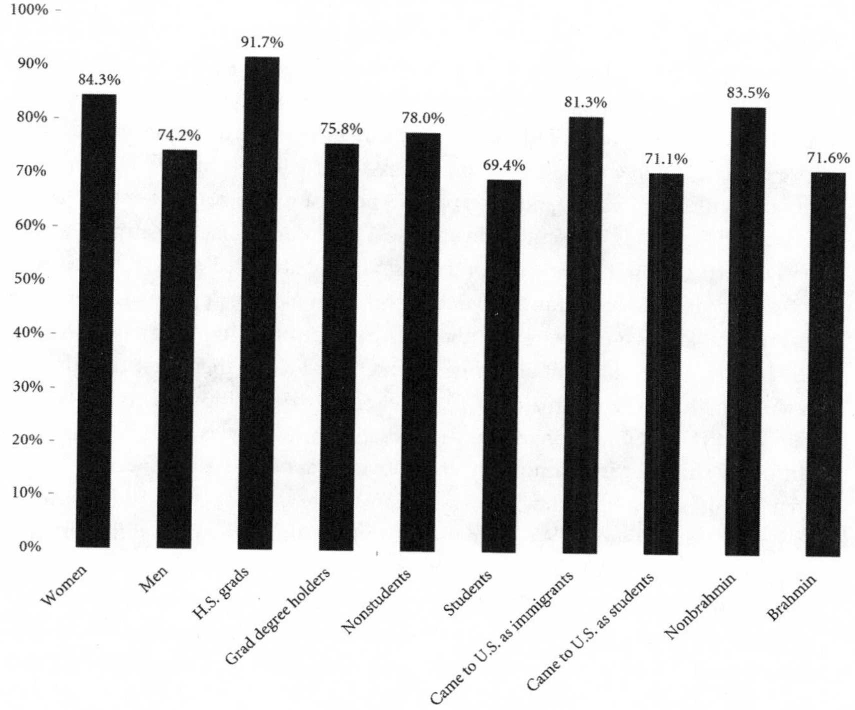

Figure 5. Frequency of temple visitations

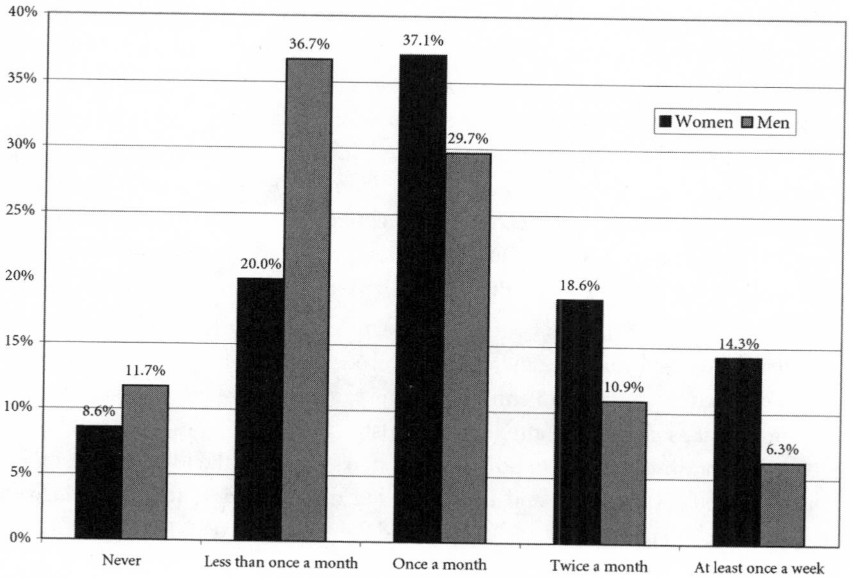

Hindu society as the "bearer of tradition" but also in light of the greater disaffection expressed by women for American society in general.

2. The second qualifying factor worth noting is that many of those attending a temple did so for other than religious reasons. For example, of those who claimed not to be religious, 31 percent went to a temple once a month, and 38.1 percent less often. Similarly, while 54 percent said the main reason for going to a temple was religious, more than 45.3 percent suggested there were other equally compelling reasons—primarily cultural and social ones. For 74.3 percent of the respondents, a temple served both religious and cultural purposes. In the first place, visiting a temple clearly affirmed family ties: 83.3 percent said they attended a temple with their spouse and/or children (only 5.4 percent ever went alone). Temple visitation also affirmed social ties: 48.5 percent indicated they went to a temple as frequently as their best friends. (Incidentally, only 1 percent indicated their best friends were drawn from the American majority.) It is clear these friendships were often linguistically related, as subgroups within the Indian community as a whole were most commonly shaped within linguistic and subcultural boundaries—Bengali, Tamil, Gujarati, and so on. Indeed, when respondents were asked to define themselves by answering the question "Who am I?" more identified themselves in terms of regional-linguistic identities than in terms of their "Indianness." It is not surprising, then, that these regional-linguistic friendship patterns were evident in the patterns of temple attendance. This is expressed in part by the choice of a temple to which a family would go. In the Pittsburgh area there were at least two major Hindu temples developing during that period (the late 1970s), the Śrī Veṅkaṭeśvara Temple in Penn Hills and the Hindu-Jain Temple in Monroeville. The Monroeville temple stressed the theme of "unity in diversity" and provided worship opportunity for Jains as well as Hindus; the Penn Hills temple was more nearly orthoprax in architectural style and ritual and was dedicated primarily to the worship of the deity Viṣṇu in his manifestation as Lord Veṅkaṭeśvara. As I shall observe, it was modeled after a similar temple that is an enormously popular pilgrimage center in the state of Andhra Pradesh. Hence, while the religious assumptions underlying the maintenance and attendance of each temple may have been quite different, it was by no means incidental that it was primarily South Indians—especially Kannada, Telugu, and Tamil speakers—who attended the Penn Hills temple and primarily North Indians who attended the Monroeville temple.

More specifically, *no* Indians who had come from any of the four southern states of India claimed, in the study, to attend the Monroeville temple exclusively, while 40.7 percent claimed to attend the Penn Hills temple exclusively—another 50 percent of the South Indians claimed to attend both Pittsburgh area temples. Conversely, 24.1 percent of the immigrants from other Indian states attended the Monroeville temple exclusively, while 14 percent said they attended the Penn Hills temple exclusively. Another 45.3 percent of the North Indians said they attended both temples.

Table 1. Temple attendance in Pittsburgh

Temple	S. Indian immigrants	N. Indian immigrants
Hindu-Jain Temple only	0%	24.1%
Śrī Veṅkaṭeśvara Temple only	40%	14.1%
Both temples	50%	45.3%
None	10%	16.5%

Whatever else these statistics suggest, they seem to illustrate several realities about the Indian immigrant community as a whole in its early years in the Pittsburgh area: (1) friendships and identity groups tended to be related to linguistic, subcultural, or regional identities; (2) religious Indian immigrants tended to identify with those religious, ritual, and architectural traditions most nearly associated with their regional identities; (3) the practice of religion, and especially the attending of a temple, was one way—though not necessarily the most common way—of affirming family ties and cultural heritage.

With these qualifications and this context in mind it is, nevertheless, clear from the history of the building of the Śrī Veṅkaṭeśvara Temple and the care that was exercised to provide an aura of authenticity to its architectural and ritual character that its construction was a social and cultural event, as well as a religious event. I turn now to the building of that temple and to some of the implications the process had for a community of first-generation Hindu Indian immigrants becoming a part of the American landscape.

The Construction of a Temple

A Brief History

It is not necessary to reconstruct the entire history of the Pittsburgh temples in great detail in this context. It will suffice to trace the events that led to the existence of two major temples in the area, including the construction of a prototypically orthoprax temple.

The story starts for all intents and purposes in December 1971.[4] A few Hindu couples had been meeting irregularly in their homes for *bhajaṉs* (the singing of devotional songs) and other expressions of their tradition. A network of some hundred families shared a concern to find ways that their children could get together and learn more of their Indian heritage. That December the University of Pittsburgh sponsored a classical Bharata Nātyam dance performance by Mrs. Jeya Mani, a Tamil artist whose husband had recently joined the anthropology department at Slippery Rock State College. Immigrant Indians attending the performance were moved to systematize their concerns for their children. Dr. and Mrs. Mani were invited to the home of a Tamil couple, Dr. and Mrs. Raj Gopal, for a meal. Mrs. Mani was asked to start a dance class for some of the girls. A basement in Squirrel Hill, in the southeastern part of the city, then being rented for use as an "India shop," was pressed into service. By January 14, 1972, the basement had become a makeshift sanctuary where families gathered on Sundays for *pūjās*, conducted by local lay "priests." Twenty children were present for the first dance class. The Gopals' own daughters, then age nine and seven, were among them.

However, Mrs. Gopal and others kept dreaming of a *pucca* (authentic) temple. That fall a Professor Somani, a Rajasthani professor at the University of Pittsburgh, was excited about such a prospect when the idea came up at a dinner he was enjoying at the Gopals. It was agreed that Dr. Alagappan of New York, who was thinking of building a temple in New York and who had been negotiating with the Śrī Veṅkaṭeśvara Temple in Tirupati, India, about that prospect, be invited to Pittsburgh to discuss various ideas. Those discussions occurred in October 1972. In the following months Drs. Gopal and Somani drove twenty thousand miles throughout the Pittsburgh area, visiting virtually every Indian family known to them. Over a two- or three-month period, the feasibility of building a temple was discussed and thirty thousand dollars was committed for the project. An ad hoc steering committee was established in December 1972 for planning and administering the project. This committee was interethnic and included Raj Gopal, Aprajita Guha, Ashok Malhotra, Robit Mehta, Lily Nath, and Bidyut Nyogi.

By March 1973 there was enough response apparent to warrant the establishment of the Hindu Temple Society of North America, Pittsburgh. This group was incorporated as the Pittsburgh affiliate of the organization discussing similar plans in New York. After the incorporation, an executive committee was elected by its membership, and a membership drive intensified, with dues charged at two levels: students could become members for an annual fee of twelve dollars; others paid twenty-five dollars.

On April 5, 1973, a Baptist church on Illini Drive in Monroeville was purchased and became the cultural center and temporary temple for the community. It housed a Sikh *gurudwāra* (ritual space) and makeshift shrines for both Jain and Hindu communities. It is said that even Muslims and some Indian Christians occasionally participated in the cultural events held at the Monroeville center.

In June 1973, representatives of the Śrī Veṅkaṭeśvara Temple in Tirupati, the most popular and wealthiest temple in India, after visiting the temple committee in New York, came to Pittsburgh. They suggested that a Śrī Veṅkaṭeśvara Temple be built on the site on which the temporary structure in Monroeville was standing. The hills surrounding the Monroeville site were said to be reminiscent of the Tirupati Hills. The officers of the temple in India offered to help in the building process. The executive committee in Pittsburgh approved that suggestion, and in July 1973 the decision was publicly announced.

Subsequently, architects at Tirupati drew up plans for the Pittsburgh temple. The plans were eventually approved in October 1974 by the board of trustees and the general body. On November 21, 1974, the board of trustees of the Tirupati Temple Devasthanam (temple office) voted to donate four hundred thousand rupees' worth of materials (icons, ritual materials, doors, etc.) and labor to the Pittsburgh project. A matching amount was to be returned to Tirupati from Pittsburgh in the form of medical supplies and scientific equipment.

Ground breaking for the new temple occurred on April 17, 1975. It was a festive occasion despite the blustery weather. About five hundred members of the local Indian community attended; representatives of the Tirupati temple office were on hand, and India's ambassador to the United States, T. N. Kaul, addressed the gathering. Pittsburgh Indians paid the expenses for the ritual (for example, the jewels buried for every such ground breaking) while the Tirupati temple paid for their representatives' travel expenses. At the suggestion of the Tirupati office, the *Pāñcarātrāgama* ritual tradition was used for these ceremonies inasmuch as it was thought more priests would be available who were trained in that tradition, and these priests would be more flexible and less conservative than the priests schooled in the alternative ritual tradition of Vaiṣṇavism would be—that is, the *Vaikhānasāgama* school.

Following the ground-breaking ceremony, brochures were printed and donations solicited. An election was scheduled for June 1975 for president and vice president of the organization. The two candidates were Dr. Sudhakhar Reddy, a Telugu who received the support of many of the North Indians who were joining the organization in increasing numbers, and Bidyut Niyogi, a Bengali nonetheless supported by many South Indians. The election proved to be a symbolic catalyst for spirited and often heated exchanges of opinion. It was evident the community was profoundly divided. Two issues, at least, surfaced during the ensuing months: (1) there was some feeling that Raj Gopal and a small group of others who had been in leadership positions had made too many unilateral decisions; (2) some did not want to commit themselves to any traditional priest or ritual school, nor make any single deity the presiding deity of the temple. This feeling was often expressed in terms that opposed a "sectarian" or "regional" temple but favored rather the idea of "unity in diversity" and a shrine that would house many deities as being more representative of Hinduism.

On July 25, 1975, a general body meeting was held to air and discuss the issues. The following is an excerpt of a resolution that was passed:

> Having affirmed that the Hindu faith is essentially universal, catholic, permissive and non-dogmatic in its ways of worship; and that the Hindu temple of Pittsburgh is and shall remain non-sectarian and broad-based, so as to meet the religious, spiritual, cultural, humanitarian, educational and social needs of all its members;
>
> It is hereby resolved:
>
> 1. That the new temple which when built shall not in any way violate the aforesaid affirmations;
> 2. That in recognition of the efforts and to respect the feelings of certain sections of the Indian community, the architecture of the new temple may remain as per the original plans and the idols of Lord Venkateshwara, Lakshmi, and Devi will be placed in the center.

The resolution went on to call for the inclusion of icons of other main Hindu deities under the same roof and for the devising of mechanisms whereby other deities could be added if and when needed, and that the new temple should be open for "personal and group worship for all its members, and all . . . religious ceremonies and festivals as per the religious spiritual needs of the members shall be permitted therein."

The resolution goes on:

> It is felt that some persons may have contributed towards the building of the new temple under the impression that this will be exclusively Lord Venkateshvara Temple. If such persons feel that the concepts of the new temple as stated herein are unacceptable to them for their own reasons, the amount of their contributions towards the building of the new temple will be duly refunded if so desired.
>
> This resolution explicitly directs the offices of the temple to abstain from any and all such commitments and acts of omission and commission which are contradictory to the words and the intent of this resolution. If any such commitments have been made or any such acts have been accomplished which stand contradictory to the words and intent of this resolution, all such acts and commitments are hereby voided and cancelled.[5]

The passage of this resolution resulted in a series of actions over the ensuing months. When the resolution was sent to the Tirupati office, the Devasthanam responded in a letter addressed to Raj Gopal, dated September 11, 1975, to the effect that because the resolution was in variance with the original agreement to build a temple exclusively to Lord Veṅkaṭeśvara, the Devasthanam therefore must withdraw its offer of support.

Efforts at negotiation and compromise continued throughout the fall and the subsequent winter. As late as April 13, 1976, a group met with Ambassador Kaul to attempt a compromise. One such compromise suggested was the building of a common hall adjacent to several shrines, each shrine dedicated to a different deity. Unfortunately, the meeting with Ambassador Kaul was too late.

On November 3, 1975, Raj Gopal wrote to the constituency reaffirming his vision that the temple should be devoted to Lord Veṅkaṭeśvara and that its ritual life be consistent with that proposed by the Tirupati office. He further suggested that additional icons be housed in a "Hall of Sculptures" and that eventually another ecumenical temple be built in which such icons could be installed. Gopal expressed the belief that a Śrī Veṅkaṭeśvara temple should be constructed and operated by an "autonomous unit" that could ensure continuity of designs already in hand. He felt the governing body for the temple should consist of "only devoted members with highest commitment in terms of time and money to the organization."

The December meeting of the general body adjourned without resolving the crisis and with hostile feelings remaining high. That same month an alternative organization, the Śrī Veṅkaṭeśvara Temple Inc., was formed, supported largely by South

Indians. The group's intent as expressed in an open letter by G. Manohar on March 22, 1976, was the "construction of an authentic temple dedicated to Lord Veṅkaṭeśvara." By May, Bidyut Niyogi had resigned as president of the Hindu Temple Society and Raj Gopal as secretary, and the SV Temple Inc. became a virtually autonomous group by April 20, 1976. Six trustees were asked by this organization to head the group's efforts. About fifty thousand dollars was raised by June 1976.

The vision of this group remained consistent with that expressed earlier. A news bulletin dated July 1976 put it this way:

> Sri Venkatesvara temple will be a beautiful representation of ancient Indian Temple architecture and of the finest aspects of traditional Hindu worship and devotion. It will meet the spiritual and cultural needs of a large number of persons in this country of Indian origin. It will also provide an exquisite example of our cultural heritage on American soil.
>
> Sri Venkatesvara temple organization will work in close harmony with (a) the Tirumala Tirupathi Devasthanam, one of the most popular and best run temple organizations in India, and (b) the Hindu Temple Society in New York, which is at present engaged in the construction of Sri Ganesh Temple, also with the help of TTD. The planning and implementation of both projects is being done jointly, especially in India.[6]

On June 30, 1976, some new property was purchased in Penn Hills by the SV Temple Inc. That same day the official ground breaking occurred with representatives from the Tirupati office present. That summer eighty thousand dollars was raised, enough to bring fifteen workmen (*śilpi*s) from India for some of the construction. No official priest had yet been appointed. In October 1976, during a meeting in Tirupati with Raj Gopal representing the Penn Hills temple, the decision to send *Pāñcarātrāgamic* priests was reaffirmed. Consequently, on November 11, 1976, the official installation of icons from India occurred, the *pratiṣṭhā*—a ten-day ceremony over which a traditional *Pāñcarātrāgamic* priest presided. A young priest, Sampathnarayanan, was brought to serve as the fledgling temple's first priest.

By June 1977 another $120,000 had been raised from all over the country. The date for the *kumbhābhiṣeka*, or official temple dedication, was set for June 8, 1977. The time had to be determined by appropriate astrological measurements, including the necessity that the ceremony be conducted during *utarayana*, or before the summer solstice. Hence, even though the temple was not completed, it was dedicated at the appointed time.

The Ritual Sequence

The construction and maintenance of a traditional Hindu temple is based on at least two classical traditions. One has to do with ritual techniques, and the other with architectural style. The ritual techniques selected for the Śrī Veṅkaṭeśvara Temple of Pittsburgh are those reflected in the texts known as the *Pāñcarātrāgama*s, recorded between the eighth and fourteenth centuries. Priests steeped in that tradition, often learning it by rote and apprenticeship from their fathers, become the ritual technicians for those temples following the tradition. Similarly, architectural details in all traditional Hindu temples are based on appropriate manuals, known as the *Śilpa Śāstras.* The specific text that served as a basis for the craftsmen (or *śilpis*) used for the Penn Hills temple was the *Kasyapa Śilpa Śāstra.* While most of the Hindu craftsmen were unable to read the original texts written in Sanskrit, a contemporary Tamil translation was available. More important, a foreman-scholar (*stāpati*) who was familiar with the textual prescriptions was to serve as the architectural and ritual leader. That is, the act of constructing a temple—including the sculpting, carpentry, and masonry—is a ritual act led by a classically trained foreman whose workmen, like many priests, have learned through rote and apprenticeship.

The construction of a traditional Hindu temple in this American city thus was an experiment in intercultural cooperation. On the one hand were craftsmen, many of whom did not speak English but were trained in classical traditions of Hindu architecture. On the other hand were American unionized workers—electricians, bulldozer drivers, and others—who for the first time were observing a very different architectural tradition at work. Compromises were sometimes struck—for example, brick was used where the Indian tradition called for stone. But, by and large, the Śrī Veṅkaṭeśvara Temple of Pittsburgh stands as a replica of Dravidian architectural style. Its central tower, or *vimāṉam,* copied the style first found in the Pallava art of eighth-century South India; its entranceway, or *kōpuram,* copies those of the Cōḻas, a twelfth-century South Indian dynasty.

Texts go into great detail regarding the appropriate dimensions of a temple's various parts and the ritual procedures entailed in constructing one. It is unnecessary here to reconstruct all such details. Suffice it to say that, in general, the construction of a temple is highlighted by a series of ritual acts, which in the case of the Penn Hills temple included the ground breaking, the installation of the icons representing the presiding deities (*pratiṣṭhā*), and the dedication (*kumbhābhiṣeka*). In each of these major ritual events, certain ritual principles were used. A small space was set apart as a sacrificial room (Sanskrit, *yāgaśāla;* Tamil, *yākacālai*), which served as a surrogate "temple" and a ritual universe. This space was purified and sacralized and the power of the divine invoked therein. Elements to be installed within the permanent temple—and figuratively that temple itself—were empowered and sacralized in the *yāgaśāla.* The power and sacrality were then transferred, in effect, from the small room to the larger temple.

The Surrogate Shrine (*Yāgaśāla*)

The focus of most of the rites of consecration, then, was the temporary sacrifice room (*yāgaśāla*). This room combined the symbolism of the universe, the temple, and the human body. A pedestal at its center represented Mt. Meru, the center of the mythical Hindu universe; four doorways and four corners represented eight cosmic directions,

Figure 6. The *yāgaśāla* used in the consecration of the Penn Hills Temple

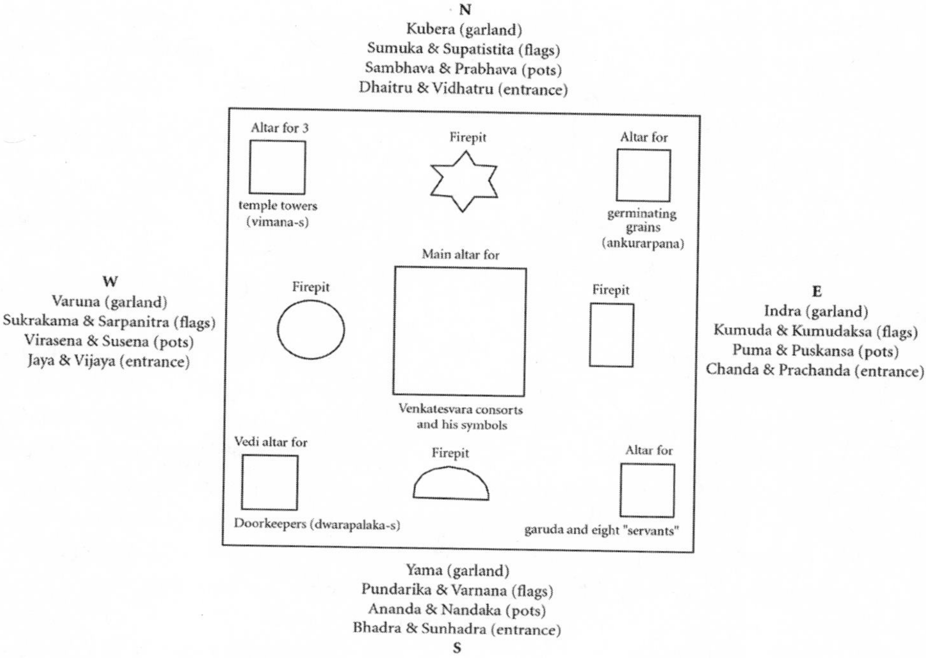

presided over by deities thought to be the guardians of the cosmic directions and represented in the ritual by earthen vessels. Four fire pits where libations were poured into the fire during the sacrifice represented mediating points between earth and heaven. Explicit in any ritual of consecrating a temple is the imagery of founding a world. But, more than that, according to the textual formulation known as the *vāstupuruṣamaṇḍala,* this minicosmos is equated to the human body.[7] That is, the symbolism of the body as used in techniques such as Tantra and Yoga is homologized to the temple. The temple, the sacrifice room, and the human body are all seen as microcosms in which life-changing rituals can be performed. A simplified diagram of the *yāgaśāla* used in the consecration of the Penn Hills temple is shown above.

In the ritual, the "deities" and various elements to be consecrated were represented by conical vessels (*pālikai*). On each altar several such surrogate objects stood. On the northeast altar were vessels bearing the germinating seeds of nine grains, implanted at the beginning of all dedicatory rituals; these growing grains would link the art of temple building to the imagery of implantation, growth, and other agricultural motifs. On the southeast altar stood vessels representing the *garuda,* or hawk, the vehicle of Viṣṇu, the presiding deity of the temple. With the *garuda* were representations of eight other entities—for example, Vāsuteva or Śiva and Puruṣa or the cosmic demiurge. On the southwest altar were representations of the guardians to the main shrines of the temple (the *dwarāpālakas*); on the northwest side were representations of the three temple towers (*vimāṇam*). On the altar at the center were representations of Śrī Veṅkaṭeśvara, his consorts Āntal and Padma, and symbols associated with Viṣṇu such as the wheel (*cakra*). At the doorways, vessels and flags represented the deities who guarded the eight cosmic directions.

Two of the major ritual sequences that must be consummated in the construction of any authentic Hindu temple are the *pratiṣṭhā* (installation of icons) and *kumbhābhiṣeka* (temple dedication). The first of these occurred for the Penn Hills temple between November 10 and 17, 1976.

Installing the Icons

The *pratiṣṭhā* is the process by which it is believed icons can be embodied with the fullness of the divine.[8] *Tiṣṭhā* literally means a "standing place" or location, and *pra* means "with greatness." The process was believed to literally implant the deity in his new home, ritually bringing Veṅkaṭeśvara in all his power to the North American continent. The icons were carved in India over three months, then shipped to Pittsburgh. An auspicious time was chosen with the help of astrologers, and a master of ceremonies (*ācārya*) was selected,[9] in this instance, one Srinivasācārya from Hyderabad, a specialist in such rituals. The ritual procedure for the installation can be summarized as follows:

First, a *saṅkalpa* was performed. This was, in effect, the solemnization of a verbal contract in which all members present vow to enter in the ritual process while the divine is invited to bless the proceedings and remove impediments. This occurred at Penn Hills on the evening of November 10, 1976. The chief *ācārya* together with his assistant, Sampathnarayanan, chosen to become the first resident priest for the temple, then proceeded with other parts of the ceremony: a sacred cord was tied around the wrists of all present, symbolizing their oath to observe the appropriate conduct as prescribed in the tradition for the seven days of the ritual. The string remained on the wrists of participants to remind them of this vow. Among other things, the participants were expected to practice sexual continence and refrain from the eating of meat. This ceremony is called *takṣabandana.*

The ritual known as *aṅkurārppaṇam* followed. The seeds of nine grains were planted in pots accompanied by appropriate chants and the pouring of libations into the four fires. These libations, repeated frequently throughout the seven days, included ghee (melted butter), cooked rice, and medicinal plants and herbs. The sprouting of these seeds throughout the week was intended to be homologous to the "planting" of the temple and its icons.

On the central altar, several vessels of silver and copper were placed. These contained scented waters and precious jewels; inserted into their tops were coconuts, mango leaves, *darbha* grass (used in the ancient sacrificial rituals), flowers, and pieces of new cloth. Into these vessels Viṣṇu was invoked and invited to be present for the entire ritual. These vessels became the surrogate presence of the god, from which his power was eventually transferred to the permanent icons. On other altars similar vessels were invoked for the consorts, the door keepers, and other deities. All these surrogate deities, once invoked, were then worshipped in the prescribed manner. These invocations and libations were repeated for seven days.

Meanwhile, on November 11, after appropriate preliminary rituals, the eyes of the icons were opened by the chief sculptor. For several ensuing days these icons were themselves purified and sacralized by the priests. This process includes several steps. The first, known as *jalādhivāsavidhi*—literally immersion—was substituted at Penn Hills by *chāyādhivāsa*—that is, immersing an effigy rather than the icon. *Chāyādhivāsa* is a ritual in which the shadows of the icons are made to fall on water in a pot; in that water, pieces of *darbha* grass had been placed (with appropriate mantras) twisted in a particular fashion to become effigies of the appropriate deities. This process is an alternative done when it is not possible to immerse the icons in running water all night. The ritual, in effect, represents a cooling and purifying of the icon. There followed worship of the presiding deity of the land (*vāstupuruṣa*) on which the temple had been constructed.

The next day, after the usual rituals in the *yāgaśāla* or surrogate temple, the icons were covered with paddy, again with appropriate mantras, and kept that way for the whole night; this step is known as *dhānyādhivāsa.* The next day the icons were covered with flowers (*puṣpādhivāsa*) and kept overnight.[10] The fourth day (and overnight) they were strewn with precious gems (*ratnādhivāsa*). The last of the processes is *śāyanādhivasa* or the keeping of the icons in beds or cots, covered with cloths or blankets. These five stages are apparently intended to represent five stages of creation and homologize the icon to the five elements and other fivefold entities such as the cosmos itself.

On the day prior to the installation, fire sacrifices were performed for the deities, representing the ten vital forces of the cosmos and the five elements, earth, water, fire, air, and space. After appropriate libations to each group, the icons were touched with ghee left over after the libation. At the same time the priests were reciting appropriate mantras and propitiating the appropriate presiding deities. Particular parts of the icon were thereby sacralized and homologized to the forces and elements of the universe. This ritual is known as *prāṇadi dasa vayunyāsa.*

The most important step in the installation of the icons followed: the giving of life itself, *prāṇapratiṣthā.* After the libations and invocations (*nyāsas*) were done, the vessels were carried from the *yāgaśāla* to the pedestals where the icons had been set up within the temple by the *śilpis* or craftsmen. The *ācārya* requested the deity to come from the pot and dwell in the icon, asking that the lord in his formless state infuse himself in the form of this representation *(parivāradevatā*).[11] An *abhiṣeka,* or bath with holy water, was given the icons again accompanied by *mantras*. The icons were dressed. A *santihoma,* or libation for peace, was performed; various deities were worshipped and invited to be present thereafter. That evening the god and goddess were ritually married, though this ritual would not be necessary where the two appear in the same shrine.

Sacralization of the Temple

Another major ritual sequence in temple building is the *kumbhābhiṣeka* (Tamil, *kumpāpiṣēkam*), literally, anointing of the "pot." This is a ritual rarely done even in India, for it represents the consecration of a new temple or a reconsecration after a major renovation. It has now been performed in North America several times, the first two times in New York and in Pittsburgh. The highlight of the ritual is the settling of golden vessels (*kalaśa*s) on top of the temple's major towers and anointing them, an act that signifies that the temple itself is set aside as sacred space. This event, even more than the *pratiṣṭhā,* can assume the character of a spectacle and has the potential of attracting many witnesses. Such was the case on June 8, 1977, when the Śrī Veṅkaṭeśvara Temple in Penn Hills held its *kumbhābhiṣeka.* The event became an electric moment for those in the Pittsburgh area who had worked and dreamed for so long for a temple, as well as an occasion for pilgrimage for immigrant Indians at a distance, some of whom came up to five hundred miles for the climactic occasion.

A *kumbhābhiṣeka,* in general, has several intentions. It incorporates much of the symbolism of the *pratiṣṭhā* rituals so that by means of the *kumbhābhiṣeka,* the temple itself, and especially the temple tower, is set up or installed as an embodiment of the divine presence. The divine presence is thought to become manifest in the temple towers through at least three processes: (1) First the *yāgaśāla* is fully sacralized and the divine invoked into the appropriate entities in the surrogate temple. The divine power is then ritually transferred into the permanent fixtures of the temple from the sacrifice room; (2) the priests fully sacralize (and cosmicize) their own bodies, then transfer that sacral power into the divine representations through the Tantric rituals known as *nyāsa*s, or invocatory prayers; (3) the deities are evoked out of the divine symbols and invited to assume their appropriate forms (rather than the formless state in which they were thought to have been previously present in the symbols) once the symbols are deemed to have become fit embodiments in which the deities may appear.

The rituals of *kumbhābhiṣeka* combine several motifs. The building of a temple becomes like the founding of a cosmos by homologizing parts of the sacrificial room and eventually the temple itself to various parts of the universe. Building a temple is also likened to the planting of a crop through rituals such as the germinating of grains, the use of paddy on the pedestal of the deities, and other devices that homologize deities or temple parts and vegetation. Further, building a temple becomes the inauguration of a king in his domain by means of various rituals, some of them directly borrowed from ceremonies associated with kingship. The deity is treated like a sovereign; the temple becomes his palace; the landscape it surveys becomes the king's domain; and the worshippers, his subjects.

Despite the important and powerful symbolism of the *kumbhābhiṣeka,* many of the preliminary rituals at Penn Hills were done in relative obscurity over a period of several days. Virtually no lay participants understood the details of the ritual sequence; yet certain themes were acted out that, in a striking way, reflected the attitudes and posture of a community that was settling in to a new home.

The rituals of the *kumbhābhiṣeka* are done in a series of eight sequences, each of which, with certain exceptions, is identical to the others.[12] The rituals are designed to sacralize the sacrificial room, cosmicize the bodies of the priests, and transfer the divine power from the surrogate temple and objects to the permanent temple features. At Penn Hills these rituals started on the evening of June 4, 1977, were repeated twice on June 5, 6, and 7, and were culminated by the climactic ritual events on the morning of June 8. The specific ritual events that became a part of the Penn Hills *kumbhābhiṣeka* are listed in an addendum.

The initial events of the ritual sequence have to do with preparation of the ritual space and its participants. These included the setting up of ritual elements, especially the planting and germinating of seeds. Several rituals were repeated after each of the first seven sessions of fire sacrifice and included acts such as worship of the surrogate deities and placing libations on their altars. Certain other rituals were performed only once in the sequence; these included acts such as immersing the surrogate deity in milk (after the fourth session) and (after the seventh session) performing some sixteen types of invocations (*nyāsa*s) by which the icons were homologized to human beings and sacralized. The apex of the sequence occurred in the *prāṇapratiṣṭhā,* in which life is breathed into the temple by way of the vessels (*kalaśa*s). Here the threefold process of causing the divine to become manifest is brought to culmination: transference of sacrality from priests to divine symbols; transference of sacred power from surrogate temple and symbols to permanent temple and symbols; and invoking the divine to change from a formless to a manifest state. The highlight of the ritual sequence occurred as priests lifted the sacralized vessels (*kalaśa*s) to the top of the temple tower (*kōpuram*) accompanied by shouts of "Govinda, Govinda" from devotees below. There the newly installed vessels were libated with water. Finally, the resacralized icons within the temple received the honors normally given to a divine being, including ornamentation (*alaṅkāram*) and the recitation of praise (*arcana*).

By the end of the ritual sequence, the temple had become the fully installed replica of the divine. The temple and its main icons had become the house of divine power and the center of worship. It was the dwelling of god and a cosmos made in the image of a human being.

Temple-Building Rituals as Paradigms

The rituals associated with temple building are a highly symbolic series of acts that, among other things, suggest the temple is much more than itself. The temple is a paradigm—symbolic of the divine presence, it is true—but, more than that, it is the embodiment of the universe of its human users. It is clear from its symbol system that the temple is homologous to both cosmos and human community.[13] Thus, the building of a Hindu temple in the American city of Pittsburgh served as an intriguing image of the acculturating community for whom the temple was meaningful. These paradigmatic themes are particularly worth highlighting.

Temple building, like acculturation, is implantation. Seeds are caused to germinate; icons are set in permanent pedestals like trees into a pit. Paddy or unripened rice serves as a base for icons or surrogate icons in certain rituals as if to dramatize the homology between icon and plant. So too the human community, mirrored in this temple, was implanted in order to have life and to grow in new soil. Temple and community were not only implanted but also transplanted and enrooted, fixed into place in a new moment of time and space, transferred from an older "nursery" of belief and practice and invited to flourish and continue under careful cultivation.

The building of a temple, further, acts out the purification of space. The potentially hostile and unknown is tamed, made subservient to god and man. This pastoral theme, which recurs in Hindu myth and ritual, is expressed in the temple-building process by various symbolic devices—for example, the deities that "sit on" the parts of the *vāstupuruṣamaṇḍala* in the surrogate temple as if to keep it under control, and the explicit purifying and sacralizing of ritual space. In Pittsburgh this pacification of space served as apt analogy for a first-generation immigrant community seeking to carve a place in a modern wilderness too often overgrown with human insensitivities.

The building of a temple, and especially the installation of its icons, is homologous to the coronation of a king and the establishment of his kingdom. Kingship, in turn, implies the identity of his subjects as a people. Implicit—and perhaps even explicit—in the rituals of *pratiṣṭhā*, or icon installation, therefore, is the affirmation of a sense of peoplehood. It is a peoplehood characterized by fidelity to a god-king who is himself transplanted from India to a new domain, thereby legitimating for all time the immigrating process. Pittsburgh's Hindu immigrants had become a people whose god-king, like themselves, while deeply rooted in the Indian tradition, had now become a permanent part of the American landscape.

Another theme in temple building that may be paradigmatic of the acculturating community is that of renewal by sacrifice. Fundamental to the building of a temple and to most creativity in Hindu ritual is sacrifice. The *vāstupuruṣa* (the personalized embodiment of the ritual place) is sacrificed in order to make it a new creation. Sacrificial libations serve to purify, empower, and renew. The community can be understood in this sense as well; new opportunities and a renewed sense of identity had not come without sacrifice and loss.

In temple building, finally, there occurs a localization of the universal. The god, who is thought to be formless and without limits, could become embodied in a local manifestation. A particular icon could become the full representation of divine power. In a similar sense, in each community of Hindu immigrants there can be practiced and expressed the full range of what it has come to mean to be Hindu: kinship systems, social relationships, heritage—all undergoing modification, to be sure—but practiced, nonetheless, in particular families. To put it in other terms, just as a local temple and icon are a localization of the full range of divine manifestations and power, so an individual Hindu, within his or her own skin, is an embodiment of Hindu religious expression, and a "drop" that shares in the full character of the ocean of Hinduism. A particular temple, like a particular community, can be understood as a part of that universal reality that gives the particular identity.

Some Conclusions and Implications: The Temple in the Indian American Experience

A Hindu temple, especially one demonstrating classical architectural style and ritual procedures, plays a significant role in the lives of some members of Indian American families as they establish themselves in their new society. It is, for them, a socially, psychologically, and religiously significant institution. This is so in several ways, but here I summarize only some of the implications.

As I have shown, the building of a Hindu temple by Indian Americans represents the founding of a world. This is so ritually, of course, in that the Hindu temple is a cosmos, a space in which cosmic processes are reenacted and maintained. But it is also so in a social and psychological sense for many Indian immigrants. A temple affirms a world—a psychic space—in which the community lives and acts out its identity. It is a world on the boundaries, no longer purely Indian, but not yet part of the American majority. It is a world that is both Indian and American, but not fully either one alone.

A temple is a public statement of that Indian American world that theretofore had remained relatively private. As a matter of fact, it is consistent with the Hindu tradition that any number of arenas can serve as the "cosmos" in which one works out one's psychic-spiritual identity. According to the tradition, that world can be bounded within one's own skin or it can be the "cosmos" of the home, which for many Hindu families had been the area of spiritual obligation and identity. Some Indian Americans had been relatively content to keep their world private, to live out their personal, cultural, spiritual identities in the personal and domestic realms. The building of a temple, however, makes that world public; it intends to say to the community itself and particularly to its children, but also to the American public, that Hinduism is beautiful and can be a viable part of the American landscape. Indeed, for many the temple becomes the favored arena for acting out these identities.

This psychosocial world takes on many dimensions within the community. At one level the experience of liminality is conveyed—that sense of being betwixt and between. Ironically, many of the ritual symbols of temple consecration are liminal symbols. The *yāgaśāla* is a temporary ritual space, the sacrality and significance of which are transferred to the later more permanent ritual house, the temple itself. The vessels blessed in ritual are liminal; they are neither the "old" representations of the deities, namely, the fire itself, nor the "new" representations, the icons. The vessels are deliberately ambiguous symbols; they are stable and mobile, human and divine, solid and fluid. The doorways of the *yāgaśāla* so frequently sacralized in the consecration ritual are passageways from chaos or profane space to order and sacred space.

The building of a temple seems to suggest the experience of liminality, culminating in a settling in, even if into a halfway house. To be sure, members of the community vary as to which end of the transitional spectrum they find themselves. The first-generation builders of an orthoprax temple would appear to be comfortable in affirming the Indian dimensions of their Indian American passage. In fact, for such persons a temple affirms a certain sense of history. Knowing who one is—having an identity—usually requires a sense of rootedness and lineage. This becomes particularly crucial for parents whose children are coming of age in a context very different from the one in which they themselves grew up. At first glance, orthopraxy appears to be a recovery of the past, even a clinging to that past as part of the tradition.

But the process is not quite so simple, as already in the reconstruction of tradition, compromise has occurred. Frequently, for example, in the architectural and ritual sequences associated with the building of the Penn Hills temple, one can see evidences of innovation and adaptation unlikely to occur in a traditional Indian context. These include the use of brick and mortar rather than rock in construction; including restrooms within temple precincts; and the openness of the inner worship area not only to nonbrahmins but also to non-Hindus. One of the intriguing compromises was the way the inner sanctum was built on the second floor. (The sanctuary is always supposed to rest directly on the earth.) Here a pillar of earth was included immediately under the sanctuary connecting it to the earth. A similar principle, incidentally, is invoked in the building of temples in urban settings even in India in recent years—the construction of a temple in Chembur, Mumbai, in the 1980s is a case in point. While changes such as these may seem small to those impatient with tradition, they nonetheless demonstrate that tradition is fluid and adaptive and that transition is the lot of even the most conservative of Hindu immigrants.

At the same time, few members of the community who see themselves close to the American end of the Indian American spectrum think that the end of the transitional process is to become lost in an American "melting pot" devoid of pre-American components. The second generation, in particular, is caught in a liminal experience of its own. Somewhat alienated from the views of their parents or, at least, not as close to the roots that had nurtured them, they are sometimes perceived, at the same time, by their American peers to be "different." Here again the temple plays a role as the venue where identity and generational differences can be negotiated. For many parents, and especially mothers, the temple has become an extension of the domestic sphere,[14] where they can retain, even if selectively, something of where they came from. Here too their children can be socialized in a context that is thought to be authentic, where the priests and the architecture are as close to being "Indian" as anywhere in North America.

Families, therefore, come to Pittsburgh from all over the East Coast for their marriages, tonsures, initiations, and commemorations of sixtieth birthdays, or they pay to have the temple priests come to them.

Rites of passage (*saṁskāras*) are performed in the temple or by temple priests on a regular basis. Most commonly performed is the tonsure ceremony (*chūḍākaraṇa*), as many orthoprax families think it essential to have an infant's hair cut, at least symbolically, before the child's first birthday to cleanse the child from the impurities of birth and infancy.[15] In a recent trimester, from October through January, tonsures done on the premises ranged in number from 63 to 155 per month, with the fewest occurring in the winter months.[16] Also relatively common is the first feeding of adult food (*annaprāśana*), generally done six months after a child's birth. During the same trimester, these rituals numbered between six (in December) and nineteen (October). Practiced rather seldom in this context is the naming ceremony (*nāmakaraṉa*), usually done within eleven days of birth. But now because children are born and names are given in settings determined by the technology of our age, the name-giving ritual has become rare, having been done an average of twice a month in the Śrī Veṅkaṭeśvara Temple. For the privilege of using the temple's premises and/or one of its priests, parents pay thirty-one dollars for any one of these ceremonies.

The more elaborate initiation ceremony (*upanayana*), traditionally marking the beginning of the Vedic education and more generally preparing one for adulthood, is performed in the Śrī Veṅkaṭeśvara Temple some thirty times a year at a cost of $120. Weddings, for a fee of $300, also occur on the premises about thirty times a year. These, of course, can become elaborate affairs bringing extended families and friends to the temple grounds for the occasion. Yet another common rite of passage is the *śrāddha* ceremony, which is part of the rituals performed for the recently deceased. In the same trimester noted above, fifty-nine *śrāddha* ceremonies were performed, usually for elderly parents who had died, whether in India or in the United States.

In addition to these formal ritual occasions, local parents can take advantage of a wide range of activities arranged by the temple's various committees. A summer camp, held each year north of the city, attracted 110 young people in the most recent summer. Also offered during the summer is a "music academy," when artists from South India, one instrumental and one vocal, are housed for three months of teaching. Sixty students, including ten adults, enrolled for the most recent opportunity. In addition, as with most religious institutions, the temple has a youth organization that attempts to provide occasions for the young to socialize. This group does everything from holding car washes to performing mock weddings. Also available are classes in "religious education," taught by a Tamil volunteer, and having twenty-five to thirty children in the under-twelve age group and another fifteen in the teen category. These classes offer lessons in chanting and vignettes of Hindu thought and ritual.[17] In addition, local parents can provide for their children opportunities to learn classical forms of South Indian dance and music and to read and write the native languages that are being forgotten. At the temple, in short, one can be "Indian" and "Hindu" irrespective of what one is elsewhere. Yet, even here, the Indian American experience is an ongoing process of interchange, hybridization, and cross-fertilization.

Finally, it is apparent the temple is also a world in which one can express one's Tamil, Telugu, or Kannada persona. For Tamilians, in particular, there is a long-standing sense that a village (*ūr*) is not home until it is centered by a temple. That is, a town becomes one's own and an impersonal geographic space becomes home when a temple centers it. Accordingly, Tamils had been very active, from the earliest days, in planning and construction of the Śrī Veṅkaṭeśvara Temple and in ensuring the authenticity of its ritual life. Indeed, so ubiquitous were the Tamils in the process that non-Tamils perceived them to be seeking a certain hegemony over temple affairs. Negotiations, sometimes acrimonious, led to a process of governance in which temple leadership came to be shared and rotated annually. Now Tamilians negotiate along with the other ethnic groups for celebrations that reflect their particularity: the celebration of the Tamil New Year in March and April and of Poṅkal in mid-January, for example. First-generation Tamil émigrés, like their non-Tamil counterparts, remain vigilant about their cultural values being expressed and passed along, especially in language and dance. In one class, for example, a dozen students learn to read and write Tamil with the help of a volunteer teacher. Meanwhile, interest in the classical dances of South India has mushroomed. While in the early years of the temple's existence, a handful of girls were taking lessons in Bharata Nātyam, a dance usually associated with Tamil Nadu, today seventy young women were so engaged.[18] A similarly significant number were learning Kuchipudi, a dance originating in Andhra Pradesh and commonly perceived as an expression of Telugu identity. Tamil musicians take their turn giving concerts along with those from other South Indian states. Various gurus from Tamil Nadu, similarly, will have their day in the temple. And, not least important, it is here one can nurture friendships that have persisted within one's ethnic group, though bonds now have frequently been forged that transcend ethnic boundaries.

This experience of Tamil ethnicity in the Śrī Veṅkaṭeśvara Temple needs to be contextualized, nonetheless. The sense of "Tamilness" or "Teluguness" is no doubt stronger among first-generation immigrants than in their children. Further, newer immigrants with young children of their own, with more recent ties to the homeland, sense the need to perpetuate this identity more strongly even than those immigrants who came two or three decades ago. The latter have learned to live with negotiated forms of governance and have developed friendships across ethnic lines. Because most of the children of this earlier group have now grown and/or married, the perceived need to maintain an ethnic option within the temple may have waned somewhat. Yet all of them remain willing to take their turn on one of the temple's administrative committees, as representatives of their ethnic community. Other forms of nostalgia still emerge as ties to the extended families back home remain strong and the propensity to invest in charities and enterprises in Tamil Nadu persist. Some still speak of retiring "back home." Some of them participate in regional or national associations of Tamils in the United States—indeed, local Tamil physicians hosted a national gathering of Tamil doctors in 2003.

At the same time, the Pittsburgh Tamils have varying interactions with other South Asians who have built their own religious edifices in the area. The Hindu-Jain Temple, for example, was completed in the mid-1980s and has become a venue wherein Hindus from various parts of North India can engage in rituals addressed to both Śaiva and Vaiṣṇava deities, as well as sponsor ethnic events such as concerts and lectures and the study for their children of their respective languages. Within the same structure, Jains, both Digambara and Svetāmbara, may offer *pūjā*s to the appropriate *tīrthaṅkaras* and celebrate the birth and *samadhī* of Mahāvīra. A few miles away, Sikhs have constructed a *gurudwāra,* mostly with their own hands, in emulation of remembered *gurudwāra*s of North India. Herein, some seventy-five families celebrate the reading of the scripture, the *Gurū Granth Sahib,* which is held weekly and for special occasions such as the birthday of the founder, Nanak. In addition, the *langar* or communal kitchen occurs regularly and the socialization of the young takes place. Similarly, a few blocks away, Muslims of South Asian descent have built a *masjid* that serves as a setting for Friday prayers and a largely Sunnī ritual life. It is also the venue for the instruction of their children and the maintenance of social interactions.

Some interaction occurs between these religious and ethnic communities in non-ritual settings—for example, through one or more of the associations for Indian Americans of Pittsburgh. And in each of the edifices is a striking parallel in intent. At the core of each institution's purpose is the maintenance of an active ritual life, socialization of the young in their respective heritages, and the opportunity to discuss issues relative to negotiating religious and cultural identity in American society. In each case, women have taken a significant role in the teaching of children and the organizing and conduct of the institution's programs. Tamil Americans in Pittsburgh, in short, much like other Indian Americans, have found ways to express their Tamil heritage while engaging in various forms of hybridization both with other Indian Americans and with the American majority.

Addendum: Ritual Sequence for the *Kumbhābhiṣeka*

Preliminary rituals have to do with preparation of the ritual space and its participants. These include the following:

swastivācanam. A preparatory ritual welcoming attendees.

ṛthvigrahaṇam. Selection of the chief priest and assignment of duties to ritual officiants. This, of course, had been done prior to the start of the public rituals. While Srinivasācārya was chief priest, he had three brahmin assistants—one was a ritual specialist flown from India for the occasion; one was the young priest, Sampathnarayanan, assigned to preside over the daily rituals for the fledgling temple; one was a lay brahmin immigrant then residing in Washington, D.C.

yāgaśālāpravēśanam. Entry in the sacrificial room (*yāgaśāla*) where the sacrifice was to take place.

mṛthsaṅgrahaṇam. Collection of pure earth with which the fire pits were made. At Penn Hills four fire pits, like the *yāgaśāla* itself, had been constructed of concrete well beforehand.

śilpipūjā. Worship of workmen. This was apparently done twice in the series—once at the second sequence, near the beginning of the sacralization of icons, and once at the end after icons had been installed.

Several rituals had to do with setting up ritual elements, especially the planting and germinating of seeds.

pālikāsthāpanam. Filling of small earthen pots with nine food grains known as *navadhānya.* The pots used at Penn Hills were ceramic rather than earthen.

sōmakumbhasthāpanam. Installation of a pot with sōma to drink (sōma is the drink of which the Vedic god Indra is said to have been very fond).

aṅkurārppaṇam. Watering the grain pots for germination and inauguration of the ritual ceremony.

bījāvāpanan. Sowing of the seeds of nine grains.

Other rituals are repeated at each sequence and include the following:

vāstuśānti. Pacification of ritual space.

dwārathōranadwara-kumbhapūjānan. Worship of the deities symbolized at the four entrances of the *yāgaśāla*—in the garland, in the pots, in the flags, and in the entrances themselves; each entrance area was believed to have seven guardian deities; their worship was tantamount to invoking their presence into the ritual space.

yāgaśālabali. Oblation in the sacrifice room, generally taking the form of the offering of cooked balls of rice at the four corner altars.

maṇṭaparadhanam. Worship of the dais or altar where the surrogate deities were installed. In the *kumbhābhiṣeka,* the *kalaśam*s or "golden" vessels to be placed at the top of the towers in the last sequence were treated as deities. The "power" of the surrogate deities was transferred to the *kalaśa*s eventually.

pañcagavyasvāpanam. Bathing the deities with five exudations of the cow (dung, urine, milk, curd, ghee).

naivedhyam. Offering of fruits and cooked rice to surrogate deities.

sōdaśakumbha-snapanam. Setting up sixteen pots full of liquid for bathing the deities.

abhiṣeka. Bathing or anointing the surrogate deities.

paryagnikaraṇam. Creating flame in the sacrificial fire pits.

nityahoma. Daily fire sacrifice, including the offering of twigs, grain, ghee, flour, and cooked rice.

hārati. Three circumambulations of the deities with burning camphor in a plate. The movements were both clockwise and counterclockwise and were believed to remove inauspicious elements. Devotees often joined priests in this maneuver.

mantrapuṣpam. Chanting Vedic recitations while holding or strewing flowers.
āsīrvādam. Offering of blessings to devotees.

Certain rituals are performed only once, at the appropriate point in the sequence:

aṅkurārppaṇahoma. The sacrificial fire, in the very first sequence of rituals, was especially intended on behalf of the germinating seeds.

sāntihoma. The sacrifice during the second sequence intended for removal of inauspicious elements.

ksīradhivāsam. Immersing the surrogate deity in milk. This was performed at the fourth sequence on the morning of June 6. The divine representation was permitted to soak until the next ritual sequence.

jalādhivāsam. Immersing the surrogate deity in water. This was done in sequence five.

māhākumbhasthāpanam. Setting up the main vessel or *kalaśa* (during the seventh sequence).

cakrābjamaṇḍalārādhanam. Worship of the wheel and the lotus, emblems of Viṣṇu, on the main dais of the *yāgaśāla.* This too was done during the seventh session.

sōdasanyāsaprānādi-dasavāyusnāsadihoma. This very important sequence was performed during the seventh ritual session. It entailed sixteen types of *nyāsas* or invocations and ten varieties of breathings into the icons by means of sacrifice. With these rituals, the icon or *kalaśa* was homologized to a human being, and the priests, believed to be fully sacralized, transferred that sacral power to the surrogate deity.

On the morning of June 8, the eighth or final session of the ritual sequence occurred. In addition to the now routine rituals enumerated above, certain special rituals were performed on this occasion, which included the following:

pūrṇahuti. The concluding full sacrifice.

dēvatdhyāsanam. Worship of surrogate deities.

kalānyāsam. Invoking power in the *kalaśa* ("golden" vessels to be placed atop the temple tower) by means of *nyāsas* or invocatory prayers.

prāṇapratiṣṭhā. Breathing of life into the temple, through the *kalaśa.* It is here the threefold process of causing the divine to become manifest was brought to culmination: transference of sacrality from priests to divine symbol; transference of sacral power from surrogate temple and symbols to permanent temple and symbols; and invoking the divine to change from formless to a manifest state.

mahābhiṣeka. Bathing or anointing of the temple tower.

alaṅkāram. Ornamentation or beautification of the divine symbols.

arcana. Recitation of praise to the temple deities.

kalyanōtsavam. Enactment of the sacred marriage.

mahānivēdanam. Great offering of the fruit nectars.

samāpti. Conclusion.

CHAPTER 3

Shrines as Cultural Spaces in Singapore

The temple has long been an institution with political, social, and economic—to say nothing of religious—significance in the lives of South Indian Hindus. It has been possible to examine political and social rapprochements through the alliances forged in the temple structures and rituals and to see economic transactions encapsulated.[1] Less attention has been paid to the ways temples and shrines serve as cultural spaces, arenas in which changes over time reflect something of a people's cultural history: their sense of values, their ethnic and subethnic relationships, even their self-definition. In iconography, architectural style, and ritual practice, people's self-expressions are reflected, often explicitly, sometimes unconsciously.

As indicated earlier, this sense of religious edifice as cultural space is especially apparent in the lives of persons who have left a motherland and settled into alternative societies. In the previous chapter I indicated how the building of a South Indian Hindu temple in a North American city was paradigmatic of the way its builders expressed concretely the acculturation process. We saw how the temple serves not only as a religious center for such persons but also as a social institution. Indeed, the temple is an extension of the psychosocial cosmos of those who interact and worship in it. It is possible, therefore, to "read" and interpret shrines as indicators of a people's cultural history and self-expression.

This chapter seeks to recapture something of the universe of Hindus of Tamil (and Telugu) background in Singapore through the lenses provided by shrines and temples that have been constructed and used over the years of that people's existence on the island. While many of the historical factors underlying the building, expansion, modification, and decline of numerous temples in Singapore are beyond reconstruction, several patterns can be discerned.

Historical Patterns

Phase One: Sojourners

The earliest phase of the Indian presence in Singapore is reflected in what can be recovered from the shrines that were built from the early to late 1800s. At least three temples, extant today, claim to have their origins in the period prior to 1870. These include the Śrī Māriyammaṉ Temple on New Bridge Road, the site for which was given to Narayanan Pillai in 1823 and which housed a wood and thatch (*atap*) structure by 1827;[2] the Śrī Śivan Temple, which housed a lingam on Orchard Road by the early 1850s, though at least three makeshift shrines had been used in different parts of the city before that time; and the Taṇṭāyutapāṉi Temple, first constructed on Tank Road by Chettiyars in 1859. Other structures, almost always of temporary materials, followed into the latter part of the century. These included at least three Kāḷiyammaṉ temples, two along Serangoon Road in Singapore's "Little India" and one on Somerset Street. In addition, the Śrī Śrinivāsaṉ Perumāl Temple was established on acreage given to one Mr. Narasingam along Serangoon Road. No doubt other temporary shrines were built, evidences of which have been entirely lost. Indeed, the temples that remain extant have been reconstructed and/or moved so often that early documents and records about the life of these temples have seldom been preserved.

From these early shrines, nonetheless, one can reconstruct something of the ways in which early Indian émigrés presented themselves. It is obvious, for example, that many of these early Indians understood themselves to be in Singapore (and in the Malay Peninsula alike) only temporarily. The shrines were seldom more than a space and a picture or simple (usually portable) representation of the deity. That these early shrines were temporary suggests the status of many of the early South Indian workers as "sojourners," living and working, usually without families, away from home. These early shrines suggest also something of the liminal character of the migrants' lives in the nineteenth century. There was, as A. Mani puts it, an "India-Singapore continuum" in which the continuation of Indian identities remained especially strong in the early stages.[3] Subethnic identities such as caste and geographic "home ties" appear to have been reflected in the construction of these shrines. Some clues suggest that intercaste reciprocities consistent with patterns in temple life in South India were also operative.

In general, there were two types of shrines constructed in this early period. One is the caste-based shrine such as that maintained by the Nattukottai Chettiyars; the other is the more eclectic, often multicaste shrine, usually constructed on behalf of lower-caste workers in the name of their foreman. Joanne Punzo Waghorne, in her discussion of the early shrines built in Chennai (formerly known as Madras), also noticed these two types of shrines but suggested a third type could be found: those that were "duplicate" temples wherein replicas of more famous temples found elsewhere were built as "branch offices."[4] In Singapore virtually all the early shrines were "branch offices" inasmuch as the deities favored were those brought by sojourners from their home areas, but no temples in the early period were intended to be replicas of any particular temple back home.

The Taṇṭāyutapāṉi Temple and the Chettiyars

The way in which the shrine reflected the caste or subethnic roots of Tamil sojourners is especially evident in the Taṇṭāyutapāṉi Temple built and maintained by the Chettiyars. Taṇṭāyutapāṉi (meaning "he who holds the staff") is the form of the popular Tamil god Murukaṉ in which the god is a bachelor ascetic, most prominently enshrined in Tamil Nadu in the town of Paḻaṉi. The Chettiyars apparently adopted

Taṇṭāyutapāṇi as their tutelary deity when they were doing business in Paḻaṉi in the seventeenth century. Eight palm leaf records from Paḻaṉi, in fact, dated from 1627 to 1805, refer to the Chettiyars and their generous donations to the lord of Paḻaṉi.[5] The deity apparently was particularly attractive to the Chettiyar community because for generations they traveled for extended periods from their homes to do business while their wives remained at home, thus emulating the life of the unattached god. For decades into the nineteenth and twentieth centuries, the Chettiyars traveled, without their families, to engage in their traditional money-lending business throughout Southeast Asia, everywhere building shrines and, eventually, fully developed temples to Taṇṭāyutapāṇi.

Initially the Chettiyars had no intention of staying. They came in alternating teams for periods of three years, sent most of their income back to their families in Karaikkuti, Tamil Nadu, then returned themselves at the end of their "terms," only to be replaced by colleagues. In Singapore their shrine was initially makeshift, centered by a *vēl*—the lance associated with their god Murukaṉ. The lance is said to have been brought to Singapore by the great-grandfather of the temple's current ritual technician (*paṇṭāram*) and left in place at the request of the Chettiyars.[6]

The Chettiyars installed as priests in these shrines not brahmin *ayyar*s (who apparently were seldom prepared for ritual reasons to cross the ocean in the 1800s in any case) but *paṇṭāram*s drawn from Nattukottai Chettiyar country—that is, from the environs of Karaikkuti. The Chettiyar-*paṇṭāram* alliance continues to this day inasmuch as all the main shrines in the Taṇṭāyutapāṇi temples of the Chettiyars in Penang, Kuala Lumpur, as well as Singapore have *paṇṭāram*s serving as the ritual functionaries.[7]

Kāḷiyammaṉ Shrines

Caste backgrounds (but more eclectically expressed) were also evident in the construction of temples for the goddess Māriyammaṉ compared with those for Kāḷiyammaṉ. The earliest Kāḷiyammaṉ temples were constructed along Serangoon Road in "Little India," which by the late nineteenth century was noted for its cattle trade, the care of horses for the nearby race course, the care of bullocks used in transportation, and the care (and slaughter) of goats and cattle.[8] The Vaṭapatira Kāḷiyammaṉ Temple was built near the watering area for many of these animals on behalf of those engaged in such work, while the Vīrakāḷiyammaṉ Temple, the first of the Kāḷiyammaṉ temples, was built farther south on Serangoon Road in the 1880s especially for those working for the municipality in the lime kiln. The Māriyammaṉ shrine, by contrast, was constructed primarily for harbor workers living in the Bridge Street area near what is now Chinatown. The distinction between these groups of people, however, appears to have been that between "tillers" and "slashers." Māriyammaṉ, found in many estates on the Malay Peninsula, had several functions in nineteenth-century Tamil Nadu. As the goddess of smallpox, for example, in barren seasons she is still occasionally petitioned by victims of the disease. She is also said to preside over the rains (Tamil, *maḻai*) and to be invoked by growers of crops.

Kāḷiyammaṉ was more commonly associated with warrior-like attributes. She appears to have been grafted into the pantheon of Tamil Nadu during the Cōḻa period, apparently brought by pilgrims from Bengal.[9] She seems to have inherited something of the aura of Koṟṟavai, the goddess of destruction in the ancient *caṅkam* landscape, and other indigenous "folk" goddesses such as Piṭāri. In Tamil Nadu she would have been found in less arable areas (e.g., Ramnad or West Madurai districts) and was more commonly associated with castes such as *kaḷḷar*s (former thieves) and those communities associated with clearing land, breaking stones, and other work related to construction. In Singapore and Malaysia, Kāḷiyammaṉ (like Muṉiāṇṭi) was more likely to receive blood sacrifices than was Māriyammaṉ and for a longer period. She was more likely to be enshrined in uncleared or "wild" spaces adjoining settlements. The difference in the significance of these two goddesses may be put in another way. Insofar as the goddess figure represents the forces resident in the natural order, forces that can be beneficent or hostile, and with which the worker must come to terms, then the perception embodied in the worker's relationship to Kāḷiyammaṉ is that of human being *versus* the world. In this relationship, the world of nature must be pacified, subdued, conquered; the goddess thus represented the worker's role in clearing and breaking the natural world in order to construct order on it. Māriyammaṉ, by contrast, was more likely to be found in settlements of growers or former growers wherein the laborer works *with* the land and causes it to be beneficent and fruitful by means of appropriate sacrifice and labor.

In sum, these goddess shrines in Singapore seem to have reflected several social and cultural phenomena. They perpetuated the caste affiliations and concomitant worship of tutelary deities brought from the homeland. They appear to have reflected the nature of their worshippers' relationship to the land in their work. They embodied the relationship between the working group and their foreman in whose name the temple land was granted. In addition, it is at least plausible that the goddess figure represented, for some male settlers, the missed element of home and the stability represented by the mother in the traditional South Indian family. In 1836 there were 9,580 Indian males for every 1,000 Indian females in Singapore, and even as late as 1891, males outnumbered females nearly 5 to 1 (4,216 males for every 1,000 females.)[10]

*Dalit*s and Their Shrines

This pattern of reflecting the Indian "home base" in temple life persisted in some respects into the twentieth century. There is no evidence, for example, that outcaste communities worshipped in these "established" temples during the nineteenth century. However, it is probable that persons brought from South India as coolies from *paḷḷar* or *paṟaiyar dalit* communities constructed private, makeshift shelters to deities such as Muṉiāṇṭi and Maturai Vīraṉ (usually in the name of higher-class foremen).

There is evidence that the numbers of coolies used in construction and the cleaning of streets and latrines had increased by the turn of the century. Concomitantly, it is evident that extant Muṉiāṇṭi temples appearing in Singapore in the 1930s and 1940s started as expressions of ethnic and subethnic identities much as did the temples to the more "established" deities earlier. In 1928, for example, construction of railway lines began throughout the Malay Peninsula, and by 1932 the first train was running. Workers helping to construct the railways favored Muṉiāṇṭi as the indispensable protector and averter of accidents. Muṉiāṇṭi was especially favored by the *chalukians*, those who had been used for sweeping and latrine work. Later, groups of four or five, working under a foreman and his assistant, constructed tiny makeshift shrines along the railroad every three or four miles, while a larger shrine would appear every sixteen miles—a stretch that was the responsibility of several groups operating under the charge of an English-speaking overseer, often a Ceylon Tamil or South Indian *piḷḷai* or Malayali who spoke both Tamil and English.[11] Muṉiāṇṭi also appeared on the estates as protector of the laborers' domain. Muṉiāṇṭi had marked boundaries in South India, protected the "hometown" (*ūr*), and, as such, designated the psychosocial space that gave the worker one's very character (*kuṇam*). In a similar way, Muṉiāṇṭi was believed in Singapore as well as on the Malay Peninsula to avert accidents and to define and protect the spaces where laborers lived and worked.

Also implicit in these early shrines (as intimated in the construction of the Muṉiāṇṭi ones) were the kinds of intercaste hierarchical reciprocities that characterized the social life of South Indians in early Singapore. The dynamics of such reciprocities are not inconsistent with those found in South Indian shrines as well, but the particular character of the relationship, of course, reflected the local scene. In the case of many of these shrines, overseers, representing a group of workers, could negotiate with the authorities for space for shrines, could have the land granted in their names, and could help provide funding for the same. In return, such overseers could reaffirm their authority and status vis-à-vis workers. The pattern for such reciprocities was demonstrated in many of the Singapore temples sooner or later. Most of the shrines built for Muṉiāṇṭi or Maturai Vīraṉ were subsequently demolished or allowed to fall into disrepair, though the occasional shrine has been upgraded.

The Māriyammaṉ Temple

The Māriyammaṉ Temple, the oldest of Singapore's shrines, provides an interesting example of this pattern of reciprocity. The land, first provided for the temple near what became Stansford Canal, was first granted in 1821 to Narayana Pillai, who had come from Penang with Raffles, an early English builder. Pillai had established himself as a community leader with the power to settle disputes among the Tamil-speaking population of Singapore. He was a building contractor who had set up the first brick kiln on the island.[12] The shrine was moved at Pillai's request four years later in 1825 to its present site. A well dug at the old site had provided only brackish water and was deemed unsuitable for temple purposes. A structure was built on the new site sometime before 1843, apparently with the help of convicts.[13] The ownership of the land was transferred in 1831, according to an inscription, as an act of charity from Sashakala Pillay of Cuddalore to Cathunda Ramaswamy.[14] It is apparent that early devotees at the temple included harbor workers, many of whom were drawn from villages and castes from Tanjore District, as the pattern of recruiting such workers often relied on a network of family and village connections. Yet the neighborhood (and the labor force) included Telugus who remained relatively active in the temple late into the nineteenth century. Eventually, as I shall note later, subsidiary shrines were built by other contributors (for example, the Ramaswamy icon by a Vaiṣṇava named Seshalam Pillai).

Rather early in the life of this temple, then, one finds *piḷḷai*s from the Tanjore District engaged in an eclectic enterprise. They were in an alliance with harbor workers, drawn from castes such as the *tēvar*s, *kauṇṭar*s, and others from Tanjore; in construction they used the help of convicts brought by the colonial government from all over India; and Telugus of various backgrounds participated in the temple life, as did Vaiṣṇavas. This pattern of reciprocity and alliance was to be an important feature of temple space in Singapore as neighborhoods became increasingly heterogeneous. Yet the pattern for forging such reciprocity was to be found in South Indian temples much before the nineteenth century. Indeed, it is interesting to speculate about why *piḷḷai*s would be involved in the construction of a Māriyammaṉ temple in Singapore, when most of the Māriyammaṉ shrines in South India that early in the nineteenth century were not necessarily of interest to *piḷḷai*s. But here again there was a South Indian precedent, as at least one Māriyammaṉ temple—that at Swamipuram—had become well established in Tanjore District early in the nineteenth century;[15] in fact, that temple and possibly a few others in Tamil Nadu and Kerala had brahmin priests installed around the start of the nineteenth century. It is plausible that the *piḷḷai*s in Singapore knew of that temple, as it is not far from Cuddalore.

The geographic and social backgrounds of the early South Indian settlers in Singapore and the Malay Straits also suggest some of the reasons why Tai Pūcam eventually became the major festival of the Indian Hindus in Singapore and on the peninsula. It is clear that the Chettiyars were involved early in the festival's celebration, as they provided facilities for it in both Singapore and Penang; Tai Pūcam, further, is most celebrated in Tamil Nadu when the deity is in the aspect of *brahmacari* with ascetic staff. As a result, the most popular place for Tai Pūcam's celebration in Tamil country was Paḻaṉi, that favored pilgrimage center of the Chettiyars. Indeed, Chettiyars became leaders of the Tai Pūcam processions at Paḻaṉi. Moreover, in the Tanjore District the harvest was completed by the Tamil month of Tai (January–February), and farmers were free enough to participate in the festival life. Tai Pūcam became particularly popular in Tanjore District as a result and probably remained part of the tradition of settlers from that area.

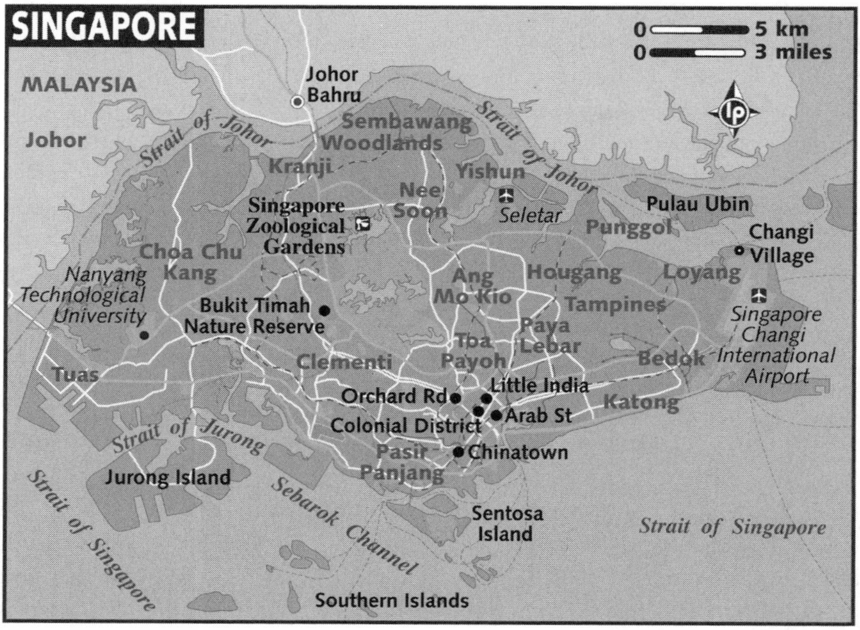

Map 1. Singapore. Reproduced with permission from www.lonelyplanet.com/worldguide © Lonely Planet Publications

These bits and pieces of historical inference based on the emergence of shrines in nineteenth-century Singapore suggest something of the internal landscape of South Indian Hindu émigrés. They were still engaged in the psychosocial passage from home with multiple caste and geographic identities still relatively fresh, yet beginning to negotiate the rapprochements that would make the new locale viable. Indeed, the very attempt to build a shrine, however temporary and makeshift, suggests the deity, like the immigrant, was a sojourner. The deity and the space he or she commanded became paradigmatic of the worshipper's world—a cultural space wherein the émigré could act out who one was and was becoming, implicit though that self-understanding was.

Phase Two: Settlers

The "line" between phase one and phase two is hardly distinct and specific and cannot be given a date. As I observed, some aspects of phase one seem to have been present well into the twentieth century, while intimations of phase two can be seen even in the middle to late nineteenth century. This second phase in the religio-cultural life of Singapore temples in many respects has continued into the present era. It has been characterized by several processes.

Generally speaking, phase two is marked by the construction and upgrading of permanent temples; the implementation of various horizontal and vertical rapprochements in the architectural, iconographic, and social life of these temples; and the embodiment of an increasing sense of comfort with a Singaporean identity, albeit still informed by the motherland.

Not least important, by early in the twentieth century, several temples had become permanent fixtures and had been enlarged, even while other newer temples were being constructed on a more modest basis. These reconstructed temples in a variety of ways came to embody a more "Singaporean" identity, reflecting a people who had begun to settle in for the long haul.

The physical growth of the "established" temples in the early and mid-twentieth century reflected various processes. There were those Indians, including Tamils and a few Telugus, who had prospered and were prepared to patronize the structures and/or their ritual life. Earlier caste identities had been tempered by increasingly eclectic neighborhoods. Trade unions and professional associations, together with neighborhood collectivities, came to supplant, in significant ways, the caste affiliations from which they had largely been derived. Temples thus reflected the vertical and horizontal alliances that had been occurring in the South Indian neighborhoods of Singapore.

The Kāḷiyammaṉ Temples

These rapprochements and changes took several forms. Not uncommonly, shrines were added and renovations made that reflected the presence and contributions of more affluent neighbors and/or sponsoring groups. Both Kāḷiyammaṉ temples along Serangoon Road, for example, from the 1890s to the 1920s profited from the presence of Bengalis in the area. The most important catalyst for the presence of this population was the thriving cattle-trading business of Mr. I. R. Belilos, whose company was based in Calcutta.[16] By 1887 Belilos had arrived in the area and started to construct sheep pens, cowsheds, and storage buildings. Judging by their names, many of his employees were Bengali.[17]

However when the Belilos company fell on hard times by the 1920s, the temples were left in financial disarray. The northernmost of the two, the Vaṭapatira Kāḷiyammaṉ Temple, was taken over by a Vaiṣṇava Telugu family, that of Govindasamy Chettiyar, who gradually upgraded the temple. Eventually (in 1982) his grandson installed a series of Vaiṣṇava shrines and Vaikhāṉasāgamic priests. The other Kāḷiyammaṉ temple on Serangoon Road—that of Vīrakāḷiyammaṉ—once managed by foremen of the lime kiln workers, came to be patronized by a series of *piḷḷai* families who donated shrines and other accoutrements through the years. In its most recent renovations, for example, the main Vīrakāḷiyammaṉ shrine was donated by the well-known business figure Govindasami Pillai; the Vināyakar shrine by the Ponnasami Pillai family; and the Periyāṭci shrine by a *muṭaliyār* family. Meanwhile, the Komala Vilas (vegetarian) restaurant and at least five goldsmith companies in the area (most of them owned by

Chinese) each donated ten thousand Singapore dollars or more to the temple. Some families, in fact, contributed to a variety of temples—the Govindasamy Pillai family, for example, patronized the building of a marriage hall and *rājakōpuram* at the Śrī Perumāl Temple, while his children later constructed a marriage hall at the Śrī Māriyamman̲ Temple on South Bridge Street in memory of their mother.

The Śrī Śrinivāsan̲ Perumāl Temple

The Śrī Śrinivāsan̲ Perumāl Temple on Serangoon Road is another that reflects a cultural history. The temple had been founded in the 1860s as the Narasimha Perumāl Temple,[18] named after the family deity of the founding patron, Mr. Narasimhan Perumāl, a Telugu naidu. It was patronized largely by Telugus, especially Vaiṣṇavas. In 1906, in the face of financial disarray, the temple and its endowments came under the management of the Hindu Endowments Board (HEB), then known as the Muhammedan and Hindu Endowments Board. In 1971 the temple was the focus of some controversy as the endowments board renovated and upgraded it and, at the behest of the Telugus on the board, installed largely Tamil Vaikhānasa Vaiṣṇava priests in place of the Śaiva *gurukkal*s and Pāñcarātra priests who had shared the ritual chores earlier. While some Telugus were unhappy with the change, most devotees were unaware of its significance and continued to patronize it, particularly (but not exclusively) Vaiṣṇavas.

The Chettiyars' Taṇṭāyutapāṇ̲i Temple

The Arulmiku Taṇṭāyutapāṇ̲i Temple, founded by the Nattukottai Chettiyars, similarly grew as the Chettiyar community became an increasingly permanent part of the city. By 1878, for example, shrines to Śiva and Parvatī were added to the original shrine dedicated in 1859.[19] Renovations and subsequent dedicatory *kumbhābhiṣeka*s were held in 1936 and 1955.[20] An imposing *rājakōpuram* of seventy-five feet has been constructed along with a *maṇṭapam,* or hall, that can be used or rented for family and public events. The facility houses a small library featuring pictures of the home temples in Karaikkuti, Tamil Nadu. The temple is the primary host for Singapore's version of the Tai Pūcam festival, but other festivals such as the Navarāttiri are also celebrated here. The temple remains under the control of the Chettiyars, who invest a considerable amount of their profits into the maintenance and expansion of the facilities. Among the other steps taken to "upgrade" the temple has been the installation of brahmin priests, who work at various shrines along with the *paṇṭāram*s who have worked with the Chettiyars for generations.

The Śivan Temple

The Śivan shrine is yet another temple reflecting the changing circumstances of the city. One of the oldest in the city, the shrine was located on Orchard Road when it got a facelift in the 1930s. The 1930s temple included a shrine to Śiva's spouse in the form of Visalāṭci, the name associated with the goddess in Kāśī or Benares. Ironically, the Visalāṭci shrine is said to have been donated by the Tamil Chettiyars, who had it installed at the same time they installed their own favored goddess, Maturai Mīṉāṭci, in their own Taṇṭāyutapāṇi Temple. To this day the Chettiyars offer monthly ablutions to Visalāṭci at the Śivan Temple, now completely rebuilt and elaborately adorned in Geylang.[21]

Yet even in the 1960s, the Śivan Temple was known commonly as the "milk vendors'" temple—"milk vendors" was the term often used by Tamils to designate "UP Wallahs," who went in significant numbers to the temple on Mondays.[22] Several South Indians attest to the coming of Uttar Pradeshis into those neighborhoods once largely peopled by South Indians; the number of North Indians attending the temple dwindled when it was moved to temporary quarters on Serangoon Road. The architectural design for the new Śivan Temple is eclectic and includes towers molded after the *śikhara* (North Indian) style, no doubt a reflection of these historical ties of North Indians to this temple.

The Śrī Śivan Temple epitomizes as well as any of these older temples the ways in which the patrons of these shrines were subject to governmental influence and the processes of development. Already moved three times before it was located on Orchard Road in the early 1850s, it was subject to several renovations and moves since then. A major reconstruction was started in 1898, thanks to the patronage of V. Nagappan Chetty and his wife. On October 18, 1915, the temple was placed under the administration of the Muhammedan and Hindu Endowments Board (subsequently the Hindu Endowments Board), joining three other temples so administered. During World War II, shelling destroyed some of the subsidiary icons and other parts of the temple; reconstruction culminated in a consecration ceremony on July 9, 1943. In 1954 Singapore's municipal commissioners wanted to widen Orchard Road. A compromise reached between the temple board and the city council led to the temple's ceding 490 square feet of land along the road and the city's providing fifty thousand Singapore dollars and permission to rebuild at the same site. This construction was completed in 1962 with the help of *śilpis* from India, and the dedicatory ceremonies (*kumbhābhiṣeka*) were held on December 9, 1964. In 1983, however, the government decided to acquire the land in order to construct a subway station on the site. The temple then was housed for a decade on Serangoon Road, beside the Śrinavāsaṉ Perumāl Temple, with all of the icons and festival events from the Orchard Road site intact.

May 30, 1993, marked the consecration of the most recent incarnation of the Śrī Śivan Temple on a three-thousand-square-meter site at Geyland East. At a cost of six million Singapore dollars, the new temple has become the most ornate and eclectic of the Singapore temples. Architecturally and ritually, the temple preserves many South Indian features (the forty *śilpis* were largely Tamil): outer walls are carved with 108 dance movements replicating those found in Citāmparam's Naṭarājaṉ temple. The deities enshrined are Naṭarāja, Sivakāmi, Vināyakar, and Taṇṭāyutapāṇi, though devotees of North Indian background often refer to these deities by terms such as Viśvanātha, Visalāṭci, and Kārtikeya. The sixty-three Tamil Nāyaṉmārs are enshrined along the walls. Similarly, the ritual calendar includes elements to be found in many Tamil Śaiva temples: the months bear Tamil names, and the Skanda Ṣaṣṭhi and Brahmōtsavam festivals held are common in South Indian Śaivāgamic temples. Yet festivals such as the Vasantha Navarāttiri (the springtime version in March and April) and Vināyakar Caturti (September) are more popular in North India. Similarly, some of the sculpting is evocative of other regions of India represented by the temple's patrons: a ground plan inspired by North Indian models; towers that resemble the North Indian *śikhara* more nearly than the Dravidian *vimāṉa;* carved arches (*toranas*) resembling those of classical western India. Also included are an elevated inner sanctum reminiscent of the Kandariya Mahadeva Temple of Khajuraho; a Kāśī *linga* on the right side, where devotees accustomed to the traditions of Benares can engage in *pūjās*; and the statuaries of five hundred saints and deities representing many regions of India.[23]

The Śrī Māriyammaṉ Temple

In a similar way, the Śrī Māriyammaṉ Temple on South Bridge Street reflected patterns of diverse patronage and support. Several shrines were added that had virtually nothing to do with the original cultus of Māriyammaṉ. In 1860, for example, one Seshalam Pillai, a Vaiṣṇava Tamil, donated some land, thereby enlarging the precincts of the temple, and installed a Rāmacāmy Perumāl shrine beside the main icon. Most of the managing committees of the 1800s were anonymous, while the temple was run by a committee chaired by the "captain" appointed by the government for Tamil Hindus. In 1906, because of some financial mismanagement, the Śrī Māriyammaṉ Temple, along with the Śrī Narasimha Perumāl Temple (both endowed properties), came to be administered by the Muhammedan and Hindu Endowments Board. Thereafter, several additions and renovations occurred. By 1935, for example, with the patronage of Govindasamy Pillai, an affluent Tamil merchant, and others, a traditional entryway (*rājakōpuram*), consistent with the style associated with temples in Tamil Nadu late in the Cōḻa era, had been erected, replacing the earlier, more nearly "makeshift" one. Earlier in the century, members of the boat-caulking community, immigrants from Podaiyar near Nagapattinam in Tanjore District, helped erect shrines to their tutelary deity, Śrī Draupaḍi Ammaṉ and the Pāṉṭava brothers. The same community initiated the now famous fire-walking (*tīmiti*) celebration in Draupaḍi's honor, as members of the community continued (at least until 1975) to hold important roles in the production of the festival.[24] At the same time, this temple, which had been the bastion of *kauṇṭar*s and *tēvar*s from Tanjore District, found many Telugus, working in the harbor district and living in the neighborhood, worshipping there; indeed some Telugus were included on the management committee of the temple (Pakrisamy Naidu Ramoo, for example, was chair from 1969 to 1971, and Soundara Rajan, a naidu, was its secretary at that time).

One of the results of these vertical and horizontal alliances was the constant upgrading of these temples. Affluence enabled the construction of additional shrines, adjunct halls, and *kōpurams*; the hiring of more staff, growing from one or two ad hoc local "priests" to full-time *paṇṭārams* (nonbrahmin ritual technicians) to the eventual installation of brahmin priests in most temples (often to work beside *paṇṭārams*, who continue to function before the shrines for which they had traditionally been responsible).

The Muṉiśvaraṉ Shrine

This changing "sociology" of shrines is also evident in certain Muṉiāṇṭi shrines (most of which have been eliminated in the context of Singapore's development). One such shrine described by Ananda Rajan in 1975 was first constructed along the railroad track in the 1930s by *adidravida* (former outcaste) railway workers.[25] Yet by the 1970s the main icon was known as Muṉiśvaraṉ, by then perceived to be an incarnation of Śiva; alongside the main icon were (and still are) Vināyakar and Bālasubrahmaṇia, and in subsidiary shrines, Śiva as Viśvanātha with his consort Visalāṭci. In 1963, when the temple was to be upgraded, English-speaking Tamils were recruited, who were assigned the leadership of the temple.[26] By this time other Indians, including Malayalis, Bengalis, and Sindhis, had moved into the Queenstown area near the temple and were invited to contribute toward the refurbishing of the temple. A painted pillar, depicting Kṛṣṇa, the herdsman-cum-flautist, bears testimony to the presence of Bengalis in the worship life of the temple; they are especially inclined to participate during the Durgāpūjā or Navarāttiri festival. Moreover, a well-placed official of the temple, a Malayali from Quilon named K. Regunayakam, who had been very active in the temple since he moved to Queenstown in 1964, was proud to point to the Ayyappaṉ shrine he helped to install around 1977; it is a shrine where one thousand devotees, especially Tamils and Malayalis, are said to gather for the Makara Vilakku festival (in mid-January) in lieu of traveling all the way to Sabarimala, Kerala. Not the least important form of "upgrading" that occurred in this temple was the installation of a Tamil brahmin priest about a quarter-century ago.[27] The temple has undergone yet another transition. The government provided some alternative land as it took over the Queenstown property. One of the issues that had to be resolved as the new temple was being built was what the name of the chief deity would be. A minority wanted to call him Dharmeśvaraṉ, which would give the deity a fully Sanskritized form and be a unique representation in Singapore besides. However, traditional worshipers who had been affiliated with the temple for a long time resisted any change from the name Muṉiśvaraṉ, a name already an elevation from the original Muṉiāṇṭi.[28]

Temples and Changing Neighborhoods

These changes in the iconographic, ritual, and architectural ambiance of the Singapore temples suggest that changing neighborhoods were reflected in the life of the temple. These accommodations were both horizontal (that is, intercaste and interethnic) and vertical (in the sense that alliances were made with more affluent and higher-placed families who often assumed control of management of the temple in exchange for contributing substantially to it). Such was the case with the Muṉiāṇṭi Temple and with the Vaṭapatira Kāḷiyammaṉ Temple on Serangoon Road, as described above. One frequent result was that a single temple would reflect the various stages of alliances shaping its development. At the Vaṭapatira Kāḷiyammaṉ Temple, for example, while S. L. P. Mohan, son of S. L. Perumāl, installed Vaikhānasa Vaiṣṇava priests as ritual functionaries for the coterie of Vaiṣṇava shrines, Śaiva *gurukkal*s continued to officiate at the Kāḷiyammaṉ and subsidiary "Śaiva" shrines—that is, Vināyakar and Murukaṉ. Meanwhile, *paṇṭāram*s remain as ritual functionaries at the plaster-of-paris shrines on the left wall at the rear of the temple—shrines, to Periyāṭci, Maturai Vīraṉ, and Karippacāmi, deities once associated with *dalit* or lower-caste communities.

Another of the ways in which these reciprocities are formalized was in the formation of *ubayam* (Tamil, *upāyam*) or participatory groups. The *ubayam* generally referred to a group who was to be responsible for certain aspects of the temple's ritual or administrative life—the patronage of one day in a festival or one ritual in a day, for example. The *ubayam* could be constituted of a family or of the Hindu members of a particular company or guild. One of the oldest of these was the *ubayam* of bullock cart drivers; one of the newest, the Hindu employees of Singapore Airlines. In between were workers for various municipal boards, the media, and other labor or professional groups. The *ubayam* was generally a generation or two removed from the older caste system in that the *ubayam* was often job based, while the job was often done originally by members of particular castes.[29] On the one hand, then, temples became more eclectic during the twentieth century, representing the changing nature of Singapore's Indian neighborhoods and the increased replacements of caste with work groups. On the other hand, paradoxically, Singapore experienced a concomitant move toward what might be called "Tamilization." The system of recruitment of labor from Tamil Nadu and the grapevine of kinfolk and neighbors who had emigrated previously brought influxes of Tamil workers into the traditional areas of Indian employment and residence early in the century and even more so by the 1930s and again in the 1950s after World War II. This pattern prevailed throughout peninsular Malaysia as well: in the 1921 census, for example, 387,509 Tamils resided on the peninsula (including Singapore); by 1931, 514,778; and by 1957, 634,681.[30] In Singapore the total Indian population increased from 12,138 in 1881 to 50,860 in 1931 to 124,084 in 1957.[31]

As a result, by the 1980 census, 64 percent of the Indian population was designated as Tamils, a total of 94,772 persons.[32] Residents recall large numbers of *kaḷḷar*s, *kauṇṭar*s, and *tēvar*s coming into Singapore in these decades. Ramaswamy Narayanaswamy, for example, who came to Singapore himself in 1930, remembers large numbers of migrants, especially *kaḷḷar*s and *kauṇṭar*s, coming from two villages in Tanjore District, Mannarkali and Athivati.[33] One of the results of this influx was the enlarged presence of Tamils in temple life.

This immigration of Tamil workers was accompanied by the attaining of a degree of affluence by some Tamil families (and also of some Telugus, aligned with Tamils.) These families, as I have shown, became affluent enough to assume the patronage, support, or ownership of a few temples as well as to occasionally visit South India to keep up with its cultural and religious life. As temples were upgraded they were generally made more consistent with South Indian (and especially Tamil) patterns. Of course, the combination of icons and rituals was the product of Singapore's social landscape, but the dynamics of reciprocities and the paradigms for emulation were fundamentally Tamil. As they became "upgraded," the temples increasingly resembled fully "āgamic" temples to be found in Tamil Nadu, albeit with the uniquely Singaporean principles of selectivity, appropriation, and modification. As a result, to put the matter succinctly, of the thirty-two or so Hindu temples now extant in Singapore, thirty of them are substantially Tamil in character with varying degrees of participation at one or more shrines and in one or more festivals by other non-Tamil Indian groups (and even by the occasional Chinese or Eurasian Singaporean). It is as if the temples reflected a certain elasticity, a push and pull between Tamil and non-Tamil and various subethnic groups. The frequency or dominance of certain forms of ritual or iconography often reflected (though not necessarily always) the character of the temple's managing committee and/or the character of its neighborhood.

These internal disputes or the uncertainty of financial support resulting from uncertain patronage in part resulted in four of Singapore's temples being turned over to the management of what was once called the Muhammedan and Hindu Endowments Board. Since 1969 these temples have been the responsibility of the Hindu Endowments Board, a body of eight persons (plus two executives) appointed by the appropriate representative of the Singapore government. The temples administered by the board are the Śrī Māriyammaṉ, Śrī Śrinivasaṉ, and the Śrī Śivaṉ temples, as well as the Śrī Vāiravimaṭa Kāḷiyammaṉ Temple, now in Toa Payoh, a subdivision of the city. The endowments board, for its part, perceives itself as setting the tone for Hindu temple life in Singapore; hence, because the majority of the board is consistently South Indian (and usually at least half Tamil), the board's instincts are to use South Indian, and especially Tamil, models in the processes of maintaining and upgrading Singapore's temples and ritual life.

Dalits and the "Mainstream" Temples

One of the eventual developments during the twentieth century was the incorporation of *adidravida* groups into the temples' ritual life. There is no evidence to suggest these groups could enter the "mainstream" temples in the nineteenth century. Further, it is difficult to pinpoint precisely when this did occur in Singapore. One former trustee of the Vīrakāḷiyammaṉ Temple claims that his was the first temple to open doors to *adidravidas*—that after large groups of them demanded entrance in 1947.[34] Other "old-timers" can remember the days before World War II when *adidravidas* had to stand outside the temples to see the deity and wait with their own plates to be fed during festivals.[35] Yet *dalit*s were admitted earlier into some temples on the peninsula—into the Kuala Lumpur Māriyammaṉ temple in the 1930s, for example. Moreover, it does seem probable that some of the deities sometimes associated with *adidravida* communities—for example, Maturai Vīraṉ (commonly associated with the Paḷḷars), Periyāṭci, and others—had been enshrined in the "mainstream" temples considerably earlier. Indeed, the Periyāṭci shrine in the Vīrakāḷiyammaṉ Temple is said to have been present by the first or second decade of the twentieth century.

Nevertheless, in the emerging social landscape of Singapore's shrines during the twentieth century (and even in Tamil Nadu itself), specific functions of deities and old caste correlations with such deities have become blurred, and deities have become less and less reliable indices of subethnic affiliations. So, for example, one can find certain "caste" families or groups with special attachments to some of these deities—some *kauṇṭar*s, for example, will have Karippacāmi as a family deity (*kulatēvatai*) and some *kaḷḷar*s, Maturai Vīraṉ;[36] even brahmin women today are known to worship at Periyāṭci's shrine when seeking a child or just after childbirth. For that matter, a deity as common in Singapore today as Kāḷiyammaṉ is said to once have had a special relationship to the so-called paṟaiyaṉ community—a group once associated with leather work and, in some cases, brought to the peninsula to clean up latrines. By and large, *adidravida*s have been incorporated into Singapore's temple life along with their deities; nonetheless, one can observe alienation between the working classes in Singapore today and the temple establishment.

The Multiple Social Roles of Temples

In addition to all of the above, it is clear that during this period that sweeps through the twentieth century, temples played still other roles in the psychosocial world of South Indians living in Singapore. Many of these functions were traditionally associated with the temple in South India, but they took on a particularly Singaporean character. For example, at least into the 1960s, temples were common gathering places for socializing, meetings, and cultural events. People came with family to visit with friends, especially on festive occasions. Along with viewing Tamil cinema and the reading of Tamil newspapers, many Tamils remember the temple as just the place to go to visit and enjoy one's friends. Moreover, one's friends, formal studies remind us,[37] were commonly drawn from one's own ethnic/linguistic groups; hence, one's presence in a temple affirmed those ethnic and even subethnic ties. Indeed, temples such as the Taṇṭāyutapāṇi Temple, built by the Chettiyars, continue to have a role in reaffirming ties to subethnic group and ancestral home.

Further, for decades the temples were the main venues for family rituals, rites of passage from prenatal ceremonies through engagement and marriage (funerals have been conducted away from temples). This role diminished with the building of halls and *maṇṭapam*s in the 1970s, but some temples even now (e.g., the Māriyammaṉ,

Perumāl, and Taṇṭāyutapāṉi temples) host major family events and take care of many of the planning details in exchange for an appropriate rental fee. And it is to the temple people often have gone—and some still do—in times of stress and need. One can still find underemployed workers, many of them on work permits from Tamil Nadu, squatting in groups on the floor of temples like the Vīrakāḷiyammaṉ on Serangoon Road, there to commiserate with each other, keep their eyes and ears open for work opportunities, and appeal to the goddess for assistance.[38]

During World War II the temples played an especially crucial role during the Japanese occupation. Many folks remember using one temple or another as a haven and a network of information about how best to avoid reprisals and other of the tragedies of that period. In some cases, temples were active in anti-British agitation. The Vīrakāḷiyammaṉ Temple, for example, was to have been the venue in which the commander in chief of the Indian National Army, Mohan Singh, was to be presented with a special sword purchased by one Mr. Maruthamuthu, a temple official. The event never occurred because Singh became "indisposed," but five of his officers came instead to set another time for the presentation. This event epitomized the attitude of Indians in the peninsula during the war. Inspired by Chandra Bose's Indian nationalism, many Indians signed up for or supported the idea of an Indian army to drive the British out of India after the war. Some were thus seen as collaborators with the Japanese during the war. In any event, the Vīrakāḷiyammaṉ Temple was active in providing shelter for those who lost their jobs either as the result of bombings or because they were fired by the Japanese during the war or by the British after the war for alleged collaboration with the Japanese. Up to twenty persons a night are said to have been given shelter by the temple and food provided by sympathetic merchants.[39]

Ritual as Expression of Social Reciprocities

The reciprocities described in the construction and upgrading of these temples are further reflected in their ritual life. As noted already, relatively affluent and elite patrons and their families have assumed ownership of entire temples and, along with trade guilds or *ubayam*s, have assumed responsibility over the years for patronizing certain ritual events during festival occasions. In exchange for these acts of patronage, they receive *mariyāti* (or honor) from temple authorities who thereby affirm the status and authority of the patrons. Such patrons are also able to assume the role of "watchdogs of orthopraxy."

Less affluent middle-class groups, by purchasing tickets for the ritual occasion, are believed to accrue benefits from the ritual in their own behalf and concomitantly gain stature and affirmation of place in the social hierarchy. Lower-class persons who wish to "purchase" patronage are able to receive the accrued benefits and gain stature and a sense of vertical mobility through alliance with temple patrons. The ritual alliances thereby enact the kinds of interdependencies and alliances that characterize the social landscape.

One moment in a ritual enactment will illustrate something of those patterns and people's various perceptions of them. The occasion was the Paṅkuṉi Pirumāmam Utcavam (Paṅkuṉi Brahmōtsavam) at the Śrī Śrinivāsaṉ Perumāl Temple on Serangoon Road. The festival now celebrated is one of the biggest of the year in this temple. On Paṅkuṉi Uttiram, the marriage of Āṇṭal to Perumāl had been reenacted. Two days later the Brahmōtsavam started. This day, the ninth of the Brahmōtsavam (Tuesday, April 9, 1991), is the highlight of the festival. This morning, on the day said to be Viṣṇu's birthday, the deity and his consort have been paraded around the temple pavilion in the silver chariot. They are dabbed with water that had been sacralized during the week with fire rituals (*homas*) and libations (*abhiṣeka*). Following viewing of the deity (*darśan*), the deities in the main shrine are offered extended libations of water, sandal paste, milk, honey, and so on (*abhiṣeka*) and are ornamented and shown the lights and insignia of kingship (*arātaṉai*). Around noon the people who have been in attendance are fed a vegetarian feast and make conversation.

A priest, whose major chores for the morning are completed, chats with a Western observer. The priest seems nostalgic for his home. He had been affiliated with a small Vaiṣṇava shrine dedicated to Aḻakār near the bus stand in Madurai, Tamil Nadu. He is in Singapore without his family on a work permit provided by the government for a period generally not to exceed two years. He is earning a better salary in Singapore than he was back home and is able to send a significant portion of it to his family. He maintains the priests are doing the rituals in Singapore just as they would back home, except for the compromises and modifications they are asked to make by temple authorities and patrons. "We do whatever the *yajamāna* wants us to do," he says; "he is like the king used to be, you know; we do his bidding." This day is a happy occasion for him, even though he is busy, as it is "Viṣṇu's birthday," and the power of the *nakṣatra* (lunar constellation) overrides the fact that it is the dark side of the fortnight. The priest reflects the attitudes of many of Singapore's early Indian sojourners—they came temporarily and without families. The temple serves as home away from home, the lifeline to the heritage and roots still missed.

The *yajamāna*, or patron of the day, is a wealthy Telugu naidu, S. L. P. Mohan, grandson of "Govindasamy Chettiar," a philanthropist given that honorary name because he had been generous in the support of temples during his lifetime. The family had assumed ownership in the 1920s of the Vaṭapatira Kāḷiyammaṉ Temple (just up Serangoon Road from the Perumāl Temple) when it had floundered financially, had assumed the patronage of festival events, and helped in the building of *kōpuram*s in several temples. Mohan's father, S. L. Perumāl, had been largely responsible for renovating the Perumāl Temple for the 1971 *kumbhābhiṣeka,* for changing its name to the Śrī Śrinivāsan Perumāl Temple, and for installing the Vaikhānasa priests (because they were perceived at the time to be more "popular" than Pāñcarātra priests). Mohan himself, when he took over after his father's death in 1982, installed a coterie of Rāma shrines in the Vaṭapatira Kāḷiyammaṉ Temple and installed Vaikhānasa priests to officiate at those shrines.

Mohan is anxious to maintain his family's obligations in Singapore's temple life. He and his family provide patronage for at least four ritual events per year at the Perumāl Temple along with their other obligations because "it is our duty" and because he understands himself to be a "religious man." "I get freedom from stress when I come to the temple in the midst of this pressure-packed city," he says. He wants to make the rituals as much as possible like those to be found in India, which he visits often, there to consult with "various gurus," especially the Kañci Śaṅkarācārya. He apologizes to the Western observer that this particular ritual is somewhat more modest than it would have been in India: "Here the government won't let us hold processions whenever we want, and we don't have access to much water, so we have to settle for this small well in which to bathe the god." He estimates that his sponsorship of temples and rituals in the city costs him about S$200,000 (US$120,000) annually, excluding the amount devotees help to defray.

Mohan is less concerned about the meanings of the rituals than with the fact that they are done "right" and without regard to expense. In exchange, he gets "peace of mind," a sense of family obligation fulfilled, the honor and status accorded one who is performing these rites for the "good of devotees," and the privilege of being a guardian of orthopraxy. He is given honors (*mariyāti*) and the first of the gifts blessed by the diety (*pracāṭam*) on this occasion.

A devotee, standing nearby, finds this to be an occasion in which he can express his identity as a Telugu. I paraphrase his comments:

> We really are a minority in Singapore, perhaps five hundred families of us [actually 8 percent of the total Indian population as compared to 75 percent Tamils, according to the 1980 census]. We often come to the Perumāl Temple, as most of us are Vaiṣṇavas—we come on this occasion, but especially for Ugadhi [i.e., New Year], which falls on the new moon of Paṅkuṉi [March 17, 1991]. I consider myself a religious person, just like my mother was (though my father wasn't). Whenever I go to India, I spend a lot of time on pilgrimage, so much so my family makes fun of me. Many of our [Telugu] forefathers came to work as stevedores in the harbor; in fact, I work in hoisting container cargo on and off ships. Occasions like this bring a number of Telugus out and we've gotten to the point we mix well without much consciousness of caste backgrounds. Of course, we still have a sort of "class system," made up of about four economic levels. Our parents were more serious about caste observance than we are, but we still tend to observe these class levels when it comes to marriage; intermarriage may take place now between levels one and two or between two and three, but not between levels one and four.

Finally, a teenage girl, standing on the fringes of the ritual event throughout, talks with the foreign stranger. She understands but a little of what is happening ritually: "I was told today they would put the deity in water, and we believe that water is auspicious once the deity has touched it, so we like to touch ourselves with that water." Within minutes she is romping about the temple precincts with teenage boys who are squirting each other with water and trying to dump each other into the small temple tank.[40]

This girl and her peers speak for some of Singapore's marginalized Indians, who do not quite understand or feel comfortable in the ritual system. For others, however, the system provides an opportunity to experience the enactment of their heritage, linking them with their lineage and the authenticating sources of their identity even as it expresses the alliances and reciprocities of their Singaporean sociocultural landscape.

Summary

In general, one finds that South Indian temples have been built, both in India and by South Indian émigrés elsewhere, in stages, except when funds suffice to construct a completed temple right away. This process usually starts with the use of a makeshift space and representation of the deity (a *paṭam* [picture] and *iṭam* [place] may serve as a temporary shrine). In the contemporary world, this may take the form of renting an apartment or a building as a "cultural center" (North America, the Middle East, etc.) and using a picture or privately owned portable icon of one of more deities. In more traditional settings (e.g., nineteenth-century Singapore or urbanized parts of India), this initial space was sometimes marked by a natural phenomenon deemed sacred (e.g., a small body of fresh water, a stone or tree). Presiding over the functions of this protoshrine is usually ad hoc—by participating devotees themselves, by resident savants, or by some other tentative arrangement. In nineteenth-century Singapore, such shrines took the form of mud and *atap* sheds with pictures of icons placed therein. This may be called a temple at stage one. It usually represents temporariness of residence, reflects a sense of liminality or marginality in the new society, and indicates that funds are inadequate or that patrons are reluctant to commit funds for more permanent structures.

A temple at stage two will include, at minimum, a more permanent shrine (e.g., brick or cement) and an icon appropriately implanted, often, at least in contemporary temples, with the accompaniment of āgamic rites, most important the *prāṇapratiṣṭhā*. It is unlikely the latter rites were performed for any of the Singapore temples in the nineteenth century, but permanent brick structures and icons were springing up by the middle to last part of the century. The Māriyammaṉ Temple, for example, had a brick structure by the 1850s and certain permanently embedded icons by the late 1860s.

At stage three, the temple's users normally signal the intention of settling in and making the deity a fellow immigrant who sacralizes and legitimates the space or neighborhood wherein they reside. At this time it is common for additional deities to be enshrined. These normally represent the alliances made with various ethnic and subethnic groups who use the temple. Added shrines can also indicate the increased affluence of new patrons or users. This affluence will also lead to the attempt to enlarge and/or update the temple generally in ways consistent with favored temples remembered or observed in South India or elsewhere. An authentic *rājakōpuram*, for example, is apt to be built at some point during the third stage. Brahmin priests are generally installed by this time to conduct "āgamic" rituals. The installation of such priests signals the increased affluence of the users, their vertical mobility, their desire to affirm ethnic and subethnic identities, and their motivation to attain "authenticity." In Singapore brahmin priests were apparently not installed until relatively late (often after World War II); yet several temples did have authentic *rājakōpuram* (e.g., Māriyammaṉ by 1935) and sets of shrines that signaled the sectarian and ethnic biases of a temple's users.

By the time a temple has reached stage four, most of these elements will have been incorporated and additional spaces will have been built for subsidiary events (e.g., a *maṇṭapam* or marriage hall for weddings, cultural events, etc.; pits for *homa*s or fire sacrifices), and brahmin priests generally see to it that the rituals follow the tradition over which they have been trained to preside, responsive nonetheless to the wishes of the temple's patrons (*yajamāna*s). The priests are normally brought from that geographical area or sectarian tradition deemed to remind the temple's patrons most of their ancestral home. In Singapore not all temples have constructed *maṇṭapam*s within the temple environs, but these still fill the social and cultural purposes the *maṇṭapam* is designed to facilitate. Most of the temples in Singapore have by now installed brahmin priests (the Singapore government, in fact, outlawed animal sacrifice across the board in 1967); yet, in almost all temples brahmin priests serve alongside *paṇṭāram*s, who in some cases (e.g., Taṇṭāyutapāṇi, Māriyammaṉ, Vīrakāḷiyammaṉ) preside at the central shrine. This accommodation is apparently intended to maintain local tradition, as *paṇṭāram*s were the first ritual technicians to be used in Singapore. It is also the case that brahmin priests have to be imported from South India with temporary work permits, in each case with the permission of the government, while *paṇṭāram*s are locally born and reared, having opted for citizenship in the early days of the republic. Temples such as those to Taṇṭāyutapāṇi (the "Chettiyar" temple), Māriyammaṉ, Perumāl, and Śivaṉ, the last three administered by the Hindu Endowments Board, may be designated stage four temples, while those of Vīrakāḷiyammaṉ and Vaṭapatira Kāḷiyammaṉ, both privately owned, are more nearly stage three temples. As of the early 1990s, the Muṉiśvaraṉ Temple of Queenstown was at stage two, moving to stage three as it relocated.

No temples in Singapore have yet attained stage five, when a temple and its associated subsidiaries become an international pilgrimage center. To be sure, several temples in Singapore have become "historical" and national landmarks and, therefore, officially designated tourist attractions. The next step, no doubt, will be the emergence of an international network and mythology whereby certain of these temples come to be seen as "must stops" for globe-trotting South Indians. That stage is not far away.

CHAPTER 4

Tirunelveli North

Nadars in God's Beloved Dharavi, Mumbai

*Nāṭar*s (anglicized as nadars) who have settled in a specific pocket of Mumbai provide an interesting example of the issues I am exploring in this volume. They are now a largely middle-class community, most of whom had humble origins in the palmyra industry of an arid part of Tirunelveli District in southern Tamil Nadu. By the latter part of the nineteenth century, many them had begun to migrate into northern Tamil Nadu and beyond, either to seek more lucrative kinds of work or to market products with which they had become associated. A significant number of them settled in the city of Mumbai, not a few of them in the area known as Dharavi, sometimes referred to as Asia's largest slum. I explore their story in this chapter. However, it should be useful first to get a sense of the larger historical and demographic context of Mumbai in which this study is set, especially inasmuch as subsequent chapters observe other groups of Tamils in the city, particularly certain brahmins and Muslims.

Mumbai: A Historical and Demographic Overview

Mumbai (or Bombay, as it had been popularly known for more than a century) has become India's largest city and one of the five largest centers of Tamil population in the world. Formed out of seven islands, the city has become not only the capital of the state of Maharashtra but also India's primary commercial, communication, and transportation center. It accounts for almost 20 percent of India's organized industrial employment, one-third of India's entire income from taxes, and almost half of the country's total foreign trade. It is the biggest film-producing city in the world and one of the most rapidly growing centers of population.

Until the thirteenth century the area now comprising the city of Mumbai was a relatively sleepy series of tropical islands populated largely by fisher folk known as *koli*s, from whose patron deity, the goddess Mumbai, the city derives its name. By the thirteenth century, mainlanders began to filter into the islands. By the mid-fourteenth century, much of the land was controlled by sultans of Gujarat, and after 1534 by the Portuguese. By the mid-seventeenth century, Great Britain had acquired control of all seven islands, much of the land presented by the Portuguese as part of Catherine of Braganza's dowry on the occasion of her marriage to Charles II. During the nineteenth century the islands became a peninsula; an architectural and cultural ambience emerged largely mingling Islamic Gujarati styles with English ones, and

Map 2. Mumbai. By permission of Maps of India (mapsofindia.com)

Table 2. Primary language of Mumbai's population, 1921–61, by percentage

	1921	1931	1941	1951	1961
Marathi/Konkani	54.2	51.1	50.7	49.0	49.7
Gujarati/Kutchi	23.4	21.4	19.5	19.7	18.0
Hindi/Urdu	14.8	17.3	19.8	17.4	18.0
Telugu	1.6	1.5	2.3	2.8	2.4
English	2.1	1.8	1.8	1.1	1.0
Others	3.9	6.9	5.9	10*	10.9*
Tamil				2.2	2.2
Kannada				1.8	1.8

* Includes Tamil

Source: Meera Kosambi, *Bombay in Transition: The Growth and Social Ecology of a Colonial City, 1880–1980* (Stockholm: Almgvist and Wiksell International, 1968), 167.

increasing numbers of persons of diverse backgrounds made their way into the growing city.[1]

Population figures suggest something of the patterns of Mumbai's growth in the twentieth century. According to the 1921 census, for example, 54.2 percent of the population was composed of persons whose mother tongue was Marathi or Konkani. Marathi is the local language of most of the people of Maharashtra, while Konkani is spoken along the coast of the mainland into the "Western Ghats" and as far south as Goa. Another 23.4 percent were primarily speakers of Gujarati or Kutchi, Kutchi being the language used along the Gujarati coast and the Rann of Kutch. Another 14.8 percent of the 1921 population were speakers of Hindi or Urdu; 2.1 percent used English as the mother tongue, representing primarily the British and Anglo-Indian population in the city; 1.6 percent spoke Telugu, and 3.9 percent represented all the other language groups. By 1951 the Marathi-Konkani population had decreased in proportion (though not in numbers) to 49 percent, and the Gujarati-Kutchi population to 19.7 percent. The Hindi-Urdu segment had increased to 17.4 percent of the whole, and the Telugu-speaking population had increased to 2.8 percent, while the percentage in English had decreased. Tamils constituted too small a fraction of the population to be separately counted until the 1950s (see table 2).[2]

The largest single increase in percentage by the 1951 census was among the speakers of "other" languages, who now made up 10 percent of the Mumbai population. This category included persons displaced by the partition of Pakistan—for example, Sindhis—but an increasing number of the new migrants were from the southern states: 2.8 percent were speakers of Telugu, 1.8 percent of Kannada, and 2.2 percent of Tamil.[3] The total population of Mumbai by the time of the 1951 census had officially reached 2,994,440, of which 72.1 percent were migrants into the city who had been born in other parts of India or the world (see table 3).[4] Of these persons, 66,000 were officially Tamil speakers.

Table 3. Growth of population in Greater Mumbai, 1951–81

Year	Population (in millions)	Net migration (in millions) in previous decade	% Migrants in population
1951	2.967	9.50	72.1
1961	4.152	.600	64.2
1971	5.971	.819	54.1
1981	8.227	1.059	50

Source: Vaitsala Narain and K. B. Gotnagar, "Bombay and Its In-Migration" in *Dynamics of Population and Family Welfare, 1983,* ed. K. Srinivasan and S. Mukerji (Mumbai: Himalaya Publishing House, 1983), 318.

In the five decades since 1951, Mumbai's population has shifted in significant ways. For one thing, the number of migrants has increased manifold, though the percentage of the population who were migrants decreased. In the decade preceding the 1961 census, 600,000 persons had migrated into Mumbai; however, the population increase of persons born in the city was almost as great. Hence, the total percentage of persons living in Mumbai in 1961 who had migrated from other areas was 64.2 percent (down from 72.1 percent in 1951). In the subsequent decade ending in 1971, another 819,000 migrants officially entered the city, making the total migrant population of Mumbai 54.1 percent.[5] Between 1971 and 1981 the stream of migrants reached 1,059,000, and the total population in the city of persons born outside it was 50 percent.[6] According to one study done in 1976, 77.4 percent of those coming into Mumbai by this time were from rural areas, and 78.5 percent of them came in search of work.[7] (Many of the women had followed husbands after marriage, and, of course, children came as dependents.)

Housing for many of these new arrivals was either unavailable or increasingly expensive. Southern Mumbai, the older part of the city, which included downtown and more affluent housing areas, was reaching the point of satiety, though sections like Malabar Hill, Cumballa Hill, and Colaba were the sites where high-rise condominiums were erected by the late 1950s. Central and north Mumbai and the extended suburbs became the place where many of these new Mumbai-ites sought shelter. Meanwhile, the corporation limits of the city were extended by the time of the 1961 census to include those northern areas once considered suburban. Mumbai's population shot up accordingly: in 1961, to 4,152,056; in 1971, 5,970,525; and in 1981, 8,243,405. The population estimated for Mumbai by United Nations agencies for the year 2000 was more than 12,000,000.[8] This makes Mumbai, at the least, India's largest city and among the seven largest metropolitan areas in the world. Mumbai's newer residents are pressed into less and less space. By the 1981 census, 27.63 percent of Mumbai's inhabitants lived in 619 officially designated slums—a total of 1,074,484 people.[9] By the mid-1980s, according to one study, slum dwellers numbered 48 percent of Mumbai's total population, totaling more than 4,000,000 persons, while

Table 4. Religious affiliations of Mumbai's population, 1921–61, in percentages

	1921	1931	1941	1951	1961
Hindu	71	68	68	71	72*
Muslim	16	18	17	15	15
Christian	6	7	7	7	6
Pārsī	4	5	4	3	2
Jain	2	1	2	3	4
Jew	1	1	1	1	1
Others	0	0	1	0	1

* Includes 5 percent of the "neo-Buddhists" converted with Dr. Ambedkar in 1956 and 3 percent "scheduled castes."

Source: Meera Kosambi, *Bombay in Transition: The Growth and Social Ecology of a Colonial City, 1880–1980* (Stockholm: Almgvist and Wiksell International, 1968), 167.

pavement dwellers were estimated to have increased from roughly 100,000 to 500,000 within that decade.[10] That figure has grown even larger since.

The religious composition of Mumbai's population during the period from 1921 to 1951 remained relatively constant, at least in terms of the broad categories used by census takers. In both 1921 and 1951, 71 percent of the population claimed to be Hindus (though in 1931 and 1941, the percentage was 68 percent). The Muslim population in 1921 was 16 percent, and 15 percent in 1951 (but 18 percent in 1931 and 17 percent in 1941).[11] What the shifting figures between 1941 and 1951 only barely intimate is the movement of Muslims to Pakistan after independence and the influx of Hindus from both the Sind and the south during that same decade. Other population figures are similarly moderately suggestive: the Christian population remained the third-largest minority in Mumbai (from 6 percent in 1921 to 7 percent in 1951). What these figures do not reveal, however, is that the Christian population was and remains primarily Catholic, composed largely of Goans and "East Indians," a group of persons claiming descent from Portuguese converts initially headquartered at Bassein, about an hour from downtown Mumbai, and since World War II, supplemented by migrations from Kerala and Tamil Nadu.[12]

The fourth-largest religious minority throughout this period were the Pārsīs, constituting 4 percent of the population in 1921 and 3 percent in 1951.[13] Descendants of Zoroastrian immigrants fleeing from Iran to Gujarat, the Pārsīs became an affluent and powerful part of the Mumbai landscape by virtue of their friendly attitude toward the British and their enterprise. Pārsī institutions and charitable endowments remain a significant part of the city today despite the dwindling size of the community itself.

The Jain population, supplemented by migrants from Gujarat and Rajasthan, grew from 2 percent in 1921 to 4 percent in 1951. Finally, the Jewish community, composed largely of "Bene-Israelis," a people claiming ancient roots and supplemented by

Table 5. Population of Mumbai by religious affiliation, 1981

Religion	Number	Percentage of total population	Percentage of increase since 1971
Hindus	5,712,443	69.30	38.96
Muslims	1,219,930	14.80	44.65
Buddhists	467,716	5.67	64.51
Christians	394,687	4.79	5.18
Jains	341,980	4.15	39.74
Sikhs	51,808	.63	20.87
Zoroastrians	50,053	.60	-
Jews	3,076	.04	-

Source: Census of India, 1981, Series 12, Maharashtra: Household Population by Religion.

"Cochin Jews" and "Baghdadi Jews," remained approximately 1 percent of the total population of Mumbai for those thirty years. All other religious groups combined, including Sikhs, remained less than 1 percent of the total population (see table 4).[14]

Like the general population of Mumbai, the city's religious population had undergone change by 1981. During the preceding decade the largest growth had been attributed to the Buddhist community (by 64.51 percent). Thanks to the mass conversion of Mahars and other formally scheduled caste persons following the conversion of Dr. B. R. Ambedkar in 1956, the population of the new Buddhist community was now 467,716, making the Buddhists the third-largest religious community in the city. The Muslim population had increased by 44.65 percent to 1,219,930; the Hindu population increased by 38.96 percent to 5,712,443. Christians remained the fourth-largest religious group (with 394,682 persons) despite a population growth of only 5.18 percent. The Jain population increased by 39.74 percent to 341,980 persons, Sikhs by 20.87 percent to 51,808; Pārsīs dwindled to 50,053 and Jews to 3,076. By 1981, in terms of percentage, these religious groups constituted a portion of the total population of Mumbai as follows: Hindus 69.3 percent; Muslims 14.8 percent; Buddhists 5.67 percent; Christians 4.79 percent; Jains 4.15 percent; Sikhs 0.63 percent; others 0.65 percent. (see table 5).

Tamils in Mumbai

The Tamil presence in Mumbai can now be viewed in light of this demographic background. The story begins in the late 1800s when two Tamil groups began to trickle into Mumbai. One of these was composed of Tamil brahmins who came to pursue career opportunities as government clerks and officials and occasionally as company managers. They settled primarily in south Mumbai and in the Matunga area in central Mumbai, at that time at the northern extremities of the city. The other stream was composed of lower-caste Tamils, including Muslims, coming from Tirunelveli District and, less commonly, from South Arcot and Salem districts. These persons were generally young

Table 6. Tamils in Mumbai as of 1961 and their years in residence

	Number	Percentage
Less than one year	7,009	8.21%
1-4 years	23,280	27.27%
5-9 years	19,694	23.07%
10-14 years	16,781	19.65%
15+ years	17,998	21.08%

Source: K. C. Zachariah, *Migrants in Greater Bombay* (Bombay: Asia Publishing House, 1968), 58.

men recruited by "maistries" or Tamil foremen and employed primarily by tanneries north of Matunga. The maistries would derive a healthy commission from the salaries of the young recruits. The migrants included significant numbers of nadars, who, like the brahmins, sought better career opportunities and were turning from circumstances deemed less than hospitable—brahmins by the 1920s felt some pressure from the Justice Party and other increasingly antibrahmin movements; the nadars felt resentment from other communities such as the *maravar*s, *tēvar*s, as well as brahmins. The tannery workers tended to settle in the area that came to be known as Dharavi, often living at first in housing with fellow bachelors.[16] By the 1920s and 1930s, certain Tamil establishments were being set up in Matunga and downtown Mumbai by brahmins, at least in incipient fashion. The Śrī Veṅkaṭeśa Devasthanam of Fanaswadi, downtown, was dedicated by Vaiṣṇava brahmins in its initial form in 1927, though land had been purchased for the structure as early as 1914.[17] Smārta brahmins were responsible for establishing the South Indian Bhajana Samajam in 1927 and the Śaṅkara Maṭam in 1939.[18] Meanwhile, the Ashtika Samajam was established in Matunga by the joint cooperation of Tamil and Malayali brahmins, especially those from the Palghat area, in 1923.[19] At this early stage, these Matunga shrines were little more than a space and a picture (stage one), but they did represent a Tamil brahmin community large and self-conscious enough to express a will to settle and become a permanent part of the Mumbai scene. The story of some of these brahmin establishments will be told in a subsequent chapter.

After World War II and independence, the migration of Tamils to Mumbai became more significant. K. C. Zachariah, in his study of migrations into Mumbai, noted that by 1961 there were 85,382 migrants from Tamil Nadu living in Mumbai as compared to 73,597 from Kerala.[20] Of the male Tamil migrants, 53.3 percent were rural born; of the females, 47.7 percent.[21] Of these émigrés only 21.08 percent (or 17,998) had been in Mumbai more than fifteen years, and 58.55 percent of them had been in the city less than ten years[22] (see table 6).

These Tamils constituted about 2.1 percent of the total population of the city and 3.2 percent of the total migratory population. One study conducted eighteen years later, in 1979, of three thousand households dispersed throughout each of Mumbai's fifteen

Table 7. Population of Mumbai by "mother tongue" (largest groups only), 1981

Language	Number	Percentage
Marathi	3,789,698	46.0
Gujarati	1,189,507	14.0
Hindi	1,003,672	12.0
Urdu	778,504	9.0
Tamil	211,584	2.6
Sindhi	195,080	2.4
Konkani	170,189	2.1
Telugu	156,227	1.8
Kannada	136,882	1.6
Malayalam	135,129	1.6
Punjabi	105,382	1.3
English	103,362	1.3
Bengali	29,091	0.4

Source: Census of India, 1981, series 12, Maharashtra: Households and Household Population by Language Mainly Spoken in the Household.

wards indicated that 17.62 percent of the migrants living in Greater Mumbai were from the southern states. Of those southern migrants, 48 percent were from Tamil Nadu, or approximately 8.46 percent of Greater Mumbai's migrant population.[23] These migrants settled into suburban areas—that is, central and northern Mumbai—and, to a lesser extent, into the extended suburbs like Thane District and New Mumbai. More precisely, 23.6 percent of the males, born outside of Mumbai and living in the suburbs, were from southern states (11.36 percent from Tamil Nadu). Of the females, 25.53 percent born outside of Mumbai and living in central and northern Mumbai were from southern states (12.25 percent from Tamil Nadu). This can be compared with 5.99 percent Gujarati males and 5.7 percent Gujarati females living in these areas, and 52.79 percent of the males and 55.72 percent of the females having migrated in from elsewhere in Maharashtra. Of the migrants living in southern (or downtown) Mumbai, however, only 4.69 percent were from southern states, approximately 2.25 percent of these from Tamil Nadu.[24]

As a result of this influx of Tamilians, the official census of 1981 (the most recent available to us) recorded the presence of 211,584 Tamils in Mumbai, 2.6 percent of the total population of 8,245,405.[25] Assuming migratory trends and population growth continued at that pace, the official number of persons for whom Tamil is the primary language at the turn of the century was at least 450,000. Officially in 1981, Tamil (at 2.6 percent) was the fifth most common of the mother tongues in Mumbai after Marathi (46 percent), Gujarati (14 percent), Hindi (12 percent), and Urdu (9 percent) (see table 7).[26]

However, many Tamils who observe the scene in Mumbai insist the census records are too conservative and that the population of Tamils may well be larger, even double the official figures. Be that as it may, the Tamil population in the city is diverse and seemingly ubiquitous. They have found jobs constructing roads and buildings, laying pipes, driving taxis, running sidewalk cafés, as longshoremen, and as proprietors of numerous shops. Mumbai even has a commensurate percentage of Tamil prostitutes, pimps, transvestites, and smugglers.

At the other end of the spectrum, Tamils, both men and women, have contributed significantly to Mumbai cultural, religious, and commercial life as brahmins and other professionals have established themselves in positions as scientists, politicians, academicians, industrialists, athletes, artists, writers, government officials, and film stars.

The Geography of Tamils in Mumbai

While some of the professional and more affluent Tamils have been scattered throughout southern Mumbai, many have settled into neighborhoods that form significant Tamil enclaves. The center of the community, culturally and religiously, is Matunga in central Mumbai. Matunga's official population in 1981 was 63,294 and its literacy rate 85.09 percent.[27] Part of Matunga is Kings Circle, where three major brahmin religious institutions exist: the Ashtika Samajam, the South Indian Bhajana Samajam, and the Śaṅkara Maṭam. Other Tamils, including a significant number of brahmins, live adjacent to Matunga in Sion (total population 265,691; literacy rate 65.57 percent), where the Mumbai Tamil Samajam is headquartered, and to the south of Matunga in Dadar (total population 343,878; literacy rate 65.64 percent), where a considerable number of Tamils live, including brahmins and other professionals, especially in Chedda Nagar, where the Subramanyam Samajam, developed primarily by Tamil brahmins, is located. Along the northeast corridor of Mumbai peninsula, following the Central Railway line, are other pockets of Tamils, each of which includes at least some families of brahmins.

Along the northwestern corridor from Matunga, following the Western Railway line, Tamils have settled in Andheri, Goregaon, and Borivili. Andheri includes a small colony of approximately one hundred families of Tamil brahmins, most of whom live in a vegetarian enclave near the railway station and work in income tax and other central governmental positions.

Goregaon houses at least two colonies with significant numbers of Tamils: Siddhanta Nagar, where a Tamil cultural center (*caṅkam*) is located, but where property has now become too expensive for most middle-class families; and Bangur Nagar, a newer, less expensive area. Bangur Nagar is home to a South Indian Educational Society that goes up to the junior college level and a Rama Krishna Bhajana Samajam, run primarily by Smārta brahmins, with cooperation by Vaiṣṇava brahmins. Nearby also is a Keralite temple and a church primarily for Malayalis and Tamils. At least six hundred Tamil brahmin families live in the Goregaon area.

Borivili, at least an hour by commuter train from downtown Mumbai, includes a settlement, or colony, of life-insurance workers, where most of the Tamils live.

Borivili houses perhaps one hundred Tamil brahmin families and an incipient Tamil *caṅkam* that sponsors lectures and opportunities for *pūjā*.

Other centers house considerable numbers of Tamils, though very few brahmins. These include Antop Hill near Dadar, which had an early attraction for the Tamil criminal element, persons whose business included smuggling, bootlegging, and prostitution. Yet Antop Hill also contains a Murukaṉ temple that was popular in the mid-1970s when its wealthy (albeit allegedly criminal) patron, M. Varadarajan, was still alive. A Bālajī temple is to be found in Antop Hill and, in a separate government colony, around five hundred brahmins live who work primarily in governmental services such as customs, railways, and income tax.

Alongside the Bhabha Atomic Research Center in Trombay (in eastern Mumbai) is a colony known as Cheetah Camp, in which a significant number of Tamil nonbrahmins live. These include Tamil Muslims, Saurashtras, and other middle- and lower-middle-income groups.

However, the largest conglomeration of Tamils in all of Mumbai (virtually none of whom are brahmins) is in Dharavi, a heart-shaped slum area extending along Mahim Creek between the two railway lines. Here over two dozen Hindu shrines, churches, and *masjid*s have been constructed or are maintained largely by Tamils, a large percentage of whom have come from Tirunelveli District.

Finally, areas outside of Mumbai, serving as exurbs along the Maharashtra coast, have begun to attract Tamil settlers. Most significant of these settlements are those in Thane District and the Vashi section of New Mumbai. In Thane District is Bombivli, which houses lower-middle-class brahmins and a Veṅkaṭeśvara temple, albeit a temple constructed by Vaṭakalai Vaiṣṇavas living outside the area. New Mumbai now has its own Tamil *caṅkam,* founded in the mid-1980s, and another Veṅkaṭeśvara temple, planned by Tamil brahmins and built in the mid-1990s.[28]

Dharavi

Dharavi is the name given to an area in central Mumbai to the northwest of the Matunga-Sion corridor, running roughly between Mahim Creek in the west and the railroad line to the east. By the 1960s it had attained the dubious reputation of being Asia's largest slum. Yet the precise size of Dharavi's population is difficult to ascertain, as census figures include no distinct entity known as Dharavi. Further, the population has continued to grow rapidly from migrations into the city; many of its residents live in temporary shelters or are part of a floating population. Many have never been issued ration cards or registered in any way with city authorities. Moreover, small housing units often provide shelter for extended families, relatives or friends who live temporarily in a dwelling that becomes overcrowded and difficult to enumerate. Rental arrangements tend to be brief because of the tenancy laws of the city. In short, most local persons assume the official census count of Dharavi is considerably understated.

Dharavi is composed of two parts. Four wards constitute "Dharavi proper" or the "developed" part of Dharavi, which runs along Dharavi Road. This is the road that fronts shops and small-scale businesses run by the more affluent of Dharavi's residents. Then there are the "notified slums," 16 of these with Dharavi in their title, according to the 1981 census (out of a total of 619 "notified slums" in Mumbai).[29] Adjacent to the 16 are kilometers of assorted shacks and temporary dwellings that constitute an extended slum area, "notified" or not. L. C. Gupta, in his discussion of migration patterns and population growth in Mumbai, indicated that by the early 1980s the slum population of Mumbai had reached 48 percent of the city's entire population: more than four million people as compared to one million in 1971, while pavement dwellers had increased from one hundred thousand to five hundred thousand over the same decade.[30] Slum pockets throughout the city were said to have exceeded two thousand by the mid-1980s.[31] That many of these people live, however temporarily, in the Dharavi area seems likely even to the casual observer riding into town from the airport or taking a train out the northeast corridor. This rapid increase in slum population has moved some observers to guess there may be five hundred thousand to one million residents in the Dharavi area, an estimated eighteen thousand persons per acre.

The population of Dharavi is quite mixed; a significant number of Uttar Pradesh Muslims, for example, live there along with migrants from Gujarat, Karnataka, Andhra Pradesh, and other states. Kalpana Sharma claims that this densely packed area holds twenty-seven temples, eleven mosques, and six churches.[32] An estimated 40 percent of the population is Tamil, at least half of whom came from Tirunelveli District, though others trace their roots to North and South Arcot, Salem, and other areas in the deep south. A significant number of the Tamils are nadars; hence, it is useful to explore the religious life of nadars in Dharavi.

Nadars and Dharavi

A Brief Historical Sketch—the Nineteenth-Century Context

The background that underlay the migration of nadars and other lower-class Tamils to Mumbai (and other places) must be seen in the context of their circumstances during the late nineteenth century. Succinctly put, these circumstances included at least the following elements: chronic underemployment and unemployment exacerbated by flood and drought; intercaste rivalries; the persistence of a landholder-serf tradition that virtually precluded opportunity for freedom and upward mobility; the tacit or complicit unwillingness of courts, upper classes, and other representatives of the government to intervene on behalf of such lower-class laborers; and active recruitment and/or reports of work opportunities outside of Tamil Nadu. The migrations to Mumbai of lower-class Tamils can be seen as part of the pattern of emigrations to other cities and countries around the world where the British Empire encouraged cash crops.

The nadars, by and large, are descended from a community known as *cāṇārs*—anglicized as shanars. In the early 1800s most of these shanars were situated in the arid southern portion of Tirunelveli District and were engaged in the palmyra industry—harvesting the sap and other products of the palmyra palm and marketing these. The physical exertion associated with their work and their production of toddy, the fermented wine of the palmyra palm, caused other communities to regard them as "polluted," and placed them at the very bottom of the classes designated as *śūdras*.[33] Nonetheless, some shanars, by virtue of their commercial skills, became more affluent. Some were landlords (known as *nāṭaṉ*s, or lords of the land) and served as representatives to the local rulers in their area.[34]

Though economic and social disparities remained within the community, efforts were made to upgrade their status throughout the 1800s. By 1829, for example, shanar women were permitted to cover their breasts (a privilege previously accorded only to higher-class women). A myth developed about the origins of the community, now known as *nāṭar*s (an honorific form of *nāṭaṉ*s): that their forebears were actually royalty of *kṣatriya* status, having descended from remnants of the Pallava Dynasty.[35] As more nadars traveled into northern Tamil Nadu and extended their trade, affluence increased to the point that certain other caste groups felt threatened. Indeed, by the late nineteenth century, virtually all castes had come to resent the nadars, especially those now living in northern portions of Tamil country. Brahmins and *vēḷāḷa* landowners seemed to resent the efforts of nadar Hindus to develop temples and a religious life that emulated brahminic principles. *Maravar*s and *tēvar*s especially resented increased nadar affluence and competition. Much of this resentment came to a head in 1899 in the infamous Sivakasi Riots. (Sivakasi is a town south of Maturai where nadars had established a commercial base.) During these riots, the homes of 886 poor nadars were burnt to the ground.[36]

Part of the nadar effort of upgrading themselves was expressed religiously. About 10 percent of them became Christians; some in the coastal villages of Tirunelveli District became Catholic, some of these as early as the 1530s under the influence of Portuguese missionaries. Most of the Christians were Protestants, influenced by Anglican missionaries, especially after the 1820s.[37] In some cases, entire villages in Tirunelveli District converted to Protestantism. Yet most of the nadars remained Hindu, upgrading their shrines and employing brahmin priests. For many of these Hindus, Murukaṉ was the deity of choice; for others, it was Māriyammaṉ. Hindu nadars, on the basis of their "noble origins," also sought entry into temples of other castes. Such groups, however, refused to let nadars into their temples, leading the latter to court several times seeking redress.

The disputes with other castes (and especially *maravar*s) over temple entrance led to a high court ruling in 1898 that decided, as Edgar Thurston cites it, that there was "no proof" that indicated nadars descended from *kṣatriya*s and that, in fact, there was no distinction between nadars and shanars, who "from time immemorial" were devoted to cultivation of "palmyra palm," "collection of its juice," and "manufacture of liquor from it." Their worship was called a form of "demonology" and their position in the social structure located just above that of *paḷḷars, paṟaiyars,* and *cakkiliyar*s, all of whom were considered unclean, and below that of *maravar*s and *vēḷāḷa*s, who were free to worship as they chose.

However, the court ruling continued, the nadars had increased in wealth, abandoned their old profession, "sought social recognition," and wanted to be treated on a "footing of equality in religious matters." They had won for themselves by education, industry, and frugality respectable positions as merchants and clerks, but "they must not invade the rights of other castes" on the basis of "unreasonable and unfounded pretensions." "They have temples of their 'own,' are 'numerous enough,' 'strong enough in wealth and education,' 'to rise along their own lines' . . . without infringing the right of others." Along those lines, the ruling concluded, the court would support the nadars.[38]

With "help" like that from the courts, it was little wonder that lower-class nadars had converted to Christianity and/or emigrated in considerable numbers. Of the nadars who came to Mumbai, some were drawn from the less-affluent families, both Hindu and Christian, often recruited by maistries or foremen serving a role not unlike that of *kaṅkāṇi*s who recruited labor for Malaysian and Sri Lankan plantations. Yet other nadars came into Mumbai as entrepreneurs (or became entrepreneurs after arriving). In fact, some nadars in Mumbai insist their families were well placed for at least seven generations (that is, as far back as they could be traced). It was a mix of nadars, then, who settled into Dharavi; though most arrived poor, some subsequently developed businesses of their own.

Early Years of Dharavi

Recruitment of Tamil laborers to Mumbai appears to have been less than systematic in the nineteenth century, though there are reports that Tamil recruiters or maistries were eventually appointed by tanneries and mills of Mumbai to recruit Tamil laborers, for which service they would receive 10 percent of the salaries paid each recruit.[39] Whether recruited or not, a small trickle of lower-class Tamils came to Mumbai in the late 1800s. R. Rajamani, an ad hoc historian of Dharavi, reports that his grandfather came about a century and a half ago from Tirunelveli District together with a group of Tamil Muslims. They rode by bullock cart to Sholapur, from where they could take the train to Mumbai. Dharavi was already a part of Mumbai municipality but on its northern outskirts and adjacent to tanneries owned largely by Gujarati Muslims, which were outside the limits. There was space to live and opportunity to work in the tanneries (as many of the Tamil Muslims and nadars did) or to set up family businesses. Rajamani's grandfather, for example, ran a beedi (cigarette) shop that was slowly nursed by his son into a more extended business until it eventually failed. As recruits came, they would walk from the Mumbai railway station to

Dharavi, often being pressed into work the very day they arrived. Even into the 1960s and 1970s, the arrivees tended to be young males who would live with one another in rented houses that became known as *poṅkal vīṭus* (houses of boiled rice). Room and board, thus shared, would require one-third to one-half of their income. The rest would be sent back home or saved for investment.[40]

By the 1930s one road passed through Dharavi going toward the Mahim railway station. There was no sewage system save for Mahim Creek, which flowed nearby and was already "filthy."[41] A few common taps of water were provided by the municipality, but virtually no electricity. Only two or three permanent buildings had been erected. The laborers worked long hours in tanneries and mills, usually from 6:30 A.M. to 7:30 P.M. Only in the 1950s were the hours reduced from 7:00 or 8:00 A.M. to 5:00 or 6:00 P.M. Persons who arrived in the 1950s report on the constant and overwhelming stench from the tanneries and the slaughterhouse near Bandra Railway Station. Pelts left over from the tanning were used as "firewood." By now the number of migrants into the area had begun to grow geometrically as people back home learned there was work in Mumbai as well as potential freedom from caste-based oppression. The area became crowded with temporary shelters, as most migrants still thought of their home villages as their permanent residences. Dharavi became known also as an area infested with crime. Only one or two policemen worked there, the nearest police station being in neighboring Mahim. Illicit liquor was manufactured by fisher folks (*koli*s) living along Mahim Creek, and peddled in Dharavi. But quarrels led to some local Tamils making their own illicit liquor; this, in turn, led to reprisals from the *koli*s, who at night would attack those Tamils living near Mahim Creek. Ethnic scraps became commonplace and boiled over in 1964. At the time of parliamentary elections, a Tamil was elected, much to the apparent chagrin of a Maharashtrian opponent, who is alleged to have engendered further strife. The Shiv Sena, said to be concerned lest migrations from outside states reduce employment opportunities for local Maharashtrians, apparently "joined the fray";[42] even police were alleged to have joined in attacking and beating Tamils. In reprisal, some young Tamil men attacked and killed a policeman and threw him in the gutter.[43] The police decided to arrest Tamils en masse, many of whom were said to have been innocent. Resentments persisted.

In addition to the interethnic battles, there were intercaste imbroglios, especially between *tēvar*s and *adidravida*s and between *tēvar*s and nadars. Peace came to the area only in the mid-1960s when a "peace committee" consisting of leaders belonging to different parties (Congress, Dravida Muṉṉetra Kaḻakam, Communists, etc.) prevailed on their various followers to live together.

Dharavi had only one school into the 1960s—that was the first Tamil-language school, constructed in Mumbai in 1924, which went only through the fourth standard. Students had to leave the Dharavi area to further their education, but relatively few parents were willing to let their children, especially their daughters, go into Matunga or Sion; girls seldom studied beyond primary school.[44] The Reverend Mother

Imelda, recalling conditions in the area when she came to live there in 1962, writes, "It was conspicuously noted that there were no schools at all in this whole slum area. Therefore, the children had a carefree life. Above all, the majority of the parents were illiterate."[45]

While five primary schools have been established in the area by now, there is still no general high school, and the literacy rate remains low. According to the 1971 census, the four wards abutting Dharavi Road had a literacy rate of 42 percent, while male literates outnumbered female literates almost three to one.

In other respects, living conditions remained difficult into the 1960s. Reverend Imelda recalls, "When we came to live in the heart of this Dharavi slum [1962], there were no proper roads, very few people were seen in the roads even in peak hours, no proper water supply, and, above all, no drainage system. Therefore, during the monsoon, we had to live in knee-deep stagnant water in our house."[46]

Things began to improve somewhat for Dharavi in the early 1970s. To be sure, there had been at least one plan for its development on the books since the 1930s. A resolution passed by the municipal council for such development, however, was never implemented for "want of funds." In 1970 a resident of Dharavi, Mr. Prabhakar Kuntai, was elected a member of the legislative assembly. A law was then pending that would clear out all the residents of Dharavi and settle them elsewhere so that the area could be used for other purposes. Kuntai introduced an amendment (which passed) to the effect that people who decided to stay in Dharavi would be accommodated in Dharavi itself. Many residents of Dharavi breathed a sigh of relief. They decided to stay and to build more permanent shelters and shops. A municipal school was constructed; otherwise, the municipality was perceived as having done very little.

A further initiative came, it is said, when Rajiv Gandhi became prime minister. While he was a member of Parliament he had made a tour of Dharavi in 1983. In 1985, during a congress meeting held in Mumbai, the central government committed one hundred crores (one billion rupees) for development in Mumbai, one-third of that for Dharavi. This development project is now in the hands of a board known as the Prime Minister's Grant Project (PMGP), which has the power to develop Dharavi further. The board is run by the central government, assisted by the state and municipal governments. Thus far, most of the funds have gone into cooperative housing complexes—that is, the construction of seven or eight apartment buildings and some transit camps for persons still seeking more-permanent shelter.

Today Dharavi has five municipal schools, though no high schools save for a Tamil-medium high school run by nadars, primarily for nadars. There is no hospital and only inadequate medical facilities. There is no recreational space or organized recreation for the young. Drainage remains a problem, and there is virtually no service by the municipality with regard to garbage removal (though in more affluent parts of Mumbai, like Malabar Hill, garbage pickup may occur three to five times a week). Yet quite a few small-scale industries and shops have sprung up. The monthly household income is said to average about one thousand rupees, though at least half the resident households earn less than that, while some earners may expend up to three thousand rupees a month. Unemployment increased dramatically in the mid-1980s when several mills closed after a prolonged labor dispute; many of the laid-off workers have not been paid severance or benevolent allowances to this day.

The population of Dharavi proper (downtown Dharavi) is estimated to be around 150,000 now (excluding temporary shelters strung along Mahim Creek and the railway lines, which may house up to 1,000,000 people). Of this "core population," perhaps 55,000 to 65,000 are Tamils. An estimated 10 to 15 percent of the Tamils who once lived in Dharavi have moved to other locales. Of those who remain, 20 percent are able to lease, on a virtually permanent basis, their housing, though relatively few actually own their housing.[47] This is the Dharavi where religion has come to play a significant role in the lives of many Tamils and serves as an interesting barometer of Tamils' attitudes toward Mumbai and life.

Nadars and the Religious Landscape of Dharavi

A significant portion of the Tamils in Dharavi are nadars, and most of them claim ancestral ties to Tirunelveli District. Their life in Mumbai is epitomized by their practice of religion. I focus here on a handful of Hindu shrines and two Christian churches to illustrate the nadar sense of their being in Mumbai.

Down several back alleys from Dharavi's main street is a small shrine dedicated to Gaṇapati. The property is part of that leased by a "society" composed primarily of nadar families who decided to remain in place once it was determined the city would not move them. The alleyway is "theirs," leased from the city for as long as they choose to remain. Once that decision to settle was made, a temple became the natural way to express the sense of being at home. Accordingly, in 1977 four elder nadar men of the neighborhood brought a small picture of Gaṇapati from Matunga and set it up in the designated space, which became a makeshift (stage one) temple.[48] In 1983, as funds became available from the member families, a brahmin *śivācārya*, Balasubramaniam, was employed as *pūjāri*. The *śivācārya* began to perform *pūjā*s, in a manner largely consistent with the way he did them back in his home village of Irulṉīki in Tamil Nadu, in this shrine and in three others for which he was employed in Dharavi. The main icon that now centers the shrine was brought from Tamil Nadu shortly thereafter and installed (albeit without the brahmanic *prāṇapratiṣṭhā* or ritual "infusion of life"). A dedication (*kumbhābhiṣeka*) for the present shrine was held in 1986 under the supervision of the *śivācārya*. The shrine remains a modest (stage two) temple with an inner sanctum (*garbha gṛhya*), an icon (*mūrti*), a small tower (*vimāṉam*), and a brahminic priest.[49]

Each morning a handful of devotees gathers around 7:30 for *abhiṣeka* (anointing of the deity): gingelly oil is applied to the icon together with water. The deity is dressed (*vastram*), and sandal (*cantam*) and vermillion (*kumkum*) are placed on the forehead.

Then flowers (*pū*) are sprinkled on the god to the accompaniment of the *gaṇapati śloka,* a mantra in praise of Gaṇapati, the precise meaning of which, however, remains unknown to both priest and worshippers. During the recitation *dūpam* is offered—that is, camphor is burnt and a candle lit. *Pracāṭam* is then passed to the few devotees. This consists of *avalpūri*—that is, crushed raw rice said to be a substitute for *poṅkal* (boiled rice), which this group of families apparently cannot afford on a daily basis. Then follows the *ārccaṉai* (Sanskrit, *arcana*) or stanza of praise, a Sanskrit *śloka* muttered in Tamil. Then the priest places the burnt ash (*vibhuti*) on the foreheads of the gathered as worshippers drop coins into the tray.[50]

The ritual procedures are replicated in the evening, when twenty to fifty devotees gather by 6:30 for *pūjā.* In fact, two or three extra wicks may burn in the oil lamp for the evening *pūjā.* Again, on most days *avalpūri,* the crushed raw rice, becomes the major offering because "god likes it and will favor us if we give it."[51] In the evening the lamp with five lights is shown to the god following his being ornamented; camphor is shown the god and then to the devotees, who pass their hands over it, then their eyes in the manner prescribed by tradition. *Vibhuti* and *avalpūri pracāṭam* is shared with all.

On Tuesdays and Fridays, Gaṇapati's auspicious days, sweet boiled rice (*cakkara poṅkal*) will replace the raw *avalpūri.* Bananas and coconuts are added to the offering, and the number of flowers offered is greater.

The shrine with its modest ritual life is maintained by a board of trustees, composed almost entirely of nadars, who make decisions on behalf of the forty or fifty members. They are proud, on the one hand, that they have built and maintained the shrine by themselves—in a way that parallels the building of their own lives and careers. As one of the board's officers remarked (as paraphrased), "Nobody helps us here—not the municipality, not the social worker [who was seated in a car not far away during an interview], not the [Tamil brahmin] establishment in Matunga." On the other hand, the trustees complain that they are too poor to pursue some of their dreams for the shrine: "We'd like to put it inside"—that is, construct a *maṇṭapam* or roof to house worshippers, especially during monsoons.[52]

I will return at a later point to a discussion of the implications of this religious orientation. First, however, it should be useful to sketch in other elements in the landscape. A second shrine in Balasubramaniam's ritual circuit is another Gaṇapati temple, this one situated at the head of still another alleyway.

Here again, families settled into an alleyway of small houses. Some 120 of the 200 or so families in the alleyway are Tamils, most of them Hindus. Some Muslims and Christians also live there, though these do not participate in the temple activities. By the late 1970s, when it became clear these families could stay, they dreamed of having their own temple. These were not only nadars who were involved but also several *maravar*s, naidus, and a few *koli*s (Marathi fisher folk). By 1979 the residents of the alleyway started celebrating the Ganeṣa Chaturthi festival (Mumbai's most popular festival, celebrating the birthday of Mumbai's favorite god). This concession to local custom took precedence over the attachment to family deities back home, as most of the nadars had been worshippers of Murukan̲, and at least one naidu claimed allegiance to the Karippacāmi in the Māriyamman̲ temple in his home village. Some twenty or so families of mixed caste formed a society in whose name the property where the shrine now stands was claimed. A picture of Gaṇapati served as the first worship center, but by 1985 the society felt affluent enough to start building. Eighteen or nineteen people paid fifty rupees each to purchase the icon; another three members donated cement.[53] By the late 1980s the families had a Gaṇapati shrine of their own and used Balasubramaniam as their *pūjāri*.

Like the patrons of the first Gaṇapati shrine, these families are not affluent. The story of one of the members of the temple board is not atypical: M. Ramakrishnan, a naidu, first came to Mumbai in 1949 to work in Worli (near south Mumbai) until he lost his job. He returned to Tirunelveli District, then set out again in search of work, first in Calcutta, then back to Mumbai in 1971, where he found work in a mill. He brought his family and settled into a place provided by the government. However, "around 1976," when the road was built "over there," "we were uprooted and moved to this alleyway."

Ramakrishnan worked in a mill until 1985, earning up to sixteen hundred rupees a month. However, the union wanted more pay and started a strike. The owners were losing money, so they closed the mill and never paid the unemployed workers their provident fund (a matter still under negotiation). "Some five thousand people must have been working for the mills which closed down," Ramakrishnan estimates.

After almost five years of unemployment, he opened a beedi shop in the alleyway, where he now nets about thirty rupees a day. However, he has two unmarried children, who studied to the "eighth or ninth standard" and are now working for contractors. One of them brings home fifteen hundred rupees a month so "we can afford to live."[54]

Given the constraints of daily life, it is not surprising that festivals provide an opportunity for celebration. Most of the Hindu Tamils in Dharavi insist that Poṅkal remains their favorite festival, when they can purchase new pots and clothes and celebrate the harvest of rice crops back home and the entrance of the sun into the northern journey. Dīpāvalī also is an occasion for celebration with its explosion of firecrackers and lighting of the shrines. Yet the celebration of Dīpāvalī in Dharavi (as in Tamil Nadu itself) is far more restrained than for the rest of Mumbai, where firecrackers explode from the first of October onward and many people purchase new clothes and some (such as the Gujaratis of Mumbai) welcome a new year.

Perhaps the most festive occasion, however, is Ganeṣa Chaturthi. During these ten days, each of the shrines will distribute sweet rice (*cakkara poṅkal*) and offer the deity more flowers. The main hall (*maṇṭapam*) of each shrine is lighted and decorated; each temple hires a piper (*nātaswaram* player). The groups get together, build a stall (*paṇṭal*), and install a temporary clay Gaṇapati. Many families perform *pūjā*s in the home without the help of their *śivācārya*, but he handles *pūjā* for the temporary

Gaṇapati icon. The last day of the festival, along with lower-middle-class groups from all over Mumbai, Dharavi's Hindu nadars will carry their icon to the sea, immerse it, spill red powder on themselves, and dance as they go to the accompaniment of *mṛidangam* and *nātaswaram.* Throughout the alleyways of Dharavi, thirty-five to forty such temporary Gaṇapati *paṇṭal*s may be set up; the processions of these Gaṇapatis to the sea, needless to say, are a time for great celebration (*tamaṣa*).

The first shrine described above is controlled virtually entirely by nadars. In the second shrine nadars retain hegemony, though members of other castes are full and equal participants in the shrine's life. A third shrine reflects an unusual business alliance forged between two nadar brothers who own an electronics shop, and the young Kannada proprietor of a restaurant next door. This too is a Gaṇapati shrine erected only recently on the sidewalk facing the street just outside the two business establishments. The businessmen saw an opportunity to combine charity and public relations.

Children would gather at this spot to await the bus that would take them to school. At first the entrepreneurs set up a small dais with a container of water for the children to drink as they waited. This was followed in 1989 by a small Gaṇapati shrine. Here again, Balasubramaniam is pressed into service as the *pūjāri* to perform the same sequence of rituals that are conducted at his other shrines. Here, however, the "worshippers" are almost entirely children from the streets and nearby homes. One of the nadar proprietors expressed the motive behind the enterprise in these terms: "People are not very religious anymore, but we have a duty to maintain and pass along our customs."[55]

Every evening children who are at hand, most of them under the age of ten, are rounded up to watch the brief *pūjā.* By 7:45 P.M. all the children are lined up while boiled rice (*poṅkal*) is passed out to them. Tuesday and Friday nights are especially exciting as, in addition, a coconut with burning camphor attached is broken onto the street and scattered. The children scramble delightedly for the scraps of coconut in the mud or dust.

Whatever the motives underlying this gesture, an observer cannot help but be moved by it. Children are taught the discipline of queuing and waiting (a lost art in Mumbai), are provided a portion of a meal each evening, and learn some sense that religious acts can actually be fulfilling.

Implications and Patterns

The religious practices illustrated here embody not a little of the self-understanding of Hindu Tamil nadars living in Mumbai and especially in Dharavi. Not least of all is the important role played by the building of a shrine. The meaning of these shrines can be summarized as follows:

1. They express a will to settle in and become a permanent part of the landscape. It is significant that these particular shrines were all built after legislation was passed ensuring that residents who chose to stay in Dharavi would be permitted (even assisted) to do so. Accordingly, the old Tamil proverb was frequently invoked by

this community: Can there be a village (*ūr*), literally, a place to call home, without a temple? Most of the Hindu nadars expressed nostalgia for Tirunelveli District; several have even retained property there, but few expressed any desire to return. There was a sense of gratitude not only for work and opportunity to earn but also for relative freedom from friction between caste groups. One nadar, in stressing that point, embraced his friend, a maravar, a member of a community that had once sought to keep nadars "down on the palmyra farm." Men insist their families are happier here, because there are fewer constraints; the women are said to be more mobile and freer from familial traditions. Going back for these families would be a "last resort," only if all other options for work in Mumbai failed.[56] Not only that, but Dharavi provides to these nadars a sense that they are, in fact, home—many of the shop signs are in Tamil; their neighbors speak Tamil; they have access to Tamil periodicals (e.g., *Marāti Muracu*). Building a shrine to the deity is a statement that they intend to stay.

2. The ownership or control of property has highly symbolic value in Mumbai. Property is often exorbitant or unavailable, and tenancy laws can seem draconian, as renters can be forced to pay enormous deposits and forced out by landowners after eleven months. To have a space one can call one's own affords status, a sense of belonging, a sense that one can stay put with one's family. Often claims to property become the bases for court battles and feuds; hence, to say "this" space is ours is a matter of no small achievement in Mumbai, particularly in light of the fact that many middle-class employees in the city still have no permanent residence or property.

   Therefore, ownership or control of a shrine becomes an expression of self-esteem and autonomy. It is a way of saying, "We did it on our own; who needs them?" As a result, a sense of "us versus them" pervades nadars' consciousness, but now the "them" are the impersonal forces of unresponsive municipalities, agencies, and people. Building a shrine to a brahminical deity complete with a brahminical ritual schedule, even bringing the initial object of worship from the brahminical establishment in Matunga as if to legitimate the fledgling shrine, without the help of brahmins and other high-class persons becomes an index of community pride, vertical mobility, and proof that nadars can progress "on their own." This is no small factor among a people who a little over a century ago were kept out of temples and dismissed as shanars (toddy tappers) even by the courts.

3. Giving the god a residence in one's alleyway makes it all right to live in that place. The deity legitimates the family's being "here." The shrine makes it as if the god has come to Dharavi with the émigrés; he lends sacrality to their space and gives a center or order to the chaos of their surroundings. Indeed, there is something compelling about providing a special space for the deity when many of the small houses for human beings are crowded with two or three families.

Apart from the building of shrines, other elements in the religious life reflect something of the attempt to mix a Tirunelveli rootedness with a Mumbai ambience. Perhaps the most obvious accommodation is the fact that the deity in the three shrines examined is Gaṇapati, Mumbai's favorite god but hardly the favorite of any one of these families back in Tamil Nadu. Various ways are used to describe and rationalize this choice: "This is Mumbai's god and we're in Mumbai." "He is the brother of Murukaṉ and, therefore, they are the same." "He is always the first god we worship; but later we will add other gods." Similarly, the celebration of Ganeṣa Chaturthi is far more akin to what their Marathi-speaking neighbors do than anything they would have done back home.

By contrast, the daily *pūjā* schedule is virtually identical to that which would have been observed in a village of Tamil Nadu. Indeed, the *śivācārya* insists he made no changes from the routine he followed in Irulṉīki, with the possible exception of the more regular use of raw rice than cooked rice in Mumbai. Other festivals of the Tamil year are also celebrated with temple rituals as they were back home, albeit on a smaller scale: the festivals to Murukaṉ, especially Paṅkuṉi Uttiram and Tai Pūcam; the new moon of Chittarai (March and April); the full moon of Māci (April and May); and the constellation Kārttikai in the months of Tai (January and February) and Āṭi (July and August). A growing group of Tamils (perhaps fifty to sixty as of 1990) is joining Malayalis to go from Dharavi on pilgrimage to the Ayyappaṉ shrine at Sabarimala. These pilgrims gather at an Ayyappaṉ shrine located near one of the nadars' temples: the Ayyappaṉ temple houses only a picture of Ayyappaṉ and has a limited number of *pūjā*s offered by a *tantri* (a Kerala priest). But in preparation for the Makara Vilakku pilgrimage, some Tamils and Malayalis meet in the shrine after work for those forty days, change into their pilgrimage shirts daily, and eat and sleep there. This too emulates to a considerable degree the practice of their peers back home, even though there are accommodations in the Mumbai context to the exigencies of the workday and the necessity to negotiate viable pilgrimage groups with Malayali neighbors.

Yet there are no reported cases of possession, piercing of the flesh, or other forms of self-flagellation such as can be found in rural Tamil Nadu. These nadars, in sum, are religiously and socially a lower-middle- to middle-class community aspiring to move up the social and economic ladder. For them religion is both an indication of their status and part of the strategy for fulfilling their aspirations. They act out differing social roles in different contexts—entrepreneurs aspiring to a better life; families obliged to make accommodations with neighbors of differing caste, ethnic, and religious orientations; ethnics seeking to maintain some sense of heritage and lineage while living and/or working in a dynamic city with access to most of the elements of a modernized, mechanized, multinationally dependent world. Religious expression often embodies aspects of all these considerations.

Christian Nadars in Dharavi

A Tamil Protestant Congregation

On two of the many hidden back alleys of Dharavi stand two churches, one the Church of the Good Shepherd of the Church of North India, the other St. Anthony's

Catholic Church. The area is bustling with activity on a Sunday morning; each church tells a slightly different story about the nature of religion in Dharavi.

The Church of the Good Shepherd is probably the largest Tamil Protestant congregation in the world outside of Tamil Nadu (and perhaps even including Tamil Nadu). Estimates of the number of persons affiliated with the church range up to seven thousand; it is also said to be the "mother" or prototypical church for Tamil Protestants in Mumbai, 75 to 90 percent of whom are said to be nadars. The congregation helps support "preaching missions" for Tamil Protestants in Sion, Chembur, and Poisar. It serves as a "feeder" for congregations elsewhere and a model for others.

One can see the Dharavi congregation in perspective when one places it in the context of Tamil Protestantism in Mumbai. All the Tamil congregations of the Church of North India (CNI) are placed under the care of two full-time pastors and two honorary pastors or "catechists."[57] Under the care of Rev. James Paul, senior-most of the two pastors, were the congregations in Byculla, composed largely of middle- to upper-class nadars; in Dobivli, where nadars constitute a majority but are mixed with other caste groups; in Andheri, composed almost entirely of nadars; in Govandi, where thirty families of all communities mix freely (Reverend Paul suggested this may be the most "Christian" of all the churches, as caste was "not important"); and in Vikroli, where virtually all the congregation is nadar.

Under the leadership of a retired layperson and honorary pastor, A. C. Asirvatha, were the congregations in Bandu (70 percent nadar) and in Thane, where nadars have a hegemony in the church wherein other communities mix. Under the "honorary pastor" J. P. Asirvatham, a layman who is a company manager, are the congregations in Goregaon, composed of nadars and *vēḷāḷas*; in Mulund; in Gurunagar (primarily nadars); and in Poisar, composed almost entirely of *dalit*s or members of scheduled castes.[58]

In addition, about a dozen Tamil Methodist congregations were created because the Methodist bishop appointed seven pastors exclusively for Tamils. These congregations are to be found in such places as Parel, Bandu, Borivli, Andheri, Mulund, Thane, Kalyan, Ambrivili, and Kivala. Many of these persons are former members of the Church of South India who simply attend Methodist churches in their Mumbai neighborhood because of the proximity.[59]

The CNI congregations at Chembur, composed almost entirely of nadars, and at Dharavi are now under the leadership of one other full-time pastor; in the early nineties, that was Rev. Ananda Maharajah. The CNI is estimated to have seventeen thousand members in Mumbai. Of these at least seven thousand are Tamils, at least three-quarters of them nadars. Most of the nadar Christians are third- and fourth-generation converts who do not remember why their forefathers became Christian.[60] Nonetheless, Christianity remains the third-largest religious community in Tamil Nadu, making up 5 percent of the total population. In Tirunelveli District the percentage is considerably higher.[61]

The building in which the Dharavi Protestants met into the early 1990s was constructed as an Anglican church in the late 1800s on property donated by an English collector in Mumbai. The congregants in those days were relatively few. The first full-time pastor appointed by the CNI was Rev. James Paul, who started working in Dharavi in 1976. He found the church had an official membership of about three hundred but that several thousand Protestants lived in Dharavi unaffiliated with any church. Within six months the membership of the Church of the Good Shepherd had grown to five thousand, virtually all of them nadars from Tirunelveli District.[62] Rev. Ananda Maharajah was appointed pastor in 1983.

The ritual life of the community as reflected in a single Sunday morning during the tenure of Pastor Maharajah embodied many of the values and much of self-understanding of these nadar Christians. The Sunday morning service attracted five hundred to one thousand folks, who crammed into the small sanctuary. By 8:30 A.M. the church was apparently full, women sitting on the floor to the left of the sanctuary, their heads covered with the end of their saris; men were seated on the floor to the right; a small choir of young men sang an a cappella prelude. The call to worship was followed by the processional hymn (an English hymn translated into Tamil). A responsive reading, a singing of the Psalter, and a reading of a psalm was followed by a hymn, a prayer, and a reading from the New Testament. All stood for the Apostles' Creed. By now (8:55) the congregation had been asked to "move up" thrice so that more worshippers could crowd into the back of the sanctuary. A Tamil *kīrtaṉai* (hymn) was sung with gusto; a woman read the scripture text of the morning while many worshippers followed in their own Bibles.

The sermon exhorted the community to pray more for the leadership of the congregation and the nation. A catechist prayed, frequently invoking the divine as "swamy"; announcements were almost as extensive as the sermon. For the offertory, two traditional *kīrtaṉai*s were sung with enormous enthusiasm: "Tēvāpitā" and "Ellām Yēsuvē" ("Jesus Alone Is Everything"). After additional prayers and the benediction was a mass exodus. Some lingered outside the back of the church for coffee and conversation, and some trickled back in for communion. Those who remained for communion listened to a prayer and remembrance of the dead; those desiring to receive communion then proceeded to the rail at the front of the church—males first, then females, the latter with heads always covered. During the distribution of the communion elements, the choir sang "What a Friend We Have in Jesus" in Tamil. Finally, the congregation sang "Onward Christian Soldiers" and left after the final benediction.

Sunday school classes for the young and committee meetings for adults followed for the rest of the morning; especially timely was the meeting of the building committee, which was overseeing the renovation of the church. A two-hundred-thousand-rupee project had been undertaken to enlarge the facility. Except for a small grant from the Anglican Church's Society for the Propagation of Christian Knowledge (SPCK), the funds for the building project had been raised almost entirely by the congregation. The new building rising that morning around the present structure was the pastor's dream, but one the congregation and the CNI bishop now came to share. Space for worship would be almost doubled; but the hope was that space would also be made available for a preschool, tailoring classes for women, a clinic offering medical help provided by volunteers, and a "good" English-language school. Reverend Maharajah hoped there would be a second stage to the building project, when four floors would be erected that could house a good high school.[63]

Some Implications

The Dharavi Protestants now meet in a new building built largely with their own hands and funds. Its present pastor finds the building disappointing—its acoustics are terrible, and his living quarters are in the church's balcony overlooking the sanctuary, a circumstance he finds inhibiting to his lifestyle. Yet disappointing as the new structure may be, the Church of the Good Shepherd reflects several patterns that embody the self-understanding of Christian nadars in Dharavi. Not the least of these considerations are the meanings to be derived from the renovating and building of the church structure.

Like their Hindu brethren, Christian nadars took great pride in their capacity to build "on their own." One shopkeeper was pleased to say that he had himself contributed three thousand rupees to the project. The same person, however, claimed that being a nadar was more important to him than being a Christian, but that he had been able to make a living despite the fact he was a Christian. That is, he had a perception that, while he had worked for the railroads, he had been passed up for promotions because of his Christian name. Christian nadars share with their Hindu counterparts a sense that anything they want to get done they must do on their own; thus, building a church bespeaks a sense of self-assurance and achievement. It is a statement that "we have arrived."

Moreover, helping to fund such a building expresses something of the mobility patterns of the Christian nadars. Reverend Maharajah mused, "It is interesting that the poorer seem to be more pious and give one thousand rupees a year at some personal expense, while the better off seem less generous." Giving patterns may be more than a reflection of piety, however; the better-off parishioners, for example, are often the older ones who have developed their own businesses. Older (and better off) Christians in Dharavi are also more ambiguous in their local loyalties and sense of rootedness. Many who were born in Tirunelveli District still think in terms of retiring back home. As James Paul put it, "Our people still think of Tirunelveli District as heaven. After all, that's where Nazareth and Bethlehem are."[64] More than that, post offices in the area between the ninth and fifteenth of each month become the scenes of queues of Tamil nadars lining up to send money orders to relatives and family back home. In addition, once a family's income reaches five thousand rupees a month (sometimes less), they may be tempted to change their church affiliation to more affluent congregations. That is one reason some nadars start attending St. Paul's Church at Christchurch in Byculla, a congregation composed of middle- to upper-class Tamils where worship remains in Tamil, albeit with occasional English translations, especially for children, whose Tamil is poorer than that of their parents. Indeed, from Byculla, more affluent nadar Tamils may "graduate" to an English-language CNI church, most commonly "the Cathedral" in downtown Mumbai or, for the most affluent, the All Saints Church on Malabar Hill.

One way to keep the more affluent Christian nadars of Dharavi contributing to the building fund was to place them on appropriate committees and elect them to significant positions in the church. Otherwise, the Christian nadars most likely to contribute may well be those who are younger (and, therefore, with less nostalgia for the "old country") and those whose financial resources are such that they expect to remain in Dharavi. Reverend Maharajah reported that about half his congregation owned their own homes or leased them on a long-term basis from the municipality. These families often subleased to other families or relations, thus enhancing their income and financial mobility. The other half of the congregation was said to be composed of renters who were obliged to move every eleven months, as the city's rental laws make it incumbent on house owners to require contracts of renters that demand large deposits upon moving in; these deposits will be lost if the renter stays longer than eleven months.

Building a new church structure thus becomes a complex index of religious, social, and economic values. It expresses varying degrees of commitment and rootedness to Dharavi and becomes a reflection of Christian nadar self-understanding.

Apart from the building itself, other elements of religious expression are suggestive. Not least of these is the pietistic and personal character of religious practice. Dharavi Protestantism seems to be the counterpart of Hindu *bhakti*—that is, of personal interaction with the divine—enhanced by a form of Protestantism imported by missionaries in the nineteenth century that stressed personal commitment and personal ethics. This personalized, pietistic form of religion is expressed in the singing of beloved songs such as "Ellām Yēsuvē" ("Jesus Alone Is Everything"), "What a Friend We Have in Jesus," and so on.

Reverend Maharajah rationalized this pietistic orientation:

> We Tamils here feel the Shiv Sena is opposed to the influx of non-Marathis into the city or state and pressure employers not to hire more than a 10 percent quota from out of state. The RSS [Rashtriya Swayamsevak Sangh] is quite active in Dharavi and is trying to educate its young into more militant forms of Hinduism. The Christian population here is only about 3 or 4 percent. Our people feel a kind of double jeopardy. So religion comforts them. Older people especially tend to be more nostalgic for home and tend to be more religious.
>
> In addition, I stress personal ethics first, so that our people develop good character. Can a person provide leadership in the community if he is not of good character? Can a drunkard say "follow me"?[65]

One of the implications of this orientation has been a noticeable lack of social concern on the part of the parish through the years. Maharajah admitted that no one has been very active in teaching good sanitary habits, for example. As a result, even in the best of economic times, Dharavi has looked and smelled like a slum because people have been socialized to defecate in the streets. The new building, with its space and impetuses for educational and medical concerns, will presumably also entail a rethinking of the role of religion in addressing social needs.

Another important marker of Tamil Protestant self-expression is its "orality." The word is significant in the ritual experience, as it mixes Tamil (perhaps even "Indian") self-expression with Protestant. The reformed Protestant emphasis on the Word (both as Scripture and sermon) relatively free of visual expression has been grafted into a language that is made for verbalization. In the course of a single service is the abundant use of oratorical devices that are consistent with Tamil usage: the telling of stories, the ornate style of oration, the use of gesture, and so on. In addition, the services use responsive and liturgical exchange and a hymnody that reflects the Anglican orientation of the congregation's forebears. English hymnody (translated into Tamil), accompanied by an electronic organ, bespeaks the influence of the West and the concomitant expression that Christianity is transcultural. Yet the use of indigenous *kīrtaṉai*s and the Tamil language indicate the local rootedness of the community in Tamil space. Constructing a new building and becoming involved in the social landscape of Dharavi suggests a community committing itself to Mumbai and its environs in a new way.

Several other expressions of religion delineate the community's identity as Christian. Funerals require the use of a coffin, a hearse for procession, and a cemetery, the last a site shared by most of the Christians of Mumbai, even though gravesites are now being reused. Dharavi's former pastor had also initiated a counseling-cum-prayer program for families that had been recently bereaved. Certain festivals are played out in public, perhaps most visibly, Palm Sunday, which calls for a procession through the streets with palms. The church publishes a ritual calendar (*pañcaṅkam,* patterned after the Hindu ritual calendar) that offers a listing of scripture readings and celebrations for each day of the ecclesiastical year.

Despite these distinctions (and others), the Christian nadars of Dharavi insist they feel a genuine kinship with their Hindu counterparts. Nadars are said to contribute to festivals and religious institutions sometimes across religious lines: officials at one of the Gaṇapati shrines insist some of its members are Christians. When push comes to shove, nadars appear to have a pronounced sense of solidarity and shared lineage; hence, incidents of interreligious conflict between them are virtually unheard of. Both Christian and Hindu nadars, however, share a sense of a menacing or unresponsive "other," be it the municipality, the impersonal bureaucracies of government, or the more chauvinistic elements of Marathi culture. Sticking together and making their own way "up" remain, therefore, important parts of nadar identity.

A Catholic Presence in Dharavi

In 1989 St. Anthony's Church of Dharavi celebrated its fiftieth anniversary. The experience of this parish provides a still different look at a minority religious presence in the area. St. Anthony's is a Quasile parish that serves as a subcenter of the Lourdes Church in Sion. It has separate registers for marriage and baptism and has a separate church council. In 1939 a shed with six rooms was obtained from the Mumbai municipality, and catechists were appointed and paid by the diocese. In 1940 the Feast of St. Anthony was celebrated for the first time; in 1965 the present building was leased from the municipality for use as a sanctuary and educational facility while the old building became the Daya Sadan—a place providing housing for young girls, a dispensary, and a maternity clinic. The facilities have grown over the years. Most significantly, a second floor was constructed for use as a sanctuary during the years 1984–86, and a "eucharistic chapel" was built and inaugurated in 1989.[66]

The parish today serves various ethnic groups in Dharavi but especially Tamils and Marathi speakers. Masses are held in Tamil at 9:00 A.M. every Sunday and 7:30 P.M. every Tuesday; the latter is followed by a novena for St. Anthony in Tamil. Masses are held in Marathi at 7:30 A.M. Sundays, 7:30 P.M. Saturdays, and at 7:00 A.M. on other days of the week. The Tamil masses are conducted by a Malayali priest who comes in for the occasions. The parish sponsors a Tamil choir; a junior and senior women's group (Marian Sodalists) in Tamil; the Legion of Mary, a Tamil service group; a Tamil youth group; and a Tamil charismatic prayer group. Somewhat smaller are the Marathi groups—a choir, youth group, and women's group. In addition, the parish sponsors four substations in various parts of Dharavi.[67]

It might be fair to say that the diocese began to take Dharavi seriously in the early 1960s. The Catholic population in Mumbai up to and throughout the 1950s was relatively large (as compared with the Protestants). As late as the 1971 census, Catholics were the third-largest religious group in Mumbai (supplanted by the new Buddhists in 1981). Up until the time of independence, the Mumbai Catholics were composed in large measure of the "east Indians," those who trace their ancestry to Bassein and the Portuguese era, and by immigrations from Goa or of people of Goan descent coming from the Mangalore area. After independence, Mumbai's Catholic population was enhanced by migrations from the south, especially Tamil Nadu and Kerala. Those who came to Dharavi were primarily Tamils from Tirunelveli District, especially the Tuticorin area.

The Helpers of Mary sisters were assigned to Dharavi in 1962. Their leader, Mother Imelda, reported that they found around three thousand Catholics in the area, most of them Tamilians and *kolis* (fisher folk), all of them "illiterate." Very few of the Catholics came to liturgy, and those who did attended irregularly. "We visited their huts," she writes, and "forced them to come." The sisters found that most of them had never had their first communion, so "we gathered them" to prepare them for communion. Adult religious classes were introduced; many in the fold were subsequently said to have improved both their religious and socioeconomic status.[68]

Nine sisters still live in the Daya Sadan, each serving six-year terms. Two of the present sisters are native Tamilians, but they insist they learn whatever language is needed for each new assignment. The nuns visit the sick and work with the poor, giving advice on how to get work and improve their circumstances. They claim that they do not proselytize in any way: "The only converts accepted are those who marry a Catholic."[69]

Other personnel are also available to help the parish. In 1988 the Canossian Sisters started walking into Dharavi from their convent in Mahim in order to teach in St. Anthony's School. That same year the "Little Brothers of Jesus" came to live among the poor. These are two men who moved into a hut, support themselves with manual labor, and try to identify with their neighbors. Theirs is called a "Ministry of Solidarity." In addition, the church staff offers several catechism classes after mass, sells informational booklets, and hires a young man at twelve hundred rupees a month to keep in touch with members of the parish, delivering materials from the church and welfare checks and performing other services.

These Tamil Catholics associated with St. Anthony's Parish have some things in common with their Hindu and Protestant counterparts. Many are nadars from Tirunelveli and/or Tuticorin who came for work. The "president" of the parish for the last fifteen years, for example, has a management position in a small local company. Like other older nadars, he aspires to return back home upon retirement. Younger Catholics, however, have little nostalgia for the ancestral home and hope to sink their roots in Mumbai or its environs. Their Tamil identity is maintained in the religious context not only through the use of Tamil medium in liturgy, classes, and available literature but also through the very names and features of the sanctuary. St. Anthony, for example, is a favorite in Tamil Nadu, one "who many Tamilians believe has performed many miracles."[70] The Lady of Vēḷaṅkaṇṇi, enshrined in the eucharistic chapel by means of a picture, has become famed on the southeast coast of Tamil Nadu for the miracles believed to have been wrought on behalf of seafarers and others. Even now the festival celebration of her birthday in early September attracts many pilgrims, both Christians and Hindus, to her shrines in Tamil Nadu and Mumbai.

Yet one gets the distinct impression that St. Anthony's Church represents more than a Tamil religious presence: Tamils share the facilities with non-Tamils; the majority of the staff is non-Tamil, as the diocese makes available clergy and nuns without particular regard to ethnic background. The diocese, in its involvement, seems to be giving the message that Catholic Christianity is transcultural and should transcend particular ethnic and linguistic lines.[71]

Further, unlike their Hindu and Protestant counterparts, Catholics in Dharavi, no doubt thanks (in some measure) to funding and personnel provided by the diocese, are actively engaged in efforts to address the social needs of the area. Theirs is an attempt to say, however successfully, that religion cares about all persons, irrespective of station, and about the total person, not just one's "soul."

Conclusion

The nadars of Dharavi are an illustration of a people negotiating a variety of identities in their ritual life. Most important, they view themselves as nadars and Tamils above all else. They maintain Tamil enclaves in their small business zones, neighborhoods, and religious institutions, and they proudly affirm their caste in their friendships, marriages, and ritual experiences. A sense of "us versus them" remains strong, with the "them" being the "establishment," be it the brahminized elites of Matunga or the impersonal municipality. Slightly less important, it would seem, is their religious affiliation, as friendships and caste identities seem to override sectarian distinctions, though the relationship of Tamil Hindus with Tamil Muslims remained ambiguous and tense both before and after the 1992–93 riots (see chapter 6).

Nadars are reasonably well ensconced in their Mumbai environment, though older members continue to have strong ties to their home district, some even longing to retire back there. This Mumbai/Tirunelveli ambiguity is enacted, for example, by Hindus in their worship of Ganeṣa as a central feature of their temple visitation, while attempting to rationalize such worship by linking Ganeṣa to the deity favored back home, and by observing the quintessentially Tamil festival of Poṅkal while joining their neighbors in the Ganeṣa Chaturthi festival. Residents experience a push-pull of Dharavi within the larger ambience of Mumbai, some settling into Mumbai for the long haul, expressed in commitments to religious edifices they have helped build and by the small businesses they have established. Others, usually the more affluent, aspire to maintain their religious and commercial ties in Mumbai, but outside of Dharavi itself. This latter group is also more likely to be anglicized.

Further, despite their obvious pride in being nadar, these people have appropriated non-nadar, even non-Tamil elements that serve to enhance status and self-image. In the case of the Hindus, this has included the employment of a brahmin priest in their shrines and brahminized ideology (for example, a fully brahminized pantheon) in a manner not unlike that which occurred in the late nineteenth century in Tamil Nadu. In addition, reciprocities have been forged with neighbors as necessary to make the maintenance of public shrines possible. The nadar Protestants have interiorized Anglican and anglicized forms of expression (such as some of the hymnody and instrumentation) that provide an aura of a transnational identity. The nadar Catholics emanate the sense, imposed by the diocese, that Christianity is transethnic, even transnational. The ritual life of the nadars, in short, enacts ethnic, subethnic, and superethnic identities and, in subtle ways, reflects generational and economic differences within the community.

CHAPTER 5

Brahmins and Their Three Shrines

In this chapter I explore the story of three institutions that express the self-understanding of their Tamil brahmin participants. Two of these are in Mumbai and are controlled by Smārta brahmins; the third is in Kuala Lumpur, Malaysia, and hosts the ritual and social life of brahmins in the southern portion of the Malay Peninsula. Each institution tells a different story about how tradition is reaffirmed and how subethnic identities are negotiated in those cities where resettlement has occurred. I begin with the story of Smārta brahmins and two shrines in Mumbai.

Smārta Brahmins and Two Mumbai Shrines

Smārta brahmins are Śaivite brahmins of South India. Like virtually all South Indian brahmins, they claim descent from *ṛṣi*s who were the authors of one or the other of the Vedic schools of hymnody—in the case of most of the Smārtas, from the Yajur Vedic hymnists.[1] Smārta brahmins are supposed to follow the household ritual traditions outlined in the *Gṛhya sūtras;* however, for centuries many brahmins were engaged in nonreligious careers, from advisers to kings to urban planners and military strategists. By the start of the twentieth century, as brahmins took advantage of English-style education and assumed positions in the civil structure established by the British (see chapter 1), many of their number found less and less time for the rigorous daily ritual calendar envisioned in classical times. Indeed, Edgar Thurston reported in 1909 that "nowadays, brahmins who lead a purely religious life are comparatively few and are found mostly in villages."[2] By this he meant that most brahmins had become less stringent in their practice of household rituals and more inclined to use the temple as a venue for their religious expressions. Thurston went on to claim that temple worship had become congruent to that done at home in the sense that the deity, once worshipped in the home with sixteen *upacāra*s (acts of homage appropriate for a king), was more likely to be worshipped on this scale in the temples only. Ironically, as temples in Tamil Nadu became increasingly accessible to those communities previously barred from caste temples, especially in the latter third of the twentieth century, one would find orthoprax brahmins more likely to enact their ritual commitments in the privacy of their homes.

Moreover, there were, by the start of the twentieth century (and still are), various subdivisions of Smārta brahmins, some more "Śaivite" (as Thurston put it) than others, some more orthoprax than others. For Śaivite brahmins generally, Śiva in his various forms is the high god, worshipped along with members of his family and retinue. Most Smārtas, however, by the early medieval period, had also claimed the philosopher Śaṅkara as one of their own and attempt to follow his legacy in believing, for example, that several forms of the divine, such as Viṣṇu, Śiva, or the goddess, are expressions of the Ultimate (*brahman*) and in affirming a monistic vision of the universe. Further, while Tamil Nadu was the home of the Smārtas for centuries, there were migrations, especially during the Vijayanagar period (fourteenth to sixteenth centuries), into Andhra Pradesh, Kerala, and Karnataka.[3] Hence, one finds Smārta brahmins who are Telugu or Kannada Smārtas, whose ancestors were users of Tamil.

Smārtas were a part of the migration of brahmins into the northern cities of India, especially into Mumbai. Something of the history and geography of this migration into Mumbai is told in chapter 4. In this chapter I focus more particularly on the ritual experience of two groups of Smārta brahmins as expressed in temples they have built in two subdivisions of the city, Matunga and Chembur.

The Śrī Śaṅkara Maṭam

As indicated in the introduction, a few Tamil brahmins were settling in Mumbai by the end of the nineteenth century, lured by professional opportunities and increasing anti-brahmin sentiment in Tamil Nadu. The trickle of brahmin migrants became a torrent by the late 1960s, when the coming to power of the DMK in Tamil Nadu made opportunities for brahmins in education and professional careers scarce in that state. But as early as the 1930s, Matunga in central Mumbai had become "Mylapore North," a bastion of Tamil brahminic culture and religion and the center of South Indian orthopraxy.

Vegetarian restaurants, with South Indian fare, shops run by Tamil proprietors, South Indian cultural institutions—all have become part of the ambience of Matunga. The landscape includes at least three major temples located within two blocks of each other in which brahmins from Tamil Nadu and/or Kerala have hegemony. Those include the Ashtika Samājam (*samājam* is anglicized as samajam or samaj), established in 1923 and devoted to the deities Ramachandran and Anjaneyar. The involvement of Keralites in the recent life of this temple is signified by the installation of shrines to Guruvayūrappaṉ (1974) and Ayyappaṉ (1978), at which Malayali Nambuṭiris preside.[4] A second temple is the South Indian Bhajana Samajam, instituted in 1927 and moved to its present site in 1935; its shrine was first dedicated to Lord Sitaramachandran, though a matching central shrine was installed for the goddess Rājarājeśvarī in 1978 with the blessing of the Śaṅkarācārya of Kāñcipuram.[5] The leadership of this shrine is exclusively brahmin.

The third temple, across the street on Telang Road and sharing some of the clientele of the South Indian Bhajana Samajam, is the Śrī Śaṅkara Maṭam (anglicized as matham). A recent brochure indicates that the matham is dedicated to the "preservation, propagation and promotion of Vedic education, Sanskrit studies and Vedanta philosophy of Śrī Adi Śaṅkara with the continuous and constant prayer for the benefit of mankind."[6] In fact, the matham has served to focus the ritual and devotional life of many Smārta brahmins in Mumbai for more than fifty years. The early years of the matham's life depicted the modest circumstances of the Smārta brahmin community. The center started in 1939 as a small apartment with two pictures used as icons. Set up by Mylapore Sastrigal with the blessing of the Kāñcipuram Śaṅkarācārya, it has been run ever since by a committee of Smārta brahmins.

By 1954 a building was purchased to house the matham, but it was not until the 1970s that the community could afford to raise money to build a *pucca* temple. In 1975 the foundation stone for the present structure was laid, and its dedication (*mahākumbhābhiṣeka*) was held in 1978. The center has been visited and/or blessed at various times by one or more of the Śaṅkarācāryas: of Puri (1941, 1986); of Dwaraka (1960, 1978, 1986); of Sringeri (1955, 1967, 1982); and of Kāñcipuram (1939, 1945, 1973, 1980, 1987).[7] The matham has sponsored a wide range of what are termed "Vedic" activities. These have included Sanskrit classes on a regular basis; "Veda" classes—that is, study of texts such as *Yajurveda Sakha, Saṁhitā,* and so on; and classes in "Vedānta" or speculative materials such as the *Kathaupaniṣad.* Also part of what the leadership is proud to call its "Vedic" rather than "āgamic" traditions are its three priests who are trained for *devī-pūjā* (worship of the goddess), especially in the traditions of the Yajurveda. It is claimed they are trained in this tradition at a school "near Trichy." They are said to be "better trained than other priests," for only they know the Vedic chants, and they "have to observe extreme purity" before performing their *pūjā*s—that is, they must bathe twice and wear a clean *dhoti* prior to *pūjā* both in the morning and the evening.[8]

The temple's ritual life is focused on a combination of deities said to be unique to this temple. An image of Adi Śaṅkara, believed to be an incarnation of Śiva, is at the center shrine and is surrounded by icons of Śiva, Subrahmaṇia, Gaṇapati, Viṣṇu, Surya, and the goddess Rājarājeśvarī, the favored goddess of Matunga's Smārta brahmins.

The ritual life of the temple is complex and orthoprax. Daily rituals, for example, include a fire sacrifice (*homa*) for Gaṇapati, libations of milk to Śiva (*rudrābhiṣeka*), showing of lights to the deities (*tīparātaṉai*), and *ārccaṉai*s (Sanskrit, *arcana*) of praise. Regularly scheduled rituals occur often: for example, every Sunday a *Suryanamaskāram* (praise of the sun) is held; new and full moons are appropriately observed; elaborate arrangements are made for *homa*s and other rituals for festivals such as spring and fall Navarāttiris and Śaṅkara Jayanthi (the birthday of Śaṅkara); Śivarātri; *Jayanti*s for the Śaṅkarācāryas of Sringeri and Kāñcipuram, and hosts of other occasions. Each occasion is celebrated with as much care as priests can execute and sponsors can afford. The *pradoṣa,* for example, the thirteenth day of both the waxing and waning moon each month, is observed with more extended libations than is true of most temples in Tamil Nadu. Eleven libations are commonly used on this ritual occasion at the Śrī Śaṅkara Maṭam: oil (which is used by lay brahmin participants to "reduce heat"); *pañcagavya* (the five exudations of the cow), which must be derived from a single cow and are brought in by special arrangement; the combination of the five sweets (such as is common at Paḻaṉi, Tamil Nadu) plantain, honey, jaggery, sugarcane, and cardamom; then, separately, ghee; milk; curds; honey; sugarcane; the nectar of fruit juice; coconut water; and *vibhuti* (the ash of burned cow dung). While one or more of these libations is common in Śaiva *abhiṣeka*s, the entire sequence is likely to occur in Tamil Nadu only in relatively affluent and orthoprax temples. The sequence also indicates that, in fact, the ritual life of the temple has incorporated āgamic as well as Vedic elements.

The Śrī Śaṅkara Maṭam embodies concretely a worldview, an orientation that is shared by virtually all the Smārta brahmins of Matunga, Mumbai. This worldview generally includes the following assumptions:

1. That Śaṅkara, the eighth-century philosopher, was an incarnation of Śiva.
2. That Śaṅkara authorized worship of up to six deities, each of whom, however, is a manifestation of *brahman,* the primal cosmic essence.
3. That the Śaṅkarācārya of Kāñcipuram and/or of Sringeri is the authentic interpreter of Śaṅkara's thought. Each member of the community is likely to think of one or the other of these as his or her own supreme guru, the choice of these depending on personal connections or the geographic background. For example, those brahmins from the Palghat area of Kerala (adjacent to Tamil Nadu) are more likely to be followers of the Sringeri Śaṅkarācārya.
4. That the ritual life requires recitation of Vedic passages and is therefore "*vaidikam*"; hence, more nearly authentic than āgamic practice.
5. That the deities, and more particularly *brahman,* equate to that which is within one (albeit in ways relatively few lay members of the community can articulate).
6. That Rājarājeśvarī is the supreme manifestation of this divine principle, both within and without. She is said to be equal to Kamāṭci of Kāñcipuram, Mīnākṣī of Maturai, the devī of Śaṅkara, and the greatest of all goddesses and embodiment of all.[9]
7. That the most sacred texts known and loved by some members of the community (e.g., the *Saundarya-Laharī,* a text describing ways the goddess is to be worshipped; and the *Tiruppukaḻ,* a hymnody ascribed to Aruṇakirinātar, claimed by Smārta brahmins to be Advaitin) are expositions of these basic principles. However, these texts are read and comprehended by very few of the lay brahmins.

This religio-social world focused in the Śrī Śaṅkara Maṭam is clearly one in which Mumbai's Tamil Smārta brahmins can express their orthoprax identity in ways that may no longer be possible in Tamil Nadu. In Mumbai there is no governmental agency like the Hindu Religious and Charitable Endowments Board to which temples in Tamil Nadu are accountable. There are no temple boards of trustees dominated by nonbrahmins—all managers, trustees, and members of the Śaṅkara Maṭam are Smārta brahmins. There are none of the political antibrahmin pressures experienced in Tamil Nadu, which tended to keep the practice of brahmin identity relatively private. There is no need of the traditional *mariyāti*, the honoring of patrons and donors who contribute to temple activities, as there are no Tamil "middle-class elites" (e.g., *vēḷāḷa*s) with whom the temple participants need to carve a reciprocal symbiosis. True, there is the solicitation of donations for big events, but virtually always from the brahmin clientele. Ads are placed in souvenir issues from various clientele, but usually from brahmin-owned businesses. State and municipal officials are invited to attend and legitimate official events, and, for such individuals, *mariyāti* is offered at brahmin-dominated temples such as the Ashtika Samajam of Matunga and the Śrī Subrahmaṇia Temple of Chembur, but at the Śrī Śaṅkara Maṭam, as at the South Indian Bhajana Samajam, only *pracāṭam* (foodstuffs offered to the deities) is offered such guests, not *mariyāti*.

Other factors contribute to the orthopraxy of this community. Many of its most active participants are retirees—men who have completed their professional careers and women whose children have become independent. A rather complex mix of motives is associated with this stage of life: for one thing, of course, there is a perceived need to maintain the centuries-old practice of using the later years to be a seeker of truth. Further, the matham is intended to foster a lifestyle removed from the constraints of householding and urban stress. In addition, some activities are triggered by other factors: these may include a sense of guilt and uncertainty about whether one's life has been lived with as much religious rigor as one might have had it not been for the restraints of career and family; uncertainty about the future and the reality of one's mortality; boredom and lack of fulfillment with the diminution of professional obligations; loneliness at the departure or growth of children and a concomitant need to maintain a sense of community.

Not least crucial in this affirmation of orthopraxy is the desire to maintain a sense of identity and lineage. The transplantation into Mumbai from Tamil Nadu's soil requires not only frequent visits back to the old homesteads but also a replanting of these roots in the present home. The Śrī Śaṅkara Maṭam seems to be a hedge against forgetfulness and the loss of identity. It is a reconstruction of "tradition" as tradition is perceived and selectively reappropriated by the builders and maintainers of the facility. It is a response to the boundary situations of Mumbai and Tamil Nadu, to mobility and encroaching mortality, and to the perceived diminution of religious and cultural values both nationally and personally. It is a peaceful fortress against the perceived challenges of change, decadence, and loss.

Not a few of the lay brahmins who participate in the life of the matham admit to being relatively uninformed as to the nature of their religious tradition. Therefore, it is thought to be important in this process of reconstructing tradition to follow the lead of esteemed gurus and leaders, most particularly the southern Śaṅkarācāryas. One lay worshipper, himself the son of a priest, observed, "I have become more religious since coming to Mumbai." Yet the matham's manager interjected, "But only the Śaṅkarācārya is religious; the rest of us compromise in these modern times; we are only able to be inclined to religion."[10]

The matham is not without its eclectic practice; it is as if the more that is done, the surer one can be of eternal results. There is, for example, that mix of deities that accommodates the tastes of all the temple's participants, as well as a mix of Vedic and āgamic rituals and the opportunity to look upon various esteemed figures and gurus of one's choice, most especially the Śaṅkarācāryas of Kāñcipuram and Sringeri. One is tempted to suggest the Śaṅkara Maṭam is a product of a reinvigorated brahminism, an attempt to reproduce what it must have been like "back when things were better," a space where the past is reenacted in the present and the future is now and the only time and space that matters is that which occurs within its sacred precincts.

The Śrī Subrahmaṇia Samājam, Chembur

The second of the temples to be described is the Śrī Subrahmaṇia Samājam located in Chembur, a relatively new middle-class subdivision in the north-central section of Mumbai. This is a temple over which Tamil Smārta brahmins have considerable hegemony, though various kinds of reciprocities and accommodations have been made with other communities. The founders were primarily worshippers of Subrahmaṇia, or Murukaṉ as he is popularly known in Tamil Nadu. They set up a temporary thatched shed in Matunga in 1945 and sought to buy land from the municipality for a permanent shrine there and elsewhere but failed to get permission.[11] In 1969 the group decided to buy land in Chedda Nagar, a part of Chembur that was then virtually an unpopulated open space.[12] Donations were sought from various sources. The Tirupati Devasthanam gave a sizable donation. The Indian Overseas Bank offered a loan (interest-free for three years and 13 percent per annum thereafter) in exchange for the right to have an office on the premises.[13] Other corporations made initial donations. In addition, cans were distributed to several thousand families in search of donations. A plot of land was purchased in 1972 for 130,000 rupees, a small temporary shrine was built, and the deity Subrahmaṇia was installed in 1974.[14]

As the temple was taking shape, people, many of them South Indians, moved into the area, building or leasing homes. Plans for the structure became increasingly ambitious. Not only was there to be a classical sanctuary built along appropriate āgamic and astrological models, with icons carved in Mahabalipuram, Tamil Nadu, but there would also be a structure for community development activities—that is, a *kalyāṇamaṇṭapam* or hall where day-to-day opportunities could be conducted. These were to include medical facilities, a yoga center, library, facilities for research and learning in the *Vedas, Upaniṣads,* and *Tirukkuraḻ* (Aruṇakiri's hymnody—see chapter 10) as well as space for various cultural activities.[15] Within a decade of this temple's dedication in 1980, an adjoining facility was indeed available. Here an ayurvedic clinic had been operating for a brief period, and students could pay for lessons in music, Sanskrit, and Vedic lore. There is space for lectures, songfests (*bhajaṉs*), and four Murukaṉ festivals a year, which are said to attract one hundred thousand Tamilians annually.[16]

The sanctuary itself was built on an upper story because "Lord Murukaṉ is . . . supposed to be placed at a height."[17] The architect had planned for a pillar of concrete, filled with sand, to connect the main icon with the earth. The secretary claimed that their architect, a gentleman from Mahabalipūram, was related to the architect who designed the Pittsburgh temple. He said, "They used our concept for rooting the deities in the earth but completed their building before we did."[18]

While Tamilians are particularly ubiquitous in the life of the temple, people from other southern states participate as well. People from Andhra Pradesh are said to come for the Murukaṉ festivals because they would have gone for such festivals to Tiruttani, a Murukaṉ pilgrimage center near the border between Andhra Pradesh and Tamil Nadu. Similarly, the secretary claimed that there were worshippers of Kārtikeya (Subramahmaṇia) in Karnataka—for example, "near Utipi"—and that is why Kannada speakers come.[19] In fact, at that time a Kannada speaker, said to be a "religious man," was chair of the board of trustees.

As for Keralites, during the planning stage several of them requested that certain deities of Kerala be enshrined in the temple. As a result, the main sanctuary does indeed include two of the most popular deities of Kerala: Guruvāyūr and Ayyappaṉ. The latter, however, is not the famed Ayyappaṉ of Sabarimala where millions of male pilgrims go each year. That bachelor form of the deity was not installed, according to P. S. Subramanyam, because "we knew his worship would have to be restricted"—for example, no women could be permitted, and extensive vows would have to be taken prior to worship.[20] Hence, the form of Ayyappaṉ installed at Chembur was that found at Aryan Kavu, Kerala, where he is known as Dharma Śāstā and is married. Both of these shrines today are maintained by two Nambuṭiri priests (*tantri*s) from Kerala, while the other shrines are maintained by four Tamil Śivācāryas, trained in Alūr, Tamil Nadu, in the traditions of the *Chintāgama*s. One of these priests, named Swamirathansivan, had served in the Chembur temple from its beginning, having come straight from his apprenticeship.

The sanctuary includes a variety of representations. Subrahmaṇia remains at the center; on either side are Durgā and Ganeṣa. There are altars for the nine planets and for Nārāyaṇa (a form of Viṣṇu) plus separate shrines for the deities of Kerala. The temple's leadership maintains that this is to serve all their neighbors from South India who have no other temple to which they may go.

The temple had its official dedication (*kumbhābhiṣeka*) in 1980. The occasion was graced by the attendance of Śrī Jayendra Sarasvatī, the reigning Śaṅkarācārya of Kāñcipuram. The sanctuary is on the third floor of the building with 108 steps leading up to it, each donated by an individual devotee. The temple is administered by a board of trustees, all of whom are Smārta brahmins, but not necessarily Tamilians. Board members theoretically have three-year terms that are renewable; however, a decade after the dedication, no elections had been held, though there had been some changes in the board's makeup because of attrition or death. P. S. Subramanyam maintained that the temple was run "like a corporation" with an annual meeting. It is registered as a public trust; the annual dues for a member were fifty rupees. By the end of the first decade since the dedication, there were said to be five hundred members, many of them brahmin householders, but apparently not exclusively so.

There is a full schedule of rituals for the various deities, for each of whom devotees can purchase the privilege of patronage. Prior to the inflation and devaluation of the rupee that occurred in the early 1990s, these rituals could cost from 2 rupees for an offering of praise (*ārccaṉai*) to 201 rupees for a full day of *pūjā*. One evening in the month of Āṭi (July and August) can illustrate the rather diverse ritual life of the temple. It is during the festival of Āṭippūram in honor of the goddess. In rural settings of Tamil Nadu, as well as in Andhra Pradesh, this festival combines a variety of purposes and activities. It is the time of the summer monsoon, when diseases such as cholera and malaria are common. It is an inauspicious time of the year when the goddess is invoked to ward off the forces of evil and to protect her people. Further, in some rural agricultural settings of Tamil Nadu (e.g., Madurai District), this is a time when the earth is being readied for planting. The goddess, representing the earth, is thought to become "impregnated" in this season so that fertility and prosperity will ensue.

In Chembur, early one morning of Āṭippūram, the goddess is evoked and honored with a special fire sacrifice (*homa*). That evening a considerable number and variety of devotees have appeared, and the presiding goddess reigns "pregnant." That is, the priests have built out the icon's tummy so that the goddess appears pregnant. She has conceived and will ensure prosperity. Yet not all the rituals are addressed to the goddess, and several of the shrines are busy. For example, a handful of women sing songs of devotion to Nārāyaṇa. Another group of Malayali brahmin male devotees are chanting at the Guruvāyūr shrine.

A sequence of rituals empowering the main deity, Subrahmaṇia, has been performed; each morning his icon has been honored with libations (*abhiṣeka*), including offerings such as milky sandal paste, the mixture of five fruits, and curds, much as it would have been done in orthoprax Śaiva temples in Tamil Nadu. This sequence culminates in the evening with the showing of twenty-seven lights (*tīparātaṉai*). These lights include that of a snake (*nāga*), a peacock, a pot (*kumbha*), and others, followed by showing the emblems of kinship—a parasol, a whisk, a fan, a mirror, and a lance (*vēl*). Praise is offered with a fivefold lamp of burning camphor as well as with flowers. Virtually all of these practices are consistent with ritual sequences done regularly in many Śaiva temples in Tamil Nadu.

A similar sequence of "honors" follows for the goddess, albeit slightly less elaborate. She is extolled as protectress and queen. Finally, a group of women gather before the *devī* to sing *bhajaṉ*s in her honor.

The character of the Chembur temple now reflects something of the religious, cultural, and ethnic ambience of the South Indian settlers in this subdivision of Mumbai. It is a largely middle-class and professional neighborhood. And, while Smārta brahmins were the prime founders of the temple and maintain hegemony over it through its board of directors, non-Tamils and certain non-brahmins, albeit mostly middle- to upper-class and upwardly mobile castes, can participate in the temple's life. People may come to worship from outside the neighborhood, usually because this is the closest temple for Subrahmaṇia or for one of the Keralite deities, but these devotees are almost invariably South Indian; indeed, most of the devotional pamphlets for sale on the temple premises are in Tamil. When asked whether *dalit*s participate in the temple's life, most officials equivocated but offered that, "in theory," they could. There was little evidence, however, of *dalit* participation during this particular season, though the temple does retain on its premises *kāvaṭi*s for rent. *Kāvaṭi*s are arches borne on the shoulder by devotees who thereby emulate the worship of Iṭampaṉ, a mythical Murukaṉ *bhakta* (devotee). *Kāvaṭi*s are normally borne (but not exclusively) by "backward" castes and *dalit*s at pilgrimage centers to Murukaṉ such as Paḻaṉi, Tamil Nadu.

Be that as it may, the character of the Chembur temple is relatively eclectic and inclusive when compared to that of the Śrī Śaṅkara Maṭam in Matunga.

Summary: Some Comparative Comments

Two temples in two different parts of Mumbai, though both run by Smārta brahmins, nonetheless suggest differing patterns of governance and expression. For one thing, the Chembur temple appears to be less orthoprax and more inclusive. This may be so for several reasons. The founders were first-generation settlers or resettlers in that part of the city and perceived the need to receive patronage and funding from a broader spectrum of potential clientele in order to fund their project. As a result, not only did several corporations contribute but also migrants from other states in South India and, apparently, from other middle- to upper-level castes. This pattern is consistent with the reciprocities that brahmins forged even in relatively early Tamil history. In dynasties such as the Pallavas, Pāṇṭiyaṉs, and Cōḻas, brahmin sectarian leaders, administering the temples, would receive land and/or patronage from royalty and landowners (*vēḷāḷa*s) and, in turn, redistribute some of the accumulated wealth and grant honors, the latter in the form of *mariyāti* or *pracāṭam* (food offered to the deity and subsequently offered to congregants).[21] It was a pattern to be found in Tamil Nadu a century ago when, as Edgar Thurston reported, middle-class nonbrahmins were visiting temples run by Smārta brahmins.[22] This pattern of reciprocity has also been evident in the way Smārtas and *vēḷāḷa*s have been involved in the recovery of Tamil poets such as Aruṇakiri, in which movement Chembur brahmins have been quite active (see chapter 10). This pattern of reciprocity may also be compared to the "new" policy enunciated by the "newer" Śaṅkarācārya of Kāñcipuram, who, after a brief sabbatical in 1987, began to include *dalit*s and tribals in his entourage and message.[23] Previously a "bastion of South Indian brahmins," the matham over which Śrī Jayendra Sarasvati presides in Kāñcipuram now offers training programs and other forms of social service to "backward" and scheduled castes.[24]

In contrast, the Śrī Śaṅkara Maṭam had been in place at least a generation longer, and its officials were more informed by the more nearly exclusive tendencies of both the older Kāñci Śaṅkarācārya, Śrī Candrasekharendra Sarasvati, who lived to be nearly one hundred, and the tradition of the Śaṅkarācārya of Sringeri, where brahminic exclusivity is blatant.[25] Indeed, when the "new" Kāñci Śaṅkarācārya helped to dedicate a *dalit* temple in Mumbai (in Cheetah Camp in 1989), some of the orthoprax brahmins of the matham expressed disappointment.

Another variation in style is that of governance. Both temples are run by a board of directors with virtual lifetime tenure (all of whom were male, at least into the 1990s). This was somewhat traditional in South India in those temples owned by a particular family or caste. This was true of the Chettiyar temples in Malaysia and Singapore and of the temples run by Ceylon Tamils in the Malay Straits (though the latter included women on their boards by at least the 1980s). This was even true in the early stages of the Śrī Veṅkaṭeśvara Temple in Pittsburgh, where, however, perceptions that Tamils had perpetual hegemony led to open revolt by non-Tamils and the institution of a system of rotating leadership spread among various ethnic groups. In Pittsburgh, also, women were on the board virtually from its inception. In both of these Mumbai temples, officers are selected from within the board and by consent of the board. The difference at Chembur, however, is that devotees, whether brahmin or not, can, by paying dues, become "shareholders in the corporation" and, at least in theory, offer an annual sanction to the board's decisions. At yet a third level in the concentric circle of participation is the opportunity at Chembur for nonbrahmins to patronize rituals on their own behalf. At least, in theory, these secondary and tertiary levels of participation are available at the Chembur temple. The Śrī Śaṅkara Maṭam may offer such participation in theory, but, in fact, most nonbrahmins feel less welcome on the premises. Brahminic exclusivity at the matham has been virtually total, inasmuch as their classes, rituals, and "social services" are intended primarily for fellow brahmins.

Several factors contribute to the ways in which these brahmins express their religious, ethnic, and subethnic orientations. For both groups, there was a time of settling or resettling after a period of mobility and uncertainty (in Chembur, in the 1970s; in Matunga, three to four decades earlier). Building a permanent temple provided a centering and stabilizing force for each community. Many in leadership positions in both temples have been those retiring from positions they had come to Mumbai to pursue in the 1930s through the 1960s. These saw the retirement years as the occasion to rediscover their roots associated with their lineage and fulfill the brahminic obligation to be the "seeker" (*vānaprastha*). There was the concomitant sense of duty to preserve the "tradition" and even to re-create it or "rationalize" it (to use Max Weber's term) in ways that selectively incorporate a modern, quasi-scientific, even technocratic vocabulary. Clearly, there is a perceived need for community in the face of Mumbai's crush, and that community is thought to be most easily sought with people who share certain ethnic and subethnic orientations. Orthopraxy, in short, is one possible response to the boundaries of the modern age. In fact, Mumbai, for all its cosmopolitan and commercial ways in the workplace, can become a patchwork quilt of ethnic and subethnic collectivities expressing themselves in the relative privacy of home and religious institution. In daily life, of course, brahmins participate in full measure in Mumbai's commercial, scientific, and artistic life, practicing what Milton Singer called "ritual neutralization."[26] In their ritual life, however, there has been a propensity, on the one hand, toward orthopraxy and subethnic exclusiveness in the Matunga matham, while in the Chembur temple, on the other hand, reciprocities with non-Tamil brahmins and nonbrahmins are expressed as deemed necessary even in the ritual and institutional life.

South Indian Brahmins in Kuala Lumpur

Compared with the brahmins of Mumbai, the number of South Indian brahmins in peninsular Malaysia is miniscule; indeed, they are a minority of a minority. Estimated at between 200 and 350 families, these brahmins trace their ancestry almost entirely to what is now Kerala and Tamil Nadu. They include several generations of families: (1) The first generation (estimated to be 10 percent of the present total) came to Malaysia for professional reasons, then sought to return to India but stayed because their children had become deeply rooted in Malaysia. (2) A second generation is composed primarily of those born in Malaysia but whose parent or parents were émigrés from India. (3) The third generation is composed of those whose parents were born in Malaysia and whose children are now growing up as full-fledged participants in Malaysian society.

The community is relatively widespread throughout the southern part of the peninsula. They have little or no social interaction with other Indian Malaysians, though professional interaction is not uncommon. A generation or so ago, marrying out was considered taboo; some admit that such a marriage would have resulted in the in-laws or their child not being accepted in the community (unless the person involved had "clout"). While such restrictions are less stringent with the third generation, many of today's brahmin teenagers accept the responsibility of endogamy and thus are perpetuating the perceived genetic line.

There is no unanimity in what beliefs or behaviors are appropriate. Several agree that there is pragmatism and compromise. Because their children tend to be less orthoprax, and because as professionals they are daily interacting with nonbrahmins or with other ethnic groups, most of these brahmins have learned to live with "ritual neutralization" in the workplace. Whether or not they are strictly vegetarian, for example, may literally depend on who they are with at the time. They tend not to wear their brahmin identity openly, for example, in the workplace, but express it more in the privacy of their homes, or more likely, at the samajam, or "common space," the families share as a meeting place. If abroad, most of them speak of themselves first as Malaysians, seeking to make their impact on Malaysian society at large; only secondarily do they see themselves as *Indian* Malaysians. As to whether they are "Tamil" or "Malayali," the lines blur. While many of the families speak of themselves as "Malayali" brahmins, in fact, the ancestors of those families were *ayyar*s (not *nambuṭiri*s) who moved to what is now Kerala from Tamil Nadu or lived in areas such as Palghat where Tamils and Malayalis interact and speak both languages. Many of these South Indian brahmins (including the "Malayali" ones) continue to use the designation *ayyar* (Śaivite), or occasionally *ayyaṅkar* (Vaiṣṇava), denoting their Tamil brahmin heritage.

Nonetheless, it is a community whose memories are blurred, especially regarding what religious obligations are appropriate and what they mean. Several parents, in conversation, concurred that there were at least four times in a lifetime when the propensity toward religion increased: (1) at the age of accountability when personal and ethnic identities and values were being formed; (2) at the time of marriage, when issues relevant to choosing the appropriate mate, and being visible within the community for that purpose, become paramount; (3) when their own children are reaching the age of accountability, because parents want them to maintain some sense of lineage, tradition, and subethnicity; (4) at retirement (or as retirement approaches), when there is an increase in available time and ultimate questions become more central.

In short, this community illustrates in fascinating ways the attempt to recover and express who they are in a pluralistic society with a strong Islamic presence, and in contradistinction to the significant minority of other Indian Malaysians. I turn to that story next.

A Brief History of Brahmins in Malaysia

The earliest brahmins are thought to have arrived in Malaysia in the 1890s as part of the old *kaṅkāṇi* system—that is, to work as estate clerks and managers (where the ability to speak both Tamil and English was important) or as assistants to medical personnel. In their spare time, some of these assisted in temple rites and astrological readings. Most came alone, though some later brought their families.[27]

In the first two decades of the twentieth century, brahmin immigrants trickled into Malaysia. This included, for example, a family of five *ayyar* siblings from Salem District, two who came as railway clerks, one as a priest (first at the Scott Road Subrahmaniam Temple maintained by the Ceylon Tamils and later at the Chettiyar temple), one to study and eventually make his way into a technical field, and the fifth, their sister, whose husband served as a priest in the new land. A handful of additional brahmins came as engineers, priests, or estate clerks. One of these engineers, Ramakrishna Iyer, helped organize and maintain rice fields in Perak. Two brothers, Ayyadurai and Somaskantha Gurukkal, came to be priests in the Subrahmaṇiam temples in Klang and Scott Road respectively.

The flow of brahmin émigrés increased in the 1920s. By then a network was developing that kept relatives and friends back home informed of opportunities in the Malay Straits. These émigrés helped establish new institutions and enriched the history of the peninsula: for example, the founder of the Mahatma Gandhi School (Subramanian Iyer, arrived 1920); the founding editor of the *Tamil Nesam* (Śrinavas Iyengar, 1924); one or two who eventually became active in the Indian National Army of Chandra Bose; and the founders of several businesses, especially restaurants. The 1920s influx also included a violin virtuoso (Ramalinga Iyer, 1920), accountants, an interpreter, and at least six priests. Shankara Saśtrigal, for example, became the first brahmin priest in Kuala Lumpur's Māriyammaṉ Temple in the early 1920s.

This influx continued through the 1930s and 1940s, bringing in brahmin professionals and technicians: lawyers, clerks, and the occasional migrant from countries other than India (for example, Kuppusamy Iyer and family from Myanmar in 1930). These brahmin settlers and their descendants have played significant roles in Malaysian society from the civil service to medicine, education, law, and the arts. The resettlement continued until 1953, when the immigration regulations were tightened. The only new arrivals thereafter were those who came by marriage to male citizens.

Under the British and in the early years of independence, several brahmins were drawn to the civil service. Most notable of these, perhaps, was G. K. Rama Iyer, who headed the Economic Planning Unit under the first prime minister, Tunku Abdul Rahman. Rama Iyer was instrumental in the shaping of the first and second Malaysia Plans and in the formation of the Malaysian Airlines System in the early 1970s and the Malaysian international shipping corporation. Another brahmin, R. Subrahmania Iyer, was a secretary to the first prime minister and personal secretary to the labor minister of the time, Tan Sri V. Manikavasagam (a nonbrahmin Indian Malaysian). R. Ramani, a noted lawyer, became Malaysia's first permanent representative to the United Nations and the first Malaysian to be appointed president of the General Assembly. Other brahmins became magistrates, civil engineers, postmasters, and civil servants in various states. However, after the 1970s, when governmental appointments became more ethnically oriented, and Malays were more frequently placed in governmental positions, brahmins became less interested in public service.[28] Indeed, relatively few brahmins in Malaysia have ever been interested in politics per se, be it Malaysian or Indian Malaysian, though at least two have been involved in local, Indian Malaysian committees. G. Mohan, a community spokesman, put it thus:

> Brahmins generally despise politics because it is a dirty game that involves fraudulence, dishonesty, wittiness, social evils such as drinking and dirty tactics[,] . . . values that are generally regarded as incompatible to religious norms that [brahmins] have been imbibed with. In addition, a lot of money is involved. Above all, Indians in Malaysia are still riddled with caste and creed discriminations and a vast number of members of the political parties lack intellectualism, discipline and far-sightedness, the essential ingredients that may attract a brahmin.[29]

Far more brahmins entered the professions in Malaysia. Those in medicine are too many to enumerate, but they include the likes of G. Srinivasan, founder of the urology unit at the nation's largest government hospital and a past president of the Malaysian Medical Association; S. Narayanan, the chief medical and health officer of the state of Selangor in the late 1960s and early 1970s; E. S. S. R. Krishna, chief medical and health officer for the state of Perak until his retirement in 1974; S. Chandrasekhar, once head of Malaysia's Biochemistry Unit and a noted researcher at the Science University in Kota Baharu; S. Raman, professor of gynecology and obstetrics at the University Hospital in Petaling Jaya; Professors S. Subrahmaniam (orthopedics) and R. Krishnan (pediatrics), both attached to the University Hospital; and many other physicians, several of whom have their own clinics or laboratories.

Brahmins in Malaysia have taken education seriously, as have their counterparts around the world. As G. Mohan put it, "One of the virtues involved and embedded in the minds of most brahmin families here is education. The concept of education as a means to social mobility and education as an investment is in their philosophy of life."[30] It is not surprising that dozens of Malaysia's brahmins are teachers; a few have served as headmasters or contributed in other ways. S. Krishna Iyer, for example, a professor of electrical engineering at the Technological University, was the first to produce a book in Malay language on heat transfer—indeed, it was the first locally produced book of any sort in engineering. Several brahmins have contributed to the teaching of English in English, though at least two have contributed to the study of Tamil in Malaysia: L. T. Rajan, a Telugu brahmin, who wrote several Tamil textbooks and organized several Tamil seminars in the 1950s; and T. Krishnamoorthy, who was headmaster of the only Tamil-language school in the state of Kelantan until 1980.

Law and the arts have also attracted many brahmin contributors. Of the dozens of brahmin men and women lawyers, the best known is perhaps G. Sri Ram, a noted criminal lawyer who became the personal lawyer of the prime minster. Of the artists, Bairaji Narayanan may be the most versatile. He was a news reader on radio and television, a playwright and dramatist, a singer of Carnatic music, a poet, an actor, and a scholar of literature. Other brahmins have enhanced the quality of Carnatic music offered in Malaysia. These include Krishna Bhagavathar, S. Ratha Sarma, and Kasthuribai Rengan.

In sum, the brahmin families of the Kuala Lumpur area have a high professional profile. Virtually all of them have completed at least a college education and successfully compete in the multiethnic Malaysian landscape. Yet despite professional success, they perceive a need to maintain a social network wherein brahminic ties and mores can be expressed. One of the most persistent ways in which these subethnic interactions are enacted is through religion.

The Samajam (Brahmin Association)

Into the early 1930s brahmins lived reasonably close to each other and visited one another socially.[31] Occasional religious functions were held in a home to which other brahmins were invited. The first mention of the possibility of forming an association apparently occurred in 1932 while a Rāma Navami observance was being celebrated in a home. But little progress was made. In the late 1940s and into the early 1950s, several brahmins would meet in the home of A. V. Sankar in Pudu (a subdivision of Kuala Lumpur). At first the gatherings on Saturdays and Sundays were strictly social, often highlighted by a game of cards. Soon Sankar decided to hold *bhajaṉs* (songfests) in his home on a Saturday after the card game. Attendance picked up. His home became the venue for the annual Rāma Navami celebrations. During the Saturday *bhajaṉ* on July 17, 1954, serious discussions were held relative to forming an association. Within two weeks, on August 1, 1954, an inaugural meeting was held. All persons present were unanimous in becoming charter members of the association, and a pro tem committee was formed.

In 1957 a drive was started to raise funds for a building to house the association. Thirty thousand Malaysian dollars was promised from within the community; land was leased in Pudu (near A. V. Sankar's home), and in 1959 a modest hall was erected. Framed pictures of certain deities became the shrines in the hall, but these were pictures with a special history. The picture of Rāma (the main deity in the hall) had been brought to Malaysia by Rama Swamy Iyer in 1925, and he in turn passed the picture along to his son A. V. Sankar. Pictures of the accompanying figures were similarly passed from Ramaswamy Iyer to A. V. Sankar—pictures, of Sitādevī, Lakṣmāna, and Anjaneyar. These pictures remain the representations of the deities to this day. Ritually pure cooking utensils were ordered from India through a brahmin restaurant and kept in a brahmin house until the hall was complete.

The first event in the samajam hall occurred in February 1960; it was the *upanayana* (initiation rite) for Viji, the son of A. V. Sankar. The first celebration of a sixtieth birthday was that of A. V. Sankar himself in 1961. The first marriage occurred in 1961. Other ritual occasions soon followed: the Āṭi Lakṣārcana (one thousand praises of the deity performed in July and August), and the monthly *paurṇami* (full moon) *pūjā* once held in the home of Laksam Vadhyar. The first worship to Śāstā, the favored god of Kerala, was held in 1964. The hall also became the venue for social events, the first of these held in October 1960 on the occasion of Dīpāvalī. This was organized by S. Balan, who also founded a brahmin youth movement that year. The hall became the venue for the youth meeting. Since then, virtually all public and ritual events held by the brahmin families have taken place in the hall.

Ritual as a Major Form of Community Formation

The single most important element in bringing families together and in developing a sense of community is the performance of rituals. What is interesting about their rituals, however, is that, despite the fact that brahmins serve as ritual technicians in most of Malaysia's temples (and in most temples of diaspora Tamils around the world), this community of brahmins had hired no one to serve as official priest or ritual technician. All the participants, that is, are lay brahmins: They conduct the ritual occasions themselves, based usually on the memories of traditions established by the A. V. Sankar family. Rituals may be added to or enriched by the memories or traditions of other families. In addition, families look to their counterparts in Singapore, as much as or more than to those in India, when questions arise about the appropriate way a ritual is to be done or what it means.

Ritual events almost invariably are followed by a communal potluck meal and opportunity for socialization. Children are part of most of these occasions, which become opportunities to pass along, somewhat anecdotally, the character of Hinduism as embodied in ritual sequences. Ritual, that is, is not only the expression of remembered Hinduism; it is the catalyst for community and the occasion for educating about the perceived tradition.

Monthly *Pūjās*

Among the ritual events that bring families to the brahmin samajam are monthly sequences. At least three such rituals are held once each month. These include the following:

1. On every full moon night (*paurṇami*), there is worship of Devī, the goddess, represented by the picture of Sitādevī, consort of Rāma. Occasionally, this ritual includes the recitation of 1,008 names of the deity. Only two of the brahmin males are deemed qualified to conduct this ritual—these are the two who have some memory of the ways these rituals were done in the past. Already the community is worried about who will take over when they are gone.
2. Every final Saturday of the month, *bhajaṉ*s (songfests) last some one and a half hours and conclude with a potluck meal. While this event seems largely a concession to the English calendar, one of the participants (Ganesan) suggested that "Saturday is important to Viṣṇu, who controls Saturn, the presiding planet of the day!"
3. The first Sunday of each Tamil month—that is, the Sunday after the sun enters the new zodiacal sign—a Ganeṣa fire sacrifice (*homa*) is held. This ritual combines several factors: Ganeṣa is the deity of "new beginnings"—hence, it is appropriate to start the month invoking his blessing; the timing also combines English and Tamil calendars; the sacrificial ritual, done selectively and, traditionalists would say, perfunctorily, evokes the archaic Vedic ritual tradition, albeit reconfigured for the contemporary moment. It is also worth noting that most of the icons and rituals of the samajam are Vaiṣṇava in character, though this particular ritual is clearly Śaiva. There are at least two reasons for the Vaiṣṇava tilt. Most important is that the founding families of the samajam (Ramaswamy Iyer and A. V. Sankar) were Vaiṣṇavas and "Malayali" brahmins; but it appears also to be the case, as more than one participant remarked, that Śaivas would go to Vaiṣṇava rituals, but Vaiṣṇavas were less likely to go to Śaiva rituals.

Annual Festivals

The brahmin families hold at least two annual festivals of consequence in the samajam. The most recently initiated and second-best attended is the occasion known locally as

Ayyappaṉ Bhajaṉ Day. This is a substitute for the Makara Vilakku, normally culminating in mid-January at the shrine to Ayyappaṉ at Sabaramala, Kerala. In Kuala Lumpur it is held on the first Wednesday in June, which is a public holiday and the birthday of the king. (The king is elected from the nine sultans who retained their titles even after the establishment of an independent democratic state. The king in Malaysia has titular responsibilities roughly homologous to those of the British sovereign.) The timing, in short, is a concession to the Malaysian polity, yet on a day when the brahmins are free from their normal jobs and can assemble. Once initiated by a Malayali brahmin family (and now conducted by his son and relatives), this occasion now seems to engage Tamils and Malayalis as ritual attendees. The morning is spent in *bhajaṉs* (singing of devotional songs); periodic chants can be heard, not unlike what one would hear on the way to Sabaramala: the leader chants, "*Cāmiyē* (O god); the devotees respond, "*Ayyappaṉ*." Worship is centered by a lighted picture of the Sabaramala Ayyappaṉ with eighteen treadmarks leading up to it, emulating the famed eighteen steps leading up to the Sabaramala shrine. The *bhajaṉs* are led in turn by musically inclined members of the community. The highlight of the day is the *pūjā* addressed to Ayyappaṉ and the showing of lights (*arātaṉai*) thereafter. There is prostration and the passing of food offered to the deity (*pracāṭam*).

One interesting variation in this ritual from that at Sabaramala (apart from the fact that this occurs in one day, in June, while the Sabaramala pilgrimage in January requires forty days of preparation) is that women fully participate in the KL ritual. Women lead in *bhajaṉs*, for example, and can approach the deity. At Sabaramala, of course, women of menstruating age are not permitted to engage in the pilgrimage or approach the shrine. One of the leaders of the KL ritual claimed not even to be aware that most women were not permitted to participate in the Sabaramala experience, though another KL participant claimed that some time ago, some "old-timers" in KL were also reluctant to let women participate but eventually decided that including the women was better than having them "sitting around." Be that as it may, 150 to 200 persons, both male and female, participate in Ayyappaṉ Bhajaṉ Day.

Other occasions mark the ritual year—for example, the "changing of the thread" ceremony in August is taken seriously—but the single most important communal event, by far, is the Rāma Navami festival held in March and April.[32] This festival has its Malaysian origins in the 1930s. C. V. Ramaswamy Iyer, who came in 1925 and brought pictures of Rāma and others still used in worship, is ascribed the honor of being the festival's initiator. First held in a restaurant in Brickfields, a suburb of KL, the festival eventually came to be celebrated in the home of A. V. Sankar, inheritor of the sacred pictures and the ritual traditions of Ramaswamy Iyer. The festival, known locally also as Haribhajaṉ, starts the day (*prādāṇa*) after the new moon of *Paṅkuṉi* (March and April). In some other settings, it starts ten days prior to this and culminates on the new moon day. Celebrations last up to ten days and consist of four parts:

1. Nine evenings of *bhajaṉs*, which grow in intensity and attendance.
2. The marriage of Rāma to Sitā, a ritual that serves as one of the two highlights of the week. The ritual is known locally as the *garppatsavam.*
3. Entry of bride and groom into the marriage chamber.
4. A climactic ritual-cum-dance known as the *anjaneya utsavam.* In this ritual, a lamp is transformed into the person of Kṛṣṇa, and male dancers do homage to Rāma and to his monkey general Hanuman.

Each evening leading up to the climactic events, *bhajaṉs* are held in the meeting hall. These *bhajaṉs* are followed by the *arātaṉai* (showing of lights to the deity), the distribution of *pracāṭam* (offerings blessed by the deity), and the serving of refreshments. Different families have volunteered to organize each evening's activities and to see to it they are carried out. The same families have been responsible for the same events for years, ensuring, as one participant put it, that time is not wasted reorganizing events every year, and that the tradition continues.

The gatherings had been growing each evening until the day of the sacred marriage. The "patron" of the *kalyāṇam* (the marriage ritual) is one of the few positions that rotates. People have signed up for this privilege fifteen years earlier. This year's patron is the brother-in-law of A. V. Sankar. He claims he was not religious years ago, but merely came to the "shed" as part of the Sankar family to help with logistics. But then he began to see how Rāma was actually helping people: in the late 1970s, for example, he had taken his family to India for pilgrimages, and because of "prayers to the deity," none of the family became sick. In addition to his duties as patron of the *kalyāṇam,* he had been serving as chief priest for the more perfunctory rituals held during the week. The person leading the singing of *bhajaṉs* is the daughter of A. V. Sankar Iyer.

The worship center for the Sītā Kalyāṇa finds pictures of Ayyappaṉ, Rāmayayam, and Veṅkaṭacalapati in the background in that order from left to right. Directly in front of them are trays of "white brass" with coconuts and bananas. In front of that are two lamps representing Rāma and Sītā.

The marriage of Sītā is conducted somewhat as a typical brahmin marriage would be, albeit in an abbreviated form and with some modifications. The rituals are accompanied by recitations from the *Rāmāyaṇa.* There is no circumambulation of a sacred fire, as would be the case in a brahmin marriage. There is no swing on which the deities sit (as would be the case in most temples). There is no exchange of dowries or gifts. However, the ritual does involve the tying of a *tāli* (the cord that represents the culmination of marriage in Tamil weddings) and offerings of coconut, banana, and camphor to the divine couple. The camphor flame is passed to the gathered families, as are sweets (for example, raisins and sugar lumps). The morning *pūjā* is followed by a feast, a full-course meal served on banana leaves. The presiding "priest" for the morning ritual has been doing this for years. He is a lay brahmin who studied briefly under a "guru," learning some of the "proper" proceedings in goddess worship, but he concedes that he must use a book to recite the mantras and that his enactments are apt to be quite different from those that may be done in India. Throughout his career he has been a legal clerk—presiding at rituals is clearly an avocation. Some 60 to 70 percent of the brahmins of the KL area are said to be present for this morning ritual—two hundred to three hundred people. It is the largest function of the year. The fact that it is on Sunday this year is coincidental, but it does help swell the attendance with people who come from out of town.

That evening the entry of the married couple into the conjugal chambers is reenacted. Known locally as the *dolotsavam,* it is performed in a manner that replicates the pattern of *bhajaṉ*s and *arātaṉai*s observed throughout the previous week.

The single most riveting ritual of the entire sequence, and among the best attended, is held on the subsequent evening. The climax of the festival week, this final ritual is known as *anjaneya* but is also called *dipapradikshāna* or *divya nāmar sankar thanam.*[33] After *bhajaṉ*s and preliminary *pūjā* (for example, the recitation of names and others), the *anjaneya* begins. A lamp is placed before the Rāma picture and lit, representing Kṛṣṇa. Twelve men enter from an anteroom, dressed in traditional white *vēstis*. These are supposed to be *brahmacārins* (celibates), but, in fact, most are married and middle aged or older. All the men are bare chested and smeared with sandal and *vibhuti* (ash of cow dung); they prostrate themselves before Rāma and sit in two columns of six each, facing the shrine. The musicians are to the side of the shrine. The director of the music is a songstress with cymbals in hand; at her side another musician plays a harmonium sounding a drone. A choir of women, following the lead of the songstress, will sing a constant stream of *bhajaṉ*s addressed to various deities, both present and absent. The songs are punctuated with cries of "Govinda."

The mythical background for this ritual reenactment is told by a father (E. S. Ganesan, a Śaivite) to his children in the presence of a Western observer: Once Rāma had vanquished Rāvaṇa and reacquired Sītā, and after Sītā had been tested for her chastity twice, Rāma needed to do penance because he had killed Rāvaṇa, a devotee of Śiva. At Rameswaram he prepared to build a lingam (an aniconic representation of Śiva) in order to worship Śiva and sent Hanuman out to get one. But because Hanuman had taken so long, Rāma became impatient, as he wanted to get back to his work, so he set up a makeshift lingam. Hanuman finally returned with a lingam. This is why Rameswaram has an outer shrine. Now whenever one worships Rāma, one worships Hanuman, and Hanuman is the prototypical devotee of Rāma.

This story clearly had several intentions in the telling; the children are "learning" not only how Hanuman is associated with Rāma but also the significance (even supremacy?) of Śiva. In addition, the children are socialized to the significance of the famed pilgrimage site "back home" and, not least of all, to the link between the local samajam and the pilgrimage center at Rameswaram.

Be that as it may, the men who had been seated rise and go forward to be garlanded by an old man who is now retiring (because of age, illness, and an accident) from the role he had held for years as chief choreographer for this ritual. The men now have become Hanuman's band of monkeys. The men start dancing with the lamp (Kṛṣṇa); one of them brings it to the center of the room, where it is placed on a tray of rice where plantains are offered. Flame is offered to the men, who are circumambulating and clapping. At first the mood is light; some of the men are smiling, their wives giggling as their menfolk trip over each other. There is some laughter as one man's *vēsti* needs to be rehitched.

But the pace quickens; the men pair off and clap each other's hands, right hands up and left hands down. Fans have been turned off so the flame will not go out, thereby signifying the eternality of the deity's power. Soon sticks are brought on for the paired men to beat together, a dance form reminiscent of the folk dances of girls, dating as far back as the *Silappatikāram* and the dances in the Indian *raslīla.* The songstress sings on and on as the temperature rises. The men drink water, brahmin style, yet begin to drag. As the rhythm gets more intense and the humidity more stifling, a man in the audience stands and starts to shout and shake his hands, apparently uncontrollably, and begins to dance. Three or four others try to restrain him, pouring *vibhuti* (cow dung ash) on his head and giving him water. Soon thereafter, the lead dancer, very intense, pumps his arms in the air and starts throwing bananas into the crowd as if he too had become entranced.

After about two hours, the dancing and *bhajaṉs* wind down. The lamp is returned to its place before Rāma; *pracāṭam* is offered and the concluding vote of thanks is offered by the chair. The Rāma Navami celebration has come to a close for yet another year.

Perceptions and Interpretations

As families are invited to reflect on the implications of these proceedings, a wide range of perceptions and self-understandings are activated. On the one hand are those who perceive themselves to be intensely religious (though not entirely for religious reasons) and, on the other, those who participate in apparently religious events who claim not to be very religious, if at all. Ritual attendees have varying degrees of comfort with their place in Malaysian society.

Take, for example, the lead dancer, who purported to become possessed during the dance. He told the researcher that he tries to become possessed on this occasion because it is an indication that a good year will follow for him. Entrancement is a form of being highly religious. Sometimes "you feel it coming on" (as when the music is of a certain intensity). The deity "gets into you as well as the icon." Religiously self-taught, he argues that possession is the giving of grace (*aruḷ*) and a visitation of "forces on high." There is a hierarchy of such spirits. Lower echelons of deities can possess those of lower standing (as during the Tai Pūcam festival), but these are not as high a religious experience as when the supreme possesses one. "We brahmins," the dancer said, are ipso facto equipped to receive such possession without prior preparation (though others need to follow strict diets and so on). He continues, "Things that happen in the universe are foreordained, but our religious activity [i.e., *karman*] can mitigate the negative effects. The deity and our worship can reduce physical suffering and assuage problems that may arise in our employment." He offers two cases in point. First, at his own office, many co-workers were once "on his back," but now either the troublemakers have left or he has learned to live with the situation. Second, once the patriarch of the community, Ramaswamy Iyer, had a heart attack. His physicians and family gave up when he was said to have two days to live. "I offered some prayers with the family and gave him some *vibhuti* very late one night"; lo and behold, the man came out of his coma and lived another six to seven years. "These kinds of rituals offer solace in a world where justice doesn't always seem to prevail."

Yet the same gentleman conceded that, though he had been religious since the age of seventeen or eighteen, religion had become increasingly important for him in the face of crises. He hinted at some tensions with his wife, who is impatient with his religious intensity. They have no children. He has experienced tensions at the workplace, apparently brought on in part by his own personality. He has some nostalgia for the old days, when the British and the early leadership treated brahmins and Indians reasonably well. Now he claims, however, to have tempered his religious enthusiasm, or at least to have channeled it, so that it is less of an issue with his wife and friends.

Entrancement, in short, appears to result from a combination of factors: (1) physiological factors such as heat, dehydration, exhaustion, intensity of rhythm, hysteria, and occasional fasting; (2) personal psychological factors, such as an unfulfilling workplace and/or marriage and a sense of communal marginality, even insularity, that may contribute to the readiness to have an intense religious experience; (3) and a social context that, despite some ambivalence, makes possession acceptable. When all is said and done, the possession is affirmed by the group and family. The possessed person even enjoys a momentary elevation of status, though some think entrancement to be unnecessary, even undignified. (4) The final factor is, of course, religious legitimation: one becomes Hanuman, the ideal devotee, and receives the grace of the divine. (See chapter 9 for a fuller discussion of these four factors.)

At the other end of the spectrum are those who not only are skeptical of the entrancement experience but also play down the religious character of the ritual sequences. Among these may be the chairman of the samajam, an eminent urologist. He does not believe in the trance experience; he believes it to be a form of "mass hysteria": possession is not a form of *aruḷ* but of *marul* (confusion, ignorance, even madness). On the occasion of the *Sītā-kalyāṇa,* he remarked lightheartedly that lunch was the highlight of the day. Indeed, the sharing of food offers a profound opportunity for the enhancement of social cohesion. Similarly, the social opportunities, the possibility of enhancing the sense of community between families that share a certain identity, become crucial for some participants.

Most other brahmins fall somewhere between these poles. One participant remarked that his generation (the second), which remembered traditions from home, wanted to replicate them here. Tamils his age had been more concerned with the need for financial stability and a career than with spiritual tradition. Pragmatic considerations "caused us to deemphasize religion." Now "we want our children to resume the traditions" and take seriously their brahmin identity." Religious tradition has become more desirable now, he continued, for several reasons: (1) His generation is more affluent and settled and has more leisure to tend to religious matters. They are concerned for their children's identity and recognize that socializing the children in their heritage, which includes religion, is part of that. (2) There is a greater balance now between the pragmatic and the religious/cultural—on the one hand, the children are pressured to succeed, but on the other, their parents do not want them to convert or "marry out." (3) His generation is trying to recover what has been lost, which has led to a propensity to turn to gurus and to find other ways to "educate ourselves and our children" to be more nearly orthoprax.

Commonly one hears the term *parakkam* (tradition) voiced as an answer to why rituals are done. It is tradition that is carried out to bring the community together and express its solidarity. It is tradition that is reconstructed from the pastitches of memory and compromised as it is purveyed to the next generation. This form of compromise was expressed by a participant in this way (as paraphrased):

> The very young are brought to the meeting hall and permitted to socialize and play with their peers. Gradually they imbibe a little of the religious atmosphere. During their teen years they (especially the boys) have other priorities, but eventually they remember and relearn something of the tradition, especially around the age of marriage. The girls, especially, are being socialized to carry on the tradition [and most of them (at least when conversing in the presence of their parents) concur that they expect to marry in the traditional way].

The community shares an ambivalence about the brahmins' place in Malaysian society. Some have a nostalgia for the "old days," when brahmins were sought out for civil service because of their facility in English and other skills. Now it is perceived that civil positions are not available (they are dominated by appointments of Malays) and that economic opportunites in general are not accessible, as the economy is seen as dominated by the Chinese minority. The brahmins have a perception that the government now is less responsive to the needs of Indian citizens in general and brahmins in particular than in the times of the first prime ministers. But the brahmin who was a former secretary to Tun Rajah and who helped formulate the first two economic plans tried to put some perspective on the situation. Here are his comments in paraphrase:

> We need to keep the big picture in mind. True, this last plan didn't do all it could for the really poor, especially estate workers, who live in a kind of isolated situation, and for that matter for all rural "bhumis" (natives), but a number of "bhumis" have been helped; the nation has been held together; the government has been supportive of all religions—for example, in the building of temples or churches on a one-to-one matching basis. The government acts to work on development and nation building,

but space is also given for ethnic groups to maintain cultural and religious identities. In this sense, the government is flexible and Indians have relative opportunities. However, should "fundamentalists" ever take over, the situation might change.[34]

It is this last possiblity that has many of these families nervous. Many have set money aside, just in case. Meanwhile, many invest heavily in their children's education, encouraging them to make careers in the professions, especially law, medicine, and teaching. And not a few hope their children can find careers abroad, most commonly in Australia.

Meanings and Memory

This rather small collection of families in the environs of Kuala Lumpur, Malaysia, is a fascinating example of a people betwixt and between. Fully Malaysian (albeit with reservations about the state of Malaysian society and their place in it), no longer Indian (yet caught in the public perception that they are *Indian* Malaysian and with ancestral linkages to a subcontinent that was not yet a nation state), they are brahmin but have a largely self-taught sense of what that means. Most of them are more than a generation removed from the days when orthoprax ritual and concerns for ritual purity were intrinsic to brahmanic identity. Yet as they struggle to forge a public persona, for themselves and for their children, as well as for those "others" who wonder who they are, they have engaged in certain evident strategies. They have sought to reconstruct or remember "brahminhood past," usually as purveyed through the grandparents of particular families and sometimes as conveyed by selected gurus; they have encouraged cultural and social interaction with one another, which in turn has helped families learn of traditions other families have perpetuated. Not least of all, they have turned to ritual as a common means for building social solidarity and enacting perceived traditions. These traditions are selectively appropriated and reinvented, sometimes enhanced by snippets of scripture or remnants of practice carried on within families. Seldom are meanings ascribed to ritual events, save as self-taught "rationalizations" in Weber's sense—that is, rituals are often meaningful insofar as they can be explained in medical or scientific language or, more commonly, in sociological or psychological terms.

Some of these memories are taking written form. Members of the community distribute photostats and typescripts, such as the ad hoc history of the brahmins in Malaysia and the recitation of professions held by them, prepared and written by G. Mohan, a schoolteacher and the historian of the group. The documents serve to enhance the self-image of the community, among other things. Perhaps more common are the typescripts or photocopied scripts that serve as how-to manuals for the performing of *pūjās*. A. Rajamani, for example, prepared two pages on the performing of four kinds of *pūjās*. The author concludes with the comment, "This is presented precisely with the aim to give some knowledge to the younger generation to know some details of Pooja as a stepping stone towards learning more in detail."[35] The reader assumes that this document also serves the purpose of informing other families how one family perceives its ritual obligations.

The strategies used by the Malaysian brahmins in maintaining their heritage are quite different from those of Mumbai Smārtas. The Mumbai brahmin communities were significantly larger in number and were much closer to the home base, which gave access to the ritual traditions as they were still practiced in Tamil Nadu. Further, they could turn to the revered gurus of the Śaṅkarācārya traditions for advice and emulation. In Mumbai they had access to religious institutions of relatively long standing and served by professional priests who could maintain rigorous ritual programs more or less consistent with the ways their ancestors had performed them. To be sure, there were "secular" brahmins in Mumbai, many of whom seldom visited the temples of the orthoprax, whereas in Malaysia "secular" brahmins interacted with their more religious peers at the samajam for social reasons perhaps more than for religious ones. The result is a much less orthoprax form of religion, one based in fading memories; borrowing between families; selective use of the word of gurus, read or heard; and, not least of all, emulation of patterns discerned in Singapore, the nearest bastion of Hindu expression, whether embodied there in fellow brahmins or through temples of the Hindu Board of Charitable Endowments.

CHAPTER 6

Double Jeopardy

Being a Tamil Muslim in a Mumbai Alley

The Muslim population of Mumbai is large and diverse—it reached 2.5 million at the turn of the century. Some are well-placed Muslims of Gujarati background, for example, some of whose ancestors established businesses and managed mills and tanneries during the nineteenth century. These were often Shīite, whether Ithnā ʻAsharī or Ismā'īlī, following different *imāms* and organized into kinship systems determined by the particular *imām* followed, for example, Bohra or Koja. Muslims have also migrated en masse from Uttar Pradesh (UP), many from rural areas seeking work in the railways, mills, or tanneries, and from urban areas already having some entrepreneurial or management skills. Many of these UP Muslims were Sunnīs, oriented to varying degrees by either the Ḥanafī or Shāfī'ī schools of interpretation. Streams of Muslim Mumbai-ites such as these have often remained isolated from their coreligionists by virtue of differing vernaculars, ethnic traditions, theological orientation, or subethnic and kinship networks.

In this chapter I focus on a different linguistic stream of Muslims: Tamils who have settled in particular pockets in Mumbai over the last several generations. More particularly, I discuss two separate subdivisions where Tamil Muslims have settled. The first is Dharavi, that sprawling, crowded area still described as Asia's largest slum; the other is Cheetah Camp, a lower-middle-class subdivision created by the government for persons displaced when the government built its nuclear reactor plant in Trombay in 1971. Cheetah Camp is northeast of central Mumbai, just off the bay north of the harbor and about one hour by car from downtown Mumbai.

I learned a great deal from these Tamil Muslims: First, that even though people share a common language and religion, there is still enormous diversity—indeed, Islam is no monolith. Second, that despite trying circumstances, people can be hospitable, cheerful, even relatively optimistic about the future. Last but not least, these Tamil Muslims demonstrate a variety of strategies to rethink and/or reaffirm their identities in response to significant challenges.

Dharavi

It is the summer of 1994. At least two major events with national or transnational implications have affected these communities' sense of weal. One is the Gulf War of 1991, the result of which was the return to Mumbai, even if temporarily, of many Indians who had been working in the Gulf states. The Indian government had provided transport ships to bring home Indian workers whose safety would be threatened by the war. In addition to this mass exodus, many Tamil Muslim men, especially from Cheetah Camp, had completed stints of three to five years working in the Gulf states and were returning to their homes. They brought with them different perceptions of the way Islam was practiced in its primal homeland.

The riots of 1992–93 were the second major event to affect the self-consciousness of Tamil Muslims, especially in Dharavi. The chronology of events leading up to the riots has been recorded in various settings.[1] Suffice it to say that years of threats and negotiations between Muslims and Hindus and between militant Hindus and state and national governments had preceded the triggering event. Then, on December 6, 1992, overly zealous Hindu pilgrims, while gathering in Ayodhya to worship at the mythical birthplace of Rāma, climbed atop the "Babri" mosque and leveled it, chipping away with hammers, rocks, and other handheld tools. Hindus claimed the mosque had been built by Bābur on the very spot where Rāma had been born and where a Hindu temple had once stood. Some historians, however, seriously doubted these claims, suggesting (1) that Bābur had never visited Ayodhya and that the mosque was probably built by Tuqhluqs or other pre-Mughal sultans; (2) that the shrine on which the mosque was built was more likely a Buddhist or Jain *paḷḷi;* (3) that there is no evidence in texts to suggest that Ayodhya was a pilgrimage center at all until after Tūlsidās (1532–1623) had rendered the *Rāmāyaṇa* in a dialect of Hindi and thereby popularized the cult of Rāma; (4) that there was no verifiable way to precisely determine where the ancient figure of Rāma was "born"; (5) that Hindus and Muslims did not squabble at the spot until well into the nineteenth century; indeed, the first claim of Hindus to the spot came in 1959, when a small shrine was installed surreptitiously within the precincts of the mosque.[2]

Whatever the historical realities, the destruction of the mosque led to several months of reprisals, counterreprisals, and tension throughout the subcontinent; Mumbai was one of the major foci of the aftermath. Spontaneous violence occurred when Muslims protested the action with looting, erecting of makeshift barricades, and other acts. Police responded by firing into crowds in an attempt to control them. The "mob frenzy" was at its worst between 11:30 P.M. and 2:30 A.M. of December 7, 1992. Forty-six people were said to have been killed that night and more than two hundred injured throughout the city, most of these the result of police firings. Nationally, more than two hundred people were reported killed and more than a thousand wounded.[3] By December 10 the *Times of India* reported that twenty-six persons had been killed in Dharavi alone, of whom sixteen were Muslim. The same article claimed that police admitted that 90 percent of the victims of police firing throughout the city were Muslim.[4]

The second wave of violence occurred a month later and appeared to be more nearly planned. While this is not the context to discuss the anatomy of this riot in detail, suffice it to say that a combination of factors contributed to the mood of Dharavi's residents and to events associated with the January 1993 riots in Dharavi, including the following:

1. Economic frustration, exacerbated by rising inflation in the wake of changes in economic policy in 1990. The rupee had been devalued. Prices of food, fuel, electricity, and rent had all escalated. This economic frustration included a profound sense of the limitations of space. Living in Dharavi requires considerable patience even in the best of times. Small rented flats often house extended families, shoehorned into narrow alleyways lined by gulleys that serve as sewers and bathrooms for the children. Garbage is picked up only sporadically, and water is made available for only two hours a day at public taps.
2. A fundamental disenchantment with the political leadership to date at the local, state, and national levels.
3. A profound distrust of the police (even before 1990), especially by Muslims, and a belief that the police were biased and inclined to use excessive force unnecessarily.
4. The cynical, deliberate use of goondas and criminal and other unethical behavior by politicians, whether of Congress or Shiv Sena parties. This writer, for example, witnessed a "shakedown" when three "goons," representing the Shiv Sena, sold "tickets" to small business owners, promising this would provide protection when needed. During the riots those establishments (primarily Muslim-owned) whose managers had not bought tickets were looted and/or burned.
5. The propensity to remain insular. Ethnic and subethnic groups often lived in enclaves within specific chawls (alleys) that represent the ambience of "back home." Hence, UP Muslims, Tamil nadars, and Tamil Muslims from various Indian villages tended to have relatively little interaction with each other. This isolation made such groups victims of demagogues and demonizers. Interestingly, Tamils retained relatively good relations with their Tamil neighbors, irrespective of religion, so that during the riots, some Hindus were known to shelter Tamil Muslims and to prevent violence to neighbors. A few Tamils, however, were known to be "goons" hired by outside agents.

Nonetheless, certain perceptions were part of the mind-set of Dharavi:

1. Communalistic rhetoric appeared in the vernacular press, especially in Hindi, Urdu, and Marathi papers, which added to the tension.
2. Factionalist groups—e.g., the Shiv Sena, VHP, RSS, and various Muslim associations —engaged in communalistic and demonizing rhetoric.
3. Deep-seated and long-standing prejudices were exacerbated by rumors circulating regarding international affairs. These were among the comments made to this observer: "Muslim countries don't let Hindus have temples" (a Hindu); "Christians are fighting Muslims around the world—look at Palestine" (a Muslim); "Western countries would come to defend the Christians" (a Muslim); "Hindus tell Muslims to go to Pakistan, but they tell us to go to the cemetery" (a Christian).
4. Mythologization of the past occurs to glorify one's own heritage, often to the detriment of another. This glorificaton makes selective use of a religious rhetoric

purporting to support violence in the name of religion—for Muslims the notion of *jihad;* for Hindus the heroic warriors of the *Rāmāyaṇa* and *Mahābhārata.*

5. Groups transmitted generalized perceptions about persons of an alternate religion. Some Muslims tended to believe, for example, that Hindus are dirty; they pour urine and spread dung around their houses, especially in certain rituals; they offer food to idols. Hindus, for their part, spoke of Muslims pejoratively as people who eat meat and kill animals; they do not follow family planning; they do not educate their women.

Whatever the factors underlying the January 1993 violence, Muslims were the primary victims of this week of rioting. And while both waves of rioting had affected many parts of the city, Dharavi was badly hit again this time. Firebombs were dropped into Muslim-occupied chawls; businesses owned by Muslims were torched; Muslim families subsequently insisted that police entered their homes and terrorized them, slashing wall hangings or pictures that indicated the occupants' Muslim identity.[5] Reports of the number of deaths in Dharavi were wildly disparate, from one thousand to two thousand by one account, to twenty-five or so by another, and two to five by yet another. People from the Dharavi alleys were arrested and jailed, a preponderate number of them Muslim.

A third series of incidents occurred almost two months later, when bombs were exploded in a few carefully chosen sites (for example, the Air India Office). That this was the work of a "criminal element" funded by "external Islamic money" was the generally assumed case (though some local Hindus insisted that some local Muslims had either known or been forewarned about the bombings, as certain Muslim establishments were said to have been vacated before the bombs were detonated).

In the face of these events, the mood in Dharavi was tense for months. Many Tamil Muslims from Dharavi (along with hundreds of their coreligionists across the city) determined to flee to their hometowns until things settled. While those men returned to their work and homes in Mumbai within two or three months, it was often the women who played a significant role in restoring a semblance of order. They organized marches—Muslim and Hindu alike—to police stations, demanding the release of their husbands. Marches of Hindu and Muslim women together were organized throughout the alleys of Dharavi to plead "for calm and reason." Similar marches occurred throughout the city. Within months, if not weeks, Dharavi returned to some semblance of normalcy, its residents nonetheless more wary of their neighbors and sobered by what had occurred.

It was more than a year later, in the summer of 1994, that I returned to Dharavi with my research associate to explore how Tamil Muslims in particular were faring and how they expressed their sense of identity.

Tamil Muslims from Paṭṭampaṭṭi

Clearly, the Tamil Muslims of Dharavi, let alone of Mumbai, are a diverse congeries of communities. For heuristic purposes I focus on a single subgroup of Tamil Muslims in

Dharavi, those who claim Paṭṭampaṭṭi as their home village (*ūr*), and explore how they are to be compared with Muslims who are émigrés to Dharavi from other parts of Tamil Nadu. Then I focus on those Tamil Muslims in Cheetah Camp who come from the *taluq* of Kallakurichi in South Arcot District. The comparisons enable a juxtaposition of differing strands of Muslims responding to various pressures.

Paṭṭampaṭṭi is a small village in south-central Tamil Nadu with a large percentage of Muslims. Back home many of the men had been small-scale farmers who hired lower-class laborers to till their farms, but many of those who emigrated to Mumbai had sold their land to pay for their daughters' marriages. The women had engaged in the traditional work of weaving mats. As the demand for handwoven mats declined in competition with mass-produced ones, it became increasingly difficult to make a living. Dozens of families migrated to Mumbai, especially as a network of fellow villagers arranged for housing and jobs in Dharavi. Today 150 to 200 families from Paṭṭampaṭṭi live in Dharavi. Most of them are living in one- or two-room flats leased from the government, clustered in alleys officially called Indiranagar. Many men found work in the railways or on the docks thanks to the network of Tamil Muslims so employed. Many of the women work in the homes engaged in "cottage industries"—for example, the making of *iṭlis* (rice cakes) for sale in the surrounding alleys. The men earn two thousand to three thousand rupees a month, the women another sixty to ninety rupees a month.

Virtually all the Paṭṭampaṭṭi Muslims are first-generation Mumbai residents, having migrated since the 1960s. Their ties to the home village remain strong, the men visiting every one to two years, the women and families less often. In Mumbai the women almost always remain in the home—the men do nearly all the shopping and conduct affairs with the outside world. The women remain extremely busy maintaining the household and family and seeking extra income with their additional work. Almost all the Paṭṭampaṭṭi women, as a result, speak only Tamil; few, if any, have learned Hindi or Urdu. None of the women have attended school beyond the seventh standard.

The same pattern holds for their daughters. Because the daughter is to be married to a relative of her mother in Paṭṭampaṭṭi, preferably a cousin by her mother's brother (a pattern common for many Tamils of whatever religious orientation), she is pulled out of school the moment her first menstruation starts and is kept at home until she can be married, parents hope within the year. Virtually no daughter of a Paṭṭampaṭṭi Muslim in Mumbai, as a result, had been permitted to continue in school after the first menses, despite frequent pleadings both by the children and their teachers. The rationale for this pattern is that should the girls be permitted outside the house after menses, they may be "spoiled" by contact with some man, however inadvertently, and people back in Paṭṭampaṭṭi would hear of such "contamination," and the girl would be deemed unmarriageable. There was now an exception to this pattern of marrying a Paṭṭampaṭṭi enate, some parents conceded, which was that, on rare occasions, a girl would be married to a relative of her father. Nonetheless, the girl's schooling in

Dharavi, so long as her education could continue, was in Tamil medium, always in a local elementary school. Trying to continue beyond sixth or seventh grade would be complicated further by the fact that one would have to leave Dharavi to get to a secondary school, and learning in a Tamil medium inhibits or precludes study in another language.[6] Boys are permitted to do this, but girls are not.

The sense of rootedness in the home village is the single most significant element marking the Paṭṭampaṭṭi Muslims' identity. It shapes their friendships and social cohesion; indeed, many of Dharavi's Paṭṭampaṭṭi-ites are related to each other. Their relationships with each other far transcend those with other Tamil Muslims, let alone with Tamil Hindus or with the UP Muslims who live only several alleys away.

But there are other markers by which Paṭṭampaṭṭi Muslims express their identity. For example, they have shared with other Tamil Muslims a connection to the local *dargah* (tomb/shrine) first dedicated to the memory of Shahulhameed, commonly known as "Nagore Āṇṭavār," who was believed to have lived in the early part of the sixteenth century. This Islamic saint is said to have visited Melapalaiyam (near Paṭṭampaṭṭi) in Tirunelveli District and to have converted locals to his faith. He is said to have reached Nagore by way of Trichinopology and the Deccan in the year A.H. 865 (1487 C.E.) during the reign of Achyuttupa Nayakka of Tanjore.[7] This Nayakka is said to have been cured of serious disease thanks to the saint and started the building of a *dargah* to him in Nagore in part to court the help of Muslims in his campaign against the Portuguese. The *dargah* had several later accretions, most notably apparently by Pratapsingh (1739–63), a Maratha governing briefly in Tanjore under the influence of Sayyid, a Muslim king maker in the Tanjore Court for years.[8] The *dargah* attracted both Hindus and Muslims in worship, insofar as its layout resembled that of a Hindu temple, including the addition of a tank. Moreover, the *dargah* was the venue for several festivals, such as the Khanduri festival, which incorporated certain Hindu customs, such as the cart-pulling ceremony in which Muslim saints were paraded as in Hindu festivals.[9]

When Tamil Muslims came to Dharavi, they erected a *dargah* emulating the one in Nagore. It seems both men and women were disposed to visit it, though the Paṭṭampaṭṭi men even less commonly than other Tamil Muslims, and the women very seldom indeed. In the 1992 riots the Dharavi *dargah* was destroyed and, in its place, a more traditional mosque was built, largely with the help of UP Muslims who now have assumed hegemony. While two hundred or so people once attended the *dargah,* now five hundred are said to do so, partially because it is now a *masjid,* is bigger, and has a second story. The Paṭṭampaṭṭi men also claim the mosque is now "pure" because the women no longer attend, but they attend themselves only occasionally, most commonly for Friday prayers. The women conduct all their religious and social traditions in their homes. Both men and women insist, nonetheless, that since the riots they have been more conscious and proud of their Muslim identities.

Islamic and other social identities are expressed by Paṭṭampaṭṭi Muslims in a variety of ways. Several terms are used in their self-presentations. First, they are rowthers;

according to one older informant, this implies that they are the descendents of Sepoys or soldiers hired to fight for one or more chieftain in Tamil Nadu and were given land by their employers and married local Tamil women some centuries earlier;[10] the term also implies that their work in recent generations consisted traditionally of mat making and farming. Second, they are sheikhs. Few were sure of the history of the sheikhs, but all were agreed that sheikhs had less status than the *sayyids*, who were understood to be descendants of the Prophet and of immigrants and who were pan-Indian in their scope. In comparison, one man insisted, the rowthers were upper crust, once landowners and cultivators of neem trees. Indeed, several of the non-Paṭṭampaṭṭi Tamil Muslims claimed to be *sayyids*; most of these were inclined to be more orthoprax in the practice of certain Islamic rituals, more likely to know Urdu and/or Arabic than the Paṭṭampaṭṭi sheikhs.[11] The *sayyids* would not intermarry with other groups, though the sheikhs claimed they would marry with *khans* or *pathans* perceived to be lower in the social scale than the sheikhs. However, most Paṭṭampaṭṭi-ites maintained they would not intermarry with *lebbas*, "backward" Muslim "caste" members who had been designated for scholarships and reservations in the 1980s.[12] In fact, as we have noted, the Paṭṭampaṭṭi Muslims marry only enates from their home village. Most of the Tamil Muslims in Mumbai proved to be Sunnī, so the Sunnī-Shīa differences were less significant than the Ḥanafī-Shāfi'ī ones. The Paṭṭampaṭṭi Muslims claimed to be Ḥanafī in orientation, one reason presumably their ritual life was less rigorous than that of the *sayyids*, some of whom, at least, were more likely to be Shāfi'ī in orientation. In sum, the Paṭṭampaṭṭi Muslims have little significant interactions with Shāfi'ī-Sunnī Muslims from other areas, even from Melapalaiyam, several miles from their home village.

The Paṭṭampaṭṭi Muslims are relatively low key in their practice of religious obligations. The women tend to be the bearers of tradition. However, the women seldom wear the *burqa* (outer covering) but may, on the few occasions they leave their flats, pull the end of their saris over the head. Relatively little attention is paid to the daily prayer cycle (*salāt*, known locally as the *namāz*); the rationale for this most commonly voiced is that the women are too busy in their work at home and that occasionally their small children urinate in the flat, and it is impossible to clean up and purify the space in time for prayers. Both men and women are likely to be more faithful to Friday prayers, the men in the *masjid*, if not at work, and the women in a home in groups of four or five. The giving of alms (*zakāt*), another of the fundamental pillars of Islam, takes the form of occasionally helping a relative or, now and then, giving bread to the poor. Again, there is no systematic pattern to the observance of *zakāt*. The annual observance of Ramaḍān is rather low key as well, though most of the families seem more faithful now to the fast than was the case prior to the riots. On the occasion of the *Īd*, which ends the month of Ramaḍān (*Īd al-Fiṭr*), families bathe, wear new clothes, visit relatives, and feast together. In addition, the Paṭṭampaṭṭi families observe two of the main festivals virtually all other Muslims in Mumbai observe. The first is

Baqar Īd, also known as *Īd al-Aḍḥā* (marking vicariously the culmination of the *ḥajj* with the Feast of Sacrifice). On this occasion many families will buy a goat for sacrifice and give at least some of it to the poor, in some cases preserving some of it for relatives and some for the family itself. Special sweets (*sīra*) are prepared for the occasion. The other festival is Muḥarram, technically a Shīite observance commemorating the assassination of Ḥusayn. The most common way in which Paṭṭampaṭṭi Muslims celebrate this occasion is with a family picnic on the last day of the commemoration, signaling the end of an inauspicious month. As for the pilgrimage to Mecca (*ḥajj*), none of the Paṭṭampaṭṭi Muslims in Mumbai has ever gone, though some in the home village have gone. Nor do any of the Paṭṭampaṭṭi migrants ever expect to go, because of their financial circumstances.

In the practice of rites of passage, slight differences appear between the celebrations of Paṭṭampaṭṭi Muslims and those of their coreligionists. The former tend, however, to call in an *imām* for these occasions as if to ensure these practices are done appropriately. At the giving of a name to a newborn, for example, it is the *imām* or *hazrat* who first blows into the infant's ear and assures the child he or she is the "descendant of Adam and Eve." This ritual occurs seven to twenty-one days after the birth and is an occasion when the child is made to taste sugar water and a feast is served for close relatives insofar as finances permit. A boy's circumcision may be dovetailed with the naming ceremony but can also be done at any time up to the age of seven. This event always occurs in the mother's parental household, albeit with the permission and participation of the father's family.

A girl's first menses becomes a major occasion for the extended family, a public event at which a girl's availability for marriage is affirmed. It may last for nine days, during which, as one informant put it, "the girl eats lots of eggs." In fact, for the first three days, raw eggs are served to her in ginger juice; on days four through six, she eats raw eggs served in sesame seed oil; on days seven to nine, her raw eggs are served in green *dāl*, a symbol of fertility in many Tamil settings.[13] On the ninth day, the girl's hair is oiled and she is bathed. Relatives are invited to a feast. From that point on she must not come in contact with any males apart from those in her immediate family.

Succinctly put, the Paṭṭampaṭṭi Muslims are less likely to be affected by the internationalizing currents affecting other Muslims in Mumbai, even in Dharavi. While the riots disrupted their lives in the short term and created a persistent sense of "living on the edge," they have, nonetheless, resumed many of the practices that characterize their identities as shaped by their home village. Self-consciously Muslim, to be sure, and particularly so since the riots, they remain relatively passive in the practice of identifiably Islamic practices. Their men will hoist a green flag in a tree near the new *masjid* when expressing a prayer or a sense of gratitude, as will all other Muslims, a practice that before the destruction of the *dargah* was done on its premises. They will engage sporadically in the pillars of Islam but without systemicity. The most important identity for them to maintain is the ties to their ancestral village.

Some Other Muslims in Dharavi

Other Tamil Muslims in Dharavi present a different picture, and all the Tamils perceive themselves to be distinct from Muslims of Uttar Pradesh, who are the majority in the alleys of Dharavi. Generally speaking, the UP Muslims have assumed hegemony among the Muslims for several reasons. They are more likely to have been in Mumbai for more than one generation. The men have often assumed roles as entrepreneurs and managers of small businesses in the area. They almost invariably know Urdu and Hindi. The women (especially the second- and third-generation Mumbai-ites) have continued into secondary school and have assumed a self-assurance that enables them to circulate both within and outside of Dharavi (albeit dressed always in the *burqa* when outside the home). They are likely to marry other Muslims who are considered Mumbai-ites. They are perceived by Tamil coreligionists to be more influenced by international Islamic principles and therefore more likely to be faithful to such principles, even aggressive in their defense. Many of these are Shīites and observe a wide variety of festivals (Mawlid-al-Nabī—birthday of the Prophet; Abd al Qādir—honoring the founder of the Qādiriyah order of Ṣūfīs; Shab-I Barat—the night in the month of Shaban when one prays for the souls of the dead and the living, etc.), and their celebrations of Muḥarram are especially colorful, with processions and the setting up of water pots at street corners to provide water in commemoration of Ḥusayn's family, which is said to have died of thirst. Yet they tend to live in an enclave with other UP Muslims known to Hindus as "little Pakistan," and their social connections are almost entirely with other UP Muslims.

Most of the Tamil Muslim groups in Dharavi tend to fall somewhere between the Paṭṭampaṭṭi Muslims and the UP Muslims. On the one hand, for example, there are those *sayyids* from South Arcot District,[14] many of whom have been in Mumbai for more than a generation and have ties to other Muslims in Mumbai outside of Dharavi. Their women are more likely to know Hindi and/or Urdu than are females of the Paṭṭampaṭṭi group and more likely to take positions of leadership among Tamil Muslim women. It was one of these, for example, who organized and led the marches of Muslim and Hindu women after the January 1993 riots. One of these women, in fact, referred to the Tirunelveli Muslims as "wimps" for having run away to home when the trouble started. Some of these women are self-employed within the neighborhood while husbands work in the Gulf, or they have been divorced or separated from them. (The researchers found no divorced women in the Paṭṭampaṭṭi cluster and none who had family members working in the Gulf.)

Yet another discernible group of Tamil Muslims in Dharavi are those who claim Melapalaiyam as hometown. This is a city in Tirunelveli District that is said to be three-quarters Muslim. Like the Paṭṭampaṭṭi folk, they claim to be sheikhs but are generally much better placed than the former. They too had stories of their origins; one woman, for example, claimed she had learned in the *madrasa* (the Muslim school) that they had been "converted by Turks some two thousand years ago!" Another more sober observer suggested that many of their ancestors had been converted when Shahulhameed (the Nagore saint) came to their town "six or seven generations" before. The Melapalaiyam Muslims claim to be Shāfi'ī Sunnīs. After probing, however, they admit that many of them are *lebbas*. Historically, many of them had been weavers who migrated to Mumbai and the vicinity seeking work. They estimate eight hundred to one thousand of them live in the Mumbai area, of whom about half live in Dharavi. These families tended to marry *lebbas* from Melapalaiyam or its environs, but not first cousins as the Paṭṭampaṭṭi folk have done. The Melapalaiyam Muslims' self-perception is that they are more sophisticated than their Paṭṭampaṭṭi counterparts. They had taken advantage of educational opportunities, including for some of their daughters who had attended a nearby college. Some of the men lived in Dharavi without their families, who were back home (a pattern also found among some of the Paṭṭampaṭṭi men). Because Melapalaiyam was said to be a "town of about 200,000–400,000 people with some 35 masjids and a population that was 90% Muslims,"[15] these Muslims claim to have had greater exposure to religious and political leaders from outside. The result, from their point of view, was that their practice of Islam was more *pucca* (orthoprax) than their village counterparts. Indeed, their children were being encouraged to learn Arabic recitations (often in Tamil transliteration), and their women traditionally wore the *dupatta* (a ritual head covering) rather than merely cover their heads with the sari's end. In fact, the women living in Mumbai were increasingly adapting the *purdah* like their UP counterparts.[16] These women were also more likely to know Hindi or Urdu or English than were the Paṭṭampaṭṭi women.

A few of the Melapalaiyam Muslims were managing their own businesses (a restaurant, for example), though most of the men worked in the mills. This group of Muslims had been active in helping to found the South India Muslim Association (SIMA) in 1965 in order to serve South Indian Muslims in several ways: to cater to Tamil Muslims in transit to and from the Mecca pilgrimage; to serve as a *panchayat* (governing body) and settle disputes; and to collect money for the marriage of poor girls. Leadership for the SIMA is elected every two to three years, drawn almost always from the Melapalaiyam men. Interestingly, most of the Paṭṭampaṭṭi Muslims purported not to know of the SIMA's existence or to have taken advantage of its services.

Being Muslim in Dharavi in the wake of the 1992–93 riots meant, in the main, trying to "get back to normal." "Normality" appeared to indicate the continuing of subethnic, often geographically oriented identities. While many of the families purported to be even more self-conscious of their Muslim identity and proud of it, there were still varying degrees to which Tamil Muslims had been influenced by attempts to homogenize Islamic practice. The Tamil Muslims of Dharavi and especially the Paṭṭampaṭṭi Muslims were more Tamil than Muslim in any abstract orthodox sense. Yes, attendance of the *masjid* by the men was more likely since 1992, and the cluster of women meeting for *namāz* on Friday noon was slightly larger. But the virtual center of their cultural-religious world remained in Tamil Nadu, especially in their hometown (*ūr*), rather than in Mecca or even Mumbai.

Cheetah Camp

The story is somewhat different in Cheetah Camp, a settlement of perhaps seventy thousand to one hundred thousand people created in 1976 by the government for persons displaced by the construction of the nuclear reactor plant in Trombay. The journalist Kalpana Sharma describes Cheetah Camp's creation: a slum named Janata Colony had sprung up in the 1960s on vacant land next to the Bhabha Atomic Research Center. The colony had become a settled slum with mosques, temples, churches, and schools.

> On 17 May, 1976, at the height of the State of Emergency declared by then Prime Minister, Indira Gandhi, 12,000 policemen entered Janata Colony and overnight threw out a community of 70,000 people. They were shifted four kilometres away, to a swampy area in Trombay which has now emerged as a large slum named Cheetah Camp. The demolition took place to free land to house BARC personnel—3,000 of them.[17]

The settlement in Trombay lies along the bay in north-central Mumbai. Its alleys are wider and cleaner than those in Dharavi, and it is not uncommon to find homes (again, generally leased from the government) with a separate kitchen, a TV set, a refrigerator, and steel cabinets. Some houses even have attached latrines. The researchers are told the average monthly salary in Cheetah Camp is six thousand to nine thousand rupees, though we find some blocks in which families are earning fifteen thousand rupees or more.

Cheetah Camp was not affected by the 1992–93 riots but had experienced a riot in 1984. The 1984 incident was triggered by a remark made by the Shiv Sena leader Bal Thackeray and reported in an Urdu newspaper as having been derogatory to the Prophet and to Muslims. As a result, on May 23–27, 1984, protest had erupted on Muhammad Ali Road, a part of Mumbai heavily populated by Shīite Muslims. In Cheetah Camp itself, some youth had tossed a bottle at a police jeep patrolling in the settlement. That instance incurred the wrath of the police, whose firings into the crowd led to fourteen deaths, including the brother-in-law of one of our hosts.

While some suspicions about the biases of the police persisted almost a decade later, nonetheless, concerted efforts were made to prevent a repeat of the rioting in 1992–93. "Peace committees" were formed before and during the 1992-93 riots whose functions were several: maintain liaisons with the police (who were now perceived to be more nearly neutral and unwilling to "attack" in Muslim-majority areas); maintain conversations within neighborhoods between various ethnic-religious groups; and, not least of all, patrol neighborhoods all day and night to ensure no incidents would occur that would give police an excuse to seek reprisals. Indeed, no incidents were reported, and Cheetah Camp had retained relative calm.

A more significant influence on the character of Tamil Muslim identity in Cheetah Camp perhaps is the role of those who have worked in the Persian Gulf. In some Muslim neighborhoods of Cheetah Camp, perhaps as many as 90 percent of the families had someone working in the Gulf. This clearly enhanced income and had an impact on people's self-perception regarding what it meant to be Muslim. To explore this issue, I focus for heuristic purposes on a particular "community" of Tamil Muslims in Cheetah Camp, those who identified themselves as coming from Kallakurichi Taluq in South Arcot District.

The Kallakurichi Muslims are not so much from a single village as from a *taluq* heavily populated with Muslims. There is considerable diversity among them; this variation is often discerned along predictable lines—those who are first-generation migrants into Mumbai (but these are not so conservative as the Paṭṭampaṭṭi migrants), those who have grown up in Mumbai, and those who have spent time working in the Gulf. Differences in self-perception can also be discerned between men and women. Generally speaking, the Kallakurichi Muslims of Cheetah Camp are more apt to mingle and interact with persons of differing ethnic and religious backgrounds than are the Paṭṭampaṭṭi Muslims of Dharavi but, nonetheless, tend to maintain their most intense social relationships with others from Kallakurichi. Parents still prefer that their children marry persons with Kallakurichi ties and, preferably, with ties to the mother's side of the family, but exogamy—marriage to other Mumbai Tamil Muslims—is increasingly common. The second-generation and older men are more apt to be affected by movements to homogenize Islam than are the women, but all of the families tend to be more religious than Dharavi's Paṭṭampaṭṭi-ites.

The Kallakurichis understand themselves traditionally to be Ḥanafī Sunnīs, though they recognize little difference between Ḥanafīs and Shāfi'īs—in fact, one woman believed the difference to be only in the posture one takes when praying. They are sheikhs, quite different, they said, from the *khan*s or the *pathan*s (who were described as "tall, strapping, bread and meat curry eaters who engaged in lending and collecting with interest [despite Islamic injunctions against it]).[18] Most of the Kallakurichis understood themselves to have traditionally been *pañjukuṭi*s (cotton ginners) by occupation, though the term is considered increasingly irrelevant, particularly by the men.

The Kallakurichi families are learning to value education. Second-generation boys and, in some families, girls are encouraged to continue in school, though in poorer families, the girls are more likely to be sent to Tamil-language schools, the boys to English- or Hindi-language ones. In those families where girls are encouraged to remain in school, their "coming of age" rituals are modified to make it possible. Both boys and girls are also normally sent to the gender-segregated *madrasa*s (the traditional Islamic-centered schooling where Arabic recitations and Islamic history are taught). Second-generation men and women are increasingly engaged in various professions—the occasional woman as a teacher or nurse especially, while men are running small businesses or have engaged in a wide range of occupations. In fact, I talked with no families who did not have at least one male member working in the Gulf. Because many of the first-generation migrants from Kallakurichi have lived in various parts of Mumbai much of their lives, they are likely to know Hindi and/or

Urdu and feel comfortable moving in and out of Cheetah Camp. They raise children who increasingly think of Mumbai as their hometown; some of these children, in fact, have lost the ability to read and write Tamil, though Tamil is still the language of choice in most of their homes.

Kallakurichi traditions are most likely to be maintained by the older generation, and especially by women of either generation. Yet the men who have worked in Saudi Arabia and other Middle Eastern countries saw a form of Islam that did not include some of these specifically Indian or Tamil customs. Hence, upon their return they tend to challenge many of these traditions as un-Islamic.

Some of these young men (and the occasional young woman) gravitate into a Tamil-based movement dedicated to the "purification" of Islam in Cheetah Camp. This is known as the Peace Propagation Council (once known as the Islamic Propagation Council), also known as the "Najat" from the title of one of the books the group disseminates. This council or *jamat* is dedicated to the spread of "true Islam." Classes are conducted in Qurānic studies, to which older men who no longer have to work and support families are also attracted. Sunday evening discussions and sermons are held, with its senior members taking the leadership role. Qurānic verses are memorized, especially those dealing with themes such as intoxication, divorce, veneration of the dead, and other issues that appear to rule out certain customs followed by Tamil Muslims. Members of the PPC insist the Qu'rān is beyond dispute. (The Qu'rāns they use are produced in Tamil Nadu and have commentaries in Tamil.) When a question of interpretation arises, letters are sent to the ten *'ulāma* (Sunnī councils) to be found in Tamil Nadu—Tanjavur, Velūr, Nagūr, Kanyakumāri, and so on—and the response deemed most favorable to the group's own interpretation is adopted.

The PPC observes only those rituals deemed consistent with Qurānic injunctions—for example, the two *īds*—and declines to participate in "un-Islamic activities" such as covering the head when praying, visiting *dargahs* (graves of the dead), or asking favors of Allah in exchange for an offering (*mannat*). They support the Sunnī *mullahs* who claim it is appropriate for women to appear publicly only in the *burqa* in order to maintain modesty (forgetting or ignoring the fact that the Qu'rān indicates both men and women should dress and behave with decorum). In addition, members of the PPC claim not to maintain identities such as "sheikh" or *sayyid*, but merely "son of the ḥadīth" (*al-i-ḥadīth*).

In recent years the PPC has also been involved in social action projects for the betterment of life for Muslims in Cheetah Camp. Most visible of these projects was the founding of an elementary school in the English medium, which in its early stages was teaching the basic three Rs. However, as the principal—a Kallakurichi Tamil and an active member of the PPC—noted, "We will soon be able to teach the Qu'rān and Sunna to our students."[19] One of the teachers in the school, a young Hyderabadi brahmin woman and a BSC in engineering, saw teaching here as a form of "social work." She claimed that even now only a small percentage of Muslim girls in Cheetah Camp studied beyond the seventh grade, and those only in an Urdu- or Tamil-language high school, none in English medium. The same woman, when asked if she would be comfortable teaching Islam, remarked that she would not mind inasmuch as "I am an atheist."[20]

It is in the practice of those rituals and customs that demarcate Kallakurichi identity that the symbolic points of dispute arise between those who maintain certain "traditional" practices and the Islamic "purists." How, for example, should women dress? The Kallakurichi women traditionally wore the *dupatta* (head cap) when going outside the home. In Mumbai more and more of them are donning the *burqa* (the full dress covering). The men folk influenced by the PPC and the *mullah*s claim this is more consistent with Qurānic teaching. It is also the young men and (those fewer) women who interact with the larger world outside Cheetah Camp who are more likely confronted with the question of Islamic identity and more likely to interact with other Mumbai Muslims who are wearing the *burqa.*

Weddings are another tradition undergoing change. In a traditional Kallakurichi wedding, the parents chose the bride for a son; a generation or two ago, she would invariably be a girl from Kallakurichi Taluq. Now first-generation immigrants in Mumbai prefer a Kallakurichi girl but are open to letting their children have some input into that choice. That choice may include Mumbai Muslim girls (but still preferably those with Kallakurichi or at least Tamil background). A pattern that persists in Mumbai is that the boy's family (once the boy has seen and approved the girl) takes a proposal to the girl's house together with a donation of candies. A day is fixed when gifts can be more formally exchanged, the girl's family still giving the larger gifts. While no rings are exchanged, some jewelry may be given to the girl.

The wedding may still take place in the girl's hometown and may include customs such as the *haldi* for three, five, or seven days, depending on the family's choice, and the *mehindi.* The boy would traditionally go to the girl's house on horseback, wearing the *sehrā* or veil of flowers. Many of these customs are challenged by the purists, including the *haldi, sehrā,* and groom's procession as being un-Islamic. One family believed that the procession was coming back into vogue after having been temporarily discarded in the wake of the riots, when the attempt was made to reduce visibility that might arouse hostilities.

The basic pillars of Islam are kept somewhat carefully by Kallakurichi Muslims in Cheetah Camp, especially by the women (but, ironically, with less care by the men in the PPC, who claimed their work limited their participation). Ramaḍān was followed in virtually all the families with which we interacted, and daily prayers (*namāz*) were more likely to be faithfully observed during Ramaḍān. Otherwise, the *namāz* is observed but with less regularity than the orthoprax would like. In some families the *namāz* is prayed quite regularly, complete with the senior male donning a beard for each occasion. Most families tried to observe Friday prayers, though some mothers and working fathers were the least likely to be observant. The giving of alms (*zakāt*) is observed by most, though each family has its own pattern. One family will give a fortieth of total income; several make donations to widows, the poor, or relatives in the *Īd* following Ramaḍān. Very few families were inclined to donate through the *masjid,* which, it was believed, would retain half the donation. As for the pilgrimage (*ḥajj*), very few families thought it to be incumbent on them; most believed they did not have the wherewithal to aspire to ever get to Mecca. Trips to *dargah* (tombs of saints) are becoming less common among Kallakurichi families. It is not uncommon, however, for families to send donations by money order to *dargah*s back in Tamil Nadu, especially that at Nagūr, and to receive blessings in return by parcel post.

Rites of passage are another area of contestation between Kallakurichi tradition and homogenized Islam. A rite of pregnancy, for example, is taken seriously by Kallakurichi Muslims, especially during a wife's first pregnancy. In the seventh month of pregnancy, the wife's family comes with candies to the house of the in-laws. There certain rites are performed (for example, applying sandal paste on her skin). This is followed by a feast, after which both daughter and son-in-law go to the home of the girl's family. There the son-in-law would stay for a day or so, though the daughter would stay until forty days after delivery. Subsequent rites associated with birth and naming would normally occur, at least for the first birth, in the girl's family's home. The naming ceremony is still commonly done with a call to prayer (*azan*) and the whispering of the child's name into the ear. Some families choose to have the senior male member of the family do the honors rather than invite the *imām* to do it, as would have been the case a generation ago. Rituals associated with the first menstruation are also still observed, though now they may be done in a more private manner, without the large feasts that once were a public announcement of the girl's availability for marriage. This more quiet approach presumably permits the girl to continue in school. Nonetheless, she still is obliged to observe eleven days of seclusion in which she cannot see the face of male members of her own family. During this period she is to eat a raw egg each day prepared with a mixture of high-protein and vitamin-packed foods—sesame seed oil, moong *dāl,* and so on.

Members of those families who are also PPC members are not at all sure that rituals are as important a part of being Muslim as "following the Sunna" (however that is interpreted). These purists are also persuaded that many of the Kallakurichi and/or Tamil rituals are but vestiges from Hindu practice and are therefore not consistent with "pure Islam." They did not see some of these practices done by Muslims in the Gulf, nor do they see their Uttar Pradesh coreligionists observing certain of these customs. The discussion, often across generational and gender lines, is a fascinating part of the changing face of Tamil Islam in Cheetah Camp.

Conclusion

These two communities of Tamil Muslims, expressing and reinterpreting their ways of being who they are in the face of often hostile and changing landscapes, are an especially apt reflection of the ways people in local places negotiate their identities in the context of global, transnational, and urban currents. The process of reinventing tradition goes on in these communities, informed by the tug of hometown ties, the pressures of various "others," and the need to juggle multiple identities at once. Are they still participants in the social network of their hometowns, or are they fully incorporated into the ambience of Mumbai? Are they Tamil or are they Muslim? Are they sheikh or rowther, *pañjukuṭi,* or Ḥanafī? Or are they all of the above, albeit selectively?

Clearly these questions are answered differently in Dharavi and Cheetah Camp, and differently from one alleyway to another and one family to another. Many factors influence these reinterpretations, and a few of these are summarized here:

1. The proximity of one's hometown, as well as the number of years or generations one is removed from it, is one of the determinants in the juggling of identities. Many Tamil Muslims in Mumbai are still geographically close enough to their hometowns that annual (or more frequent) visits are possible. Further, the Tamil tradition of marrying daughters to the mother's relatives remains strong in first-generation settlers in the city's subdivisions and keeps ties to the home area necessary. For second-generation settlers, those ties (and therefore those traditions) are less compelling.
2. The degree to which one has access to and interaction with alternate forms of Islam helps shape one's practice of it. Many forms of Islam are practiced in Mumbai's alleys; traditions representing different areas—even different villages—of Tamil Nadu are evident, for example. So too are the practices of Muslims from Uttar Pradesh, of Shīites from Gujarat, or of those who have returned from a working stint in Saudi Arabia. Rubbing elbows with people who practice disparate forms of Islam makes families increasingly conscious of their own expressions and leads either to reaffirming the differences or to bridging them.
3. The nature and extent of one's educational background helps shape the choices. If a young woman has access to only a few years of Tamil-language schooling, her world is more likely to remain circumscribed by the Tamil background of her peers. If she has had access to an English-language education beyond the first few standards, a different world opens up to her. If the Tamil Muslim is comfortable with Urdu or Hindi, interactions with other Muslims and with non-Muslims present additional challenges and opportunities. Further, does she know Arabic and have access to Qurānic teaching, and, if so, who are the teachers and how do they represent the tradition? Beyond that, does one have a knowledge of the broader world of history and of religion? Few, if any, of our interviewees had had the opportunity to study religion comparatively or critically, whether their own tradition or that of others. One is left to wonder what difference that would make in one's self-understanding and practices.
4. Economic status seems to play a role in self-presentation. However, an increase in income or affluence is not necessarily a ticket to a "global" outlook. It does

sometimes make more accessible international currents in Islam, including those efforts to homogenize or "purify" its practice.

5. The socialization and networking process in the face of pluralism plays a significant role in solidifying or fuzzying boundaries. The degree of comfort with which persons interact across religious or ethnic lines helps form interethnic friendships, on the one hand, yet encourages greater self-consciousness of one's own uniqueness and place in the larger socioreligious fabric, on the other. One of the tragic outcomes of the 1992–93 riots in Dharavi was an increased ghettoization of some groups, including the literal building of walls to demarcate one community's space from another's.[21] Mumbai's cosmopolitanism does not guarantee interreligious amity. In fact, it may invite deepened parochialism. That it be otherwise requires will and a mutual willingness to understand and be understood.

The shifting identities of Muslims who are also Tamils have been dichotomized by some scholars as the difference between Tamil Muslims and Muslim Tamils.[22] While this categorization is somewhat simplistic, it has some utility with reference to the groups described in this chapter. The Muslims from Tamil Nadu living in Dharavi are more nearly Tamil Muslims, especially those from Paṭṭampaṭṭi. That is, their Tamil and geographic identity has taken precedence over their Muslim identity. The riots, however, did serve to move these groups closer to being Muslim Tamils insofar as religion has become a more important indication of their self-presentation. In contrast, the Muslims of Cheetah Camp are more nearly Muslim Tamils, influenced as they are by the international and pan-Indian forms of Islam.

CHAPTER 7

Libations with 1,008 Pots

Ritual Rules and Changing Circumstances

Special circumstances call for special events. The apparent ritual of choice for expatriated South Indians who wish to make a statement is the ritual of libations with 1,008 pots *(sahasrakalaśābhiṣeka)*. The ability to perform such an elaborate ritual is a mark of status, influence, affluence, and orthopraxy. On at least four occasions in the space of a few years, in two cities halfway around the globe from each other, the *sahasrakalaśābhiṣeka* was performed, two of these for the first time in their respective countries. Those performances reveal much about the communities that sponsored them, the purposes of ritual, and the dynamics of selective orthopraxy.

Starting June 9, 1986, as part of the tenth anniversary of the Śrī Veṅkaṭeśvara Temple in Pittsburgh, the libations with 1,008 pots were performed for the first time in North America. The same temple performed the ritual again in 2002 as part of its twenty-fifth anniversary. In late December 1990 the ritual was conducted for the first time in Kuala Lumpur in Malaysia under the sponsorship of the Malaysian Hindu Sangam. Within four months, in April 1991, the ritual was done once again in Kuala Lumpur, this time at the Śrī Kandaswamy Temple sponsored by the Ceylon Saivites Association. Apart from the performance of this ritual in Singapore in the mid-1980s, the 1986 and 1990–91 rituals were the first performances of the libations outside of India. It was the privilege of this writer to be present for each of these performances and to have access to the most widely known textual description of the *sahasrakalaśābhiṣeka*—that of the *Padmasaṁhitā*—translated into English as backdrop for the 1986 Pittsburgh performance. The following discussion is based on these five presentations—four enactments and one textual description.

Purposes: Classical and Contemporary

Why perform such an elaborate and apparently arcane ritual in the contemporary world? It takes two to four days to perform and requires the presence of up to twenty-four ritual specialists, elaborate planning, and not a little expense. The text of the *Padmasaṁhitā* (chapter 9, verses 6–9) states the following:

> 6) This [ritual] has the singular aim of removing all sins; it is the means to the [attainment] of all kinds of welfare and this also prolongs the lives of people, of the whole world and of the king.

7) It is performed by men wishing to have sons yearning for victory. This destroys completely dreadful things like famine and bad omens.
8) This brings in all kinds of wealth and also becomes the only means to the attainment of the objects of human pursuit.
9) By honoring me according to rules with this kind of worship, you become free from confusion, devoid of sins and competent enough to create the world.[1]

The text indicates that even Indra, who had fallen from the kingdom of the gods for killing a brahmin, regained his position by performing this sacrifice (verse 2), and other kings "shook off" the greatest of their sins by means of this propitiation (verses 3, 4).

Unspoken in the text is the reality that only kings with enough wealth could perform this ritual and that its performance therefore afforded considerable status and merit. Quite explicit is the belief that performing the ritual has pragmatic consequences: for example, the attainment of prosperity, sons, and human desires as well as the ridding of "confusion," sin, famine, and bad omens.

The contemporary laity who decided to perform the ritual outside of India did not have access to these textual suggestions. Their reasons for having the ritual performed, nonetheless, were similarly a mixture of the religious and the pragmatic. The brochure advertising the April 1991 performance in the Ceylon Tamil temple of Kuala Lumpur draws attention to the "majestic" temple where the ritual will be performed in the "garden city" [Kuala Lumpur] of the country "blessed by Mother Nature with beauty and natural resources." In this temple, the brochure assures us, "Lord Subrahmaṇia . . . brilliantly radiates divinity and grace on His devotees, and readily responds to the calls of those who fervently pray for his help."[2] The ceremony was to be held over a three-day period in conjunction with the Tamil New Year in order for the world to "enjoy peace, pleasant life and prosperity." Tacit and understated in this declaration is the assumption that the ritual would demonstrate that the Ceylon Tamils were the proper exponents of orthoprax Śaivism and had the sufficient means to do the ritual with the care and thoroughness it deserved, especially in light of the earlier presentation of the ritual in another temple by the Malaysian Hindu Sangam.

The Malaysian Hindu Sangam is the umbrella organization for some forty Hindu associations in Malaysia. It seeks to represent Hindu interests to the government of Malaysia, coordinate Hindu activities, and establish hegemony and a degree of homogenization over Hindu temples and groups. Why did the sangam sponsor a ritual of 1,008 libations in December 1990? According to the president of the association, at the time it was to prove to all Hindus of the peninsula that the sangam was interested not only in ideological and political activities but also in the proper performance of ritual.[3] In other words, the performance of ritual enhanced the sangam's credibility as the authoritative representative of *pucca* (authentic) Hinduism.

The reasons underlying the Pittsburgh Śrī Veṅkaṭeśvara Temple's performance of the ritual on two occasions were similarly a mix of the religious and pragmatic. Orthoprax Hindus were concerned that the rituals be done correctly for a variety of reasons.

The ritual is ascribed several religious purposes. It is intended to invest the presiding deity Veṅkaṭeśvara with all the power and honor that elaborate libations can bestow. It is as if all of creation in both the divine and human worlds is brought in propitiation to the deity, while all of creation, in turn, receives his blessings as the vessels are returned to patrons and the flowing libations to the world at large. The ritual also is expected to counteract any "deficiencies" in conducting services or the architectural construction of the temple, to remove calamities afflicting a community or the world, and to offer atonement (*prāyaśchitta*) for any omissions or commissions in the course of conducting religious services.[4]

Yet the performance had pragmatic purposes as well: it would attract pilgrims from across the eastern seaboard; it would enable all ethnic groups associated with the temple to work together for common purpose; it would demonstrate the orthopraxy and authenticity of the temple for all South Indians in North America. It would show, even as newer temples were springing up in other cities, that the Śrī Veṅkaṭeśvara Temple was still the prototypical one—one that could afford to sponsor such a ritual and to maintain authenticity despite costs. Not least of all, the ritual would raise money: sponsors were asked to pay for each vessel (at $100 apiece in 1986 and $150 in the 2002 performance), donations came in from across the country, and an influx of pilgrims enhanced the temple's coffers considerably. As a result, the money budgeted by the temple board was returned in each instance more than threefold. And, of course, the fact that the ritual was part of the temple's tenth and twenty-fifth anniversary celebrations would remind one and all that this temple was the oldest "authentic" temple in North America. (The Gaṇeṣa Temple in Flushing Meadows, New York, was dedicated at the same time but was deemed less "authentic" by Pittsburgh locals because of the New York temple's more eclectic propensities.)

Text and Performance

The role and interplay of text and performance were intriguing elements in the presentation of the ritual of 1,008 pots, especially in Pittsburgh in 1986. Two years before the presentation and apropos of the ten-year anniversary, the Śrī Veṅkaṭeśvara Temple's Board of Trustees commissioned the translation of some texts of the *Pāñcarātrāgamas* that would be relevant to the rituals associated with the temple. Dr. Lakshmi Swaminathan, then a research associate in the Department of Religious Studies at the University of Pittsburgh, was asked to translate the Sanskrit text of the *Padmasaṁhitā,* using an edition that is part of the H. Daniel Smith Collection, housed in the Cleveland Museum of Art. While the translator, and presumably the board, wanted the entire text of the *Padmasaṁhitā* to be translated, in fact, the project proved to be more daunting and time consuming than expected. As a result, the work and the concomitant funding for it ended before the text was completed. Instead, only certain sections of the text, especially those salient to the *sahasrakalaśābhiṣeka,* were done. Nonetheless, the implications of the experiment are worth noting. The secretary of the board at that time—and the gentleman most instrumental in getting the board to commission the project—was a sixty-year-old Kannada Lingayat. When asked why he believed this to be an important project, he offered two reasons: (1) to ensure "our children" will have access to the textual prescriptions and (2) to make sure that the priests do the rituals "right."[5]

Each of these two stated responses is worth some comment. The concern for "our children" was indeed a generic concern for these immigrants, voiced frequently by members and officials of the temple community. Our research has confirmed that from the time the immigrants started to dream of building a temple in Pittsburgh, most of them had children who were then reaching the age of accountability. By 1978, as noted in chapter 2, the typical immigrant family averaged 1.5 children, the elder of whom was eight, the younger of whom was just over six. The concern for steeping these children in their Indian heritage has underlain a great many of the religio-cultural events sponsored, from the building of the temple itself, to the starting of dance, music, and language classes, to the production of ritual and artistic events. In fact, younger Indian Americans did participate in the 1,008 pots ritual to some degree, whether to set up a stall offering American-style fast foods to visitors who might favor nontraditional foods or to use the ritual as a showpiece at which to host non-Indian friends.

Yet there was some irony to this claim that much is done for the "sake of the children." For one thing, some parents had been spending so much time in planning and administering temple activities that less time was spent with families, to the point that some children found temple activities a source of alienation. Further, some children for whom these activities were purportedly staged had already grown to young adulthood and had begun to shape their own self-identities, balancing in varying ways their Indian heritage and their American experience. Moreover, the planners' involvement in the details of temple governance and in the minutiae of its administration suggests that such things were done not only for the children but also to fulfill adults' own needs and express their own identities. The decision to have ritual texts translated, in other words, like most other activities done in the name of the temple, is part of a collage of self-expressions.

Similarly, the concern for making sure the priests do the rituals right is partially comprehensible in the context of the ritual tradition here. A succession of five priests had officiated at the Śrī Veṅkaṭeśvara Temple by that time. The first, Sampathnarayanan, was less a traditional priest as he was a student of Sanskrit. Uncomfortable in the role of temple functionary and a short-term expatriate, he returned to India to marry and teach. The second priest, Manavala Iyengar, was the more traditional *ācārya.* Having spent his life officiating in Vaiṣṇava temples, he spent three years as the chief priest in Pittsburgh before returning to India, then coming back to the United States and becoming the chief priest in a temple near Washington, D.C. His style and those of at least two of his successors were perceived as being more improvisational and impromptu. Doubts grew about his familiarity with the tradition. (Manavala Iyengar did not read Sanskrit; nor did he speak English well. This combination may have contributed to the perception by some laity that he was not very "learned.") The succeeding three priests, like Manavala Iyengar, were respected to varying degrees for their scholarship. One of these, in fact, was a Tamilian who had limited experience as an apprentice priest in Tamil Nadu. He came to the Penn Hills temple initially as a cook and was pressed into service as a priest because of the workload of the other two priests. He did not read Sanskrit; most of his training as a priest consisted of that which he acquired by watching and emulating his two Pittsburgh colleagues. The other two priests had more traditional training as *ācārya*s: Bhatta was a native Telugu but was nonetheless raised in Karnataka and in the Pāñcarātra traditions with his father since the age of ten. His father, Srinivasācārya, was the specialist priest who was brought to Pittsburgh for all the main rituals, including the *kumbhābhiṣeka* and *sahasrakalaśabhiṣeka.* The other priest, Venkatacarlu, a Telugu and the son of a priest in the Tirupati complex, did read Sanskrit, apprenticed in the Tirumala Tirupathi Devasthanam, and spent twelve years learning the Pāñcarātra ritual traditions. Perhaps it is because he also spoke English well that he gave the impression to other Hindu immigrants that he was more "learned"; yet even he was given to improvisation and abbreviation in conducting rituals in the Pittsburgh temple. Further, because the latter two *ācārya*s were trained in different family traditions, their ways of performing ritual did not always coincide; indeed, they had been known to differ on occasion on the procedure, each claiming the authentic lineage in ritual performance.

The perception that the priests need to be checked by the "text" was exacerbated by a practice that had occurred during a brief period before the temple board changed its policy. During that period the laity, by plying the priests with tips, could have certain rituals done especially on their behalf. The perception developed that ritual events were custom made for paying patrons. The temple has long since implemented a standard rate for all patrons who want to contribute more generously. These are practices consistent with those followed in temples in India.

Yet there was more to the decision to translate the *Padmasaṁhitā* than these stated reasons. One unstated factor was the interethnic (even intercaste) rivalries that had surfaced on occasion in the early years of the temple's existence. A striking feature of the ritual traditions as developed in those early years of the Penn Hills temple (at least in the perceptions of some non-Tamils) is that it was primarily Tamil brahmins who had sought to preserve and expand the temple rituals and to ensure their authenticity through the inception of systematic *pūjās.* The priests (*ācārya*s), by and large, had been supported by the Tamilians as authentic purveyors of the tradition. Further, rituals such as the putting of the deity to bed each evening (*ekanta seva*) and the songs of praise intended to waken the deity in the morning (*suprabatham*) were instituted as the result of the urging of Tamil brahmins who were both professionally well placed and members of the SV Temple Board of Trustees. Especially important, the first executive of the temple was a Tamil naidu whose "unilateral" decisions and actions were generally supported by Tamil compatriots and came to be resented by Telugus and Kannadas. A grim divisiveness in the temple's ranks and committees resulted; Tamils and non-Tamils aligned against each other. Many decisions were therefore made along ethnic lines, including this one, at least initially, to translate the ritual texts. Ironically, a Tamil was engaged in the translation, and Tamils shared in the pleasure of having the texts accessible.

The temple authorities eventually came to adopt a system of shared governance wherein administrative positions were rotated on an annual basis and members of different ethnic groups were ensured representation in any given year. The planning and presentation of the ritual of 1,008 pots, because it was a mammoth undertaking, caused members of the community to work together, thereby implementing those new patterns of governance. In fact, it is probably fair to report that the planning and implementing of this ritual served to effect a spirit of cooperation and interdependence in a way that few events in the previous years had done.

Yet another unstated reason why the decision to translate the text was made was that such a translation would serve to further make the rituals intelligible and "legitimate" them for the American context. Inasmuch as English has become the international language of discourse, an English rendition would make the ritual accessible, authentic, and contemporary. The translated text would become an expression of the "rationalism" that characterizes the South Indian communities in the United States.[6] Using and following the text, however, whether Sanskrit or English, is another thing. It is worth turning to the role of the text in the performative work of the priests themselves.

The text in question, at least in an oral form, is more than likely a product of the Vijayanagar period, almost certainly after the late thirteenth or early fourteenth century. However, the written Sanskrit text available to us is a recent publication, translated from a text that, while Sanskrit, is transliterated from Telugu script. That script in turn was derived from an earlier source or sources, likely Telugu, that were originally oral. The Sanskrit text itself (particularly that describing the ritual setting but *not* that intended for oral recitations) is often fraught with a style, syntax, and grammar that is awkward or erroneous. In the first fifty verses of chapter 7, describing how the *sahasrakalaśabhiṣeka* is to be performed, for example, there are fifteen grammatical irregularities, thirteen of them in adjectival or verbal forms that do not agree with the noun in gender and number. This appears to suggest that the writer (or perhaps, more accurately, the reciter) was unable to think in Sanskrit but was transcribing into Sanskrit what had been expressed in the mother language. Further, that "mother language" had enough Tamilizations to suggest the process of transcription occurred in what is now southern Andhra Pradesh, where Telugu and Tamil languages interact.

If this process of the emergence of a Sanskrit text were restated in reverse, it would appear to be something like this: The rituals described were performed by specific families of priests following the Pāñcarātra style and retained orally. The chants would have been retained orally in Sanskrit form and the descriptions in the vernacular form of Tamilized Telugu, apparently. These descriptions (how-to manuals) would have been retained in handwritten form, presumably on palmyra leaf, for use within specific families of priests. These descriptions were written in Telugu script as if to preserve them, while the oral Sanskrit chants were transliterated into Telugu script (that is, Sanskrit words were transcribed in Telugu). Finally, the Sanskrit text appears on palmyra leaf with its grammatical flaws, and apparently only poorly comprehended and seldom used by most Telugu priests themselves. In short, the Sanskrit "text" may have been in place by the fourteenth or fifteenth century and the ritual itself for some time before that.[7]

If this is at all a fair approximation of the "biography" of a Sanskrit text, we can only speculate about why the text was written in a Sanskrit form at all. There seem to be several plausible reasons: (1) A patron king or noble family wanted to legitimate the ritual traditions of this Pāñcarātra school by rendering it in the sacralizing Sanskrit script. (2) It was deemed important by patrons and/or certain priests to make these ritual traditions accessible to non-Telugu speakers outside of Telugu country and thereby "nationalize" the ritual traditions. (3) There was an effort to offer these Pāñcarātra traditions as viable alternatives to the rival Vaikhāṉasāgamic traditions established at Tirupati and elsewhere and/or the Śaivāgamic traditions being established in Śaiva temples.

Be that as it may, it is not altogether clear what the practical purpose of the earlier written text was, whether Sanskrit or Telugu. Did priests, even then, follow it, or did they follow rather their own familial traditions (*parakkam*)? Did the text state how some *ācārya*s actually performed the rituals, or did it indicate how the writers wished it to be performed? I am persuaded that, even at the point of the texts' being written in the first instance, it is not the text that informs performance, but performance that informs text. Hence, the temple ritual traditions have been preserved less in the form of the text than in the form of the performance itself, passed down from father to son.

The Pittsburgh priests' own view and use of the text bear out this observation. Extensive conversations with the temple priests and with the elderly savant-priest (Srinivasācarya) brought for the major rituals, including the *sahasrakalaśabhiṣeka* in 1986, suggest certain common patterns: three kinds of written texts are available to each priest, in descending order of significance. Most commonly referred to in times of need is the manual each priest possesses that was handwritten by his father or grandfather. This is an abridgement of things to do and how to do them, concerning most of the commonly performed rituals. The second reference, used only when needed, is a more extensive vernacular transliteration of the *Padmasaṁhitā* or other text. The third and final textual referent is the Sanskrit text. None of the priests we observed referred to a Sanskrit edition during or in preparation for the performance of rituals, even though all of them could recite mantras in Sanskrit and at least two of them could read Sanskrit. The Sanskrit text is known, at best, only in its oral form and is mediated to the priest by a past master. When there were questions of what to do, as in rarely performed rituals, the vernacular text is used, but only as a last resort. All of the priests stressed, in conversation, the importance of memory and practice, the need for improvisation and innovation as dictated by the circumstance. They likened themselves to surgeons who had to know what they are doing from experience. It was as if greater status accrued from performing the rituals without the necessity of referring to the written texts.

The actualization of ritual performance bears out these perceptions of the priestly role. To be sure, the textual prescriptions provide a silhouette of the ritual performance, the fundamental legitimating framework. Yet at a variety of points, the ritual performance diverges from textual description, sometimes because remembered performance takes precedence over textual description, sometimes because the exigency of moment does. Yet when the chief priest was asked why practice diverged from written text in the performance of the *sahasrakalaśabhiṣeka,* he invariably remarked that the apparently divergent performance was derived from a "different," albeit unspecified, text; however, he never did produce the textual reference to which he alluded.

In sum, the texts most embodied in the performance of the libation with 1,008 pots are oral "texts" of two types: remembrances (jogged by reference to written text only when needed) of how the ritual is to be performed, and recited chants. It is important to repeat that the mantras recited in Pittsburgh for the 1986 *sahasrakalaśabhiṣeka* were, for the most part, not the mantras presented in the written *Padmasaṁhitā* text. Rather, with the apparent exception of the chief preceptor, the general body of priests used five standard sets of mantras used generically for a variety of occasions. These were the *Bhūsukta*—praises to the goddess Bhū; *Śrīsukta*—praises to the goddess Śrī; *Nārāyaṇasukta*—praises to Viṣṇu in the form of Nārāyaṇa; *Viṣṇusukta*—praises to Viṣṇu; and *Puruṣasukta*—praises to Puruṣa. Moreover, these chants were done repetitively as vessels were sprinkled out of sequence (at least *not* in the sequence described in the *Padmasaṁhitā*). When asked why these chants were used, the priests replied it was because "they are used at Tirupati."[8] In fact, the oral chants are much older than the performed rituals, as some of them date back to Vedic times but are appropriated to accompany any number of performed rituals, even in a contemporary North American setting. The connections between oral chants and the performed ritual are sometimes playful or based on homophones or pun. For example, in Pittsburgh when an *abhiṣeka* is performed on Śrī Veṅkaṭeśvara on a Sunday morning, the *Puruṣasukta* (the hymn to the thousand-headed deity, once used in a Vedic context) is recited when the waters are poured on the icon through a thousand-holed sieve at the climax of the ritual. The hymn was repeated while the water from 1,008 pots was poured on the presiding icon on this occasion. Similarly, the *Śrīsukta* (mantras to the goddess used differently in classical times) is recited at the time that turmeric is applied to the icon, during which Śrī Veṅkaṭeśvara becomes androgynous and his feminine attributes are extolled. Or, again, during the *sahasrakalaśābhiṣeka,* the waters represented by the various pilgrims in attendance (the Ohio, Allegheny, and Monongahela rivers, Lake Erie, etc.) were homologized to the Ganges, and the blessings that could accrue for those near the Ganges are evoked for those in attendance.

What implications can be drawn from these observations of the role of text and performance in ritual reenactment? First, it is clear that temple rituals are "cultural performances" in the sense that Milton Singer used that term several decades ago. A cultural performance, as Singer suggested, represents what a community wants its children, or visitors, or the world, to know about themselves, albeit enacted in a particular time and place.[9] Temple rituals express a "tradition," an ethos, that embodies what planners and participants want to say about who they are to themselves, their children, and the pluralistic society at large. And because the rituals are performed, they are never performed twice in the same way. To be sure, certain rules or a skeletal sequence is maintained, but each performance accommodates the time and place of its particular patrons.[10]

Second, the Tamil term *parakkam* ("tradition" or "custom") is not so innocuous a term as some observers have believed. *Parakkam* is the answer most often given regarding why Tamil Hindus perform certain rituals. The term suggests that tradition is selectively preserved and reenacted through the doing. It suggests that each such doing affords a sense of lineage and hence of identity. It is the performance itself, both oral and gestural (perhaps even more than literal text), that embodies the dynamics of continuity and change within the tradition and is the expression, aesthetically and dramatically, of Hindu identity.

Third, the will to textualize—that is, to translate a written text, much like the initial writing of a text—appears to reflect a new moment of self-consciousness in the face of pluralism or change. There is a "sociology of text," expressed not only in the evolution of a ritual text in post-Vijanagaran India but also in North America. Today the translation of a Sanskrit text into English gives contemporary legitimation and a "neo-rational" authenticity to the performance the text is intended to describe. It preserves the performance, indeed, "for our children."

The Ritual Itself

The libations with 1,008 pots can be summarized as follows: 1,008 vessels filled with water and other elements are arrayed on a pavilion in such a way as to represent a miniature universe. Through a series of fire sacrifices (*homa*), the pots and their contents are sacralized by means of chants and the invocation of divine power. After several sequences lasting more than one day, the sacralized water from the pots is poured on the central icon representing the deity being honored. Patrons are honored and the deity, now present in the fully sacralized icon, is worshipped. The details of performance vary—for example, in the alignment of vessels and the sequencing of events. In fact, the rituals performed in Pittsburgh in the Śrī Veṅkaṭeśvara Temple were fundamentally Vaiṣṇava. Both those performed in Kuala Lumpur were Śaivite. Yet the skeleton of the ritual transcends sectarian and ethnic variation. I focus here on two aspects of the ritual: the alignment of space and the sequencing of events.

Space

In both Śaiva and Vaiṣṇava versions, the ritual space set aside for this event becomes a miniature cosmos. The fundamental difference is that the Vaiṣṇava space assumes the form of a *maṇḍala* outward from a center where Mt. Meru or the "house of *brahman*" is symbolically represented. The Śaiva space, in contrast, takes the form of a lingam set in an oil lamp *yoni;* that is, the base or *yoni* of the lingam (an aniconic representation of Śiva) has the form of an oil lamp. The 1,008 pots in each instance are arranged in multiples of nine to represent various quadrants of the universe, ranging from the divine to the human spheres.

More specifically, the ritual space in the Vaiṣṇava arrangement is divided into three sections homologous to the cosmos. The first, where representations of the main deities are displayed in the center of the *maṇḍala* on an elevated altar, is the "house of *brahman*." Here sit nine groups of 9 vessels each (a total of 81). The central vessel, bigger than the others, is wrapped in a cloth and is to be filled with precious stones, fragrances, medicinal herbs, metals, and fruits. This vessel (*kalaśa*) represents Viṣṇu known here as Veṅkaṭeśvara.

Surrounding this central configuration is a concentric circle representing the realm of the divinities. This space is divided into eight quadrants, one for each of the four cardinal directions, in each of which deities are represented by 81 vessels (total of 324), and the four intermediary directions, in each of which there are 49 vessels (total of 196). Within the vessels in the cardinal directions are to be placed fruits, scents, water from various sources, and grains. Each vessel represents an incarnation or attribute of Viṣṇu. In the vessels in the intermediary directions (also representing deities) are to be placed a variety of substances, including milk and other exudations of the cow, honey, oil, and various kinds of water.

The outer circle representing the human world is divided into sixteen quadrants, each bearing 25 vessels (total of 400). Each represents a protective deity and is to be filled with substances such as clay, tree bark, seeds, grains, and water.

In each cosmic sphere the central quadrant is arrayed in nine equal squares, each with 9 pots in it:

9	9	9
9	9	9
9	9	9

In each sphere the adjacent quadrants have a 9-pot square at the center, surrounded by 4-pot squares at each corner and 6-pot oblongs on each side:

4	6	4
6	9	6
4	6	4

On the outer fringes of each quadrant, a 9-pot square is surrounded by a 1-pot square on each corner and a 3-pot oblong on each side:

1	3	1
3	9	3
1	3	1

While pots may represent different deities and be filled with different materials, each quadrant has a persistent motif. For example, at the central quadrant representing the "house of *brahman*," each pot is to contain a precious jewel plus a pearl. In the first quadrant to the east, in the "domain of the gods," each pot is to contain a different fruit plus the jujube fruit. In the first quadrant to the south, in the "domain of the gods," each pot is to be filled with a fragrant thing (e.g., sandal, flowers, pollen) and a *tamala* leaf. In the first quadrant to the west, each pot is to be filled with water from a different source plus water from a lotus pond and from a waterfall, plus golden images of a fish and a tortoise. In the first quadrant to the north, each pot is to contain a different grain plus rice. Other quadrants are to contain exudations of the cow, waters mixed with other liquids, spice mixtures, and so on.

Such are the textual prescriptions for the pots. No reason is offered in the texts for why pots are so numbered or why certain things are to be put in each pot. One can only make inferences. Water, for example, especially as it comes from various sources, is universal, primordial, creative, purgative, refreshing, and so on. Clay is that of which human beings are made, and trees and other flora are part of the natural order with which human beings interact.

However, as laypersons sought to find the materials to be placed in the pots, many accommodations were made. Yes, water was collected from a variety of sources and kept faithfully in jars until the appropriate time. But "exudations" from the cow, rather than coming fresh, came from grocery stores. A variety of substitutes were used representing contemporary North American surrogates for the classical prescriptions. Attempts by the ritual's priests and patrons to explain the reasons for the inclusions in the pots or the meanings to be expressed in them were modest. Engineers, scientists, and academics struggled to make the ritual contemporary or scientifically credible: "The sages really knew a lot about science, didn't they?" "Notice how many of these combinations have medicinal qualities: some are acidic or alkaline, suggesting their therapeutic quality." "Some of the substances cool" (e.g., lime). Not least commonly heard was "The metallic vessels [copper in 1986, silver in 2002] are conductive—that is, they convey heat." The whole process is likened to the channeling of electrical energy, first into the pots, then into the icons themselves.

The laity in Kuala Lumpur were even less engaged in preparing the vessels or in offering analyses thereof. To be sure, the sponsoring agencies served as ritual patrons (*yajamānas*) to whose bidding the priests are supposed to respond. But the priests, Śaiva *gurukkals* who were already serving in their respective temples (from Tamil Nadu for the Malaysian Hindu Sangam and from Tamil Sri Lanka for the Ceylon Śaivites), were clearly the ritual technicians, and their authority was final. Unfortunately, they had little to add about the meaning or reason for the pots' ingredients.

In sum, the ritual space becomes a universe in which vessels represent the realms of humans and of deities. The natural world becomes symbolically congruent to the social world (even as in Vedic ritual), and each is made part of a cosmography, a mythical geography in which humans are ushered into the realm of the gods. The pots, whether metal or earthen (and those in Malaysia were earthen), are liminal and multidimensional; they embody the realm of nature and society, purified and sanctified, their contents then offered to the gods, only finally to be returned to those who had paid for the privilege of patronizing them. Understood or not, the mystery of the event, its enormity and ambiguity, and not least of all, the nostalgia and sense of heritage it evoked, afforded many observers a genuinely religious experience.

The Sequence

The sequence of the ritual, as prescribed in the *Padmasaṁhitā,* is equally complex. In its simplest terms, fire sacrifices are performed at four separate fire pits over a four-day period. These fire sacrifices are intended to sacralize and invoke the divine power into the vessels representing the deities. Once this process is completed, each vessel is to be taken, one by one, in offering to the main deity. Starting in the human realm, priests are told to circumambulate the cosmos with each pot, always keeping the "house of *brahman*" on their right, then pouring the libations out on the presiding deity's representation (*mūrti*).

While the text is quite precise regarding the sequence in which vessels are to be removed, in the actual performance that sequence was not followed. Several vessels would be taken at one time from different realms by several priests. Then, once the libation from each pot had been completed, individual patrons would retrieve the vessel each had sponsored.

When we turn to the first Malaysian performance of this ritual, we find many variations. As already noted, inasmuch as this was a Śaiva function, the vessels were earthen and set up in the form of a lingam. Further, whereas the Vaiṣṇava text prescribes that sixteen *ācārya*s and eight additional priests are supposed to preside at the ritual (and the Pittsburgh temple imported officiants from India to fulfill this role), the presiding priest for the first Malaysian function was the same one who served as resident chief priest in the host temple. This first ritual in Kuala Lumpur was completed within twenty-four hours, while the Pittsburgh rituals (and the second Kuala Lumpur ritual) took four days to complete. The Kuala Lumpur priest (V. Shanmukam Gurukkal) referred to no Sanskrit text but to the Tamil sequence embedded in his own memory.

The ritual sponsored by the Malaysian Hindu Sangam was held at the Śrī Irāmaliṅkeśvar Ālayam, a Śaiva temple in suburban Kuala Lumpur. The basic structure of the ritual as summarized by the chief priest (in Tamil) follows:

Permission is sought of brahmins (and other honored patrons) to proceed with the ceremony (*aṉuñcai*).

Oblations are offered to Ganeṣa for his blessings on the proceedings (*viknēsvara-pūjai*).

The place for the performance of the ritual is purified (*puṇṇiyāvācaṇam*). This involves offering gifts of hospitality to the goddess of the earth.

Auspicious clay is taken from an ant hill or a river bank and brought to the ritual premises (*mirutacaṅkaraṇam*).

Seeds are placed in a vessel so that they will sprout during the ritual (*aṅkurārp-paṇam*).

Presiding priests tie an amulet around their wrists, signifying their readiness to commit themselves to the rituals and maintain their ritual purity (*raṭcāpantaṇam*). In addition, *darbha* grass—with which sacrifices were traditionally started—is tied to the priests' fingers.

Worship is directed to the four directions (*tuvārapūjai*).

Worship is offered to 1,008 deities—the deities embodied in 1,001 pots, plus the "planets" (*parirāpūjai*).

Worship is directed to the deities housed in the main pots—that is, to Śiva and his consorts (*pitāna kalacapūjai*).

Worship is offered to the deities presiding over the eight cosmic directions (*aṣṭataṭikku pālakarpūjai*).

Worship is offered to the five fires (*ōmakuṇta pūjai*). Five temporary fire pits had been set up to receive the fire sacrifice (*homa*). Twigs and clarified butter are the major offerings. The fire, in turn, "carries" the offerings to the gods.

Offerings are made, by way of the fires, of nine grains, milk, fruits, rose water, curds, and sandal and other fragrances (*tiravya ōmam*). As in most *abhiṣēka*s, these are intended to honor the chief deity (currently resident in a pot) as king and to fully empower and sacralize the deity.

The fire sacrifices conclude with the offering of coconut wrapped in red silk (*pūrṇukuti*). The coconut serves as surrogate offering of the self and substitutes for the Vedic practice of offering animals.

These rituals have served to fully sacralize the deity resident in the main vessel. Fire offerings accompanied by *nyāsa* (sacralizing of the priest's body through the invoking of sacred sound) have enabled the priest symbolically to direct the sacred through his own body and the medium of fire into the vessels representing the high god. The vessels are then ready for the customary patterns of worship, which follow any *abhiṣeka* or libation:

Lights are shown in honor of the deity (*tīparātaṉai*). These may include up to twenty-one lamps representing various elements of creation doing obeisance to the deity.

Patrons are blessed (*ācīrvātam;* Skt. *āsīrvāda*) and offered *pracāṭam* (gifts offered to the deity are shared with patrons).

Flowers are thrown on the deity, accompanied by chants (*mantira puṣpam*).

*Bhajaṉ*s (devotional songs) are sung from the Śaiva Tamil canon (*Tevāram*).

Once the vessels have been fully consecrated and worshipped, Śiva in the form of the water from the 1,008 pots is poured in libation on the main temple icon, Śrī Irāmāliṅka Iśvarar, a form of Śiva. The main temple icon is then dressed (*alaṅkāram*) and worshipped as were the surrogate deities, with the showing of lights (*tīparātaṉai*); the blessing of patrons (*ācīrvātam*); throwing of flowers (*mantira puṣpam*), and singing of hymns from the Śaivite canon (*Tevāram*). At this point viewing of the deity (*darṣan*) is most auspicious and devotees are most likely to seek the deity's blessings.[11]

Variations on this pattern may obtain, depending on the particular school of priests; steps may be added, repeated, or done in a different order, all of which was the case in the Ceylon Śaiva temple in Scott Road for their April 1991 libations. There, for example, the fire sacrifices (*yāka pūjai* or *homa*s) were done four times; worship (*pūjā*) was added for the specific locale—for example, a "Ganges worship" (*kaṅka pūja*) for the sacred well on the temple precincts from which water would be used in the rituals; and special *homa*s were performed to sacralize the Ganeṣa vessel and the lance of Subramaṇia, the presiding deity.

Summary: Rules and Reasons

In their book *The Archetypal Actions of Ritual,* based on an examination of Jaina temple rituals, Caroline Humphrey and James Laidlaw suggest, among other things, that the formalized temple rituals in the Indian setting are primarily a matter of following certain "constitutive rules" and that meanings are ascribed later; people do ascribe meanings to specific ritual actions after the fact. Yet rituals such as these appear to be dialectical. Reasons and rules are interwoven. Clearly, each of the presentations of this ritual was done for reasons, both stated and unstated, and each was done according to rules determined by priests. This interaction of rules and reasons takes on specific connotations when performed on behalf of expatriated communities.[12]

The *sahasrakalaśābhiṣeka* is a complex and expensive ritual, rarely done even in India. Yet it embodies in some ways the experience of transplanted Indians. It has an archaic lineage that evokes a sense of heritage, rootedness, and antiquity, especially when performed outside of India. At the same time, it is fluid, changing every time it is performed and adapting to the exigencies of each time and place of its performance.

Its performance demonstrates the capacity for "continuity through homologization" —that is, the capacity to make correspondence and linkages between what is new and unfamiliar to that which is ancient, a principle evident in the Vedic rituals themselves. We have noted illustrations of this above: water from the Allegheny River stands in for that from the Ganges; milk brought in cartons replaces that freshly drawn from the udder. The chants themselves demonstrate this constancy and this malleability; mantras extolling *madhu,* once used to accompany the "sweetness" of the *soma* libation, are used now to accompany the libation of honey or molasses; *dadhi,* once extolling the strength of a horse in sacrifice now accompanies the libation of "strong" curds; *gandha,* referring to the fragrance apparently of cow dung (*kariṣa*) in earlier ritual, now often accompanies the libation of sandal paste.

Despite this variability and change, there is a constancy to the ritual. It is the constancy that comes from following certain rules, as maintained within specific families of priests. The "rules" may differ from one priestly family to another, yet the result of following the rules in each case is the successful completion of the ritual. In this sense, performing a ritual of this kind is not unlike cooking. Certain steps are followed to make an apple pie, for example. One family, following "Gramma's" recipe, makes an apple pie that is particularly flavorful. Were that family to publish a cookbook, their recipe for apple pie would differ from that of another's, yet both families would have rules for apple pie. Similarly, families of priests pass their ritual rules down to descendants. Their rules may differ from those of another family. "Ritual texts" that emerge will reflect the rules of specific families. The rules themselves may be modified from generation to generation within a family, even from occasion to occasion, depending on circumstance. It is the officiating priests themselves, together with their patrons (apparently even more than the text reflecting their family's sets of rules), who determine that a ritual has indeed been successfully completed. And, of course, once one tradition of rules has been set in place in a given temple, it is that tradition that is normally to be followed in that temple. This is the case with the Śrī Veṅkaṭeśvara Temple of Pittsburgh, where the rules followed are those particular Pāñcarātra rules observed by the priest who presided over the dedicatory ceremonies (*kumbhābhiṣeka*) in the beginning.[13]

This dialectic of rules and reasons is an apt mirror of the ritual experience of diasporic South Indians. Both rules and reasons have been a part of the ritual experience of Hindus for generations. The rules, insofar as they remain relatively constant, link participants in the modern moment to those authenticating moments that shape their lineage. Yet, as we have seen, the rules themselves may vary within priestly families, thereby delineating more specifically the lineage with which one identifies—that is, is it Vaiṣṇava or Śaiva? The priestly traditions of one temple or of another? Ceylon Tamil Malaysian or other Tamil Malaysian? Similarly, the reasons, both religious and pragmatic, have varied with the particular era and community that sponsors the ritual event, from those stated in the legitimating texts of the early modern period to those expressed by Tamils in Pittsburgh or Kuala Lumpur.

Ritual, in sum, is more a performance than a text. It is a slowly unfolding drama that is nonetheless always processual, evocative, fresh. Perhaps it is not too much of a stretch to suggest that the immigrant communities for whom the ritual has been performed are themselves performances of sorts, still unfolding dramas, so many vessels filled with elements of the remembered and of the newly experienced. The story of *those* dramas is still being recorded and described. But no written text will fully describe what requires the engagement of all one's senses to comprehend.

CHAPTER 8

Navarāttiri

Nine Nights with the Goddess in Mumbai

A celebration that has taken on the character of a spectacle in much of Mumbai is the Festival of Nine Nights (Navarāttiri; Navarātri in Sanskrit). It is a festival especially popular with Tamils, Gujaratis, and Bengalis (who know it as Durgāpūjā), though each linguistic-ethnic group has its own patterns of celebration. Further, subethnic groups and families bring their own particular traditions to bear during the nine-day affirmation of the goddess. In Mumbai the festival has been significantly secularized and commercialized thanks largely to the popularization for the young of the *garbha* (dance) that has its roots especially in Gujarati tradition. This dance has become the Mumbai version of the disco, an opportunity for the young to get out at night and mix with one another. Yet despite the public visibility of certain parts of the festival in Mumbai and despite the fact that certain myths and rituals are shared by Bengalis, Gujaratis, and Tamils, the actual celebration of Navarāttiri most frequently takes place within ethnic (and even subethnic) boundaries and along the lines that are thought to reflect the specific heritages of the celebrants.

The Festival of Nine Nights, celebrated in September or October, takes its name from the belief that over a nine-day period, the goddess—or, more accurately, goddesses—grows in strength and does battle with demonic forces until at last, having attained the fullness of her power, she destroys all the forces of evil. The festival not only celebrates the goddess's rise to supremacy but also affirms the role of women—indeed, places women front and center throughout the period. It is primarily the women who set up the decorations in the home and serve as hostesses and interpreters for their invited guests. In Mumbai, primarily women attend the daytime rituals in the temples and are explicitly honored in these rituals. And the role of women in passing along family traditions to daughters and daughters-in-law is especially manifest throughout the Navarāttiri season.

To be sure, Navarāttiri is a popular festival with Tamil Hindus of all walks of life—men as well as women, brahmin as well as nonbrahmin. Yet while Navarāttiri is celebrated by Tamils globally, in this discussion we focus particularly on some of the practices of Tamil brahmins in Mumbai and compare these briefly to those of Gujaratis in Mumbai and to those of Tamils in Pittsburgh. First it is useful to sketch briefly some elements of the festival's history.

The origins of the festival are obscure. P. V. Kane speculates, on the basis of references in the *Kumārasambhava* and certain numismatic evidence from the Kuṣāna king Kaniṣka, that worship of the goddess is to be found in classical sources by the first two centuries of the common era.[1] No doubt, goddess worship is much older in folk and rural settings. The festival appears to have agricultural roots, as there have been (and continue to be) in states such as Bengal and Bihar at least two celebrations, apparently associated with the coming of spring and autumn crops.[2]

That the festival had agricultural and/or "folk" antecedents is suggested by a variety of additional factors. One of these is the long-standing practice in agricultural settings of celebrating Durgā's (or a predecessor's) defeat of the buffalo-demon Mahiśāsura, especially at the time of the rainy season and/or the planting of crops.[3] Another is the continued practice of goddess worship in rural settings, albeit at different times of the year, in ways that seem congruent to the classicized forms of worship in brahminized settings: these include the embodiment of the goddess in earthen vessels known as *gatham*s or *karakam*s in the south; the offering of vermilion and turmeric, but also of animals such as goats as food (which of course has been replaced in classical settings by vegetarian fare); and the evocation of the goddess both for protection from disease and evil forces during inauspicious times (such as rainy seasons) and for the bringing of fertility and prosperity. Indeed, many of the offerings to the goddess in classical settings (e.g., rice, fruit, flowers) are clearly derived from agricultural settings.

Textual references to Navarāttiri and/or Durgāpūjā abound. The *Devīpurāṇa,* for example, states that performing the festival does great benefit:

> This is a great and holy *vrata* [vow] conferring great siddhis, vanquishing all enemies, conferring benefits on all people, especially in great floods; this should be performed by brahmins for solemn sacrifices and by kṣatriyas for the protection of the people, by vaiśyas for cattle wealth; by śūdras desirous of sons and happiness; by women for blessed wifehood and by rich men who hanker for more wealth; this was performed by Śaṅkara and others.[4]

The *Devīmahātmya,* that text describing the coming of the goddess to her place of supremacy, is, nonetheless, somewhat more succinct about the purpose of the festival: "a man becomes free from all troubles and becomes endowed with wealth and agricultural products by my favor."[5]

The festival is prescribed for all, even (according to the *Skandapurāṇa*) tribals who offer wine and meat. Indeed, some of the texts indicate that the offering of certain animals, especially the goat or buffalo, is desirable, while other animals such as the lion or elephant ought not be sacrificed.[6] There is even indication that the sacrifice of human beings was once thought appropriate, as the sacrifice of a human is said to satisfy Durgā for one thousand years while the victim goes straight to paradise[7]—though some substitutions are approved even in the *Kāḷikapurāṇa,* where human sacrifices are enjoined. All such sacrifices were said to be especially appropriate on the ninth day of the festival and presumably represented the destruction of the demonic forces and the gratification of the goddess, for it was to be accompanied by the recitation of the Devī's beheading of the demon Mahiṣa.

Quite apart from sacrifices, texts prescribed other ritual activities. The recitation of mantras is said to have great benefit, their sound even more important than their meaning.[8] *Pracāṭam* was to be offered to family, friends, and guests, and one thousand brahmins were to be fed.[9] According to the *Lingapurāṇa,* the four most important rites of Navarāttiri are bathing the image of the goddess, *pūjās* of various kinds, offering a victim (*bali* here expressed in the form of vegetarian food), and *homas* or fire sacrifices.[10] On the eighth day (*tithi*) of the waxing moon, "maidens" were to be honored. The *Devīpurāṇa,* in several instances, specifies that Durgā is honored less by *homa,* gifts, and prayer than by honoring girls, especially those between the ages of two and ten. The *Skandapurāṇa* confirms that prosperity is ensured for those who so honor girls.[11]

On the tenth *tithi,* the "sending away" of Devī should include merry making and the exchange of greetings. Indeed, according to the *Kāḷikapurāṇa,* this merry making may include "verbal orgies," sports revelry, and the throwing of dirt and mud at one another—activities, in short, designed apparently to make all participants equal.

Needless to say, many of those textual injunctions suggest considerable variation in practice and are no longer carried out (if, indeed, they ever were). The sacrifice of animals, for example, while still a part of the worship of Durgā in parts of Bengal and in Nepal and in rural and folk settings throughout India,[12] has long since been eliminated as part of the ritual life of brahminized Tamils. The Tamil brahmin celebration of Navarāttiri is much more restrained than texual descriptions appear to countenance and more sedate, in fact, than the Navarāttiri celebrations of their Gujarati and Bengali counterparts.

Another interesting aspect of Navarāttiri's history is the way in which it was celebrated in the courts of southern "kings" and would-be rulers. The fall festival assumed special importance in South India, partially because of its appropriation by kings and regional potentates, especially from the Vijayanagar period, as an expression, in part, of status and regal authority. Indeed, Navarāttiri (or Mahānavamī, as it also was called) replaced the older Vedic tradition of the *aśvamedha* (horse sacrifice) as the means by which a king established his "credentials." In fact, certain features of the *aśvamedha* were apparently incorporated into the Vijayanagar celebration of Navarāttiri. These included the parading of horses, especially one bearing the king's emblems of grandeur, and the public promenading of women in a manner reminiscent of the *Satapatha Brāhmaṇa*'s description of the *aśvamedha.*[13]

The Mahānavamī festival, under the Vijayanagars, also incorporated elements of the mythology of Rāma, wherein Rāma's defeat of Rāvaṇa was suffused throughout the celebrations but was especially highlighted on the final day of the festival, known as Vijaya daśamī. One result of the fusing of various mythological strands was that

Navarāttiri became the spectacle par excellence in medieval South India. As described by Portuguese travelers such as Paez and Nuniz and the Italian observer Conti, the festival took on mammoth proportions: the construction of large pavilions, the hosting of foreign dignitaries, processions of bedecked women and dancers, athletic contests, firework displays, and the sacrificial reconsecration of the king's weaponry (e.g., soldiers, horses, elephants). The festival became the symbolic expression of the king's status and worth, his role as "fructifier" of his domain, and his earthly congruence to the celestial warrior Durgā.[14]

Not only the Vijayanagar kings, but also the Wodeyar Dynasty of Karnataka (where the festival was combined with Rāma's conquest of Rāvaṇa and was known as Dasara) and certain regional potentates who succeeded the Vijayanagars used the festival to demonstrate their claim to kingship. The practice in varied form continued late into the nineteenth century as demonstrated in 1892 by the rājā of Ramnad in attempting to establish his worthiness for kingship.[15]

Clearly in its historical setting, the Navarāttiri combined several features. It had agricultural implications when it was held in March and April in some portions of North India, where it came at the time of the rabi harvest. When it was held in the fall (September and October), as in Bengal and most of the south, it came after the harvest of the *kār* crop and before the onset of the cool season.[16] The festival was intended to evoke the goddess's presence and bring her to full power so that she could subdue the forces of evil and fructify the earth.[17] It was intended to be eclectic in that many different communities, from the twice-born to tribals and "barbarians" (*mleccha*s), could celebrate it.[18] For kings and warriors, it clearly had political and military overtones as earthly potentates sought to equate themselves in power and authority to the goddess. It was an opportunity to honor women (and to some extent, brahmins). For all, it was an occasion to invite the goddess to bestow boons appropriate to the celebrant's wishes—that is, Navarāttiri had a very pragmatic intent. Whatever the purpose, the fall festival is prescribed to occur during the first half of the waxing moon of the month of September or October (though some texts suggest it should start a few days earlier).[19]

Navarāttiri and Tamil Brahmins in Mumbai

The Temple

Tamil Hindus of all stripes celebrate Navarāttiri in Mumbai. But in this discussion I focus primarily on brahmins in the city. Navarāttiri is celebrated by Tamil brahmins in Mumbai in two main venues: the temple and the home. Of the two, the rituals and activities associated with the temples are by far the more elaborate. It is useful to focus on the activities at the South Indian Bhajana Samajam and the Śrī Śaṅkara Maṭam, bastions of Smārta brahmin orthopraxy, and compare these with activities at the Śrī Subrahmaṇia Samajam in Chembur, a temple in which Śaiva Smārta brahmins have hegemony but where some participation by nonbrahmins is countenanced. (The story of the latter two of these institutions was told in chapter 5.) For Navarāttiri each of these temples publishes its calendar of events, advertising the thoroughness and authenticity with which each does the ritual and inviting devotees not only to attend but also to help fund the ritual activities. It is useful to view the skeleton of the temple activities from two perspectives: the structure of the ten days as a whole and the structure of a single day's ritual sequence.

The Weekly Sequence

We start at the South Indian Bhajana Samajam (SIBS) and the Śrī Śaṅkara Maṭam (SSM). At the SIBS each day is highlighted by two fire sacrifices (*homa*s), each one offered to different deities (most often goddesses) and for different purposes. The (SSM) starts a day earlier than its sister shrine for *pūjā* and *homa* to Ganeṣa in order to "overcome all difficulties to attain all desires."[20] There then follows, on successive days, fire sacrifices in the SIBS addressed to different deities: Aṉṉapūṉeśvarī (the goddess made famous at Benares, on day two); the nine planets and Rājamātaṅki (day three); Swayamvara Bāla Pārvatī (day four); Bhuvaneśvarī and Asvarūdā (day five); Vāgvātiṉi and Vārāhi (day six); Durgā and Navākstar (day seven); Pratyaṅkirā and Vityā (day eight); and a large *homa* for Sarasvatī (day nine). Several of these days are given special significance: the first day, for example, starting at 8:00 A.M., marks the beginning of the festivities with a major *homa*, exchanging of vows, bathing of the nine vessels to be used in the rituals, and so on. Devotees are invited to patronize this ritual sequence for 1,001 rupees. On day four, the day of celebrating the *svayamvara* (self-selecting of a wedding partner for Parvatī, a day which happened to fall on a Sunday that year), a "marriage meet" was held at 2:00 P.M. at a nearby hall. A sign had been posted on the temple walls inviting eligible boys and girls to come with their parents and/or guardians for exchange of conversation. The invitation had made it clear that only Iyer, Iyengar, Madhva, Telugu, and Kannada brahmins were invited. The festival climaxed on the ninth and tenth days: the ninth day had a major *homa* sequence for Sarasvatī and included a feeding of the "poor" and of brahmins; the tenth day (Vijayadaśamī Day) culminated with a grand procession of the supreme goddess Rājarājeśvarī, she who embodies the power and attributes of all goddesses combined.[21]

The intentions of this nine-day sequence are variously interpreted. One apparent intention is to honor and empower each of at least nine goddesses, the power of each of which will be integrated at the end of the festival into the favored goddess of the Smārta brahmins of Mumbai, Rājarājeśvarī, thereby enabling her to conquer all evil forces and to preside "in state" for the rest of the year. Some of the intentions associated with Navarāttiri at other temples in Tamil Nadu are either absent or only implicit in the SIBS's presentations. For example, C. J. Fuller, in describing Navarāttiri in the temple to Mīṉāṭci in Maturai, where the presiding goddess is equated to Rājarājeśvarī, suggests the festival integrates the goddess's warrior prowess with her eroticism and fructifying power. Further, it is said that Rājarājeśvarī integrates the character of the brahminic ascetic with that of the royal warrior.[22] However, in none of these three brahmin temples of Mumbai is the cosmic battle with the demon Mahiṣasura explicitly acted out, and the goddess's "eroticism" is only hinted in the heartlike shape of the sacrificial fire pit at the SIBS. And while "sacrifice" may remain a central theme (as when the goddess's slaying of the demon was seen as a sacrifice that saved and fructified the world), the daily sacrifices in SIBS's Smārta brahmin context are given a more "Vedic" nuance—that is, the daily *homa*s serve to renew a sociocosmic contract. The goddess (or goddesses) is invited to retain her dominion over the cosmos, while, more implicitly, humans agree to serve as her stewards in the city, the goddess's earthly domain.

In other settings (for example, in Bengal and at the Chembur temple in Mumbai), still other interpretations may apply. The festival is said to be addressed to three goddesses in particular, Durgā or Kāḷī, Lakṣmī, and Sarasvatī (variously identified in different settings), who, in turn, are said to represent three forms of the great goddess, three levels of the social and cosmic order, and the three "essences" (*guṇa*s) of the cosmos—*tamas, rajas,* and *sattva.*[23] These three attributes are sometimes linked to the three chief duties of human beings (*artha, dharma,* and *kama*) and to the character of the entire cosmos.[24] By that reading, the week's sequences would entail no less than the reinvigoration of the entire universe, including the social, natural, and divine order.

Meanwhile, at the SSM *homa*s are held each day at 8:00 A.M. and 6:00 P.M. for specific purposes. These *homa*s are intended to "ward off diseases" (*pala paramēcvari pūjā*) and to "attain mental peace" (*vityā pūjā*) on day two; for "education, art and culture" (*rājā matānki pūjā*) and to "ward off dangers due to accidents" (*vaṇaturkā-pūjā*) on day three; to "ward off all types of invisible enemies" (*mahā vārāhi pūjā*) and to "ward off skin diseases" (*taksiṇa kaḷika pūjā*) on day four; for "attaining scholarship" (*parā paṭṭārikā pūjā*) on day five; to "acquire property" (*puvanēcvari pūjā*) and "protection from enemies" (*carapa pūjā*) on day six; for "relief from debts" (*suvarṇa akarsaṇa pūjā*) on day seven; to "ward off evil spirits" (*piratyaṅkara pūjā*) and for "marriage of boys and girls" (*syamvarā pārvatī pūjā*) on day eight; and for attaining ultimate bliss (*mahāṣōṭākṣari pūjā*) on day nine. Again, devotees are invited to patronize any one of the *homa* sequences for 501 rupees. Devotees are assured in the announcements of events that all rituals will be performed by experienced Vedic officiants "to invoke the blessings of goddess Durgā for the welfare of the entire humanity."[25]

The Subrahmaṇia Samajam of Chembur, not to be outdone, promised a festival of equal efficacy. "Learned sivachariars" were conducting "Nava Chandi Homa" to enable devotees to "receive the divine blessings of Devī." These *homa*s, it was promised, "will not only bring peace and prosperity in [a devotee's] family but also save the universe from escalation of war and violence."[26] While fire sacrifices were indeed conducted every day, the temple made an effort to ensure that the first, ninth, and tenth days were special spectacles. The first day, for example, included the obligatory *homa* for Ganeṣa, libations (*abhiṣeka*), showing of lights to Durgā, and the recitation of the goddess's thousand names (*lakṣārcana*).[27] Each day the ritual cycle of libations and showing of lights to the goddess was performed. As one male devotee put it, "Every night we put the water that's been consecrated onto the goddess. She is energized gradually; otherwise we could not withstand all her energy." The ninth day included a special ornamentation of the goddess (*alaṅkāram*), another libation (*abhiṣeka*), and other āgamic rituals in the evening for the convenience of working devotees. The tenth day (Vijayadaśamī Day), which happened to fall on a Saturday that year, included a fire *pūjā* for "ladies," classes in dance, instruments and *Tiruppukaḻ* singing, and, of course, a grand procession of the goddess in the evening.[28]

The rituals associated with this temple's celebration of Navarāttiri clearly combined the tradition of *homa* (a Vedic ritual) with the āgamic rituals centered by the icon in a manner more commonly found throughout Tamil Nadu. In fact, it is clear that less-orthoprax believers frequent this temple as well (despite the hegemony retained by āgamic Smārta Śaiva brahmins), as there are on the premises *kāvaṭi*s (arches with peacock feathers) with which devotees can dance in praise of the presiding deity, Subrahmaṇia or Murukaṉ. Indeed, one staff person reported that the previous year someone came to the temple with a lance (*vēl*) in his cheeks, while another was dragging a cart with hooks in his back.[29]

The Chembur temple, in short, reflects a tacit relationship between brahmin and nonbrahmin participants. Śaiva brahmins maintain the traditions and retain hegemony over the temple's ritual and cultural life. Rituals on nonfestival days are consistent with āgamic norms. Nonbrahmins who participate are usually middle- to upper-middle class professionals (Chembur and this subdivision, in particular, reflect that economic status) who participate not only for religious reasons but also as a means of vertical mobility, thereby expressing their sense of equality with brahmins.

For the fire rituals of Navarāttiri, each temple has installed a temporary worship center, fire pit, and display: each temple, for example, centers the week's *homas* by means of a ritual space known as the *yākacālai,* an elevated platform on which representations of the goddess are displayed. At Chembur there are thirteen vessels plus three more prominent ones, representing Lakṣmī, Durgā, and Sarasvatī. At the more orthoprax temples, there were nine garlanded vessels (*kalaśa*) adorned with coconuts, flowers, mango leaves, and threads. Next to the ritual space, in the Matunga shrines, was a surrogate shrine for the goddess: at the SSM, a miniature throne on a pedestal surrounded by objects used in the *pūjā*—conch, vermilion, ghee lamps, scarves, betel flowers, plantains, perfumes, and grains. At the SIBS, the miniature shrine consisted of a multicolored rice cake (*maṇḍala/yātra*) on which were placed the nine grains and fruits to be used in worship. In front of this display was the fire pit/altar (*vedī*). The altar at the SIBS was different from the others in that it was shaped like a heart with the pit for the fire at its center.[30] Before the *vedī,* finally, is a representation of the goddess: a pot (*kalaśa*) with flowers, coconut, and threads (Chembur); a statue of the Devī on a tiger (SSM); or a picture of the goddess on a tiger plus a pot with coconut and flowers (SIBS). At the Chembur temple the representation of the goddess was dressed in different attire each day so that she could embody different goddesses favored by Tamilians (e.g., Mīṉāṭci of Maturai).

The Daily Sequence

The activities associated with each day of the festival in a temple are long and complex.[31] I focus only on the South Indian Bhajana Samajam for heuristic purposes. Each day started with a *homa* for Ganeṣa at 5:30 A.M. This was followed by libations (*abhiṣeka*) (6:00); rituals for goddesses and the Vedas (7:30), and *pūjā* for blessings on the nine-night celebration (*navāvaraṇa pūjā*) (9:00). The morning *homa*s ran from 8:00 A.M. to 12:00 P.M. Priests sanctified their own person with tantric *nyāsa*s and chanted, primarily from the *Devīmahātmya* (the myth of the great goddess's origins and exploits) and the *Lalitā Sahasranama* (a series of verses reciting the goddess's names), accompanied occasionally by men who may be present and know the chants. Into the fire were poured things believed desirous to the goddess: "sticks; *darbha* grass, such as was used in the ancient sacrifices; fruits; grains; turmeric; a winnowing basket; flowers; scarves; and a sari. By 11:00 A.M. women were singing *bhajaṉ*s, and by 11:45 the women would stand and gather around the goddess, while two women showed camphor to her. These participants were invariably brahmin.

Toward the end of the *homa,* between 11:00 A.M. and 12 P.M., a ritual popularly known as *cūmaṅkali pūjā* began. This was actually a ritual done on behalf of an unmarried boy (*brahmacāri pūjā*); a girl (*kaṉṉiyā-pūjā*); and several representative women (*sūvāsini pūjā*). In this ritual a girl, a boy, and four women (all of them brahmin and no one of which may be a widow), who have been seated on a bench in front of the ritual during the chanting, were honored. The women were each given a tray of fruit and flowers and a scarf and received prostration from a family. An orange sari was then given to each woman, who subsequently retired with the accompaniment of mantras and thrown flowers to change into the new clothes. When the women returned in their new attire, they were garlanded by other women, and flowers were put in their hair. The honorees looked discreetly toward the floor (like new brides) while priests chanted mantras and other women tossed flowers on them. This ritual is repeated each morning with a different set of honorees.

There was a break in the ritual day because afternoon (*cayaṅkālam*) is deemed an inauspicious time. By 6:00 P.M., however, further rituals were done to honor the goddess. These included the recitation of 1,001 names (*lakṣārcana*), ornamentation (*alaṅkāram*), and the showing of lights (*tīparātaṉai*), all rituals consistent with the āgamic traditions. The day concluded with lectures delivered by a visiting dignitary, starting at 8:15 and going on into the evening.

These temple rituals, particularly those sponsored by the Smārta brahmins of the Matunga temples, are more elaborate than any found in places where other Tamils have settled. In Pittsburgh, for example, the Śrī Veṅkaṭeśvara Temple has become a major venue for celebrating Navarāttiri, and many women find it easier to fulfill their festival agendas in the context of the temple than at home. The Pittsburgh temple does have an elaborate *maṇḍala* as the center of worship during Navarāttiri. The worship center includes representations of the temple deities—in this case, Veṅkaṭeśvara and his Vaiśnava entourage. The focus of worship includes various representations of Viṣṇu, such as Sudarsan (the personified *cakra* or wheel of Viṣṇu), germinating seeds, and Durgā and Sarasvatī. A fire pit receives libations each evening, culminating in a *homa* for Sarasvatī on the last evening. As in Mumbai, no cosmic battle is enacted on the last day, though the presiding deity (in this case, Veṅkaṭeśvara) is empowered through the daily *homas*. At the side of the sanctuary is the traditional display of dolls (*kōlu*), arranged each year by children and their mothers.

While several dozen devotees will attend the culminating libations at the Pittsburgh temple, at no point do the rituals match in intensity or complexity the activities of the Matunga temples. It is estimated that 250 worshippers a day will come to the SSM in a day during Navarāttiri; the matham budgets three hundred thousand rupees for the festival and gets a goodly portion of it back from the patronage of devotees. Similarly, the SIBS will welcome a few hundred brahmin devotees a day who have given back to the temple by the first day of the festival more than the temple board had budgeted for it. Clearly, one of the intentions of such elaborate celebrations is the very pragmatic one of raising funds for further developments of the temple premises; the SIBS board, for example, has dreamed of a more elaborate structure, of founding a school for the study of the Vedas, and other projects.[32]

What other factors can account for the elaborate nature of the temple-oriented celebration of this festival? For one thing, one is tempted to suggest that these temples are assuming the role, however unconsciously, of the medieval kings—that is, they are establishing their claim to hegemony, status, and orthopraxy. They seek to be the "fructifiers" of their respective domains—and even compete, one must point out, for enlargement of their domains. Further, the goddess who is protectoress of all domains and the most powerful of all the deities must be appropriately honored and kept on one's own side. Requests made to her are pragmatic, asking for a wide range of things, from freedom from disease and accident to success in wealth and education. She who protects villagers from dangerous threats seems to protect her premises in Matunga or Chembur—and perhaps those districts themselves—from threats of all kinds, including from those who are deemed religiously less than orthoprax. These temples provide a buttress against the secularization of the festival to be seen throughout Mumbai.

The observer is struck by the sense of obligation enacted in the Matunga temples. This community of Smārta brahmins understands itself to be the "preservers of tradition" and the watchdogs of orthopraxy. As observed in chapter 5, given the relative freedom of Mumbai, as compared with life in Tamil Nadu, these devotees find they can openly enact their identity as Smārta brahmins in public space and participate in the community that identity entails. The orality of *homam* chants and the cultural performance of fire sacrifice represent the heritage that informs one. Devotees also bring personal agendas to ritual events: these may include a sense of guilt at having given so much attention to a career; uncertainty at one's personal station on the journey to ultimate fulfillment; or dissatisfaction with the circumstances of family and work. Women in particular seem to find fulfillment. Those still in the process of socializing their own children in the "tradition" are reinforced and supported by the week's celebrations. By contrast, those whose children are grown may bring a sense of boredom or of expectations unfulfilled. Honoring women in public spaces and worshipping a goddess with elaborate ritual may well serve as a reminder that it is indeed good to be a woman.

The Home

This brings us (much more briefly) to the other venue in which Navarāttiri is played out in Tamil brahmin lives in Mumbai: the home. The home has been the center for Navarāttiri celebrations in many communities, Tamil and non-Tamil, going back for generations. Pratapachandra Ghosha in 1876, describing the Durgāpūjā as it was done in Bengali brahmin homes then, offers details more akin to the observance in the Matunga temples today: among other things, the home observances included the setting up of a frame in which effigies of the deities were displayed (still done today in many homes, both brahmin and nonbrahmin, in Tamil Nadu and Mumbai). Those displays featured Durgā, Lakṣmī, Sarasvatī, Śiva and family, Kāḷī, and the entourages of various gods. This setup was to be kept pure from "unbelievers" through the dark half of the moon's cycle. On the ninth day of the waning moon, the goddess was to be roused and prepared for worship. After the new moon officiating priests were appointed, the pot representing the goddess was sacralized and bathed, and various preparatory rituals were performed (e.g., sacralizing of the priest's body, purifying of the carpet). These rituals were repeated through the sixth day of the waxing moon as a priest would chant the *Devīmahātmya.* By the eighth day the main combination of rituals was to be performed, including vivifying and adorning the goddesses, *homa* offerings with libations to the fire, and worship of a brahmin virgin. Some Bengali families sacrificed a goat. On the ninth day the rituals of the previous day were to be repeated but on a grander scale: more animals could be sacrificed, the showing of lights to the goddess occurred, household priests were given their ritual gift (*dakṣini*), and family members bowed to the goddess and embraced and forgave each other. Guests could visit more families where the *pūjā* was done, sometimes accompanied by singing and dancing. On the tenth day the goddess's representation was immersed. She was carried out of the house on a bamboo pole, accompanied by music, loud noise, and the throwing of dirt and mud. Devī was put on a boat, then "thrown" overboard.[33]

Clearly, contemporary home practice has become more modest. However, in some Gujarati homes, rather elaborate observances are still maintained, especially where familial traditions are passed on. One Gujarati brahmin woman in Mumbai described how Navarāttiri is observed in her home:

I've been observing this festival for thirty-seven years, since I married into this family. We worship Ambika, who was born when all the gods appealed to Brahmā, Viṣṇu, and Śiva to destroy the demons. The goddess received weapons and gifts from other deities and incorporated the strength of other goddesses, for example, Brahmaśaktī, Maheśvarī, Kumarī, Vaiṣṇavī, Indraśaktī, Chandika, etc. She became the most powerful of them all, fought the demons for nine days, and destroyed them on the ninth day.

We keep the devī in a pot [*kumbha*]; the pot is covered with a red cloth and we attach red and green bangles, a coconut, and mango leaves. For nine days we have priests direct *pūjā*s to the goddess—each *pūjā* takes about one and a half hours and culminates in garlanding the goddess and showing her lights.

On the eighth day we have a *homa* in our house between 11:00 A.M. and 4:00 P.M. Here all the gods are marked in a brick fireplace. The four sides of the fire pit are marked by banana trees in pots with *aśoka* tree leaves strung along the four trees to make an enclosure. Into the fire the priest puts ghee, fruits, and coconut in a cloth [representing what used to be an animal]. Though some temples still observe four Navarāttiris a year, we only observe one: ours comes at the end of the monsoon before the harvest occurs. We mark the season by planting seeds in the pots; those spring up by the fourth day.[34] We keep grains in the house and distribute them to friends as if to say there will be food to eat all year.

By the ninth day feasting begins at our house. For eight days men had not cut their hair. Now we celebrate by carrying around the *garbha* [pot], and people contribute donations into it. We usually do the *dandi* dance, which is supposed to reenact the dance of the *gopis* (for we also celebrate Rāma's defeating of Rāvaṇa on this day). Now in Gujarat and Mumbai the *dandi* has become a secular disco and a social occasion.[35]

Practices in the homes of Tamil brahmin women in Mumbai vary widely, but, generally speaking, observances in the home have become much more modest, and families depend on the temples for the more elaborate ritual events. One thing that does persist is the home display of dolls or icons. Normally set up in the room set aside for *pūjā* will be a frame (*kōlu*) like a short staircase in which deities are arranged. One such arrangement illustrates the pattern. In the home of Mrs. Venkitesvaran of Sion (near Matunga), the goddess at the top of the frame is Rājarājeśvarī, the favored goddess of Mumbai's Smārta brahmins and others, including this Vaiṣṇava family. This is said to have been the grandmother's (Mr. Venkitesvaran's mother's) deity, and it is she who performs the *pūjā* each morning of the year. (The grandson insists the *pūjā*s are no different during Navarāttiri.) To the right of Rājarājeśvarī is Durgā and on a step below, the various avatars of Viṣṇu. Other deities fill out the frame. Lights and tinsel surround the display. Below it is a *kōlam* (a geometric design made of rice flour). The hostess says she uses the same decorations each year but arranges them differently.

The highlight of the week in this home is the "open house" held on two evenings—the fifth and sixth nights of Navarāttiri between 5:00 and 8:30 P.M. Formal invitations are sent out. Known as the "Navrathri Kolu," celebrating guests are invited to view the display, engage in conversation, and partake of sweets. Those who walk come before dark, those with cars after dark. The network of invitees is drawn mostly from the Tamil brahmin friends known to the host and hostess, supplemented by couples who "live in our building" or who "work with my husband." The hostess chats with female guests; the husband or son entertains the males.[36]

Some Tamil homes in Tamil Nadu and around the globe engage in more elaborate activities. M. Arunachalam, for example, writing in *Festivals of Tamil Nadu,* suggests that one often finds a "*kōlam* over the whole house" and that books are often venerated and placed on a pedestal. As in the Venkitesvaran home, the devī, by whatever name, is almost universally given a "durbar" where she sits in royal splendor on a "gallery" (*kōlu*) of seven to nine steps. Food offerings consist of cooked rice, ghee, coconut, jaggery, banana, and betel offered on banana leaves. Even in homes where worship will not occur on all nine days, Arunachalam suggests, there will be an invocation (*avahara*) on the seventh day, the worship of Śaktī on the eighth day, and Sarasvatī *pūjā* on the ninth day, though he concedes in "poorer homes" just the Sarasvatī *pūjā* will occur.[37] Penny Logan reports that in Tamil Nadu, Sarasvatī *pūjā* on the ninth day of Navarāttiri is especially popular. Commonly, on this day an image or picture of Sarasvatī is set up in front of the *kōlu,* together with displays of books, musical instruments, and other "tools" of one's trade, all decorated with sandal paste, vermilion (*kumkuma*), and flowers. Sarasvatī is offered foodstuffs such as chickpeas or *pāyacam* (sweet pudding). The veneration of instruments (even those that may be used in an office, such as machines or ledger books) is known as *āyadha* (weapon) *pūjā,* a vestige of the day when the festival was associated with kingship and warfare. Some families in Mumbai and Pittsburgh similarly use the occasion to honor instruments of their home and profession.[38]

As with Gujarati families, the conclusion of the festival for many Tamils may dovetail with Rāma's overcoming of Rāvaṇa. Tamil celebrations of Navarāttiri do not include the immersion of the goddess's effigy, a practice found in nineteenth-century Bengal and in Gujaratis' homes in Mumbai. The practice of immersing the deity, at least among Gujaratis in Mumbai, may have been borrowed from the practice of immersing Gaṇeṣa in the sea during Mumbai's most popular festival, Gaṇeṣa Chaturthi.

Implications

What is it all about, this celebration of the goddess during nine days in September? Asked this question, Tamil brahmin women articulated several reasons they found the festival enjoyable and important. One evoked the mythology to reassert that it commemorated the victory of Rāma over Rāvaṇa and of Durgā over the demons. Another suggested that this cosmic battle was, in fact, to be interiorized. The festival provided the occasion to seek the goddess's help in destroying unhelpful passions and in focusing the mind toward the pursuit of wisdom. Another offered that the festival integrated several elements of one's landscape at once: the "traditional" and remembrance of the past as well as the "modern"; the sacred dimensions of life as well as the secular; and the "institutional" such as temple and home along with the personal. Yet another suggested that the festival was an aesthetically enriching experience with its multiplicity of colors, displays, sights, and sounds and that, at the same time, it was a season of warm social interaction. Another respondent suggested it was a time for the "redistribution of goods" and the reaffirmation of friendships, identities, and history.[39]

Perhaps one can summarize some of the reasons why Navarāttiri has retained its popularity (in some form) among these particular Tamils of Mumbai: for one thing, it combines seasonal, theological, and social themes. Even though the seasonal aspects of the agricultural cycle are no longer operative in Mumbai, the festival does fall after the heavy southwest monsoon and is commensurate with the resumption of the normal postmonsoon period—the social new year, if you will. More important are the theological themes of the deity's conquest of evil and her reinstallation in the home, the temple, and the heart. Socially, the festival provides the opportunity to keep in touch with those who help define one—an interaction that can easily fall by the wayside in the bustle of urban life. Further, it embodies something of the character of historical change brought on by the exigencies of urban life. These include the movement of "tradition" from home to temple, and from palace pavilion to temple; the deselection of certain past activities and the mutual exchange of "traditions" between differing ethnic/linguistic streams; and the accommodation of and resistance to contemporary circumstances. Not least important is the way it expresses and celebrates the role of the woman—on the one hand, affirming her traditional status as wife, mother, and bearer of tradition; on the other, moving her closer to the center of public celebration and affirming her role as professional and leader.

Finally, Navarāttiri in Mumbai expresses the ambiguity of urban life. On the one hand, the city is made the domain of the goddess; on the other, the city is "demonic" or chaotic, and within that chaos miniature universes (e.g., the temple and the home) are created in which the goddess can reign supreme, protecting all within those smaller precincts from external threat. Within those abodes, community is possible, roots and legacies are affirmed, and one can express in multiple ways what it means to be who one is.

CHAPTER 9

Trance and "Sacred Wounding"

Interpretations of Tai Pūcam at Kuala Lumpur, Malaysia

The most visible and significant religious event for Malaysians and Singaporeans of South Indian descent is the celebration of Tai Pūcam, a festival occurring in January or February (Tai) when the full moon falls on or near the constellation Pūcam. Ostensibly dedicated to the worship of Murukaṉ, the festival has become a spectacle attracting tourists as well as Malaysians of Chinese descent. Most of the larger urban areas have witnessed the growth of Tai Pūcam processions, including Ipoh and Pulau Pinang. Yet Penang and Kuala Lumpur remain the major Malaysian venues for the festival, while Singapore continues to witness growing participation in the festival, albeit in a relatively sanitized form.

For Malaysian Tamils the festival serves many purposes and can be interpreted at various levels. It is a means for expressing and affirming identity as Indian Malaysians, as Tamils, and as members of subethnic communities. It becomes a way of expressing political power within the Indian community and especially to the Malaysian Indian Congress and through that party to the government. It embodies the fractures and discrepancies between some lower-class Tamils rooted in the plantation ethos who are frequent participants in extreme penitential activities and middle- to upper-class Indians whose vision of Hindu identity is quite different. It becomes the occasion for demonstrating individual worth as in a rite of passage, wherein one proves one's merit to oneself and one's social network. Not least of all, the festival provides an occasion for expressing gratitude and paying off debts to the deity, and for seeking a change in life's station.

The features of the festival that are most widely reported are the more extreme forms of vow fulfillment. Some forms of offering entail trance, the inflicting of wounds, and possession by one or more deities. This type of activity is officially discouraged in Singapore and, in fact, has diminished slightly since 1987, while overall participation in more moderate forms of expression has nearly doubled there in that period. In the Kuala Lumpur setting, however, despite ongoing attempts by some Hindu reformers to curtail this form of activity, these more extreme forms of penance continue to flourish even as overall participation in the festival grows.

In this chapter I attempt to explore some of the dynamics that underlie these festival activities and summarize some of the interpretations that can be brought to them. I will focus especially on the festival in its most popular, expressive, and diverse form: that observed on the outskirts of Kuala Lumpur.

The Context

Brief Historical Sketch

Seven miles north of Kuala Lumpur is a limestone knoll in which several caves are to be found, known as Batu Caves. The largest of these caves, about three hundred feet high, was discovered in 1891 by emissaries of Thamboosamy Pillai, then responsible for managing the Mahāmāriyammaṉ Temple in Kuala Lumpur.[1]

Mr. K. Thamboosamy Pillai had come in 1872 from Pondicherry District by way of Singapore as assistant to the lawyer J. G. Davidson. Thamboosamy Pillai was soon recognized as a *kapitan* or leader of the Indian community and, on its behalf, erected a temporary Māriyammaṉ temple in 1875. Soon thereafter the temple was moved to its present spot, a piece of land donated for use of the community by the sultan of Selangor.[2]

Plantation workers living around the Batu Caves area urged the Māriyammaṉ temple officials to designate one of the caves as a shrine to Murukaṉ. Accordingly, two "scouts," one a *piḷḷai* and one a *tēvar,* found the caves in 1891, planted a bamboo *vēl* (lance—the insignia of Murukaṉ), and claimed the cave as a shrine to Murukaṉ. Tai Pūcam was declared the official festival of this temple of the *vēl* at Batu Caves that year.[3]

Along with *piḷḷai*s and *tēvar*s, Chettiyars were active in the early patronage of the Tai Pūcam festival. Chettiyars, who came to Malaysia to do business, brought with them their patron deity Taṇṭāyutapāṇi, the form of Murukaṉ enshrined at Paḻaṉi. Chettiyars helped establish and have been centrally involved in the Tai Pūcam celebrations in Penang and Singapore.[4] The Chettiyars had become patrons of the deity at Paḻaṉi in the seventeenth and eighteenth centuries while they were trading in the area.[5] The affinity between the Chettiyars and the Paḻaṉi Taṇṭāyutapāṇi is said to have been established by virtue of their traveling to do business without their wives (that is, as celibates) and the deity's being an ascetic there.[6] In fact, the Chettiyars, through the person of Kumarappa, a Chettiyar trader selling salt in Paḻaṉi, were given a major role in leading the pilgrimage to Paḻaṉi for the Tai Pūcam festival there. As Kumarappa's profits had increased, his endowments to the Paḻaṉi temples increased. Other Chettiyar traders became involved who endowed the festival at Paḻaṉi in perpetuity and, in exchange, were given honors and the right to manage all the donated funds for the festival.[7]

To the present day, nonetheless, the Mahāmāriyammaṉ Temple has retained sponsorship of the festival, though Chettiyars have remained active patrons, a fact recognized during the procession of deities from Kuala Lumpur to the Batu Caves during the Tai Pūcam festival. The procession stops for an extended period, for example, in Sentul, just north of KL, where is housed a temple to Taṇṭāyutapāṇi, patronized by Chettiyars. In 1929, after a court ruling, the management of the Mahāmāriyammaṉ Temple was passed to a board composed largely of *tēvar*s (who had been active much earlier in that temple), while the *piḷḷai* family theretofore involved was assigned the ceremonial role of stanikar, including that of "executive officer" in the small *devasthanam* (office) that stands at Batu Caves.[8]

The Śrī Māriyammaṉ Devasthanam, with the help of private donors and the state government of Selangor, has made improvements to the caves over the years. In 1939, for example, a two-way cement staircase of 272 steps was constructed, giving pilgrims easier access to the shrine.[9] In 1940 seven acres were purchased for further development, and a Tamil school was started.[10] Several caves were developed to extol the virtue of Tamil culture. One of them became an "art gallery" in 1972, in which figures of Nāyaṉmārs and other Tamil saints are depicted in sculpted form.[11] In 1982 another cave became a "Valluvār Kottam," an area with sculptings honoring the Tamil poet Tiruvallar.[12] In the 1980s a group of Malayali Malaysians independently developed a cave about a mile from the main cave into a shrine for the Ayyappaṉ of Sabarimala. In 1991, preparatory to celebrating the centennial, several sculptings and other renovations were installed in the main shrine.

A Brief Reconstruction of the Festival

The Tai Pūcam festival as performed at Batu Caves encompasses three days. However, by 1991, for a variety of reasons, activities leading up to the festival constituted a virtual season. The first of these factors, unique to that year, was that the Mahāmāriyammaṉ Temple was gearing up for the centennial of Batu Caves. Centennial activities were to culminate in a *kumbhābhiṣeka* scheduled for June 1991. These preparations were feverish for months prior to Tai Pūcam as temple authorities, volunteers, and employed craftsmen were engaged in extensive renovations around the caves: the installation of lighting; crafting of statuaries depicting the six sacred sites of Murukaṉ in Tamil Nadu; cleaning up and refurbishing facilities; and construction of a small new shrine at the foot of the caves.

A second factor, more subtle, was the attempt by the Indian community, primarily catalyzed by the Mahāmāriyammaṉ Temple, working through the Malaysian Indian Congress (MIC) and the press, to make the Indian community more visible in Malaysia and Tai Pūcam the official national holiday for Indians. While Tai Pūcam had been declared a public holiday in four states, including Selangor, where Batu Caves is located, it was not so recognized by the federal government, which does recognize Christmas, the Chinese New Year, Hariraya or the Ramaḍān season, and Dīpāvalī as official public holidays. Mr. Swami Velu, the president of the MIC, a cabinet minister, and the most prominent Indian Malaysian politician, was especially visible in the season preceding Tai Pūcam, though cynics thought he was primarily seeking to restore his credibility with the community. For whatever reasons, Poṅkal, the mid-January Tamil festival, was more evident in 1991 than in earlier Malaysian history, meriting several pages of "educational" discussion and promotion in the pages of the Tamil daily. In the period from early January through Tai Pūcam, public lectures and conferences celebrated the history and character of Tamil culture and the arts. These were often patronized by the government, dominated by the United Malays National Organisation party (UMNO), which, while predominantly Malay and Muslim, nonetheless seeks to retain support of Chinese and Indian minorities to stay in power. The season included an exhibit of *kāvaṭi* makers, or artisans. (The *kāvaṭi* is the display carried by devotees on their shoulders.) Another activity given public attention was the *kōlam* (ornamentation) competition held for the third straight year at the Putra World Trade Center. While Indian youngsters were the primary contestants (and eleven-year-old twin boys won the first prize of a round trip to Bali), at least two pairs of entrants were non-Indian. The PWTC public affairs minister Encik Zainal Epi was quoted as saying, "The competition was organized to strengthen social interaction among the various races in the country. You can only learn and understand other people when you know their culture and their way of life."[13]

Other preparatory activities occur each year. Space for five hundred stalls in the cave grounds is advertised in Tamil papers well ahead of time, then subsequently allocated, and usually rented, on the basis of a lottery draw. Various *ubayams* (patronage groups) of the Māriyammaṉ temple have agreed to provide certain services to pilgrims at a reduced rate. Tickets are sold to pilgrims for the right to climb the steps with their offerings. In 1991 about fifteen hundred registered as bearers of *kāvaṭi*, though many others carried *kāvaṭi* of various kinds, some of them without buying tickets and hence theoretically not permitted to go up the steps to the main shrine. That year the Mahāmāriyammaṉ Temple collected forty thousand Malaysian dollars from *kāvaṭi* bearers who bought tickets and about five hundred thousand Malaysian dollars from the festival overall.[14] Pilgrims themselves had been preparing for the occasion with several days of fasting and meetings with their lay advisers.[15]

Paṇṭārams (rather than brahmins) serve as priests at Batu Caves. This is consistent with the tradition carried on by Chettiyars in their Taṇṭāyutapāṇi temples who have continued to employ *paṇṭārams* as their chief priests since first coming to the Malay Straits. Accordingly, sixty to seventy *paṇṭārams* are engaged by the chief priest at Batu Caves for the duration of the festival.

The festival itself occurs over a three-day period. The first day starts before dawn in the Mahāmāriyammaṉ Temple with *pūjā* addressed to the festival icons of Murukaṉ and his two consorts by the resident brahmin priest. This *pūjā* sequence includes *abhiṣeka* (libations), *vastram* (dressing), *alaṅkāram* (ornamentation), *lakṣārcana* (recitation of one thousand names), and *ārccaṉai* (praise). The images are circumambulated around the temple three times then placed on a silver chariot. *Paṇṭārams* take over as the chariot leaves the temple grounds around 4:00 A.M. followed by perhaps twenty thousand devotees, many carrying vessels of water or milk and other gifts for the deity.

The procession winds through several main streets then makes its way to Sentul on the north side, where it stops twice. Sentul was once the residential quarters for Indian railway workers for Malaysia and is still heavily populated by Indians. The procession stops first for *darśan* (viewing of the deity) by shop owners who have tied banana trees to their doors, and second near the Chettiyar temple dedicated to Taṇṭāyutapāṇi. At both stops devotees can receive *darśan* and perform *ārccaṉai* with the help of the *paṇṭāram.* Shortly before noon the procession will arrive at Batu Caves, there to be greeted by a throng of devotees and a carnival atmosphere. At stalls various foodstuffs and souvenirs are sold; from "truth booths" literature and pamphlets are disseminated by volunteers. On into the evening there will be speeches by itinerant gurus from India, *bhajaṉ* performances, and Tamil movies. By the cool of the evening, pilgrims have begun their trek of three or four furlongs carrying *kāvaṭi* up to the main shrine.

The second day is the highlight of the festival, the day on which the Pūcam *nakṣatra* presides. The festival icons are given a water libation (*abhiṣeka*) at the riverbank shortly after dawn, and pilgrims are offered *darśan* before the icons are returned to the *maṇṭapam* at the foot of the caves. A brahmin priest presides over this *pūjā* sequence. Meanwhile, vow takers have gathered by dawn at the riverbank to begin their trudge to the temple steps and up into the cave shrine.

Several kinds of offerings are made, most of them not necessitating trance or wounding. Most common is the *pāl kāvaṭi,* milk offered in small containers covered at the mouth with a banana leaf and a yellow cloth. Usually this is carried on the head; occasionally, however, vessels of milk are attached to the flesh with hooks or, more commonly, at the end of an arch borne on the shoulders. Other *kāvaṭi*s carried on the head include a pot (*kalaca*), sometimes made of betel leaves and shaped in the form of a temple entrance (*kōpuram*) and generally offered to Gaṇeṣa; the *cantaṉam,* a *kōpuram* made of sandalwood; or various metal *kāvaṭi*s that become miniature *vimāṉa*s or temple towers. These are sometimes stabilized by attaching them to the body with hooks. Some offerings are carried by hand, such as the *agni kāvaṭi*—pots of fire usually carried for Śakti or Māriyammaṉ—or *pannīr kāvaṭi*—pots bearing water scented with jasmine. *Karumpu kāvaṭi* is borne by couples whose wish for a child has been granted. In this offering a child with a shaved head is carried in a cloth sling up the steps to the shrine. Relatively common in the penitential parade is the *vēl kāvaṭi,* wherein a lance, anywhere from six inches to several feet long, is used to pierce the tongue or the cheeks in honor of Murukaṉ. Other offerings can be attached to hooks in the flesh or to the arch borne on the shoulders—*puṣpam* (flowers), *mayil iraku* (peacock feathers), *pavalam* (beads or gems), or lime.[16]

Each devotee is generally surrounded by a supportive group, be it family or friends. These will circle the devotee, shout or sing encouragement, and provide liquid refreshment. Some will occasionally become entranced themselves or become possessed by a deity on whose behalf they will serve as a medium. Those who become entranced, including those believed to become possessed by deities, usually prepare for the experience beforehand and start in procession with other vow takers by the riverbank. Certain prescribed behaviors characterize the deitites who are believed to possess devotees: those possessed by Muṉiāṇṭi or Muṉiśvaraṉ, for example, will wear colorful turbans and sashes, smoke cigars, and flagellate themselves, sometimes pulling a chariot with ropes skewered into their back. Those possessed by Maturai Vīraṉ walk on large knives held by supporters until the activity was discontinued by temple authorities. Possession by Hanuman results in behavior emulating a monkey, such as leaping around or scratching oneself. Those possessed by Kāḷiyammaṉ cut their tongues.

While devotees are supposed to stop at the Iṭampaṉ shrine at the foot of the cave, many will go straight up the steps to the main shrine. The end of the pilgrimage comes at a modest white shrine to Murukaṉ at the left interior of the huge cave. After dancing vigorously or in other ways making offerings at the shrine, pilgrims are revived and will have their skewers removed and their offerings are shared with supporters.

By late afternoon the festival is winding down. Speeches are given by politicians. In 1991 both Swami Vēlu and his chief political rival for the MIC leadership, Subramaniam, were asked to give speeches. A public reconciliation was enacted and both were recognized with ritual *mariyāti* (the sharing of honors).

After dawn of the third day, the *vēl* of Murukaṉ is brought down from the main shrine and reinstalled on the chariot. By midmorning the procession back to Kuala Lumpur has begun. Once again the chariot is stopped in Sentul, this time at the artisan quarters. To the accompaniment of pipe (*nātaswaram*) and drum (*mridaṅkam*), devotees receive *darśan* once the images have been set up on a *paṇṭal.* At midafternoon the *paṇṭāram* performs *abhiṣeka,* and the images of the deity are once again made available to devotees until evening. At dusk the procession returns to the Śrī Mahāmāriyammaṉ temple and Tai Pūcam is concluded for one more year.

Some Interpretive Remarks

As intimated in the description and context of the festival, Tai Pūcam has come to have significance in the Indian Malaysian context at many levels, and people choose to participate in a great variety of ways. The metaphor of a ripple is sometimes used in describing the impact of festivals of this kind.[17] At an outer level there is a general Malaysian population that is being reminded yet again of its Indian minority community. This will include employers whose Indian employees are missing for the day and government functionaries and others who learn of events through press coverage and word of mouth reports. This will also include those tourists, foreign and domestic, who come to the Batu Caves out of curiosity, sometimes taking pictures. Closer to the center is that ripple representing the general Indian Malaysian population, some of whom may actually come to Batu Caves as an opportunity for a family outing. Some of these may think of the festival as a statement of Indian Malaysian ethnicity, a political statement, or merely a holiday. Then there are those who participate as pilgrims, making their way to the top of the steps, having made vows of various sorts, and getting *darśan* of the god in the cave. These may also combine their piety with recreation, enjoying with their families refreshments, carnival rides, and the general ambience of the occasion. There is, however, an inner circle of participants who undergo the more extreme forms of trance, possession, and "sacred wounding." It is the dynamics of this group of pilgrims I wish to examine more fully inasmuch as their ritual behavior, I believe, has affinity to certain ritual expressions to be found in other contexts—the flagellations that occur, for example, among certain Christians on Good Friday, or some Shīite Muslims during Muḥarram, or the trances that appear to be present in the phenomenon of glossolalia in Christianity, or possession in the folk practices of South and Southeast Asia. Simply put, I want to explore the interpretive connotations that can be gathered around four considerations: (1) personal boundaries—that is, life historical, psychological, and/or personal issues that make people candidates for this sort of experience; (2) contextual boundaries—the contexts, at both a macro or political level and a micro or familial level, in which these enactments must be viewed; (3) physiological factors that stretch the body beyond its normal capacities; and (4) religious and ideological factors that give to the festival and this experience its significance and legitimation.

It is clear that the activity of some participants in Tai Pūcam represents forms of what is generally called "altered states of consciousness." To be sure, not all pilgrims or vow takers enter into trance, become possessed, or wound themselves. Indeed, most do not. Yet a significant number do engage in one or more of these forms of participation. Some will enter a trance in order simply to carry a *kāvaṭi* of milk or other offerings. The trance of others precedes their being skewered; in fact, assistants will not proceed with the skewering procedure unless the pilgrim is in a trance. In most instances trance is the sine qua non for becoming possessed by the deity and emulating the deity's actions and words.

The process of becoming entranced can be described in two stages.[18] The first stage is preparatory. During this stage, which may last from a week to forty-eight days, the pilgrim follows a daily regimen of meditation (*tapas*) and abstinence (*viratam*). Each is expected to rise before dawn, take a cold bath, then enter the *pūjā* room for prayer, reciting stanzas of praise (*stotra*) to Murukaṉ and waving lights (*ārati*) to the deity's image. This *pūjā* should be repeated at noon and after sundown. The devotee is discouraged from sleeping in comfort and encouraged to limit social relations and maintain relative silence. Sexual abstinence is expected, as is strict fasting. The daily diet will start with a glass of milk mixed with *tulsi* leaves drunk right after awakening. No food or drink is taken again until evening.[19] Pilgrims are encouraged to cook their own food, usually with separate utensils and certainly without meat.

During this period the vow taker will generally meet on several occasions with the guru or mentor (usually an older lay male). During these meetings the adviser will perform *pūjā*, recite mantras, and lead in singing of *bhajaṉs* (devotional songs). He seeks to develop rapport and a sense of trust and mutual participation within his group of advisees. When he senses they are ready, he initiates them into a trance. If they are not deemed ready, pilgrims will be advised to intensify their *tapas* or discontinue their preparations altogether.

The second stage occurs on the banks of the river running along the Batu Caves, hours before the actual vow is to begin. Raymond Lee describes this process as follows:

While the penitents take their ritual baths by the watertanks, the advisor performs *puja*, cuts lime, and waves *arathi* before a picture of Murugan. More *puja*s are performed when the penitents appear dripping wet before him. They clasp their hands in a posture of prayer, close their eyes, and concentrate on Murugan, while the advisor smears ashes on their chest, backs, arms, necks and foreheads. As the supporters sing devotional songs and chant, "*vel, vel,*" the advisor burns *sambrani* [Tam. *campirāṇi*] . . . and waves the fumes to be inhaled by the penitents. When they show initial signs of trance by moving rhythmically forward and backward, he applies ashes on their foreheads at a point between the eyes (*netrikan*) and rubs it. Most penitents lose consciousness at this moment and the advisor inserts needles and skewers into their bodies. If a penitent bleeds or cries out in pain, the advisor will stop the piercing and instruct him not to continue because he has no blessings from Murugan or he has not observed his fast properly. When the piercing is completed, limes are fixed to the ends of the skewers or hung on hooks attached to the penitent's torso. The advisor pats the penitents' cheeks gently, bringing them to a level of consciousness sufficient for carrying *kavadi* to the shrine. He accompanies his charges into the cave to complete his spiritual responsibility. After the penitents dance in front of the Murugan shrine, the advisor massages their foreheads making them unconscious while he removes all sharp objects from their bodies. The exhausted penitents are revived and instructed to go home, wash, pray, and sleep. In the evening they are required to pray at the nearest Hindu temple and to continue their fast for another three days.[20]

Personal Boundaries

Why are people willing to undergo the stringent discipline of entrancement and wounding that characterize Tai Pūcam? One of the reasons, clearly, is the agenda that individuals bring to it—their needs, vows, expressions of gratitude, and so on. While Tai Pūcam always has a public character, individual participants bring to it personal agendas and understandings. The individual's sense of what the festival means is informed by one's historical situation. Hence, there are as many personal reasons for participation as there are participants. Generally speaking, one may describe the life experience of each participant as having included a "boundary situation" or life crisis. Personal boundary situations come in many forms. Clifford Geertz has described at least three kinds of "experiential challenges" as occasions when religious activities become especially meaningful: when intellectual questions persist without easy answers; when moral ambiguities exist in social and political arenas; and when one is confronted by one's own finitude and mortality, as during illness.[21] Similarly, Peter Berger has written of alienation and the loss of meaning (anomy) as such an occasion.[22] For Tai Pūcam participants there are several kinds of boundary situations or experiential challenges, one or more of which have been a part of the life of individuals. Usually a vow has been taken that if the particular crisis is resolved, the deity will receive a special offering. Sometimes, however, the pilgrim is still seeking resolution of the crisis when the vow is offered. Illnesses have been overcome; examinations have been passed; job situations have improved. A young father whose infant son was seriously ill vowed two years earlier that if the child recovered, he would carry vessels of milk from his small shop in northern Kuala Lumpur to Batu Caves during Tai Pūcam for three consecutive years.[23] A university girl vowed to engage in *pāl kāvaṭi* if she passed her exams, and the stress of worrying about these and her mother's health was reduced;[24] accordingly, she went under the tutelage of a lay adviser and experienced trance at the appropriate time so she could carry her offering of milk. A university student from a plantation vowed to perform *kāvaṭi* if his father was healed from a life-threatening illness; the young man felt he was not ready to assume his family's financial responsibilities in the event of his father's death.[25] Such instances could be multiplied by the hundreds. Vows are taken for a year, three years, or a lifetime, often because a crisis has been resolved, but sometimes until an appropriate resolution to the crisis is made.

At the same time, many participants, especially those who engage in the more extreme forms of wounding, use the ritual as something of a rite of passage. It becomes an opportunity to demonstrate mastery of a difficult enterprise, self-worth, and, even more important, the capacity to evoke the miraculous grace of the deity. Indeed, participants speak of the experience as being life transforming, as the high point of their lives, and as the visitation of divine grace (*aruḷ*).

Both men and women participate in the sacred wounding, and participants come from various walks of life. They include some middle-class Hindus, some Sikhs or other non-Hindu Indian Malaysians, occasionally Chinese, and, even more rarely, foreigners. One foreigner who spoke of the experience of bearing *kāvaṭi* with hooks in the body as life transforming, nevertheless, did participate in the event from a context in which he was experiencing both frustration in the workplace and chronic health problems.[26] For most of these participants, even if relatively educated or well off, a sense of need brings them to the experience.

Yet many of the pilgrims who engage in the more rigorous forms of sacred wounding are young (eighteen to thirty), not a few of whom are college students, some of them finding in these vows a way of affirming their Hindu/Tamil identity. Some observers note that the majority of such participants are drawn from the working-class Tamil population,[27] many of them with a plantation background, either still living in rural settings or relatively new to an urban working environment. That is, these are often persons who feel economically or politically marginalized. Several factors feed into this sense of marginalization in the contemporary context.

Economic Factors

The first set of relevant data indicates the economic plight of Indian Malaysians (of whom 80 percent are Tamils) is critical. By the end of the New Economic Plan, initiated in 1969 and ending in 1990, 1.2 percent of Malaysia's wealth was in the hands of

Indians, as compared to 19.8 percent in the hands of Malays and other indigenous peoples (Bumiputras) and 32.6 percent in the hands of Chinese Malaysians.[28] Of the Indian earners, the most affluent 10 percent of the Indian population received 33.2 percent of the total Indian income, while the lower 80 percent of Malaysian Indians received less than 50 percent of the income earned by the Indian community.[29] As of 1979 (the most recent figures available), 60 to 70 percent of all Indian households lived below a hypothetical poverty line of seven hundred Malaysian dollars annual income.[30] In 1975, 75.4 percent of all Indians employed worked as manual laborers, while another 12.2 percent were unemployed.[31] Further, between 1950 and 1985 the percentage of Indians working in agricultural production declined from 50 percent to 32 percent, and those in industrial production rose from 25 percent to 36 percent.[32] That is, an increasing number of the Indian Malaysians are first-generation urbanites born into working-class families whose salaries remain marginal and are scarcely keeping up with inflation. Those who remained on estates have experienced even more economic hardships in this period. While estate workers received a 10 percent raise in income between 1979 and 1986, inflation actually increased by 32 percent in that period;[33] further, a rubber tapper's real wages had declined by 7 percent between 1960 and 1981, while productivity actually rose by 12.8 percent.[34] A 1984 survey of Malaysian plantations found that nine of ten households had children aged between six and fifteen working. Usually these worked for the parents and received no direct wage. Nonetheless, 60 percent between the ages of ten and twelve in rubber estates were so employed, and 60 percent between ages six and ten in the palm estates.[35]

Identity Factors

This generation of Tamil workers are the descendants of Tamils brought to the plantations as indentured servants or as part of the *kaṅkāṇi* system in the mid- to late 1800s and whose treatment and fortunes have been well documented.[36] The class system established on the estates had replaced the caste system of South India, with the European overlord at the top and the chief *kaṅkāṇi* (recruiter, foreman) or *kirāṇi* (clerk, accountant) serving as mediator for the British owners. These *kirāṇi*s were upper-class Indians who knew both Tamil and English, usually Tamil *piḷḷais,* Ceylon Tamils, or Malayalis. Working-class Tamils had access to Tamil schools up to the sixth grade and to the shrines, primarily shrines to Māriyammaṉ, but also to Maturai Vīraṉ, Muṉiāṇṭi, and other attendants, depending on caste and geographical background.

The Tamil schools available on the plantation were often understaffed and poorly equipped and usually had the result of inhibiting mobility into wider Malaysian society. Indeed, as one critic put it, these schools often taught a hidden curriculum of "unquestioning respect for authority" and had become instruments of "labourer control in the hands of planters."[37]

Many of the historical elements of estate life remain part of the persona of newly urbanized working-class Tamils, including elements of folk religious practice and self-image. Beginning to fade from this persona, however, is the systematic use of Tamil language and particularly the ability to read and write it. Since the government mandated the adoption of Bahasa Malay as the national language of Malaysia in 1971, opportunities for studying Tamil systematically have diminished. Hence a perceived need has arisen to engage in activities and/or opportunities that are thought to reflect that Tamil heritage. The practice of religion remains an important part of that effort.

This leads to the further consideration that engaging in various activities of Tai Pūcam, including those associated with wounding, becomes a means of perpetuating and enacting self-understandings. Precisely what Tamil identity means, however, is part of what is being negotiated during Tai Pūcam, for the festival falls right along the fault lines of the Indian community's self-definition. These matters will be discussed further later. For the moment, suffice it to say that another of the factors impelling working-class vow takers to participate in forms of trance and wounding is the perception that participation in these forms of religious practice acts out a sense of Tamil Hindu identity in the face of the Indian establishment's different sense of the nature of Hindu *bhakti;* in the face of the government's insistence on a national Malaysian identity; in the face of a Malay Islamic majority presence in the country, together with resurgent forms of Islamic religious expression; and not least of all, in the face of a virulent form of evangelical Christianity seeking conversions on the estates. To participate in Tai Pūcam is perceived to be Hindu, Tamil, and faithful to one's heritage.

Gender Factors

A visible feature of Tai Pūcam participation is the presence of women in the penitential parade. A young girl, no more than eight or nine, dances in trance by the riverbank, her tongue and cheeks skewered with small lances, while her parents stand nearby with some trepidation and not a little pride. Three girls of college age have just completed a pilgrimage for the third straight year into the upper shrine at Batu Caves. They had just walked from Kuala Lumpur with their mother with milk offerings. They chat among themselves, in English, as a Western observer eavesdrops: they conclude that the experience has been "psychologically" good for them even though they had resisted their mother's wishes to do this at first. Another young woman, exhausted and drawn, has just arrived in the upper shrine. Attached to her fingers are tiny vessels filled with milk. She had just crawled on elbows and knees for several furlongs and up the 272 steps. She now looks into the eyes of her husband and mother-in-law accompanying her with a telling gaze. She has proven her mettle to them, has done all they expected her to do by way of becoming pregnant with a first child. Other women, dressed in yellow saris and wet from the water poured on them at the river well,[38] have joined the penitential procession. Some carry *pāl kāvaṭi,* and many are entranced; a few smoke cigars and dance bawdily as if possessed by Muṉiāṇṭi.[39] These women represent the presence of vow takers with their own gender-based concerns to be added to those factors already identified. Again, many, though by no means all, of these young women come from backgrounds rooted in the plantation economy and its value systems, nonetheless representing generational changes with still-emerging newer roles for working-class women.

Studies confirm that women have fared considerably worse than men in the rural economy. The migration of Indian women began to rise after the late 1920s. By 1957, women contributed 47 percent of the plantation workforce, and as of 1969, 80 percent of Indian women who worked were doing so in agricultural pursuits.[40] By 1947, of 50,068 women workers in the rubber industry, 81 percent were tappers while the rest were reported to be in supervisory positions.[41] Moreover, the United Planting Association of Malaysia in 1946 recommended women be paid fifty-five cents a day, while men be paid seventy cents a day.[42] Women had less access to health and educational opportunities and generally worked primarily out of economic necessity.

Women also continue to have the major responsibility for household chores and for purveying the tradition to children. One study of Indian women on a plantation indicated 90 percent of the women had sole responsibility for all household activities; 85 percent of the women surveyed were married; 81 percent lived in households averaging 5.9 members; 65 percent had more than five children; 78 percent practiced no form of family planning; 54 percent of them had encountered some health complications either at a prenatal or postnatal period; another 49.8 percent fed their husbands and children the better portion of the meals and hence were experiencing various degrees of malnutrition. Of the women surveyed, 51 percent had been demoted, retrenched, or forced to accept lower wages at some time in their lives. The majority, 78 percent, claimed to have been victims of uncalled-for verbal assaults; 21 percent said they had experienced physical abuse by male workers and supervisory staff; and 9 percent said they had been raped on the plantations.[43]

The pressures on these women increased as they sought to juggle employment and household responsibilities; their menfolk were often not supportive of their employment save as it helped their family's economy. Decision making and ultimate authority often lay with the men. R. Kurian summarized the plight of the plantation women:

> Whether on the estates or in the home, she is confronted by a system of wage rates and by a division of labor that discriminates against her by the man's claim to manage the household's financial affairs and by a system of indebtedness for which she is never herself directly responsible. And yet, in almost all cases, she is the one who suffers most. Her wages are lower; she continues working long hours even when her children are full time workers; she is the one who suffers from lower nutritional levels; she suffers the loss of jewelry and dowry to pay off debts that her husband has accumulated; and she suffers the violence when her husband objects to her protests about what she endures."[44]

Indian families have been leaving the plantations over the last generation (replaced by Javanese and Filipino workers) and have sought work in Kuala Lumpur. While the lot of the women may have improved somewhat, many of their older patterns have persisted among the working classes, exacerbated by unemployment or underemployment. It is in this historical context that the penitential rites of Tai Pūcam take on added significance for the female participants. Mothers want their girls to have it better than they; girls long for upward mobility and enhanced power both in marriage and in the workplace; husbands and mothers-in-law want their wives and daughters-in-law to bear children; wives in turn seek redress from such pressures. The parade of Tai Pūcam becomes a way to make a public statement about one's self-worth and the capacity to master trying situations. Given these considerations, it is not surprising that women are a significant part of the Tai Pūcam parade.

Contextual Boundaries

Such personal agendas as are described above are shaped and modified by the total context in which people are set. The vow taking and total significance of Tai Pūcam in Malaysia are no exception. The festival must be seen in the context of the historical, political, social, and cultural factors operative in Malaysia. It would not be an overstatement to say that the dynamics of Tai Pūcam participation are enactments of the place Indians negotiate for themselves in the west Malaysian peninsula. Some aspects of this economic, historical, and political context have been intimated above. A detailed discussion of these dimensions is beyond the scope of the present chapter, but some summary comments are appropriate.

In brief, it may be said that individuals participating in Tai Pūcam do so in a complex social dynamic that operates at both a micro and macro level. This dynamic is one that finds support and affirmation within certain social configurations at both the micro level and macro level and, at the same time, reacts against certain social and political configurations at both the micro and the macro levels.

Individual vow takers in Tai Pūcam are not mere loners or iconoclasts who operate in isolation. Rather, virtually every participant is part of a network and is surrounded, in the procession, by representatives of at least one support group. One of those support groups, as we have seen, is the family, though often the penitent is acting out a request for greater respect and power within the family. The social group may be the peer group—friends who help ease the burdens of penitential activity—or a group that has been undergoing training for the event under the tutelage of a guru. More implicitly, the network of which the individual is a part may be one associated with caste, economic class, and other intimations of being a minority within a minority.

Some remnants of caste remain in the activities of Tai Pūcam. This is so even though many of the younger generation either claim to have forgotten their caste backgrounds or are the product of intercaste marriages over several generations, and even though, on the surface, the festival is a unified, pan-Indian religious celebration. Plantations had been characterized by a four-tier hierarchy. At the top was the European overlord or his owner-successor, who had often been expected to serve as patron of religious festivals and distribute *pracāṭam* after ritual events to demonstrate his hegemony and overlordship. Under this proprietor were the chief *kaṅkāṇi* (recruiter, foreman) and *kirāṇis* (clerks and accountants); the former was usually a member of the caste being recruited; the latter role was filled by somewhat Westernized English-speaking persons who could nonetheless speak the Tamil language of the laborers. These persons were generally *piḷḷais*, Malayali nayars, or Ceylonese Tamils, all of whom also acted as go-betweens in other contexts as well—for railway and construction workers, for example. At the third tier were people of caste sometimes categorized as *śūdras* who generally engaged in agricultural work. These included *kauṇṭars*, *tēvars*, *reddiars*, and *karuvoors*. Also included in this category were those engaged in skilled labor such as *vaṅnārs* (washermen), *anbattars* (barbers), and others in small numbers. The fourth category, generally recruited from the ranks of the *dalit* or *adidravida* communities, were unskilled laborers—for example, *paraiyars* (scavengers), *cakkalis* (leather workers), and *kuruvars* (gypsies and trinket sellers).[45]

In the plantation context, the established temples were usually those of Māriyammaṉ, perceived as the goddess of rain or agriculture as well as protectoress from smallpox. The temples were usually established in the name of the *kaṅkāṇi* or *kirāṇi* (often *a piḷḷai* or *vēḷāḷa*) in quasi-alliance with the casted communities, especially *tēvars* and *kauṇṭars*. This quasi-alliance between *vēḷāḷas* such as *piḷḷais* and other agricultural groups such as *tēvars* had been present in certain Māriyammaṉ temples in South India, especially in Tanjore District, from where many of these plantation workers had come.[46] In the plantation context, however, the *kaṅkāṇis* and *kirāṇis* maintained power in the temples, just as they did in the estates, through the management and fund-raising committees. The *dalit* groups had not always had access to some of the Māriyammaṉ temples on the plantation until the postwar era. These groups generally maintained worship of their attendant deities. Certain *dalits*, for example, as well as the more highly placed *kaḷḷars* and other nonagricultural "slasher" communities, were said to be worshippers of Kāḷiyammaṉ.[47] Indeed, Kāḷiyammaṉ temples were usually to be found in those places—boundary areas—where clearing and construction were to be done on the fringes of urban zones.[48] Similarly, other *dalits* were said to worship Maturai Vīraṉ or Muṉiāṇṭi. In the early 1900s in the plantation context, however, only the *kaṅkāṇis* were permitted to go into trance to represent the goddess Māriyammaṉ, while *dalit* groups had access to possession only by their own deities.[49]

As the plantation economy changed and workers became unionized and later began to leave for the cities to seek work, leadership patterns also changed. The urban Māriyammaṉ temples began to reflect these shifting patterns. As early as 1928 a group known as the Hindu Mahājana Sangam was formed on the premises of the Mahāmāriyammaṉ Temple in Kuala Lumpur; the group started a civil suit and, in 1930, won a court order permitting them to become the managers of the temple, albeit under the name Śrī Mahāmāriyammaṉ Temple.[50] This decision effectively removed the *piḷḷai* family theretofore responsible for temple management into an otiose position of "stanikar" and gave to the *tēvars* and their allied groups de facto control of the temple. Part of the management structure established at the same time was the institution of the *ubayam* (patronage groups). These *ubayams* are composed of Tamils of South Indian origin who constitute employment groups such as smiths, merchants, writers, masons, or workers of specific departments or industries (e.g., Malaysian AirSystem).[51] These *ubayams* are more nearly occupationally or class-based groups that, nonetheless, are the inheritors of the old caste structures insofar as smiths, for example, often were the descendants of a particular caste that used to do the work of smiths.

The relevance of these considerations for the celebration of Tai Pūcam at Batu Caves is severalfold. The festival is primarily sponsored, planned, and managed by the Śrī Mahāmāriyamman̲ Temple of Kuala Lumpur, which thereby maintains authority over the festival as well as much of the religious life of Kuala Lumpur. This gives to *tēvars* and their allies considerable hegemony, including a negotiated participation by those groups once considered *adidravidas*. Such groups perpetuate the worship of Mun̲iāṇṭi and Maturai Vīran̲, even while having access to trance and possession by deities who were once deemed the sole right of upper-class communities.

The Śrī Mahāmāriyamman̲ Temple is reluctant for several reasons to alter the kinds of religious wounding done at Tai Pūcam that are deemed excessive by intellectual Hindus. The festival in its present form perpetuates the relative control of the temple over rural and working-class communities and embodies a de facto alliance with these groups. Not least important, it generates considerable revenue for the temple. At the same time, temple management negotiates participation and support from the other power brokers of the Indian Malaysian scene. The Malaysian Indian Congress, for example, is regularly wooed in order to get leverage and funds from the government.[52] Indeed, the federal government has provided matching funds for renovation both to the Mahāmāriyamman̲ Temple and its Batu Caves complex. Other Hindu groups, most notably the Malaysian Hindu Sangam, maintain ties with the government in order to get help, including funds for renovations and permissions for priests from India to enter the country with long-term visas.

On the one hand, participation in penitential activities acts out and affirms a variety of social relationships at the micro and macro levels: family, caste, or quasi-caste identities; reciprocities with the new leadership of the Hindu communities; and a sense of being Tamil and religious in at least some aspects of the tradition of plantation and South Indian life. On the other hand, such flagellants are often acting in ways that defy the expectations of a significant portion of Malaysian society. In the first place, the Indian community itself is divided regarding what is the most appropriate way to express one's Hindu beliefs. Within the Indian community, Chettiyars, the earliest worshipers of Taṇṭāyutapān̲i in Malaysia, and among the early supporters of Tai Pūcam, remain generally unimpressed by and distanced from the more extreme forms of penitential participation. The same is true of the Ceylon Tamils who have been consistently patrons of Subramaṇia in the form they have brought from their home district in the Jaffna Peninsula. The Chettiyars had come as money lenders and tended to remain relatively insular and orthoprax. Ancestors of the Sri Lankan Tamils, for their part, had taken advantage of Western education established in the mid-1800s in Jaffna, then took civil service exams (often failing to get jobs in Sri Lanka but finding them in the Malay Straits). These had come as clerks and English-speaking assistants to the British. Their descendents work in the professions and tend to remain religiously orthodox followers of Śaiva Siddhāntha. Similarly, the handful of brahmins to be found in the Kuala Lumpur area, themselves groping for ways to express authentic Hinduism, for the most part (despite such exceptions as noted in chapter 5), think that possession and wounding are not forms of *aruḷ* (the grace of god) but rather of *marul* (delusion, confusion, ignorance, even madness). A whole range of anglicized Indians continue to be active in efforts to reform, modify, or eliminate practices deemed to be excessive, not by governmental intervention (all agree that would be a mistake) but by attempts to "educate" participants.

One such attempt will illustrate this attitude. The Rudra Devi Samaj of Kuala Lumpur arranged to set up a booth on the grounds of Batu Caves during the festival of 1991. This group is composed largely of young professionals who meet regularly for study and the uplift of the Indian community. Their adviser, Śiva Śrī Muta Kumara Śivachariar, prepared a two-page leaflet in English, which the group distributed from their "truth booth" during the festival. The tract attempts to distinguish between the bearing of *kāvaṭi* as an authentic form of penance addressed to Murukaṉ and the "degeneration" associated with the practice today. The swami and his followers critique the use of skewers as "un-Hindu" because (1) the body is considered a sacred temple in Hinduism and ought not to be violated, (2) blood ought not be spilled on temple premises, (3) God is merciful and does not take satisfaction in a devotee's pain, and (4) the carrying of *kāvaṭi* has become too much a spectacle and demonstration of a devotee's prowess and not a "highly symbolic and philosophical act."[53]

A significant consideration in this dispute, quite apart from the question of political and religious hegemony within the Indian community, is the character of Indian/Hindu/Tamil identity. Educated elites, including those anglicized Tamils identified above but also including the 20 percent of the Indian Malaysian population that is non-Tamil, seek to distance themselves from the common perception of Tamils as "keling." The history of the term "keling" is unclear,[54] but Tamils themselves believe it denotes "low status," drunkenness, uncouth behavior, and dark and dirty demeanor.[55] The terms "Tamil," "Indian," and "Hindu" have different connotations in Malaysia, and Tai Pūcam falls right at the junctures of these connotations—a Sri Lankan Tamil, for example, would rather not be identified with the kind of "Tamil" or "Hindu" who engages in the flesh-skewering activities of Tai Pūcam.

These renegotiations of identity have been exacerbated by the larger landscape of Malaysian politics and society. An important dimension of this landscape is the visibility in the economic arena of the Chinese minority (35 percent of the population and of the wealth) and the political visibility of the Malay majority. The Malay population is represented in the dominant party in Malaysian politics, UMNO, which nonetheless seeks to maintain its power by garnering support from the Indian and Chinese minorities. Indians perceive Malays to receive favored treatment in many arenas—political appointments, mandated appointments in industries, scholarships for study abroad, and a host of other ways. The establishment of Bahasa Malay as the national language and its mandated use in 1971 as the lingua franca in all public schools (including universities) meant Tamils had to compete in Malay language with persons whose mother tongue was Malay. It also meant opportunities for systematic study of the Tamil language were sharply reduced, resulting in a generation of Indian youth who often can speak Tamil but cannot read or write it. Not the least important element of the Malaysian landscape affecting Indian identity is the resurgence of a more visible, puritanical Islam fueled by a variety of factors: alienation caused by the uneven distribution of wealth even among Malays in the capitalist Malaysian economy; reaction against perceived Western hegemony in the global economy; growing familiarity with and appreciation for the experiments in Islamic nationalism tried elsewhere (for example, Iran); the very propensity in a pluralistic society to redefine oneself; a perception that the nominally Islamic government has excluded more conservative Islamic groups from opportunities for power; and others.[56]

These elements of the Malaysian sociopolitical landscape lead to a strategy of distantiation and of accommodation by the Indian minority. On the one hand, there is the will to reassert, usually through religious expression, the nature of one's Indian/Hindu/Tamil identity against the majority culture. On the other hand, there is a subconscious co-opting of certain features of an Islamic culture. Friday noon, for example, has become the most common time during the week for religious meetings among Hindus. Similarly, the celebration of Tai Pūcam is increasingly taking on the character of a Hindu/Indian counterpart to the Malay/Muslim celebration of Hari Raya and the fast of Ramaḍān. That is, it may be no coincidence that Tai Pūcam is increasingly the conclusion of a "festival season" celebrated by Indians in Malaysia, which season stresses the necessity of fasting and other austerities leading up to the activities of Tai Pūcam itself. Similarly, the fact that Chinese occasionally participate in Tai Pūcam penitential activity is said to be an indication of the festival's popularity and acceptability. It is even possible that certain features of the penitence—including the use of long lances and other paraphernalia—may have been borrowed from Chinese popular religion.[57] At the least, the use of trance by spirit mediums, forms of self-flagellation, incense, and other symbols of possession among the Chinese serves to support, at least implicitly, the belief of working-class Tamils that these ritual techniques have universal efficacy.

To summarize this discussion, a push-pull dynamic is at work between the flagellating participants in the Tai Pūcam festival and their social contexts at both a micro and macro level. At the micro level, they are part of a family or peer group that is supportive during the festival procession, but to whom the individual pilgrim is obliged to prove himself or herself. At the macro level, they function as participants of certain (often lower) strata of Indian Malaysian society often at odds with anglicized Indian Malaysian "intellectuals" and in contradistinction to the larger communities of Muslim Malays or Chinese, from whom, nonetheless, they appear to borrow certain accretions. The boundaries become both exacerbated and blurred.

Physiological Factors

It is clear that, in addition to the personal and contextual factors discussed above, the trance and wounding experience of certain pilgrims during Tai Pūcam stretch the body beyond its normal "boundaries." Something clearly occurs that is physiological in nature. While the personal and social considerations will have their particular forms in the Tai Pūcam context, I believe both personal and social factors will be present in virtually *all* the experiences of trance found in religious contexts. So also, the physiological factors involved in the trance experience will have their particular manifestation in Tai Pūcam but are salient to all experiences of trance.

A vast literature on the phenomena of trance and "spirit possession" describes it in psychological, psychopharmacological, neurophysiological, or neuropharmacological terms. Considerable attention has been given to the role of hypnosis and dissociation in the phenomenon of trance. Elizabeth Collins, for example, has offered an extended discussion of the role of hypnosis and dissociation in the celebration of Tai Pūcam in Penang, Malaysia.[58] It is not my intention here to review or replicate this discussion. My concern here is simply to affirm that *one* of the elements present in trance experiences such as those that occur during Tai Pūcam is physiological and to explore the salience of one possible explanatory hypothesis. The hypothesis I wish to explore is a neurophysiological one employed by a group of medical anthropologists, psychiatrists, and others. These include Charles Laughlin, Barbara Lex, Eugene d'Aquili, and Colleen Ward.

A Neurophysiological Model

This experience of entering trance at Tai Pūcam appears on the surface to be consistent with the hypothetical model developed by some medical anthropologists in discussions of the neurophysiology of altered states of consciousness. This model, first presented in 1975 and refined thereafter by Eugene d'Aquili, Charles Laughlin, and others, sought to explain the attainment of altered states of consciousness by integrating W. R. Hess's ergotropic-trophotropic model with the split-brain research emerging from the work of R. Ornstein, R. W. Sperry, J. E. Bogen, C. Travarthan, and others.[59] This model may be summarized in its simplest terms by indicating that there is believed to be a distinction in the central nervous system between the ergotropic, or energizing, subsystem of nerves and the trophotropic, or relaxing, subsystem of nerves. Each of these subsystems is said to cause the secretion of hormones and other physiological changes. Neurochemicals such as melatonin, serotonin, dopamine, and cortisol are believed to activate parts of the parieto-occipital region of the brain in various ways. Depending on the nature and combination of such chemical influences, various sensations are engendered, including quiescence, trance, and/or a sense of unitary wholeness. In actual trance and other forms of intense excitation, both the ergotropic and trophotropic subsystems are thought to be operative at the same time. D'Aquili, for example, argues that both sides of the brain (the right side being tied to trophotropic and the left to ergotropic) are activated while both of these neural subsystems are discharging. The result of these mixed discharges, at their height, is expressed, as Barbara Lex puts it, "in the form of chronic or intense excitation, physiological states such as orgasm and rapid eye movement (REM), or paradoxically, sleep; learned behaviors, including Zen and Yogic meditation and ecstatic states; and pathological states such as experimental and clinical neurosis, psychosomatic disorders, and psychosis."[60]

This neurophysiological phenomenon is said to be "entrained" by "driving mechanisms" such as external stimuli.[61] A. M. Ludwig (1966) had earlier enumerated five major strategies for the induction of altered states of consciousness: (1) increase in exterceptive stimulation (auditory, visual, olfactory)—for example, rhythmic drumming, chanting, singing, dancing, and burning of incense and pungent herbs; (2) reduction in such stimuli (fasting, sexual continence, deprivation of light, etc.); (3) increased alertness; (4) decreased alertness; (5) and the presence of psychosomatic factors such as those hypothesized by Lex, d'Aquili, and others.[62]

The result of these stimuli and somatic changes is said to be expressed in the symptoms of ritual trance: shaking and trembling; changes in speech and facial expression; pupil dilation and glazed eyes; postural changes; muscular rigidity; spatial disorientation; sensation of timelessness or floating; and intense emotional response, including loss of the capacity to sense pain.[63]

This neurological hypothesis may be applicable to the trance experience of Tai Pūcam where drumming, chanting, and other external stimuli may help stimulate trance. Yet another stimulus may be olfactory, for as d'Aquili puts it, "The use of incense and other powerful fragrances directly affects the limbic system."[64] In the Tai Pūcam experience, at least two "incenses" are reported by observers as used during stages preparatory to the inducing of trance. One of these incenses as reported by Raymond Lee used during Tai Pūcam at Batu Caves is *campirāṇi* (benzoin, anglicized as *sambrani*), which is apparently derived from a gum resin found in the benzoin tree (*styrax benzoin*) or the *nytta* tree of Africa (*parkia biglandulosa*). It also appears to be derived from the *salai* tree, found in Malaysia. In folk etymology, *campirāṇippotu* (the pla̧cing of *campirāṇi*) evokes the descent of a spirit into a person.[65] Priests speak of the effects of breathing the fumes of *campirāṇi* to be very "powerful," but chemical analysis of the substance remains incomplete.

Another incense, reported by Elizabeth Collins as used in Penang, is camphor (*kapur* in Malay).[66] Camphor is a tough, gumlike crystalline compound ($C_{10}H_{16}O$) obtained from the wood and bark of the evergreen camphor tree (*cinnamomuim camphora*). Chemical studies of the effect of camphor on human beings have yielded interesting results. Once used as a stimulant in clinical medicine and certain preparations intended for ingestion, it is now banned from the American market, for internal use, though it is still a common ingredient in liniments, ointments, and nasal decongestants. The ingestion of two grams of camphor, it is now known, can produce dangerous effects in an adult human, including epileptiform convulsions, depression of the central nervous system, and even death.

Ingesting or inhaling camphor in smaller quantities can result in less-severe symptoms within five to ninety minutes. These include nausea and vomiting, a feeling of warmth, and headache. Most interesting, from the point of view of this inquiry, is the capacity of camphor to cause "confusion, vertigo, excitement, tremor, delirium and hallucination; increased muscular excitability, tremors and jerky movements."[67]

These results of camphor use, of course, leave several questions unanswered relative to its potential use in inducing trancelike states. When camphor burns, for example, its chemical character changes and its toxic effects presumably are mitigated. Further, some persons appear to enter trance during Tai Pūcam spontaneously when no camphor fumes are present. Conversely, priests and other mentors appear to have access to camphor fumes without experiencing its deleterious effects. Not least important, the use of camphor and other such materials alone do not account for the total experience and significance of Tai Pūcam and its trance. Nonetheless, this pharmacological dimension of the trance experience does seem to warrant further investigation of ritual substances such as *vibhuti* (the ash of burned cow dung, which some local Indian physicians suggested may help staunch the flow of blood because it contains calcium) and *kaṅkaṇam* (turmeric root), both used commonly during Tai Pūcam.

Whatever one decides about the applicability of this model to the trance experience, it is insufficient in itself to explain the meaning and significance of the phenomenon. In fact, most of those who have espoused this neurological model of the physiology of "altered states of consciousness" insist that social and cultural context is essential for understanding the content and meaning of these experiences.

Colleen Ward, for example, argues that this neurosomatic profile, outlined above, is consistent with the trances practiced during Tai Pūcam. Nonetheless, like Lex, d'Aquili, and other of the medical anthropologists, she insists that the meanings associated with these physiological occurrences must be derived from the cultural context. Possession, for example, is seen to be a form of trance. Yet, building on I. M. Lewis's work, she agreed that central or ritual possession (in contrast to peripheral possession) is valued by at least some segments of society and supports those segments' moral, political, and religious assumptions. Ritual possession, she suggests, is a "temporary, desirable, generally voluntary, and usually reversible form of trance exhibited in the context of religious ceremonies and attributed to the power of sympathetic spirits."[68]

Thus, ritual trance and possession, she concurs, are not only dependent on physiological factors but also involve psychosocial factors: expectations, beliefs, suggestion, costuming, group participation, and so on—all may affect trance induction.[69] Similarly, learning and socialization are necessary ingredients to the individual's readiness to enter trance and are an important part in interpreting it.

In sum, whatever the plausibility of the neurological model posited by the Laughlin-d'Aquili school, the phenomena associated with ritual trance cannot be interpreted exclusively in physiological terms; to do so would be a form of medical reductionism and leaves unexplored a host of elements present in a festival like Tai Pūcam. These include the personal, cultural, economic, and political factors we have just discussed and the religious dimensions we explore next.

Religious and Ideological Considerations

Despite (and perhaps because of) all the elements that make Tai Pūcam a pageant and a political performance, the festival is perceived quintessentially to be a religious event. It is the religious and ideological context that affords the event its meaning and significance. These religious factors provide a sense of history and of being rooted in antiquity even while they are reflective of the contemporary sociopolitical moment. These factors need only be summarized here.

One begins with the experience of possession and trance itself. Possession by the deity, especially by Murukaṉ, was described in early Tamil literature as a viable, if not preferred, way to gain access to the deity's presence.[70] In rural South India to this day, the deity is understood more likely to become manifest in a person than in iconic form. The visitation of the deity is believed to be the deliverance of grace (*aruḷ*), and the "fact" that the visited vow taker feels neither pain nor weariness while possessed is deemed proof of the occurrence of a miracle. The offering of incense (*cāmparāṇippotu*) is considered an act that invokes the descent of a deity's spirit on a person.[71] Many entranced persons have spoken later of the moment of trance as the high point of their lives, when their consciousness was totally subsumed into that of the divine, at least as selectively remembered.

Vow fulfillment similarly has a long history in Hindu and Tamil religious practice. More particularly, the bearing of *kāvaṭi*s was associated with worship at Paḻaṉi and given mythical sanction in the primordial devotion of Iṭampaṉ, the first devotee presumed to have worshipped Murukaṉ at Paḻaṉi. It is probable that the ancestors of current pilgrims to Batu Caves, who came largely from Tanjavur and surrounding districts in Tamil Nadu, followed an agricultural cycle that freed them for pilgrimage to Paḻaṉi at the time of Tai Pūcam (that is, shortly after the rice harvests associated with Poṅkal). Moreover, vow taking was commonly practiced subsequently on the Malaysian plantations, though these vows were usually fulfilled to Murukaṉ or Māriyammaṉ at shrines nearer to the respective plantations.[72] The fulfillment of the vows is intended to bring an individual to a place of acceptance and relatedness to the deity in a way that replicates the summum bonum of the *bhakti* experience, when the devotee experiences the divine in a manner that transcends speech and cognition. The voiceless of Malaysian Indian society clearly believe that they too can have access to the divine through the fulfilling of such vows and that this experience is in the tradition of *bhakti* devotionalism. At the same time, such vows have a public character, as if the taker embodies his or her acceptability to the divine in a context where worthiness may be publicly displayed.

Pilgrimage is a part of this religious enactment. While Batu Caves is only indirectly understood to be a *tīrtha* in the classical sense, the tradition has developed that Batu Caves is the place to be on Tai Pūcam in Malaysia. The first planting of a bamboo *vēl* by the discoverers of Batu Caves in 1891 is perceived to have been an act of worship engendered by the very awesomeness of the site. Pilgrims speak of miracles that have occurred here, not least of them healings. Clearly, the shrine of Murukaṉ is elevated as all such shrines to Murukaṉ must be, and as are most of those built to Taṇṭāyutapāṇi by Chettiyars in the Malay Straits. Batu Caves, that is, participates in the aura of the *ārupaṭai,* the six sacred centers of Murukaṉ. (In fact, many of these centers are replicated with sculptures in the environs of the Batu Caves.) It seems quite plausible that once Murukaṉ is perceived to be a global deity by overseas Tamils, Batu Caves will be mythically upgraded to one of his six "global" centers. In any case, trekking to Batu Caves on this festival occasion has assumed many of the trappings of pilgrimage, complete with pageantry and pain, work and play, participation and spectation; as with much pilgrimage, there is a recentering of life, a reenactment of an authenticating *arché,* and an embodying of one's basic identity.

These dimensions of pilgrimage and *bhakti* are given sanction by myth. All the deities brought to Malaysia by earlier Indian immigrants are integrated into the cultus of Batu Caves. Māriyammaṉ, as represented by the trustees and patrons of Śrī Mahāmāriyammaṉ Temple, is the mother of Murukaṉ here. The Murukaṉ of Batu Caves is the ascetic, penitent god known at Paḻaṉi and to Chettiyars as Taṇṭāyutapāṇi, to Ceylon Tamils as Subramaṇia, the brahminized god of the Jaffna Peninsula, and to the *adidravidas* of the working classes as the god accessible to all persons as mediated not by brahmins but by *paṇṭārams*. At the same time, deities such as Muṉiāṇṭi, Kāḷiyammaṉ, Maturai Vīraṉ, and Iṭampaṉ are believed to attend the festivities by virtue of their possession of duly prepared penitents.

Like the *kāvaṭi,* the lance (*vēl*) has a special place as Murukaṉ's symbol in Tamil history, but also at Batu Caves and throughout Malaysia. Frequently, the lance was the first representation of Murukaṉ to be implanted in shrines in the straits, as it was a portable expression of the deity's power and presence. This was the case, for example, with the Chettiyar temple at Tank Road in Singapore.[73] As Indian immigrants settled, more elaborate iconography followed. Moreover, the lance or the staff (*taṇṭa*) is the focal instrument of Tai Pūcam, a festival that enacts the power of the deity to rout evil and malevolence cosmically and internally. It is no coincidence also that the lance and other of the military paraphernalia of deities such as Murukaṉ came to be revivified, albeit with special spiritual significance, at times when religious options like Islam were a part of the landscape.[74] Implicitly at least, the lance of Murukaṉ expresses for Hindus the capacity for power and spiritual integrity in the context of today's Islamicized Malaysia. One might even speculate that, for some wounding pilgrims, the use of the lance on one's own person is an attempt to render the body a purified and pacified space for the deity's presence.[75]

Summary

The ritual enacted at Tai Pūcam, then, serves at many levels to express the character of the Indian/Tamil presence in Malaysia. It is understood to represent perceptions of the Hindu tradition, especially as reconstructed by the Tamil majority within the population. Despite differences of interpretation of what Hinduism is, the festival brings together virtually all the elements of the Hindu community in ways that reflect the reciprocities between subethnic groups in that community. Those reciprocities are negotiated largely under the hegemony of the *tēvar*s and their allies, including increasingly those drawn from the *adidravida* communities who share the current leadership of the Śrī Mahāmāriyammaṉ Temple and the larger Indian community. That leadership itself indicates there has been a religious changing of the guard, as a result of which religious participation and leadership in the "establishment" are now available to those once marginalized. The festival and the season preceding it have become a national expression of the psycho-social-cultural religious space that characterizes Indian Malaysians—an Indian counterpart to the Malay Ramaḍān and Hari Raya (celebrated in March in 1991) and the Chinese New Year (celebrated for a fortnight in February). Many of the young Indian Malaysians find in religious practice (more than in language or in other cultural expressions) the primary way to act out who they are or believe they are. As with many rituals, Tai Pūcam invites participants to see, feel, even smell the tradition and to embody experientially that which they understand to be Hindu.

CHAPTER 10

Singing on the Boundaries

Bhajaṉs, *Saint Makers, and the Reinterpretation of Aruṇakiri*

Once a month, on the day that the constellation Kārttikai (Pleides) presides, a group of women in Mumbai gathers at a local temple from 9:30 to 11:00 A.M. to sing hymns from the *Tiruppukaḻ,* a masterpiece of Tamil hymnodic creativity. The group is led by Mrs. Kalyani Raghavan, who since 1981 has been teaching several scores of Tamil brahmin women the intricate nuances of this music. Musically inclined for most of her life, she discovered the *Tiruppukaḻ* in 1973, three years after moving to Mumbai from her native Tamil Nadu; she was immediately struck by the winsomeness of the music and the beauty of her guru's voice. Her guru was the Tamil singer Rajalakshmi Balasubramanyam, niece of "Delhi Raghavan," who has become known for starting *Tiruppukaḻ* song groups all over India and for creating attractive *rāgas* for the original meter. Rajalakshmi Balasubramanyam and her husband, since 1972, have taught about four hundred people in Mumbai (most of them Tamil brahmins) one hundred stanzas and thirty metrical combinations (*tālas*) of the *Tiruppukaḻ.* These students have, in turn, sung the hymns for special occasions, while four of them, including Kalyani Raghavan, have taught other students.

The first public performance of these *Tiruppukaḻ* stanzas in Mumbai by these singing Tamils was in 1975 on Vinayaka Chaturthi (the "birthday" of Mumbai's favorite god, Ganeṣa). Today these singers perform *bhajaṉs* (devotional songfests) on several occasions important to Tamils in Mumbai. Kalyani Raghavan's group, for example, comes to the Subramaṇia temple in Chembur, a subdivision of Mumbai, not only for the monthly Kārttikai celebration (the day popularly said to be the god Subramaṇia's "birthday") but also for certain annual events. January 26, for example, India's Republic Day, attracts five hundred singers, including Delhi Raghavan himself, who sing their way up the 108 steps in the temple with the one hundred plus *Tiruppukaḻ* stanzas. The group also sings on August 18, the "birthday" of Aruṇakiri, presumed composer of the *Tiruppukaḻ;* on *Āṉi Mūlam,* the day during August or September when *gurup-pūjā* (worship of one's teacher) is performed; and on main festival days of Subramaṇia or Murukaṉ, in whose honor the *Tiruppukaḻ* was first composed.[1]

What has been happening in Mumbai has been occurring in other places where Tamils have settled. In Pittsburgh, for example, for years Sunday morning *bhajaṉs,* once led by Dr. Lakshmi Swaminathan before she moved to Long Island, included the singing of selected stanzas from the *Tiruppukaḻ.* The *rāgas* and meter (*tāla*) are challenging, so it takes a while for the lay participant to learn the stanzas from a leader. Accordingly, the group of Pittsburgh singers, at first a relatively small group of Tamil brahmin women, has been supplemented by non-Tamil brahmin women, by men, as well as by other nonbrahmin professionals, both Vaiṣṇava and Śaiva. In Malaysia and Singapore, Aruṇakiri's songs have become well known enough, thanks to the performance over the years by professionals, that on some occasions, large crowds may join in the singing of a familiar *rāga,* while a guest artist is performing at special festival occasions. Very few devotional books, such as are popularly available at Hindu (and especially Śaiva) shrines, will fail to include at least one stanza ascribable to Aruṇakiri, and Tamils from all strata of society will listen at mass rallies during the singing of Aruṇakiri's hymns.

T. Arunachalam, writing of Aruṇakiri in a popular devotional booklet distributed from Singapore, puts it aptly, if with some rhetorical excess:

> His songs are sung along the length and breadth of the land [India] by scholars, bhaktas, men, women, and children, by wandering minstrels and pedlars, and by musicians in concerts. Even today his songs have helped gifted bhaktas to sing and keep order over large multitudes of people wherever millions are gathered for a temple festival. The singer begins a familiar song of Aruṇakiri and the entire mass of humanity follows and the result is a pindrop silence among a surging sea of humanity numbering a million. The cadence and rhythm, the elegance of his diction; the meaning and sweetness, the lilt and dance of his words have today such a magical effect. The choice use of Sanskrit by the saint heightens the effects.[2]

This phenomenon reflects several patterns that have become a part of the resurgence of religious and ethnic affirmation both in twentieth-century Tamil Nadu and in the diaspora. The first is the role of group singing. The *bhajaṉ* serves many functions. It provides a sense of community to like-minded persons (occasionally transcending the lines of caste) who, in the face of urban depersonalization and fragmentation, welcome the opportunity to bond. *Bhajaṉ*s express the importance of orality, speaking and hearing the "tradition," even feeling it within the body. Singing gets one in touch with the great poets and saints of the past, thereby reaffirming a sense of lineage by the re-presentation of a "giant" of one's vernacular heritage.

These *bhajaṉ*s also embody a kind of "saint making." In the context of contemporary piety, saints, poets, and other creative figures of the past are reperceived in terms that speak to the present. Like biographers of a saint, who recast the life of a saint in ways that reflect the biographer's own values, so other appropriators (like singers, commentators, and translators) are wont to perceive the saint in their own image. Both singing and saint making, in other terms, celebrate pregnant expressions of a legitimating past but also reflect the exigencies of a perceived present.

Also reflected in the rediscovery of Aruṇakiri is the role of text and performance in conveying the essence of religious and cultural identities. On the one hand, texts, expressed orally and propositionally, their being written, translated, and commented on, express something of the belief systems of the various moments when the textualizations occur. On the other hand, enactment and performance can convey the ethos of a people. Especially in the Tamil tradition, the *act*—the gift given, the deed done, a musical or dramatic presentation reperformed—is a time-honored way of expressing a community's essential nature. The reperformance of an Aruṇakiri composition is a form of ritual, and, as in any ritual, the presentation of a community's identity is experienced, lived, sensed, and reconceived. Tradition, like Aruṇakiri's work, refuses to be reduced to words.

It is no coincidence that this resurgence of interest in Aruṇakiri, and in the songfest as a devotional form, occurs in a time when increased mobility, the press of urban and professional constraints, and the increased visibility of ethnic and religious pluralism all give one the sense that one is living on the boundaries. As we have noted throughout this volume, these boundaries embody spaces and times of personal and social crisis of various kinds—transitions, migrations, the threatened loss of rootedness or personhood, and others. In just such times does the rediscovery of a saint-cum-musician from the past provide mooring.

I will return to these themes again. But first it is appropriate to offer a brief review of the poet and the process by which he has been rediscovered.

Aruṇakiri's Life: History and Perception

The reconstruction of Aruṇakiri's life is itself a reflection of the dialectic between the traditional saint and the modern saint maker. The traditional view of Aruṇakiri's life, known and assumed by many Tamils to this day and passed on from generation to generation, is based on the first written work on the life of Aruṇakiri, a romantic poetic treatise titled *Aruṇakirinātar Cuvāmikal Purāṇam.* This hagiography is said to have been written between 1865 and 1880 by a saint called Taṇṭapāṉi Cuvāmi and also known as Murukatāca Cuvāmi. This account weaves legend and myth around Aruṇakiri in such a way as to depict him as a paradigmatic Tamil poet inspired by the gods and a prototypical devotee of the god Murukaṉ. The author was a Murukaṉ *bhakta* headquartered in Paḻaṉi, a pilgrimage center of Murukaṉ just beginning to undergo renovation in the 1860s as an expression of Tamil self-consciousness and the affirmation of Murukaṉ as the quintessential Tamil god. The legend of Aruṇakiri's life as first depicted in the *Purāṇam* includes the following elements with minor variations.

Aruṇakirinātar is said to have been born and to have lived for most of his life in Tiruvaṇṇāmalai in North Arcot District on the northern fringes of Tamil country. He was born, it is said, of a courtesan or temple prostitute named Muttu. As a young man he lived the life of a profligate, delighting in the company of prostitutes and cheap friends. His inheritance was squandered by the time he reached manhood, so he turned for help to his sister, Āti, who was very fond of him despite his weaknesses. He took advantage of his sister's affection and soon exhausted her possessions—jewels, money, and property—as gifts for his prostitutes.

By now Aruṇakiri's body had lost its youthful vitality and was diseased. The better class of courtesans began to shun him and make fun of him, but his lust persisted. Yet again, he turned to his sister for funds, even though she had nothing left to give save the clothes on her back. She said to Aruṇakiri, in effect, "If your lust is so irresistible, then, here's my body. Use it to satisfy yourself."

His sister's words hurt Aruṇakiri deeply. In recognition of the miserable state to which he had come, he had no recourse but to end his own life. So he climbed the northern *kōpuram* of the Tiruvaṇṇāmalai Temple, intending to jump to his death. But at that moment the god Murukaṉ appeared as an old man, touched Aruṇakiri's tongue with his lance, and said, "Sing!" (*pāṭuṅkaḷ*). A torrent of verse rushed from Aruṇakiri's lips, the first line of which was composed and uttered by Murukaṉ himself.[3]

Several elements of this mythical account cannot be corroborated historically, though other features are based on allusions in the corpus of poetry ascribed to Aruṇakiri. The poet, for example, does refer frequently to his intense desire for women (e.g., *Kantaralaṅkāram*, stanzas 29, 30, 32, 34, 35, 40). He refers quite often to the north tower of the Tiruvaṇṇāmalai Temple as the place where he received the grace of Murukaṉ (*Tiruppukaḻ*, 540; *Kantaranapūti*, 3, 35). Whether he was in fact the son of a courtesan seems dubious because he refers to his parents, wife, and other relatives (*Tiruppukaḻ*, 392, 413, 1131) and to his mother as having good character (690). The allusions to his wife indicate he was married, though at least one passage suggests his interest in prostitutes persisted even after his marriage, for his wife is said to ridicule him for it (392).

It remains most difficult, however, to date and isolate any single individual as being the definitive Aruṇakiri and to distinguish such a historical figure from later perceptions. The traditional view, generated in the context of Tamil nonbrahmin self-consciousness, is that the poet was nonbrahmin, a possibility that seems to be suggested by several hints: the poet's apparent consumption of meat (*Tiruppukaḻ*, 26); his condemnation of brahmins for the sacrifice of goats in rituals (*Kantarantāti*, 31); and his willingness to criticize those who do not "practice what they preach" or "share their wisdom with those who ask" (*Kantaralaṅkāram*, 6). This view also seems consistent with the fact that his music was retained primarily in the households of *tācis* (temple dancers) and of *piḷḷais* who were pipers or *nātaswaram* artists.

However, brahmins have claimed Aruṇakiri as one of their own, identifying him with a famous Tintima Kavi named Aruṇakirinata, said to have been descended from a *kauta* brahmin family brought from Benares by a Koṇṭan Rājentiraṉ Cōlā and settled in Mettaipatti. This Aruṇakiri, said to have been born in 1299, is mentioned in a Sanskrit text, generally ascribed to the seventeenth century, known as the *Vipaka Patra Mālā*. Further, the brahmin argument continues, the poet was obviously completely fluent in Sanskrit and knew "from the inside" the customs of brahmins that he criticized. Problems nonetheless persist with either view inasmuch as other inscriptions and allusions suggest a discrepancy in dates. Various references in the poetic corpus (for example, in *Tiruppukaḻ*, 1056, to the Vijayanagar Pirauta Tevaraya, who ruled from 1422 to 1456) and inscriptions that may indirectly allude to Aruṇakiri (for example, one dated 1370 referring to Cōmanāta Jēyār, a name also mentioned in *Tiruppukaḻ*, 828) suggest our poet may have written during a period falling somewhere between 1350 and 1450. One also cannot rule out the possibility that more than one poet was writing under that name, a possibility made plausible by the differences in style between the *Tiruppukaḻ*, for example, and more restrained compositions such as the *Kantaranupūti* and the *Kantaralaṅkāram.*[4]

Aruṇakiri's Poetic and Religious Vision

Whatever the circumstances of the poet's life, the broad corpus of literature ascribed to Aruṇakiri is a remarkable achievement in Tamil poetics, and his verses are widely sung by Tamilians today. He was a skilled musician, best known for his use of meter and rhythm as dance accompaniment. His use of alliteration; his homophonous rhyming of the first several syllables of each line in a single poem; and his innovative use of metric repetition (*cantam*) make him, along with Kampaṉ, one of the two most skilled users of the stylistic canons of Tamil poetics. Further, for this poet, sound and meter were themselves part of his message: sound was numinous and cosmogonic, for it was the form of the divine itself.[5] Meter had cosmological and sacral implications, for rhythm was the beat of the cosmos, homologous to the dancing of his god Murukaṉ (*Kantaranupūti,* 17); similarly, the varieties of metric repetition (*cantam*) were said to be created by the dancing feet of Murukaṉ (*Tiruppukaḻ*, 1269).

More than that, Aruṇakiri's work was a significant expression of the ultimate religious vision of his time. He was the most prolific hymnist of the god Skanda-Murukaṉ in the history of Tamil literature. Yet his poetry was eclectic, knitting together the mythology of much of the Hindu pantheon, incorporating images of Viṣṇu and the goddess as well as the thought of classical Śaiva Siddhānta with many of the folk and indigenous expressions of religion in Tamil country. His verses combined conceptual and experiential, metaphysical and mythic, abstract and particular, austere and sensuous, Sanskrit, Telugu, and Tamil. He thus served to make religion accessible. He was a harbinger of the resurgence of *bhakti* in the post-Cōḻaṉ south and an exponent of a Tamil self-consciousness after a period of considerable Sanskritization.

Aruṇakiri's religious vision was rich and often paradoxical. He exulted in the experience of the divine—an experience said to be suprasensual and beyond articulation: "Be still; think not" (*Kantaranupūti,* 12) is the invitation of his deity. Yet he reveled in the images of the senses to describe the deity, the deity's exploits, and the world in which the deity cavorts. Everything was intense and vibrant for Aruṇakiri, whether it be living a worldly life or experiencing god. He identified with the common man, including the will to profligacy and the need for the basic amenities of life. He criticized the religious elite for their snobbishness and their reluctance to share what they had with others (*Kantaralaṅkāram,* 20, 51, 53, 57, 66). He romanticized the Tamil language and landscape, even while incorporating Sanskrit and Telugu idiom (cf. *Kantaranupūti,*

1, 10, 17, 29). His was a poetry fraught with apparent paradox: it celebrated the world, the human condition, and the religious experience often in passionate and sensual terms, yet it bespoke a profound quiescence, a serene space beyond the world's vicissitudes, human ambiguities, and intellectual and ethical categories.

The very paradoxes found in the poetry ascribed to Aruṇakiri stimulate the varying claims of his contemporary appropriators. Śaivite devotees find in Aruṇakiri the quintessential exponent of Śaiva Siddhānta thought and devotionalism. Especially in collections such as the *Kantaralaṅkāram* and the *Kantararanupūti,* one finds the articulation of the classic principles of Śaivism: the existence of the Lord (*pati*), the soul (*pacu*), and the bonds (*pāca*); the need for transcending the three bonds (*malas*) so that the soul (*pacu*) can be made inseparable with the lord (*pati*); and others.

Some passages, especially in the *Tiruppukal̲,* lead certain Advaitins, including Smārta brahmins, to claim Aruṇakiri as one of their own. One finds, for example, extended praise to the goddess and to Viṣṇu, as Murukan̲'s uncle and/or brother-in-law. One finds the occasional passage that appears to collapse all polarities and celebrate the unity of existence—all evidence, claim the Advaitins, that Aruṇakiri was influenced by Śaṅkara's monism and the philosopher's sense that the divine is equally present in several specific deities.[6] Aruṇakiri's multivocality and eclecticism, in short, contribute to the possibility that many people today see in him reflections of themselves.

Rediscovery of Aruṇakiri

Of special interest in the present discussion is the rediscovery of Aruṇakiri and the use of his verses in the context of contemporary Tamil devotionalism. Until the 1860s and 1870s, Aruṇakiri seems to have been known and honored by a small circle of people. Some musicians and poetic literati, of course, knew his work; his stanzas were played by *nātaswaram* pipers and sung by members of the *tāci* community (that is, the descendants of the temple dancers). Yet relatively few families, primarily of the *piḷḷai* community, had preserved some of his songs on palmyra.

In 1871 V. T. Subrahmanian Pillai, a devotee of Murukan̲, was moved at hearing some recitations of the *Tiruppukal̲* and determined to start a collection of stanzas. His collecting was continued by his sons; indeed, one of them, Chengalvaraya Pillai, who had an M.A. in Tamil literature, proceeded to arrange them in twelve sections to make them comparable to the twelve collections of the *Tevāram,* Śaivism's canon of Nāyan̲mār hymns.

Yet other scholars, both brahmin and nonbrahmin, were collecting Aruṇakiri's songs during the nineteenth and into the twentieth centuries. Nineteenth-century figures included Melavi Mahalinga Ayar, who printed one hundred stanzas in 1839, Tiravoor Subbaraya Mudaliyar (1846), and V. Pushparatha Chettiar (1888–90).[7] Aruṇakiri's popularity increased in the twentieth century, thanks in part to collections and publications done by several editors and agencies. M. R. Kanthasami Kavirayar, for example, once editor of the *Vidhya Bhanu* of Maturai, published collections of the *Tiruppukal̲* in two parts in 1933–34. A commentary on 150 stanzas was written in 1926 by a Tiruvilankam of Jaffna, Sri Lanka. More recently, Kripananta Variar, a popular Tamil Śaivite orator, has edited a collection of 1,323 *Tiruppukal̲* songs. The most comprehensive collection, said to include all of Aruṇakiri's work, was published by the Śaiva Siddhanta Mahasamajam in Madras in 1935. This edition includes 1,361 *Tiruppukal̲* songs.[8]

Increasing numbers of musicians and pundits were instrumental in popularizing Aruṇakiri's stanzas. T. M. Krishnacami Ayyar, for example, an advocate and upper-middle-class brahmin, led pilgrimages to the Murukan̲ temple of Tiruttani, gave *Tiruppukal̲* concerts throughout Tamil Nadu, and organized *Tiruppukal̲ capa*s (groups) in and around Madras City. Madurai Somu, a popular vocalist in the 1970s, was especially skillful in portraying Aruṇakiri's intricate meters in ways that engaged the very bodies of his audience. K. V. Jagannatha lectured and wrote popularly on the Aruṇakiri material; Kalyanacuntaram Ayyar, K. V. Karthikeyan, and Swami Annanandar all published material on or about Aruṇakiri in the popular press. Not least important, hosts of traditional Tamil pundits regularly lecture or rhetorically re-present or sing Aruṇakiri's stanzas throughout Tamil Nadu.

The spread of Aruṇakiri's songs beyond Tamil Nadu is aptly illustrated in the devotion and work of two men. The first was a Mysore-born brahmin, popularly known as Satchidananthan Swami, who became entranced at hearing an Aruṇakiri stanza while on pilgrimage in Pal̲an̲i in May 1908. He learned Tamil, memorized much of the *Tiruppukal̲*, and sang his verses throughout India, founding many Aruṇakiri *capa*s. By the time of his death in 1950, the swami had witnessed a virtual explosion of interest in his beloved hymns. He had established *bhajan̲* groups throughout Tamil Nadu, twelve of them in Madras City (Chennai) alone, but also in Mumbai, Delhi, and Calcutta (Kolkata).[9] The other musician instrumental in the spread of *Tiruppukal̲ capa*s outside of Tamil Nadu is a Smārta brahmin named A. S. Raghavan. Born in Mumbai, he enrolled in a Carnatic music academy there in 1942. Over the years he learned *Tirruppukal̲* stanzas from his uncle and other members of his family and began to create *rāga*s where some of the original *rāga*s had been lost. In time he set to music five hundred of Aruṇakiri's compositions, began to teach the *Tiruppukal̲* in New Delhi where he had settled, and in 1958 founded a group known as *Tiruppukal̲-an̲parkal* (*Tiruppukal̲* lovers). He or his students have subsequently started groups or offered courses primarily to Tamils, in Indian cities such as Calcutta, Bhopal, Bangalore, Hyderabad, and Mumbai, and outside of India in Toronto, Canada, and Penang, Malaysia. Proceeds for the groups' singing have been used for renovation of religious institutions, the holding of special ritual or cultural events, charitable donations, and the publishing of translations of the *Kantaranupūti* in Malayalam, Kannada, Telegu, and Hindi and of the *Kantaralaṅkāram* in Hindi.[10]

Some Implications

Milton Singer,[11] commenting on the *bhajan̲*s he observed in Madras City in the 1960s, suggested that urban songfests served three functions:

1. Providing an easier path to salvation in an age when the paths of strict ritual observances, religious knowledge, and ascetic withdrawal have become difficult or inaccessible.
2. Reducing the consciousness of caste, sect, and regional differences and the tensions generated by this consciousness.
3. Providing a philosophy of devotion for believers.

The contemporary pattern of singing Tamil *bhajaṉs* in cities such as Mumbai and Pittsburgh reflects certain aspects of Singer's functions but also considerably more. It is true that songfests are an expression of devotion, though they do not necessarily replace other forms of devotion such as participation in temple *pūjās* and festivals. To be sure, many of the *bhajaṉs* of expatriated Tamils occur in temples or public cultural spaces, suggesting that public sacred space has increasingly either replaced the home or become an extension of the home as the appropriate venue for acts of *bhakti.* Further, most of the participants in the *bhajaṉs* Singer observed a generation ago were male. Many of the overseas *bhajaṉs* groups today are composed predominately of women and are often led by women, suggesting women find empowerment and bonding in such groups in the face of the challenges expatriated women share: how, for example, is one fulfilled, especially when children are grown or professional careers leave little time for maintaining extensive patterns of traditional *pūjā?* Nor is singing a particularly new phenomenon in Tamil devotionalism—I will point out momentarily that singing is as old as *bhakti* itself. Do *bhajaṉs* "reduce the consciousness of caste"? Perhaps to a certain degree, insofar as upper-class nonbrahmins participate in the songfest with *Smārtas* and other brahmins. For such nonbrahmins, the opportunity may represent a way of being upwardly mobile. But the Mumbai groups are composed primarily of brahmins who are, in the singing, affirming their religious and subethnic kinship; further, even Singer reported that nonbrahmins admitted to him, regretfully, that the sense of egalitarianism experienced in the *bhajaṉs* did not last beyond the *bhajaṉs*.[12]

No doubt, other elements in these songfests are worth reflection. First, the experience of *bhakti* has always been, at least in the Tamil case, expressed in or accompanied by song. Second, just as contemporary singers sing "on the boundaries," so too (as I shall presently argue) has devotional singing always occurred. In addition, in those periods when devotional singing has occurred, there has been selective appropriation of past forms, reinterpretation in terms of the values of the present. In short, a dialectic between a perceived past and a perceived present takes place, a remaking of saints and musicians past, if you will. The creation of new *rāgas* for Aruṇakiri's stanzas is one way in which the saint is made contemporary for our time. A brief summation of the history of Tamil *bhakti* may illustrate this dynamic.

Perhaps it is not oversimplification to suggest that we are currently witnessing the third major era of Tamil devotionalism. The first of these eras, of course, is the well-documented "golden age" of Tamil *bhaktas* during the seventh to ninth centuries of the common era. It was ushered in with the singing of the Āḻvārs and Nāyaṉmārs, witnessed the building of temples under the aegis of the Pallavas and Pāṇṭyaṉs, and resulted in the Hinduization of Tamil country. The second was a "silver age" ushered in by Aruṇakiri himself, along with Tattuvarāyar. It was an era lasting roughly from the fifteenth through the seventeenth centuries and was characterized by the enlarging of temples and the including of folk and popular participation in temple ritual. The poetics of Aruṇakiri provided a certain inspiration for the *bhakti* spirit that persisted into the seventeenth century in the work of Tāyumāṉāvar and, to a lesser extent, that of Kumārakuruparaṉ and Kacciyappacivam.

The third era is that which started in the late nineteenth century and has been characterized by the renovation of temples, the increased incorporation of certain village deities into orthodox temple cults, and the recovery of considerable earlier *bhakti* literature. By the 1920s and 1930s, temples were opened to the previously disenfranchised; pilgrimage centers became increasingly accessible because of improved transportation facilities, and there was an explosion of festival and ritual celebrations. We are now in the second century of this era of devotionalism, which may be appropriately called "neo-*bhakti*."

It is no coincidence that each of these periods was an era in transition. Old social, religious, and political configurations were giving way to newer ones. The Nāyaṉmārs and Āḻvārs, for example, were, in significant measure, reacting against or singing in the context of a landscape largely influenced by Jain and Buddhist communities. In their early songs was a marked hostility and disaffection for Jains and Buddhists. Even so, in time there was an effort, both explicit and implicit, to reincorporate aspects of these movements that had been critiqued. In addition, there was borrowing from brahminic sources and the selective use of Sanskritic myth and idiom. Pallava temples largely emulated those of the north; mythologies of the *Tevāram* poets made frequent reference to the Epic Śiva; and *brahmadeya*s or brahminic communities became major cultural centers in the south. Yet, all the while, the poets gave to the *bhakti* experience a quintessentially Tamil cast: it evoked a celebration of Tamil land as the abode of the gods, stimulating pilgrimage to Tamil sites; gloried in the availability of the divine to the individual; alluded to a certain "classlessness" in religion; celebrated the idiom of love as a way of relating to the god; and, especially in Māṇikkavācakar, expressed the relationship to the god in terms of intoxication and madness. All of these images appear consistent with those expressed in earlier Tamil poetry. A Tamil self-presentation was thereby expressed that evoked the perceived imagery of earlier Tamil moments during a transitional period, a period moving from one social order into a more explicitly Hindu one.

A similar scenario can be articulated in *bhakti* eras two and three. Aruṇakiri's work was done in the context of considerable transition. The historians Burton Stein and Noboru Karashima speak of the thirteenth and fourteenth centuries as a transitional age. Aruṇakiri was living in a post-Cōḻaṉ period; the preceding era had witnessed relative political stability and a high degree of Sanskritization in geographical place names and in literature and thought. Aruṇakiri's was also a post-Islamic period in the sense that Muslim marauders had entered the south and had set up temporary headquarters in Maturai and other towns. Aruṇakiri's music reflected this spirit on the boundaries. His was a poetry of Hindu and Tamil romanticization, for, like the Nāyaṉmārs and Āḻvārs, he gloried in the Tamil language as the dance of the god and in Tamil country as Murukaṉ's beloved domain. Further, he incorporated into his poetry the imagery of Sanskrit, Vaiṣṇava, Śakta, and possibly to a lesser extent, Islamic motifs.

The Sanskritizations in Aruṇakiri's work are abundant and beyond dispute; the impact of Islam is much more implicit. At the very least, Aruṇakiri's style demonstrates an awareness of the images of battle and political instability. An occasional stanza, for example, used the staccato sound of racing hooves (e.g., *Kantaralaṅkāram* 92, where the hard Tamil phoneme *ṇṭ* [nd] was repeated twenty-one times) as he elevated militaristic imagery to a cosmic level in a way that reified older Śaiva themes: Murukaṉ thunders across the heavens to rout demonic forces, even as, within the poet, the god routs destructive passions (7, 43, 59, 88). But beyond the *religious* reasons underlying this imagery, there is at least a hint that it had *political* overtones as well. One scholar, Anuananda, believes references in Aruṇakiri to political "confusion" refer to circumstances around Tiruvaṇṇāmalai during the latter part of the fourteenth century, when Bokkaṉ I lost power to his commander in chief Tirumallināta. And, on the larger stage of South India, it is likely Aruṇakiri was aware of those Muslim marauders who had raided Tamil country. The times seemed appropriate for the musician to evoke Murukaṉ's militaristic imageries, as if to suggest his beloved god would vanquish the forces of instability and establish a reign of bliss. One is reminded of the Nāyaṉmārs' inclination to evoke Śiva's terrifying warrior-like attributes under similar circumstances.

But, beyond that, it is possible that when Aruṇakiri sang of the transcendent character of the divine, he was articulating a vision not only entirely consistent with Śaiva Siddhānta thought but also conscious of a Muslim understanding. In any case, whether or not such a connection is conscious in Aruṇakiri's work, most Muslims would not have been uncomfortable when the poet speaks of the god as the teacher of eternal truth (*Kantaranupūti,* 8, 11, 13, 15, 20, 36) and as the source of wisdom (17, 28, 50), or when he sings of the divine as the essence of existence (15), its goal and way (5), the elixir of immortality (28), quiescent and unmoving (9), beyond birth and death (12). He is being and nonbeing, formed and formless (51), the giver of grace (15, 33), and sustainer of the cosmos (6).

More compelling for the contemporary *bhakta* is the way Aruṇakiri weaves Vaiṣṇava themes into his religious vision. In the god Murukaṉ, Śaivism and Vaiṣṇavism are reconciled, for while he is the son of Śiva, he is son-in-law (or in some stanzas, nephew) of Viṣṇu (e.g., *Kantaralaṅkāram,* 22, 39, 41, 43, 50, 54, 90, 91, 95).

Aruṇakiri was singing on the boundaries when he appropriated virtually all that had now become a part of the Tamil landscape: the fluid use of Sanskrit idiom; imageries that may be responsive to Islam; the subtle philosophical nuances of Śaiva Siddhānta; and, not least of all, images drawn from Vaiṣṇavism and the worship of the goddess. In the spirit of the Vijayanagar era, many are invited into the temple of *bhakti.* On the one hand, Aruṇakiri was profoundly Tamil, evoking primordial identities long consistent with a Tamil spirit (whether perceived or real): sensuality, celebration of land, and openness to all of the religious experience. On the other hand, he represented an eclecticism that incorporated Sanskritic, and apparently Islamic, images and made them Tamil.

A similar process may be said to characterize the contemporary experience of Tamil *bhakti.* It was born in a colonial era. Intimations of an anti-British cast to religious devotionalism were at times explicit in the folk tales of South Indian village deities wherein various village *vīraṉ*s and Aiyaṉars are said to have done heroic feats against the English. More implicitly, the renovating of temples and other religious practices bespoke a self-conscious effort to be Hindu in the face of a Christian other. Yet the new devotionalism co-opted strategies of Christianity and has made use of technology and other trappings of the modern era.

As we have observed, many contemporary Tamils, especially those who live outside their homeland, live on the boundaries. They are obliged to self-define not only in the face of postcolonialism but also in the context of other majority cultures, be it the Hindi or Marathi of Mumbai, the Malay Islam of Malaysia, the Chinese of Singapore, or the post-Christian culture of North America. Further, in some quarters (e.g., Malaysia and North America) Tamil Hindus worry about conversion of their young to Christianity. Self-definition occurs on these boundaries through the singing of music that represents the best of a Tamil past and through the reinterpretation and re-presentation of a classical saint—especially one whose stanzas embody contemporaries' self-image.

Performance and Textualization

Finally, the dynamics of recovering a saint in the image of the present are reflected in the dialectic of performance and textualization. Both are basic ways in which Tamil self-definition is expressed; both are present in the work of Aruṇakiri and in his recovery and re-presentation.

On the one hand, Aruṇakiri's stanzas are untranslatable and irreducible to literary text. His work must be performed, played, sung, and acted out in the ambience of performer and audience. Contemporary singers put it aptly when they comment on their performing of the *Tiruppukaḻ:*

> In the beginning there was Śiva; then came *Ōm. Ōm* is the sound of the ocean, the sound of the waves. From *Ōm* came all other sound and music at the instigation of Śiva. Therefore, the cosmic rhythm is re-enacted in musical rhythm.
>
> Feel, then think; you don't understand it the first time.
>
> It's the music, not the words, that is important.

> Pitch (*surthi*) is the mother; meter (*tāla*) is the father. Meter is strict, disciplined, uncompromising; pitch is kinder, more flexible, more willing to be varied by those with a sore throat.[13]

Singing Aruṇakiri in *bhajaṉ*s, in other terms, is an experience that defies conceptualization. It is visceral, even somatic. It is no accident that Aruṇakiri's work was best known and reenacted into the twentieth century by performers—*nātaswaram* pipers who played his *rāga*s and meters and *tāci*s who sang and danced them. Aruṇakiri *bhajaṉ*s are a form of ritual. Participating in them affirms one's identity and enacts who one is. It can also be transformative, enabling the singer to enter into a closer relationship with fellow singers. It evokes a sense of rootedness even while offering, however momentarily, a new mode of being.

At the same time, of course, Aruṇakiri has been textualized in ways that further reflect nuances of self-definition. The writing, collecting, or translating of a stanza serves to refine, define, and make self-conscious understandings that once were expressed in more fluid oral and performative symbols. Once written, texts preserve, even freeze in perpetuity, perceptions and experiences that may otherwise be fleeting. Texts legitimate; they make accessible to a literate elite and invite acceptance from that literate elite that which may otherwise remain inchoate and unspoken. Texts, in short, move perceptions from the visual to the cognitive, from being experienced to being thought about. Texts "logify" the experienced reality in such a way as to make it comparable to the understanding of an outside world.

More specifically, the textualization of Aruṇakiri has elevated him to ever-growing status as an exponent of Tamil tradition. Tāyumaṉavar, for example, himself considered to be a saint, in his own work and perception presented Aruṇakiri as the paradigmatic Śaiva saint. Taṇṭapāṇi Cuvāmi, in his hagiography of Aruṇakiri, became saint maker, presenting the poet as a prototypical everyman fraught with human frailty but made saintly and poetic by inspiration of the god. In a manner consistent with the mythological tradition associated with virtually all Tamil poets, Aruṇakiri was said to be given his gift by the god. Aruṇakiri was thereby presented as paradigmatic Tamil poet/singer and the Murukaṉ *bhakta* par excellence. V. T. Subrahmaniam Pillai's collecting of Aruṇakiri's songs served to systematize and collate the work and make it accessible to the nonperformative communities, especially to a literate Tamil public. Aruṇakiri's work thus became a hymnal, at once the most extensive collection addressed to Murukaṉ and, at the least, implicitly rendered comparable to other hymnodies such as the Vedic corpus. Chengalvaraya Pillai's lifetime of organizing and commenting on Aruṇakiri took the work to a new level in the Tamil consciousness. Not only was Aruṇakiri explicitly equated to the canonical saints of the *Periya Purāṇam* by Chengalvaraya's organizing of the corpus into twelve sections, but also, as a master of arts in Tamil literature, Chengalvaraya Pillai depicted Aruṇakiri as poet and literateur, thereby bringing him to consciousness as a significant exponent of the Tamil literary tradition. Translations (or the attempts at translation) elevate Aruṇakiri's status further. Rendered into English, Aruṇakiri's work is legitimated by the "new" postcolonial international lingua franca and becomes presumably comparable to other figures of his genre. Unfortunately, no translation does justice to Aruṇakiri as poet, but Karthikeyan in his paraphrase attempts to depict him as mystic and saint on par with any in the pan-Indian tradition or with any saints in other traditions who are known to the comparer. V. S. Devasenapati, with his philosophical orientation, attempts to portray a figure who is both saint and philosopher, available for critical analysis as well as for inspiration, even to those who do not know Tamil.

The textualization of Aruṇakiri, in short, recasts him in the image of the textualizer. This textualizing serves to enhance one's ethnic self-image. The intellectual Tamil further finds that his or her visceral, ritual response to Aruṇakiri has been given a rational, intellectualized, and cognitive basis: it is okay to be Tamil, and Aruṇakiri gives one an idiom in which to both feel and think Tamil. Further, the various attempts to express Aruṇakiri in textual forms, such as collating, commenting, and translating, illustrate a pattern that has been present in the rediscovery of many of early Tamil poets and saints. Publishing, indexing, translating, and commenting on their works, even the rhetorical glorification and extolling of their presumed virtues in public orations, epitomize the nature of Tamil renaissance in the twentieth and early twenty-first century. Aruṇakiri, like other classical Tamil figures such as Appar or Tiruvalluvar, is made a model and paradigm of those values the Tamil wants to espouse in the modern world—scholar, performer, politician, as well as saint.

CHAPTER 11

Conclusion

In this volume I have examined the ritual experience of several Tamil communities living outside their ancestral homeland in the urban areas of Singapore; Kuala Lumpur, Malaysia; Mumbai, India; and Pittsburgh, Pennsylvania. In all these communities I have found an attempt to negotiate and/or maintain viable ethnic or subethnic identities while living and interacting to varying degrees with other South Asian and non-South Asian peoples. I found a virtually universal desire to establish local "spaces" in which families could maintain religious and cultural lifestyles. These spaces have served as venues, not only for worship but also for the serving of food, the display of dress, and the performance of music, lecture, and dance. These communities have sought to deal with intergenerational issues through cultural reproduction, and change with expressions that range from the reinventing of orthopraxy to various forms of hybridization.

I have claimed that these communities are all "living on the boundaries." This is so, I have argued, in many different senses, not least of all that the common boundaries of late-twentieth- and early-twenty-first-century urban life are exacerbated by the specific challenges that these communities are facing in diaspora. These include the necessity of sorting out issues of identity maintenance in the context of pluralistic settings quite removed from an ancestral homeland. This sense of boundaries may be least evident in the case of Mumbai brahmins, who, after all is said and done, may seem closer in time, space, and disposition to the patterns of their Tamil forebears. But, even in Mumbai, and perhaps especially in Mumbai with its highly commercialized and apparent cosmopolitan aura, where daily professional interactions occur with a highly diverse population, there is a perceived need to do precisely what people on boundaries do. That is, some families seek to forge a sense of community, establish spaces that they can call their own, reaffirm their humanity and personhood in the crowd, and find a way to pass on their values to their heirs.

I do not want to claim that rituals arise *only* when they are catalyzed by the kinds of boundaries identified in this volume—rather that such boundaries stimulate the propensity to ritualize. Nor do I claim that ritualizing is the *only* response, even of Tamils, to boundaries—only that for many Tamils, ritualizing serves multiple purposes in diasporic settings. Demonstrated in the preceding chapters have been some of the ways ritualizing serves these communities. These purposes are perhaps summed up by a series of dialectic oscillations: the need for continuity as well as the desire for innovation; the interactions of textualizations and performance; the discourse of ritual rules and ascribed reasons for such rituals; the propensity to distance selves from "others," yet the willingness to accommodate, even appropriate from, others; the linking of geographies from the homeland to those of the new home; and others.

Attempts at continuity are forged in these communities by reconstructing traditions and myths from pastiches of the past. Øivind Fuglerud, speaking of the Tamil refugees from Sri Lanka settling in Norway, writes, "The only way to create a coherent present is to connect it to a past through which it was produced and from there to work one's way forward to a correct image of the now which one seeks to understand. In this cognitive process 'history' is understood selectively; past events are emphasized by a present which allows them to stand as causes for what is."[1] Fuglerud goes on to quote P. Connerton in this regard: "We experience our present world in a context which is causally connected with past events and objects . . . which we are not experiencing when we are experiencing the present. And we will experience our present differently in accordance with the different pasts to which we are able to connect the present."[2]

Accordingly, in this volume I have observed that all the communities sought to make connections to a past, albeit different pasts for each subethnic group. The "past" selectively appropriated by Smārta brahmins in Mumbai, for example, is a "past" different from that of the shanars/nadars or the Tamil Muslims in the same city. Each such appropriated "past" is reconstructed in myth and enacted in replicatory ritual events, especially by first-generation émigrés.

Continuities are expressed in other ways as well. The very need for a sense of connectedness, for example, has deep roots in Tamil culture. In classical Tamil culture, being a person implied being connected to one's social and cosmic order. Rituals served, even in early Tamil settings, to establish and maintain such order. When one was removed from the purvey of these rituals, it was thought one was susceptible to various forms of bodily distress known as *tōṣam.* As Fuglerud puts it, "The breaking or circumventing of ritual rules . . . puts one outside the social context in which cosmological principles are embedded."[3] To experience *tōṣam* by the avoidance of appropriate rituals was also to experience "aloneness disorder"—that is, "being disconnected from other human beings with whom one ought to be connected."[4] Tamil exile life exacerbates the possibility that the individual will be disconnected. Ritualizing helps to reinforce the sense of community and of being connected to the sociocosmic network of which each individual is thought to be a part.

Yet another continuity is the notion that boundaries themselves are not new to Tamil culture. As made explicit in the last chapter and intimated in others, the most recent wave of devotionalism and of ethnic and subethnic resurgence has its roots in the colonial period, especially by the late nineteenth century. This wave has not a little relation to the presence of a colonial government and the challenge of a missionary and Western presence. It was during the nineteenth century, for example, that colonial policy exacerbated the boundaries between castes. It was not by coincidence, then, that nadars, as a case in point, began in that century to contest their place in both Hindu and Christian settings or that, by the early twentieth century, tensions between brahmins and *vēḷāḷa* communities grew. Nonetheless, at the same time, in instances such as the recovery of the Aruṇakiri legacy (chapter 10), Smārta brahmins and *vēḷāḷa*s continued the kinds of reciprocities found in earlier Tamil history. These same reciprocities are to be found in Chembur, Mumbai. Nor is it a coincidence that the recovery of classical texts and the inclination to translate and publish them, a phenomenon that accompanied a Tamil renaissance, was occurring by the late nineteenth century. This resurgence of interest in Tamil language and literature had been stimulated in part by the interest of Western scholars, including, ironically, missionary scholars such as E. Enriquez, B. Ziegenbalg, G. U. Pope, and Robert Caldwell. The nineteenth century, in short, when much of the resurgent interest in temple building, the recovery of festivals, the heightening divisions, and the recovery of Tamil literature was spawned, was a century when cross-cultural, even global, boundaries had become part of the South Asian landscape. While the boundaries of the diasporic experience bring new challenges, the sense of living, thinking, and ritualizing on the boundaries is not necessarily new.

Other strategies have been used as well in attempting to affirm continuities. Those that we have observed in this volume have included the construction of sacred spaces, a practice that goes back in Tamil history to before the Pallava period (seventh to ninth centuries). Throughout history such shrines and temples served to center and/or protect habitable areas; to localize a deity in such a way as to sacralize space; to provide opportunities to ritually enact the reciprocities of the social-political order, and other purposes. In addition to the construction of these spaces, the observance of certain rules in the performing of rituals goes back at least several generations, whether it be possession or the keeping of festival vows as at Batu Caves, the performance of elaborate temple rituals, or the keeping of more streamlined rituals in the home. Of course, the performance of the rituals changes, each expression molded by the moment it is done and the community for whom it is done. So too do the reasons for each performance reflect the new moment in which it is done.

These attempts at continuity are close to what David Chidester has called "indigeneity." Indigeneity has to do with differentiating of selves and communities from colonial or globalizing structures and therefore asserts the "authenticity" or "purity" of local traditions, engages archaic metaphors, and privileges self-representation.[5] The term indigeneity may be appropriate for the communities I have been examining here, though the explicitly political and strident tones critiquing colonial or global structures tend to be understated or absent in the ritualizing process. There is, to be sure, a desire to recover the "indigenous," to link the present to defining or authenticating moments, events, or rituals of the perceived past; and the researcher will hear concerns expressed about the role or intent of majority cultures and/or governments. But the ritualizing may be less a form of protest and more a form of self-expression. This is what Roland Robertson has called glocalization.[6]

In addition to the evident attempts at forging continuities are evidences of innovation and hybridization. These have taken a variety of forms. Even while distancing themselves from other South Indians (or even other Tamils), from other South Asians or non–South Asians, Tamils have the inclination to engage in various reciprocities with these "other" communities, to appropriate from them selectively. The propensity to so interact is itself not new, however, as there are abundant evidences of it in Tamil history. These have included ways in which Tamils, in settling in Thailand, Cambodia, or Myanmar in the premodern centuries, forged ties with other Indians and with indigenous populations. It was observable for centuries in Tamil Nadu itself, where brahmin, king, and landowner expressed their relationships in the ritual life of temples. It was also evident in the ways brahmins and upper-class nonbrahmins cooperated in the recovery of Aruṇakiri's music (chapter 10).

"Hybridity," Chidester suggests, is a strategy common to those who are émigrés. One finds it operative in "migration and diaspora, contact and contingency, margins and mixtures." It displaces rigid distinctions between cultures and communities and is expressed in the "translations, negotiations, and improvisations of the displaced."[7] Hybridizations and innovations in the ritual life of today's diasporic Tamils are abundant, if often subtle. A Singapore temple with a Tamil priest provides space and opportunity for the worship of a favored deity of Kerala and the celebration of a popular festival of Bengal (chapter 3); the Śrī Veṅkaṭeśvara Temple of Pittsburgh, while constructed along lines consistent with traditional South Indian architecture and ritual, nonetheless improvises a way to put the sanctuary on the second floor and bathrooms on the premises (chapter 2). The same temple affords opportunities for governance and celebration accommodating not only Tamils but also Telugu and Kannada speakers. Nadars in the alleys of a Mumbai slum find ways, despite decades of intercaste disputes, to include nonnadars in the governance and participation of a neighborhood shrine (chapter 4). Tamil Muslims in the same slum practice rites of passage that share many elements with their Hindu neighbors (chapter 6). Smārta brahmins, when constructing a temple in Chembur, Mumbai, find ways to accommodate nonbrahmins and non-Tamils in an effort to make the temple both affordable and accessible (chapter 5). Reasons for performing the elaborate libations with 1,008 pots vary in accordance with the sponsoring group, and the respective performance and invocations incorporate the particular landscapes in which they are performed (chapter 7).

Illustrations can be multiplied. In the final analysis, ritualizing has a way of blurring boundaries and catalyzing interactions across strictly ethnic and subethnic lines. Not least important, the ritualizing process is fluid, always changing, as are the sponsoring communities themselves. And like these communities, ritual events and the shrines in which they usually occur bring the past into the present and the present into the past. Thus, temporal as well as spatial and social boundaries are both highlighted and made fuzzy at one and the same time. This is one reason ritualizing works so well on these boundaries.

NOTES

1. Introduction

1. H. G. Rawlinson, *Intercourse between India and the Western World: From the Earliest Times to the Fall of Rome* (Cambridge: University Press, 1936), 19.

2. Ibid., 30.

3. R. Ramasamy, *Sojourners to Citizens: Sri Lanka Tamils in Malaysia, 1885–1965* (Kuala Lumpur: Sri Veera Trading, 1988), 4, citing J. E. Tennent, *Ceylon* (London: Longmans Green, 1859), 2:539.

4. Ibid., 5.

5. Ibid. Ramasamy cites the Tamil poet Vaiyapuri Ayyar, who claims ships to Sri Lanka carried more than twenty-five social groups, including royalty, musicians, and merchants.

6. Ibid., 7.

7. Ibid., 17.

8. Michael Aung-Thwin, *Pagan: The Origins of Modern Burma* (Honolulu: University of Hawaii Press, 1985), 34.

9. Ibid., 36.

10. J. Filliozat, "The Role of the *Śaivāgamas* in the Śaiva Ritual System," in *Experiencing Śiva: Encounters with a Hindu God,* ed. F. Clothey and J. B. Long, 81–86 (Delhi: Manohar Books, 1983).

11. George Coedès, *The Indianized States of Southeast Asia* (Honolulu: East-West Center Press, 1968), 22.

12. Ibid., 38.

13. Ibid., 52.

14. Ibid., 246.

15. Ibid., 248.

16. Ibid., 158, citing K. A. Nilakanta Sastri, "A Tamil Merchant Guild in Sumatra," *TBG* 72 (1932): 314.

17. Paul Wheatley, *The Golden Khersonese: Studies in the Historical Geography of the Malay Peninsula before A.D. 1500* (Westport, Conn.: Greenwood Press, 1973), 67.

18. Coedès, *Indianized States,* 142.

19. Ibid., 143.

20. Ibid., 148.

21. Eleanor Manikka, *Angkorwat: Time, Space and Kingship* (Honolulu: East-West Center Press, 1996), 24–25.

22. Ibid., 231–60.

23. Vasudha Narayanan, "From Angkor to Atlanta: Hindu Migration and Culture" (unpublished paper), 59.

24. Catherine Bell, *Ritual Perspectives and Dimensions* (New York: Oxford University Press, 1997), 219.

25. "Introduction: Themes in the Study of the Indian Diaspora," in *South Asians Overseas: Migrations and Ethnicity*, ed. Colin Clarke, Ceri Beach, and Steven Vertovec (Cambridge: Cambridge University Press, 1990), 8.

26. Ibid., 9.

27. S. Manickam, *Slavery in the Tamil Country: A Historical Overview* (Madras: CLS, 1982), 47–48.

28. Frank Heidemann, *Kanganies in Sri Lanka and Malaysia* (Munich: Anacon, 1992), 110.

29. Manickam, *Slavery*, 66.

30. William Goudie, "The Pariahs and the Land," *Harvest Field* (July 1894): 492–93, cited in Manickam, *Slavery*, 47–48.

31. Ramasamy, *Sojourners to Citizens*, 42, citing C. R. De Silva, *Ceylon under the British*, 2 vols. (Colombo: Colombo Apothecaries Co. Ltd., 1954), 1:284.

32. Ibid., 47.

33. Ibid., 54.

34. Ibid., 123.

35. Øivind Fuglerud, *Life on the Outside: The Tamil Diaspora and Long Distance Nationalism* (London and Sterling, Va.: Pluto Press, 1999), 1.

36. Ibid., 2.

37. David West Rudner, *Caste and Capitalism in Colonial India: The Nattukottai Chettiars* (Berkeley: University of California Press, 1994), 85.

38. Ibid., 87.

39. Ibid., 133–35.

40. R. Ramasamy and J. Rabindra Daniel, *Indians in Peninsular Malaysia: A Study and Bibiography* (Kuala Lumpur: University of Malaya Library, 1984), 5–6.

41. Ibid.

42. *Sucked Oranges: The Indian Poor in Malaysia* (Kuala Lumpur: Institute for Social Analysis, 1989), 38.

43. Ramasamy and Daniel, *Indians in Peninsular Malaysia*, 5.

44. Ibid.

45. Eugene Irschick, *Politics and Social Conflict in South India: The Non-Brahmin Movement and Tamil Separatism, 1916–1929* (Berkeley: University of California Press, 1969), 12.

46. Ibid., 14.

47. Ibid., 19.

48. Ibid., 331–47.

49. Roger Daniels, *History of Indian Immigration to the United States: An Interpretive Essay* (New York: The Asia Society, 1989), 41.

50. Ibid.

51. Ibid., 42.

52. Ibid.

53. Milton Singer, *When a Great Tradition Modernizes: An Anthropological Approach to Indian Civilization* (New York: Frederick A. Praeger, 1972), 67–74.

54. Roland Robertson, *Globalization: Social Theory and Global Culture* (London: Sage Publications, n.d.), 173.

55. The Supreme Court in Kuala Lumpur ruled that the Śrī Mahāmāriamman Temple of Kuala Lumpur was to have its responsibilities shared by appropriate "ubayams."

56. Valentine E. David, *Fluid Signs: Being a Person the Tamil Way* (Berkeley: University of California Press, 1984), 61–104, 197–223.

57. The Greek term "diaspora" refers to dispersal or scattering, as in agriculture, away from the place of origin.

58. Jonathan Z. Smith, *Map Is Not Territory: Studies in the History of Religions* (Leiden: Brill, 1978), chap. 1.

59. This term is borrowed from Williams and Boyd, *Ritual Art and Knowledge*, 20–22.

60. Compare with Douglas, *Purity and Danger*, 114–39.

61. In a 1978 study by the author, 60 percent of Indian immigrant women in Pittsburgh indicated their preference for living in a neighborhood with other Indian families.

62. Compare with Jonathan Z. Smith, *To Take Place: Toward Theory in Ritual* (Chicago: University of Chicago Press, 1992), 86.

63. B. Smith and W. O. Flaherty, trans., *The Laws of Manu* (London: Penguin Books, 1991), xxii–xxiv.

64. Compare with D. Haberman, *Journey through the Twelve Forests* (New York: Oxford University Press, 1994), 68–76.

65. For this discussion on ritual space, I am indebted to a variety of sources. These include Jonathan Z. Smith, *To Take Place;* Mircea Eliade, *The Sacred and the Profane: The Nature of Religion*, trans. W. Trask (London: Harcourt Brace Jovanovich, 1959); and T. N. Madan, ed., *Religion in India* (Delhi: Oxford University Press, 1991), especially part 2, "Sacred Space" (97–171). There are many studies of Hindu temples; of these Stella Kramrisch's *The Hindu Temple* (Delhi: Motilal Banarsidass Publishers, 1991) remains a classic.

66. Discussions on rites of passage that inform this section include the following: Arnold van Gennep, *The Rites of Passage*, ed. Monika B. Vizedom and Gabrielle L. Caffee (Chicago: University of Chicago Press, 1960);Victor Turner, *Ritual Process: Structure and Anti-structure* (New York: Aldine, 1997); and Rajbali Pandey, *Hindu Saṁskāras: Socio-Religious Studies of the Hindu Sacraments* (Delhi: Motilal Banarsidass Publishers, 1987).

67. Aparna Rayaprol, *Negotiating Identities: Women in the Indian Diaspora* (Delhi: Oxford University Press, 1997), 86–106.

68. Surprisingly little has yet been written on the experience of young South Indian expatriates, though there is work pending, most notably by Aparna Rayaprol, Khyati Y. Joshi, Niloufer Mody, and Barbara D. Miller. See especially Joshi, "Patterns and Paths: Ethnic Identity Development in Second Generation Indian Americans" (Ph.D. diss., University of Massachusetts, 2001); Mody, "The Development of Ego Identity and Ethnic Identity in Asian Indian Adolescents Living in America" (Ph.D. diss., California School of Professional Psychology at Fresno, 1994); and Miller, "Precepts and Practices: Researching Identity Formation and Indian Hindu Adolescents in the United States," in *Cultural Practices as Contexts for Development: New Directions for Child Development*, ed. Jacqueline J. Goodenow et al., 71–85 (San Francisco: Jossey-Bass, 1995).

69. Caroline Humphrey and James Laidlaw,*The Archetypal Action of Ritual* (Oxford, U.K.: Clarendon Press, 1994), 88-110.

2. The Construction of a Temple in an American City and the Acculturation Process

This chapter is a revised and updated version of an article first published under the same title in my book *Rhythm and Intent.* It is reprinted here with permission.

1. All statistics cited here are based on the study conducted in the spring of 1978, directed by Fred Clothey and funded by the Public Committee for the Humanities in Pennsylvania. Names of persons interviewed were drawn at random from several mailing lists, primarily those of the Indian Association, the Hindu Temple of Monroeville, the Śrī Veṅkaṭeśvara Temple of Penn Hills, the faculty and staff of two universities, the Pittsburgh telephone directory, and the Sikh Association of Southwestern Pennsylvania. The sampling, therefore, may not fully represent the Indian population as a whole. However, the mailing lists of the two temples and the Indian Association were consistent with a basic "master mailing list" of the Indian community. Hence, the sampling, especially of the Hindu population, should be representative.

2. It should be noted that in recent years, as the earlier immigrants brought in parents and other family members, the percentage of professional and graduate-degree-holding Indian Americans has declined.

3. It is important to note that not all Indian immigrants are Hindus. In my study, 81.2 percent of the sampling was Hindu; 5.4 percent was Sikh; 5 percent was Jain; 2.5 percent was Muslim; and 2 percent was Christian. These figures should not be considered representative of a national norm, inasmuch as, in the Pittsburgh study, among random lists from which respondents were selected was a listing of Sikh families in the area.

4. This history is reconstructed from conversations with several individuals, including some founding couples; from letters; and from news sheets published under the title the *Hindu Temple.*

5. *Temple Times* 3, no. 3 (August 1975).

6. *Saptagirivani* (Silver Jubilee Commemoration) (Pittsburgh: Śrī Veṅkaṭeśvara Temple, 2002), 20, citing an unspecified news bulletin of July 1976.

7. In the commentary to the *Kāsyapa Śilpa Śāstra* (2:22–27) that describes the nature of ritual space, there is an allusion to a myth that illustrates this body-temple equation. A personified demon named Vāstupuruṣa (literally: space-body) is troubling the world. The gods who guard the cosmic directions (for example, Isāṇa and Nīṛṛti) chase the demon and pin him down to the ground at the spot where the ritual space is consecrated. The deities sit on his legs, arms, and so on in such a way as to indicate the demonic force has been conquered and the appropriate space has been made safe, but also cosmicized, sacralized, and equated to the human body.

8. H. Daniel Smith, *A Descriptive Bibliography of the Printed Texts of the Pāñcarātrāgama* (Baroda: Oriental Institution, 1975) 1:219. This ritual is described in the Pañcarātrāgamic text known as *Padmasaṁhitā.* The ritual as done at Penn Hills varied from the textual prescription in some details. The description that follows is a summary provided by A. Sampathnarayanan, assistant priest for the ritual. Variations from the text will be pointed out occasionally.

9. The *ācārya* is supposed to be well informed in the Pāñcarātra traditions, attractive and healthy, morally blameless, properly initiated, and so on (ibid., 218).

10. H. Daniel Smith makes no mention of this ritual.

11. H. Daniel Smith, *Descriptive Bibliography,* 221. Sampathnarayanan does not mention this event.

12. For descriptions of these rituals I am indebted to the officiating priest, Srinivasācārya Iyengar; to Professor Narayana Rao of the University of Wisconsin; and to Mr. K. T. Narasimha, formerly curator of the Southern Circle of the Archaeological Survey of India.

13. See the *Padmasaṁhitā,* xxx; and H. Daniel Smith, *Descriptive Bibliography,* 223. I have shown that the ritual space is homologized to a human body, as well as to a cosmos, as in the *vāstupuruṣamaṇḍala.* The texts explore these homologies both vertically and horizontally.

14. Rayaprol, *Negotiating Identities.* Rayaprol demonstrates that women have made the SV Temple an extension of the domestic sphere.

15. This rationale for the performing of the tonsure is that of Mrs. Anusuya Chandrasekhar, accountant and office supervisor of the Śrī Veṅkaṭeśvara Temple. Pandey in *Hindu Saṁskāras,* 94, concurs that "removing impurities" is the reason given in medical texts for the early tonsure, while other texts also suggest life is prolonged by performance of the tonsure (citing Vasiṣṭha, *Dharmasūtras,* 1:296).

16. The trimester cited is from October 2004 through January 2005. All these statistics were made available by Mrs. Chandrasekhar in a conversation.

17. I am very grateful to Mrs. Chandrasekhar for her discussion of these matters in a conversation on February 25, 2005.

18. From a conversation with Jeya Mani, instructor of the Bharata Nātyam classes.

3. Shrines as Cultural Spaces in Singapore

1. See, for example, Burton Stein, ed., *South Indian Temples* (New Delhi: Vilkas Publishing House PVT, 1978), especially essays by Arjun Appadurai, "Kings, Sects and Temples in South India, 1350–1700 A.D." (47–74); and Carol Breckenridge, "From Protector to Litigant—Changing Relations between Hindu Temples and the Raja of Ramnad" (75–106). See also Stein, *Peasant State and Society in Medieval South India* (Delhi: Oxford University Press, 1980).

2. Jean Mialaret, *Hinduism in South India* (Singapore: Asia Pacific Press, 1969), 40. Mialaret's date for Narayana Pillai's receiving deed to the land for the Māryiammaṉ temple (1823) is contested by Soundara Rajan in an oral history taped by the Oral History Department of Singapore. Rajan's date is 1821.

3. A. Mani, "The Changing Caste Structure amongst the Singapore Indians" (Singapore, 1977), 17, cited in Sharon Siddique and Nirmala Purushotam, *Singapore's Little India: Past, Present and Future,* 2nd ed. (Singapore: Institute for Southeast Asian Studies, 1990), 12.

4. Joanne Punzo Waghorne, "The Diaspora of the Gods: Hindu Temples in the New World System, 1640–1800," *Journal of Asian Studies* 58, no. 3 (August 1999): 648–86.

5. Conversations with Dr. Thinnappan in March 1991. See also C. Chandrasekhar, *The Nagarathars of South India* (Madras: Macmillan India Press, 1980), 31; and Rudner, *Caste and Capitalism,* 135.

6. From a conversation with the chief *paṇṭāram* at the Chettiyar temple in February 1991.

7. One Chettiyar suggested to me that one reason *ayar*s could not serve as priests for Taṇṭāyutapāṇi was that brahmin priests were married, whereas the deity was *brahmacarin;* yet *paṇṭārams* may also be married, while many of the priests who have come to the straits came temporarily and without families. A *paṇṭāram* serving in the Singapore Chettiyar temple may have come closer to the truth when he suggested the Chettiyars "thought of us as their 'friends' from long ago and trusted us."

8. Siddique and Purushotam, *Singapore's Little India,* 20.

9. Paul Younger, in *The Home of the Dancing Śivan* (New York: Oxford Press, 1995), 187, indicates that Kāli had replaced Piṭāri by the thirteenth century at Citamparam.

10. Siddique and Purushotam, *Singapore's Little India,* 25. A brahmin woman, referring to the early worshippers of the goddess Kāḷiyammaṉ, remarked in a conversation with the writer that "they must have missed their mothers."

11. Conversations with Ahoran Pillai on April 30, 1991. Mr. Pillai's grandfather had come to Malaysia in 1915 to work on the estates. Ahoran Pillai worked most of his career with the Malaysian railways as a porter.

12. Hindu Endowments Board: http://www.heb.gov.sg/mariammantemple/smt-history .html (accessed 2002).

13. Nilaya Muhammed Ali, "Hindu Mother-Goddess Worship in Modern Singapore," (academic exercise, NUS, 1984–85), citing Soundara Rajan "The History of the Śrī Māriyammaṉ Temple," *Singapore Śrī Māriammaṉ Temple Mahā Kumbhābhiṣeka Souvenir Magazine* (1971): 168.

14. From an inscription displayed in the environs of the Śrī Māriyammaṉ temple. How the deed had come from Narayana Pillai to Sashakala Pillay is not clear.

15. This temple is said to have been upgraded and installed with brahmin priests two hundred years ago by one Sarobhaji, who believed himself to be cured of smallpox by Māriyammaṉ at that spot. This account was afforded by an *ayyar* priest in a Māriyammaṉ temple in Rawang, telling the story of his home temple, where he insisted his forefathers had been priests for seven generations. The existence of the temple and the traditional participation of *piḷḷai*s in its life were confirmed by Professor S. Singaravelu of the Department of Indian Studies, University of Malaya.

16. Siddique and Purushotam, *Singapore's Little India,* 45.

17. Ibid.

18. The reason for this change in name remains unclear. Mr. Athisdam, then the secretary of the Hindu Endowments Board, in a conversation in June 1991 indicated he believed the change was at the insistence of certain Telugus then on the board. Mr. Soundara Rajan, in a statement recorded by the Oral History Department of Singapore, believes the change was made in "ignorance" of the distinction between Pāñcarātra and Vaikhānasa "sects" in Singapore—a change that in India would have been a cause for a court case. Mr. S. L. P. Mohan indicated in a conversation (July 1991) that his father, S. L. Perumal, a Telugu Naidu then on the HEB, was instrumental in changing the priests because Vaikhānasa priests were to be found in the "important" temples of India, like that at Tirupati.

19. M. K. Narayanan, "Murukan Temples in Singapore," http://murugan.org/temples/singapore_temples.htm (accessed November 1, 2002).

20. Ibid.

21. From conversations with the clerk at the Chettiyar temple in April 1991.

22. Reported by Mr. Athisdam in a conversation (June 1991).

23. This information comes largely from Radhika Srinivasan's "A Symphony of Sacred Arts" on the Web site for the Śrī Śivan temple produced by the Hindu Endowments Board, http://www.heb.gov.sg/sivantemple/tem_architecture.html (accessed 2002).

24. This historical sketch is reconstructed from an oral history provided by Mr. Soundara Rajan for the Oral History Department of Singapore. Mr. Rajan was once secretary of the Śrī Māriyammaṉ Temple.

25. Ananda Rajan, "The Ecological Study of Shrines" (academic exercise, Sociology Department, National University of Singapore, 1975).

26. Ibid., 53–64.

27. When Mr. Regunayakam was asked (May 1991) why an *ayyar* from Tamil Nadu was appointed rather then a Nambuṭiri from Kerala, he replied it was a matter of finance: the Nambuṭiri would have cost $1,000 (US$600) while the *ayyar* cost only $350 (US$200).

28. From a conversation with Mr. K. Regunayakam in May 1991.

29. Note, as an example, the schedule by which various *ubayams* or families were responsible for events during the Paṅkuṉi Uttiram Brahmotsavam in the Perumāl Temple in April 1991.

> Paṅkuṉi Uttiram (Friday) Śrī Āṇṭal Tirukkalyāṇam
>
> Responsible Group: P. Govindasamy Pillai, Mr. G. Ramakrishnan Family and S. L. Perumal Family
>
> First Day (Monday) Patrons: Mr. C. Paramjothy Family
>
> Second Day Patrons: M. P. Lingam & Sons (Pte.) Ltd.
>
> Third Day Patrons: Mr. A. Narayanaswamy Kandiar
>
> Fourth Day Patrons: Sri Srinivasa Perumal Thondargal
>
> Fifth Day Patrons: Komala Vilas Proprietors
>
> Sixth Day Patrons: Dhaksi a Bharatha Brahmana Saba
>
> Seventh Day (Tirukkalyāṇam) Patrons: C. Yogarajah, S. Yogeswaran
>
> Eighth Day Patrons: Mr. C. Balaguru Family
>
> Ninth Day Patrons: S. L. Perumal Family
>
> Tenth Day Patrons: P. Govindasamy Piḷḷai, Mr. G. Ramakrishnan Family
>
> Vaiṭaiyātri Festival (Thursday) Patron: Mr. S. Renganathan
>
> Puṣpayākam Patron: Mr. Azagarsamy Naidu Family
>
> Sunday Chitra Pournami Ubayam Patron: Dakshinathargal

These patrons generally expect to repeat their role annually.

30. K. S. Sandhu, *Indians in Malaya: Some Aspects of Their Immigration and Settlement, 1786–1957* (London: Cambridge University Press, 1969), 237.

31. Siddique and Purushotam, *Singapore's Little India*, 64.

32. Cited by Nirmal Purushotam, "The Social Negotiation of Language in the Singaporean Everyday Life World" (unpublished thesis, Singapore National University, 1976), 130.

33. Oral history recorded by the Oral History Department of Singapore.

34. Mr. Chidambaram in a conversation in April 1981.

35. Mrs. Lakshmi Naidu in a conversation recorded for the Oral History Department of Singapore.

36. A brahmin *gurukkal (ayyar)*, recently arrived in the Vīrakāḷiyammaṉ Temple from Tamil Nadu, admitted in a conversation in April 1991 that his *kuladevam* was Maturaivīraṉ.

37. See chapter 2 of this volume.

38. Young men (some estimate up to ten thousand of them a year) still come on temporary work permits from Tamil Nadu. The pattern often is that they will have paid an "agent" back home (the present-day equivalent of the old *kaṅkāṇi*) up to forty-five thousand rupees. In exchange the immigrant receives a work permit, good for a year, but renewable, usually one-way passage, and the assistance from another "agent" in Singapore to get piece work. These

workmen apparently often live in the buildings they are helping to construct. (From a conversation with a group of such recruits in May 1991.)

39. This account is taken from Gopal Das, "The Kāḷiyammaṉ Temple, Serangoon Road" (unpublished academic exercise, Singapore National University, March 1958), 29–30.

40. From conversations and observations on April 9, 1991. This summary of festivities associated with the Paṅkuṉi Uttiram festival in Singapore first appeared in my essay "Rituals and Reinterpretation: South Indians in Southeast Asia," in *A Sacred Thread: Modern Transmission of Hindu Traditions in India and Abroad,* ed. Raymond Williams, 127–46 (Chambersburg, Pa.: Anima Press, 1992). It is reprinted here with the permission of Bochasanwasi Swaminarayanan Sanstha Inc. (Flushing, N.Y.), which currently holds the copyright to the volume.

4. Tirunelveli North

1. This brief sketch is common knowledge and can be found in most introductory brochures to Mumbai, one of the best of which is produced by India's Department of Tourism and has text written by Pushpa Pal and Vidya Srinivas.

2. Figures from Meera Kosambi, *Bombay in Transition: The Growth and Social Ecology of a Colonial City, 1880–1980* (Stockholm: Alquist and Wiksell International, 1988), 167.

3. Ibid.

4. Vaisala Narain and K. B. Gotnagar, "Bombay and Its In-Migration," in *Dynamics of Population and Welfare, 1983,* ed. K. Srinivasan and S. Mukerji (Mumbai: Himalaya Publishing House, 1983), 318.

5. Ibid.

6. L. C. Gupta, "Migration and Population Growth—an Experience of Greater Bombay," in *Bombay by 2000 A.D.,* ed. Rashmi Mayur and Prem Ratan Vohra (Mumbai: Prem Ratan Vohra, 1986), 177.

7. Ibid., 179.

8. Neil Grant and Nick Middleton, *Atlas of the World Today* (New York: Harper Row Publishers, 1987), 36.

9. Census of India, 1981, series 12, Maharashtra.

10. Gupta, "Migration and Population Growth," 180.

11. From Kosambi, *Bombay in Transition,* 167.

12. From an interview with Dr. John Correia-Alfonso in July 1990.

13. Kosambi, *Bombay in Transition,* 167.

14. Ibid.

15. Census of India, 1981, series 12, Maharashtra. Household Population by Religion, 4–7.

16. From interviews conducted with workers of these communities in Mumbai in July 1990.

17. Brochure, Śrī Veṅkaṭeśa Devasthanam, Mumbai, 10, 11.

18. "The South Indian Bhajana Samaj, Sri Sarada Navarathri Souvenir" (1989), n.p.; "Fifty Years of Dedicated Service" (unpublished document prepared by Śrī Saṅkara Maṭam, 1989), n.p.

19. The Ashtika Samajam, Matunga Souvenir (1989), n.p.

20. K. C. Zachariah, *Migrants in Greater Bombay* (Bombay: Asia Publishing House, 1968), 32.

21. Ibid., 56.

22. Ibid., 58.

23. Narain and Gotnagar, "Bombay and Its In-Migration," 324.

24. Ibid.

25. Census of India, 1981, series 12, Maharashtra. Households and Household Population by Language Mainly Spoken in the Household.

26. Ibid.

27. Ibid. Some observers think this official population figure is unrealistically low.

28. Based on observations and conversations in the summer of 1990, especially with Professor K. K. A. Venkatacharya, then director of the Anantacarya Indological Research Institute.

29. Census of India, 1981, series 12, Maharashtra.

30. Gupta, "Migration and Population Growth," 180.

31. Conversation with Dr. Shekhar Mukherji, professor and head of the Department of Migration and Urban Studies of the International Institute for Population Studies in Mumbai, September 1990.

32. Kalpana Sharma, *Rediscovering Dharavi* (New Delhi: Penguin Books, 2002), xxvii.

33. Dennis Templeman, *The Northern Nadars of Tamil Nadu: An Indian Caste in the Process of Change* (Delhi: Oxford University Press, 1996), 20–21, citing Robert A. Caldwell, *The Tinnevelly Shanans: A Sketch of Their Religion and Their Moral Condition and Characteristics as a Caste* (Madras: Christian Knowledge Society Press, 1849), 50–56.

34. Ibid., 21.

35. Robert L. Hardgrave Jr., *The Nadars of Tamil Nadu: The Political Culture of a Community in Change* (Berkeley: University of California Press, 1969), 29–30; and Templeman, *Northern Nadars,* 21.

36. Templeman, *Northern Nadars,* 26; Hardgrave, *Nadars of Tamil Nadu,* 29.

37. Templeman, *Northern Nadars,* 25. Susan Bayly in *Saints, Goddesses and Kings: Muslims and Christians in South Indian Society, 1700–1900* (Cambridge: Cambridge University Press, 1989), 420–60, includes an extended discussion of shanar/nadar Christians in the nineteenth century.

38. Edgar Thurston, *Castes and Tribes of Southern India.* 7 vols. (Madras: Government Press, 1909; New Delhi: Asian Educational Services, 1993), 6:365.

39. From a conversation with Rev. James Paul in Mumbai in August 1990, speaking of the history of Tamil migrations into Mumbai.

40. Much of this historical information, except where otherwise noted, is derived from an extended conversation with R. Rajamani, a former teacher and current advocate who was born and lived his entire life in Dharavi. He wrote a series of articles on the area for the Tamil daily *Bold India.* He is, in a sense, the ad hoc local historian.

41. R. Rajamani's term.

42. This perception of the Shiv Sena attitude is shared by many Tamil residents in Dharavi. Eventually, as one informant put it, "We beat up the Shiv Sena people, threw them dead into the mud, and they surrendered" (P. Perumal's recollection).

43. P. Perumal in an interview in August 1990.

44. Conversations with a Sister of Mary in July 1990.

45. Mother Imelda, writing in *Souvenir Golden Jubilee St. Anthony's Church and School, Dharavi, Mumbai, 1940–90,* (Mumbai: St. Anthony's), 17.

46. Ibid.

47. This historical account, including these estimates, is derived largely from Mr. R. Rajamani. I am most grateful to him for his kind help.

48. See chapter 3 in this volume.

49. This historical sketch is reconstructed from conversations with devotees and trustees at the shrine.

50. Descriptions of these rituals are derived from conversations with Mr. Balasubramaniam, the *pūjāri* at this and other shrines in Dharavi.

51. Comment by an anonymous devotee (August 1990).

52. From conversations in August 1990 with an anonymous informant.

53. Ibid.

54. Reconstructed from a conversation with M. Ramakrishnan in August 1990.

55. From a conversation in August 1990.

56. M. Ramakrishnan, a naidu, expressed it without sentiment: "Home is where my salary is." Yet even he expects to marry his children in his home village because "that's where the relations are."

57. The "geography" that follows of Tamil Protestants in the Church of North India in Mumbai is derived from a conversation with Rev. James Paul, the seniormost of Tamil Protestant clergy in the city; the estimated percentages of Nadars that follow are also his.

58. Reverend Paul reported that there was a young man of dalit or "scheduled caste" background who was a potential pastor, but Nadars would not let him preach in their congregations. In *Saints, Goddesses and Kings,* Bayly reports that, in the late nineteenth century, Nadar Christians often contested vigorously for entry and leadership in Tamil churches (444–48).

59. Note that Methodists declined to become part of the Church of North India when the latter was formed in 1970 for a variety of reasons, not the least of which was that its clergy would have had to take a cut in salary.

60. The story of a (now rare) first-generation convert now living in Mumbai is suggestive: She was born into a Tamil brahmin family living near Bangalore. Her family had a lot of children, but her mother's sister had none. Accordingly, she was offered to her aunt for adoption. Her aunt treated her well, but her uncle did not, for he allegedly beat her. Finally, she ran away from home as a teenager and went to the office of a Christian mission for refuge and advice. The missionary in charge went to the home to inquire into the matter, only to be told "the girl would no longer be welcomed at home, as she had touched a pariah." She chose then to remain at the mission until she was eighteen, at which time she decided to convert and was baptized as a Christian. By this time her family, which was said to be fairly affluent, was prepared to take her back, but she refused. She went on to prepare for a career in teaching. (Rev. James Paul recounted the story of his wife's background in a conversation in August 1990.)

61. Census of India, 1981, series 12, Maharashtra. Household Population by Religion, 8–9.

62. Interview with Rev. James Paul, August 1990.

63. Interview with Rev. Ananda Maharajah, August 1990.

64. Interview with Rev. James Paul, August 1990.

65. Ibid.

66. Derived from *Souvenir Golden Jubilee of St. Anthony's Church and School,* 3–4.

67. Ibid.

68. Ibid., 3.

69. Conversations with a Sister of Mary in July 1990.

70. Brought to Tamil Nadu by French Jesuits, Saint Anthony became especially popular with peasants because he was perceived to enhance the agricultural process and to protect the

lands from evil influences, thereby fulfilling the role of certain village Hindu deities (Professor Selva Raj in a conversation, June 11, 1005).

71. The difference between the support network of St. Anthony's Church and the Church of the Good Shepherd is illustrated dramatically in the souvenir booklets each had published, Good Shepherd in 1987 and St. Anthony's in 1989. The souvenir booklet of Good Shepherd included 15 ads, all of them placed by local (Dharavi) advertisers, 5 in English, 4 in Tamil, and 6 in both English and Tamil. St. Anthony's souvenir booklet (to be sure, a fiftieth-anniversary booklet) placed 180 ads; 123 (68 percent) of these were in English; 47 (26 percent) were in Tamil; 8 were in both English and Tamil; but only 3 were in Hindi or Marathi. Of these ads, 35 (19 percent) were greetings placed by religious individuals or groups, 13 of them (7 percent) by church agencies.

5. Brahmins and Their Three Shrines

1. Thurston, *Castes and Tribes,* 1:268. This is a reprint of his work first published in 1909 as part of the British attempt to classify India's communities.

2. Ibid., 308.

3. Ibid., 356.

4. The Ashtika Samajam, Matunga Souvenir (1989), 21.

5. "The South Indian Bhajana Samajam, Sri Sarada Navarathri Souvenir" (1989).

6. From the cover of the unpublished document "50 Years of Dedicated Service," prepared for the fiftieth anniversary of the Śrī Śaṅkara Maṭam in 1989.

7. "50 Years of Dedicated Service."

8. From a conversation with the manager of the Śrī Śaṅkara Maṭam in August 1990.

9. The Rājarājeśvarī icon (*mūrti*) became a major part of the Matunga brahmins' world in the early 1970s. Venkatesvara Sastri came from Madras to offer discourses at the South Indian Bhajana Samajam. Attracted to a picture of Rājarājeśvarī, this swami recommended an icon of her to be installed. Sometime thereafter a certain Maunaswami (a swami, sworn to silence, from Ambattur, a suburb of Madras) stopped in Mumbai overnight while on pilgrimage to Benares. To this swami the community expressed their desire to install an icon for that goddess. Upon his return to Madras in 1978, he arranged to send a *mūrti* of Rājarājeśvarī (from a conversation with M. V. Ganesh Sastrigal, chief priest of the South Indian Bhajana Samajam, on August 3, 1990). Sastrigal believed that Rājarājeśvarī is a "new" form of the goddess, and therefore "greater" than all other forms of the goddess. In fact, the goddess has roots in Tamil Nadu. She was the consort of Rājarājeśvara (Śiva), the guardian deity of the Cōḻa kings in the ninth and tenth centuries (Fuller and Logan, "Navarātri Festival," 88). C. J. Fuller reports that she is linked to Mīnāṭcī (Sanskrit, Mīnākṣī), the goddess of Madurai, where she is extolled in the Navarāttiri festival for her power in subduing the demon Mahiṣasura and for her erotic powers (ibid., 89). Rājarājeśvarī was also the tutelary deity of the *rājas* of Ramnad (and possibly other dynasties) from the seventeenth through the nineteenth centuries. In Ramnad she was linked to all the protective deities of the domain and served as patron/celestial exemplar for the royal family. In fact, the priests in the temple of Rājarājeśvarī in the royal palace were provided by the matham of the Śaṅkarācārya of Sringeri, that bastion of Smārta brahmin orthopraxy (Pamela J. Price, "Resources and Rule in Zamindar, South India, 1802–1903: Sivagangi and Ramnad as Kingdoms under the Raja. [Ph.D. diss., University of Wisconsin–Madison, 1979], 307–10). Hence, Rājarājeśvarī is linked both to royal traditions of Tamil Nadu and to ancestral Smārta brahmins, especially those associated with the Sringeri Śaṅkarācārya.

10. From a conversation at the matham in August 1990.

11. From a conversation with P. S. Subramanyam, honorary secretary of the samajam, in August 1990. He came to Mumbai in 1957 and had served as the chief accounts officer for the Indian Cancer Society for thirty years.

12. From a promotional booklet produced by the temple (n.d.).

13. From a conversation with an anonymous officer of the samajam, August 1990.

14. P. S. Subramanyam in conversation.

15. From the promotional brochure seeking funds for the project.

16. P. S. Subramanyam in conversation.

17. Promotional brochure.

18. P. S. Subramanyam in conversation.

19. Ibid.

20. This is the account of P. S. Subramanyam.

21. Arjun Appadurai, "Kings, Sects and Temples in South India, 1350–1700 A.D.," in Stein, *South Indian Temples,* 52–55.

22. Thurston, *Castes and Tribes,* 333.

23. William Cekner, "The Sankaracarya of Kanchi and the Kamaksi Temple as Ritual Center," in Raymond Williams, *Sacred Thread,* 62.

24. Ibid., 62. The quoted phrase is Cekner's term.

25. Glenn Yocum, "The Coronation of a Guru: Charisma, Politics and Philosophy in Contemporary India," in Raymond Williams, *Sacred Thread,* 81–90. Yocum noted that the Sringeri Śaṅkarācāryas in recent years have been Telugu Smārtas and that the comments made about *dalits* by the present Śaṅkarācārya at the time of his inauguration in 1989 were deeply offensive to various dalit activist groups.

26. Singer, *Great Tradition,* 325–27.

27. The historical discussion that follows is derived largely from an unpublished typescript compiled by G. Mohan and titled "The History of Brahmins in Malaysia and the Formation of the Samajam."

28. Discussion of the role of brahmins in Malaysia's society is derived from a typescript prepared by G. Mohan and titled "Outstanding Contributions of Brahmins in Malaysia up to 1990."

29. Ibid., 1.

30. Ibid., 4.

31. This discussion is derived from Mohan, "History of Brahmins."

32. Observation of the Rāma Navami festival and all interpretive conversations were done in the brahmiṇ samajam in Pudu, Kuala Lumpur, in March and April 1991.

33. Participants seem to collapse differences in their perceptions of this event. The names Kṛṣṇa and Rāma appear to be used interchangeably; further, the ensuing dance, said to be emulating Hanuman's army of monkeys during homage to Rāma, appears to be a vestigial replication of the dance of *gopīs* and Kṛṣṇa done in many a *raslīlā* (cf. Norvin Hein, *The Miracle Plays of Mathura* [New Haven, Conn.: Yale University Press, 1972], 147).

34. From a conversation in April 1991.

35. A. Rajamani, *Pooja* (unpublished typescript).

6. Double Jeopardy

I am especially grateful to Ms. Tasqeen Macchiwalla, who served as my research assistant during the summer of 1994, when this research was done. Her help was especially invaluable in getting access to many women for extended discussion and for interpreting what we heard. In addition, her notes, when added to my own, have become a significant resource for this final draft.

1. See, for example, Platvoet, "Ritual as Confrontation," 185–226.

2. See, for example, Sushil Srivastava, *The Disputed Mosque: A Historical Inquiry* (Delhi: Vistaar Publications, 1991).

3. *Times of India,* December 8, 1992, 1.

4. Ibid., December 10, 1992, 1.

5. In a subsequent conversation with the writer, the superintendent of police insisted the police were neutral and not against any particular group.

6. A. Asaraf Ali, in his Ph.D. dissertation, "Services of Muslims to Higher Education in Tamil Nadu, 1902–1984" (Madurai Kamaraj University, 1999), notes that Muslim women lagged behind other women in Tamil Nadu in taking advantage of educational opportunities. He cites a survey done in 1931–32 by the Muslim Educational Association of South India indicating the reasons given by Muslims for this resistance: (1) the "conservatism" of people toward "modern" education; (2) the system of *purdah,* which necessitated the segregation of women from men; (3) the absence of "proper" religious instruction in the existing colleges; (4) a strong aversion to coeducation; (5) lack of qualified Muslim women teachers; (6) "unsuitable" curriculum—that is, college curricula did not yet include courses in Arabic, Islamic History, and so on (98). One of the results of these attitudes was that the first Muslim women did not receive a BA degree in Tamil Nadu until 1931 (99). In 1929–30 there were 11 Muslim women enrolled in colleges in Tamil Nadu as compared with 270 Christian women; by 1945–46 there were 7 Muslim female students enrolled in arts colleges and 21 in professional schools (16 of these in medical schools); by 1948–49 there were 11 arts colleges for women in Tamil Nadu and 2,195 women students, of whom 96 were Muslim, 33 of these in professional schools (121).

7. Rahim, "The *Dargah* of Nagore and the Culture of the Tamil Muslims," in *The Bulletin of the Institute of Traditional Cultures* (Madras: University of Madras Press, 1973), 95.

8. Ibid.

9. Ibid., 103. Bayly in *Saints, Goddesses and Kings* cites the *Nākaiyantāti,* a famed Tamil Muslim poem, as describing the Nagore *dargah*'s tomb as a "haven of sweetness and comfort" where "afflictions are soothed and supplications are met" (134).

10. Susan Bayly reports that the term "rowther" was used in the nineteenth century simply as a way to claim higher status, though, in fact, there was a history of Muslims with military prowess who were brought to Tamil Nadu from the north (in the case of "authentic rowthers" from the Deccan) by various rulers, Hindu and Muslim, in the south (ibid., 99).

11. While the term *sayyid* is associated with those who are believed to be descended from the Prophet's family, the sheikhs are believed to be descended from the Prophet's tribe (Jackie Assayag, *At the Confluence of Two Rivers: Muslims and Hindus in South India* (New Delhi: Manohar Books, 2004), 43).

12. The *marakkāyar*s were elite Tamil Sunnī trading families living near the port cities and maintaining close ties to Arab centers of trade and pilgrimage. It is they who "stigmatized" the majority of Tamil Muslims as *lebba*s or indigenous converts to Islam (Bayly, *Saints, Goddesses and Kings,* 83).

13. Note that many of these customs associated with rites of passage are shared by Tamil Hindus as well, including the whispering of the infant's name and the feeding of solid food. Indeed, rural Muslims in Tamil Nadu, as well as other parts of South India, share several rituals

in common with their Hindu counterparts. See, for example, Mattison Mines, "Islamization and Muslim Ethnicity in South India," in *Ritual and Religion among Muslims in India,* ed. Ahmad Imtiaz, 65–88 (Delhi: Manohar, 1981). In *Confluence of Two Rivers,* Assayag demonstrates a similar phenomenon in rural Karnataka (125–29).

14. In "Services of Muslims," Ali noted that Muslims in South and (especially) North Arcot districts included those who were among the most wealthy and progressive Muslims of Tamil Nadu and who were active in developing educational opportunities for Tamil Muslims in the south (45–49).

15. In an 1823 village census commissioned by the East India Company, Melapalaiyam was said to have five thousand *lebbas* in a total population of fifty-six hundred and to have eighteen mosques and forty Ṣūfī shrines (Bayly, *Saints, Goddesses and Kings,* 83).

16. The system of *purdah* necessitated the segregating of women from men.

17. Sharma, *Rediscovering Dharavi,* 13.

18. This was the characterization of a non-Kallakurichi woman whose father was a Pathan and whose husband was a sayyid.

19. From a conversation on August 11, 1994.

20. Ibid.

21. Sharma, *Rediscovering Dharavi,* xxxi.

22. See, for example, Mines, "Islamization and Muslim Ethnicity," 68. Mines speaks of rural Muslims in Tamil Nadu primarily as Tamil Muslims, while urbanized Muslims near Chennai (Madras) are described as Muslim Tamils.

7. Libations with 1,008 Pots

1. Translated by Lakshmi Swaminathan.

2. Temple flyer: "Navothara Sahasra (1009 Kumbam) Kalasa Abhisegam, Skanda Yakgya Mahayagam and Shanmuga Archanai" (Kuala Lumpur: Sri Kandasaswamy Temple, March 15, 1991). Note that the number of pots varies between 1,008 and 1,009.

3. From an interview in January 1991.

4. Prabha Reddy, "Sahasrakalaśābhiṣeka: A Pāñcarātra Consecration Ritual with One Thousand and Eight Vessels," in *Saptagirivani* (Silver Jubilee Commemoration) (Pittsburgh: Śrī Veṅkaṭeśvara Temple, 2002), 10, citing the Śrī Veṅkaṭeśvara Temple *25th Anniversary Celebration* brochure, 2001–2.

5. From a conversation in April 1986.

6. Sociologists of religion, following Max Weber, have used the term "rationalization" to refer to the propensity of religious communities to restate or make more coherent their ideas and practices in the face of urbanization or modernization. See, for example, Susan E. Ackerman and Raymond L. M. Lee, *Sacred Tensions: Modernity and Religious Transformation in Malaysia* (Columbia: University of South Carolina Press, 1997), chap. 1.

7. This "history" of a text is reconstructed from conversations with the translator and Narayana Rao of the University of Wisconsin.

8. From conversations with the SV Temple priests over an extended period before and after the 1986 *sahasrakalaśābhiṣeka.*

9. Singer, *Great Tradition,* 56–58.

10. See Humphrey and Laidlaw, *Archetypal Action of Ritual,* chap. 4

11. This sequence was summarized, in Tamil, by the chief officiating priest at the Śrī Irāmalinksvarar Alayam in suburban Kuala Lumpur.

12. Humphrey and Laidlaw, *Archetypal Action of Ritual,* 89.

13. Indeed, the libations of 1986 were presided over by the very same priest, Srinivasācarya, who had conducted the dedicatory ceremonies. However, because of his death, another priest led the 2002 libations, one Srī Varada Ramanujan, the *Pāñcarātra-Āgama vidvān* from Tirupati (Prabha Reddy, "Sahasrakalaśābhiṣeka," 10–12).

8. Navarāttiri

I am indebted to Dr. V. Parthasarathy of the Anandacarya Institute of Indology for her help in doing this research. She enabled me to have contact with many articulate Tamil brahmin women relative to the Navarāttiri celebrations of 1990. It is largely thanks to her influence that this chapter focuses primarily on the celebrations and perceptions of these women.

1. P. V. Kane, *History of Dharmaśāstra,* 1st ed. (Poona: Bhandarkar Oriental Research Institute, 1962), 5:186.

2. Ibid.

3. See, for example, David Kinsley, *Hindu Goddesses* (Delhi: Matilal Banarsidass, 1987), 97.

4. Translated and cited by Kane, *History of Dharmaśāstra,* 156.

5. Cited in ibid., 156.

6. Ibid., 164–65.

7. Ibid., 168, citing the *Kāḷikapurāṇam* 71, 6–18.

8. Ibid., 172.

9. Ibid., 173.

10. Ibid., 179.

11. Ibid., 170.

12. See Mary Anderson, *The Festivals of Nepal* (Calcutta: Rupa and Co., 1975), 150. The slaughter of black buffaloes to Durgā, the "wife of Bhairab" on the ninth day of Navarāttiri, is described. Certain military honors are also performed on her behalf, including the honoring of swords and other military equipment.

13. Stein, *Peasant State and Society,* 387–88. P. Ghosha also noted that Devapūjā incorporates some elements of the *aśvamedha.* These include the preparation of Lajica rice and the use of ten articles in *pūjā,* prescribed in both festivals: ghee, honey, rice, flattened rice, baked rice, powdered barley mixed with ghee, fried barley meal, baked barley, masusi, and grains of *panicum italicum* (P. Gosha, *Durgā Pūjā with Notes and Illustrations* [Calcutta: Hindoo Patriot Press, 1871], 11–42).

14. See the description in Stein, *Peasant State and Society,* 384–86.

15. Carol A. Breckenridge describes the Navarāttiri performed by this personage in her essay "From Protector to Litigant—Changing Relations between Hindu Temples and the Raja of Ramnad," in Stein, *South Indian Temples,* 75–88. Another extended discussion of Navarāttiri as performed in the Ramnad court appears in Pamela J. Price, "Resources and Rules in Zamindari South India, 1802–1903: Sivagangai and Ramnad as Kingdoms under the Raj" (Ph.D. diss., University of Wisconsin–Madison, 1979).

16. Stein, *Peasant State and Society,* 384–85.

17. Kane, *History of Dharmaśāstra,* 1:158.

18. Ibid., 157.

19. Ibid., 158.

20. From the bulletin announcing the schedule for the "Sarada Navarathri Mahotsavam" from September 19 to 29, 1990.

21. This schedule is derived from the announcement of the South Indian Bhajana Samajam. For discussion of the history and character of Rājarājeśvarī, see chapter 5, note 9.

22. Fuller and Logan, "*Navarāttiri* Festival," 92–94.

23. Ākos Östör, "Cyclical Time: Durgāpūjā in Bengal," in Madan, *Religion in India,* 178–79. Östör, of course, is describing the festival in a Bengali setting.

24. Ibid., 180.

25. From the announcement published by the Śaṅkara Maṭam.

26. From the announcement of "Navarathri Mahotsvam" of the Śrī Subrahmaṇia Samajam, July 20, 1990.

27. Conversation with an anonymous participant in September 20, 1990.

28. "Navarathri Mahotsavam."

29. From a conversation on September 20, 1990.

30. This particular altar, shaped like a heart, resonates with agricultural images of the goddess's form, including the *yoni* (womb-pedestal) in which offerings are made and the iconography of Lajjāgauri, the goddess on the haunches, genitalia exposed, who personified the fertility of the earth.

31. The description is based on observations and conversations from September 20 to 29, 1990.

32. From a conversation with Mr. Srinivasan, a vice president of the SIBS.

33. Gosha, *Durgā Pūjā.*

34. The agricultural roots of the Navarāttiri are clearly reflected here.

35. From a conversation with Mrs. Lekha Chandrakas Mehta on October 11, 1990.

36. Observed at the home of Mrs. Lakshmi Venkitesvaran on September 25, 1990.

37. M. Arunachalam, *Festivals of Tamil Nadu* (Tiruchitrambalam: Gandhi Vidyalayam, 1980), 142–46.

38. Fuller and Logan, "Navarātri Festival," 84–85.

39. From discussions held throughout my stay in Mumbai, 1990.

9. Trance and "Sacred Wounding"

This chapter results from observations I made in January 1991 during a research project in Malaysia and Singapore while a Fulbright Fellow. The writer is indebted especially to R. Rajoo and S. Singaravelu of the Department of Indian Studies of the University of Malaya and to several descriptions of Tai Pūcam published earlier by colleagues, especially Raymond Lee and Colleen Ward, writing on Tai Pūcam at Batu Caves in the 1980s; Alan Babb, writing on the festival in Singapore in the 1970s; and Elizabeth Collins, writing in the 1990s on what was observed in the 1980s in Penang. Collins's book *Pierced by Murugan's Lance: Ritual, Power, and Moral Redemption among Malaysian Hindus* (DeKalb: Northern Illinois University Press, 1997) is a particularly rich study of Tai Pūcam. Other valuable studies are two volumes by Carl Vadivella Belle, the first a privately published autobiography, *Towards Truth: An Australian Spiritual Journey* (C. V. Belle, 1992); the second a still unpublished dissertation, "Thai Pusam." The present essay merely offers a footnote to this earlier work.

1. *Role of Sri Maha Mariamman Temple Devasthanam in Malaysia* (booklet produced by the Śrī Mahāmāriyamman̲ Temple Devasthanam for the first Asia Pacific Hindu Conference in Singapore, April 1–8, 1988), 16.

2. Ibid., 2–3.

3. Ibid., 16.

4. From conversations with Dr. Thinnappan in Singapore, March 6, 1991.

5. S. Chandra Sekhar, *The Nagarathars of South India* (Madras: MacMillan India Press, 1980), 31, citing records (*pattyams*) of the Paḻaṉi devasthanam, dated between the seventeenth and nineteenth centuries.

6. Dr. Thinnappan in conversation, March 6, 1991.

7. Rudner, *Caste and Capitalism,* 135–37.

8. *Role of Sri Maha Mariamman Temple,* 5–6.

9. Ibid., 16.

10. Ibid., 17.

11. Ibid., 19.

12. Ibid., 20–21.

13. *Malay Mail,* January 26, 1991, 18–19.

14. Estimates were provided in a conversation with Mr. Cekaram, the chief clerk of the Māriyammaṉ Temple.

15. This brief description of the festival is based on observations made in 1991, and in significant measure, abbreviated from Raymond Lee's article "Thaipusam in Malaysia: Ecstasy and Identity in a Tamil Hindu Festival," *Contributions to Indian Sociology* 23, no. 2 (1989): 317–37.

16. Raymond Lee has described these offerings in greater detail (ibid., 323–25).

17. Frank Korom, *Hosay Trinidad: Muḥarram Performances in an Indo-Caribbean Diaspora* (Philadelphia: University of Pennsylvania Press, 2003), 7.

18. These descriptions are condensed from Lee, "Thaipusam in Malaysia," 328.

19. It may not be coincidental that the fasting associated with Ramaḍān in the Muslim majority community prohibits the ingestion of food or drink between sunrise and sunset.

20. Lee, "Thaipusam in Malaysia," 329.

21. Clifford Geertz, "Religion as a Cultural System," in *Reader in Comparative Religion: An Anthropological Approach,* ed. William A. Lessa and Evon Z. Vogt, 4th ed. (New York: Harper and Row, 1979), 83–84.

22. Peter Berger, *The Sacred Canopy: Elements of a Sociological Theory of Religion* (Garden City, N.Y.: Anchor Books, 1967), 23–28.

23. From an interview with a young shopkeeper in 1991.

24. Reported by Lee in "Thaipusam in Malaysia," 330.

25. From an interview with a college student, 1991.

26. Belle, *Towards Truth.*

27. Ackerman and Lee, *Sacred Tensions,* 104.

28. *Asiaweek,* March 30, 1990, 30.

29. *Sucked Oranges,* 19. These figures, for the year 1979, are taken from a graph derived from Yukio Ikemoto, "Income Distribution in Malaysia: 1957–1980," *Developing Economies* (1985): table 3.

30. Ibid., 2.

31. Ibid., 19.

32. Ibid., 4.

33. Ibid., 6–7.

34. Ibid., 9.

35. Ibid., 13–14.

36. See, for example, Ravindra K. Jain, *South Indians on the Plantation Frontier in Malaya* (New Haven, Conn.: Yale University Press, 1970); S. Arasaratnam, *Indians in Malaysia and Singapore* (Kuala Lumpur and New York: Oxford University Press, 1979); Paul Wiebe and S. Mariappen, *Indian Malaysians: The View from the Plantations* (Delhi: Manohar, 1978).

37. *Sucked Oranges,* 31, citing N. J. Colletta, "Family Background and Education of Children in a Malaysian Rubber Plantation: A Collection of Articles" (publication data not cited).

38. The yellow saris are variously interpreted by participants: "It is India's color"; "The god likes it"; "It is *parakkam*" (tradition). The symbolism of yellow gives to the female penitent the legitimation of the sadhus' saffron and provides links to the colors gold, red, and yellow common in the symbolic heritage of the sacrificial system and the worship of Murukaṉ (see Clothey, *The Many Faces of Murukaṉ* [The Hague: Mouton, 1978], 177–80).

39. Vignettes from the festival of 1991.

40. *Sucked Oranges,* citing C. Gamba, *The Origins of Trade Unionism in Malaysia: A Study in Colonial Unrest* (Singapore: Eastern University Press, 1962), 274, and Sandhu, *Indians in Malaya,* 245.

41. *Sucked Oranges,* 62.

42. Ibid., citing Gamba, *Origins of Trade Unionism,* 274.

43. Ibid., 65.

44. Ibid., 67–68, citing R. Kurian, *Women Workers in the Sri Lanka Plantation Sector: An Historical and Contemporary Analysis,* Women, Work, and Development 5 (Geneva: International Labour Office, 1982), 96.

45. Wiebe and Mariappen, *Indian Malaysians,* 71.

46. One such temple to Māriyammaṉ—that in Swamipuram in Tanjore District—was cited by more than one informant in Malaysia as having included *vēḷāḷa*s in its governance and brahmins as priests around the start of the nineteenth century.

47. Elizabeth Collins, "*Bhakti* Devotionalism and Class Consciousness: A Malaysian Case Study" (unpublished paper), 12, citing Jain, *South Indians,* 277.

48. Note that Kāḷiyammaṉ temples as well as those of attendant deities were also frequently built in Malaysia in the name of *piḷḷai*s who served as *kaṅkāni*s (foremen).

49. Jain, *South Indians,* 277.

50. *Role of Sri Maha Mariamman Temple,* 5–6.

51. Ibid., 9.

52. Swami Velu himself, though a *kaḷḷar,* has been active on the board of the Śrī Māriyammaṉ Temple. Cynics suggest his religious activity has been in inverse proportion to his popularity in the Indian community (i.e., the former goes up when the latter goes down) and, in any case, results from the fact that his wife is a *tēvar* (from a conversation with R. Rajoo).

53. From a tract distributed by the Rudra Devi Samaj, Tai Pūcam, 1991.

54. One hypothesis is that "keling" derived from the term "Kalinga," which referred to the southeastern coast of India and was those Indian merchants (Chettiyars?) who were operating in Malacca in the 1500s. Because of their alleged collaboration with the Portuguese, they were viewed with disdain (S. Singaravelu in a conversation). In the Chinese idiom, the term "keling qua" is said to mean "devil" (R. Rajoo in a conversation). Indeed, the term "tamin" in certain Thai dictionaries connotes a cruel or bloodthirsty person, a term said to be brought to Thailand by Sri Lankan Buddhist monks (S. Singaravelu in a conversation).

55. R. Rajoo in a conversation.

56. Discussed more extensively in Chandra Muzaffar, *Islamic Resurgence in Malaysia* (Petaling Jaya, Malay.: Penerbit Fajar Bakti Sdn. Bhd.), 1987.

57. This is the suggestion of Lawrence A. Babb, "Thai Pusam in Singapore: Religious Individualism in a Hierarchical Culture," Working Paper 49, Department of Sociology, University of Singapore at Chapmen, 9, citing A. J. A. Elliot, *Chinese Spirit-Medium Cults in Singapore* (London: Athlone Press, 1990).

58. Collins, *Pierced by Murugan's Lance,* 106–26.

59. Eugene d'Aquili, "Social Historians Entranced; or, The Medium Is the Message," in *Social History and Issues in Human Consciousness,* ed. Andrew E. Barnes and Peter N. Stearns (New York and London: New York University Press, 1989), 131. See E. G. d'Aquili, C. Laughlin Jr., and J. McManus, *The Spectrum of Ritual: A Biogenetic Structural Analysis* (New York: Columbia University Press, 1979); or C. D. Laughlin and E. G. d'Aquili, *Biogenetic Structuralism* (New York: Columbia University Press, 1974).

60. Barbara Lex, "The Neurobiology of Ritual Trance," in d'Aquili, Laughlin, and McManus, *Spectrum of Ritual,* 137, cited in Andrew E. Barnes, "Ces Sortes de Penitence Imaginaires: The Counter-Reformation Assault on Communitas," in Barnes and Stearns, *Social History,* 70.

61. These are Barbara Lex's terms, cited in Barnes, "Ces Sortes de Penitence Imaginaires," 68.

62. Colleen Ward, "Thaipusam in Malaysia," *Ethos* 12, no. 4 (Winter 1984): 309–10, citing A. M. Ludwig, "Altered States of Consciousness," *Archives of General Psychiatry* 15 (1996): 225–34.

63. Ibid., 311–12.

64. D'Aquili, "Social Historians Entranced," 130.

65. *Tamil Lexicon* (Madras: University of Madras, 1982), 3:1375.

66. Collins, *Pierced by Murugan's Lance,"* 200.

67. I am grateful to Dr. Balwant Dixit of the Department of Pharmacology, University of Pittsburgh, for this information. He distilled for me findings recorded in numerous publications, including R. Gosselin, R. P. Smith, and H. C. Hodge, *Clinical Toxicology of Commercial Products* (Baltimore: William and Wilkins, 1984); and M. J. Ellenhorn and D. G. Barceloux, *Medical Toxicology: Diagnosis and Treatment of Human Poisoning* (New York: Elsevier, 1988). Dr. Dixit reports that camphor is included in the mixture known as *pañcamīrta,* offered routinely to devotees as *pracāṭam* after ritual. He reports that he no longer ingests *pañcamīrta* because of what he knows about camphor.

68. Ward, "Thaipusam in Malaysia," citing Sheila S. Walker, *Ceremonial Spirit Possession in Africa and Afro-America* (Leiden: Brill, 1972).

69. Ibid., 311, citing E. Bourguinon, "Trance Dance," in *Highest States of Consciousness,* ed. J. White, 331–43 (Garden City, N.Y.: Doubleday, 1979); A. M. Ludwig and P. Veraer, "Trance and Convention in Nago-Yoruba Spirit Mediumship," in *Spirit Mediumship and Society in Africa,* ed. J. Beattie and J. Middleton, 50–66 (London; Routledge and Kegan Paul, 1969).

70. See, for example, *Tirumurukkāṟṟupaṭai,* 230, 280–90.

71. *Tamil Lexicon,* 3:1375.

72. Jain, *South Indians,* 135. Interestingly, the year in which Jain observed Tai Pūcam celebrated on one plantation (1963), there were four females and only one male penitent; none of these, however, went to Batu Caves or engaged in self-wounding.

73. The chief *paṇṭāram* at the Tank Road temple in Singapore claims his grandfather provided the lance that served as the first *mūrti* for the early Chettiyar worshippers there. Because

the Chettiyars (like some other workers) stayed only for three-year periods, and that without their wives and families, the lance represented this more mobile nature of the Indian sojourners' lifestyle.

74. Note, for example, the way the fifteenth-century Tamil poet Aruṇakiri evokes Murukaṉ's military imageries for spiritual intent in the context of Vijayanagar hegemony in a post-Islamic setting (see next chapter).

75. The use of the lance or *vēl* in worship is said to be sanctioned by its use in ancient Tamil culture. While it is true the lance was commonly linked symbolically to Murukaṉ in ancient times (see Clothey, *The Many Faces of Murukaṉ,* 33–34), I know of no evidence suggesting it was used to pierce the flesh of devotees in early Tamil society. However, there is evidence of various forms of self-immolation in medieval Śaivism, including decapitation and skewering of the abdomen and/or knees with swords wielded by "heroic" devotees (see R. Chandrasekhar Reddy, *Heros, Cults and Memorials: Andhra Pradesh, 300 A.D.–1600 A.D.* [Madras: New Era Publications, 1994], 130–43). Similarly, self-flagellation is to be found among certain folk or tribal peoples of contemporary Andhra Pradesh: in northern Andhra Pradesh, for example, priests of the shepherd community (Oggu Pujāris) are known to hit their stomachs with the tip of a spear when possessed. Similarly, the Goravas—a hill people of southern Andhra—pierced their knees with rods during an October festival (conversation with Nagarajan of the University of Hyderabad in 1998).

10. Singing on the Boundaries

Portions of this chapter are excerpted from the introduction to Clothey, *Quiescence and Passion: The Vision of Aruṇakiri, Tamil Mystic* (Bethesda, Md.: Austin and Winfield, 1996). It is reprinted here with the permission of the publisher.

1. From an interview with Mrs. Kalyani Raghavan Iyengar on July 25, 1990, and with Mr. G. Balasubrahmaniam on August 21, 1990, both in Chembur, Mumbai.

2. T. Arunachalam, *Tamil Hinduism* (Singapore: EVS Enterprises, 1953), 28.

3. This is taken from my more extended study of Aruṇakiri: *Quiescence and Passion.* The account is also found in Sadhu Anuāṉanda's essay "Arunagirinathar—Traditional View Challenged," *Indian Express,* November 26, 1970, 10–11. See also V. S. Cenkalvaraya Pillai, *Aruṇakirinata* (Madras: Liberty Press, 1947); and Kamil Zvelebil, "Arunagirinathar—Confessor of Beauty," *New Orient* 4, no. 5 (October 1965): 155–56.

4. For more extended discussion of Aruṇakiri's dates and work, the reader may turn to earlier studies by the author, especially *Quiescence and Passion* and "Some Aspects of Aruṇakiri's Significance for Tamil Bhakti," in *Śrinidhih: Perspectives in Indian Archeology, Art and Culture,* ed. Niharranjan Ray, et al., 261–66 (Madras: New Era Publications, 1983).

5. *Tiruppukaḻ Kāti Mati:* nātā rūpa mānāta rākut turaivōnē.

6. This is the claim, for example, of G. Balasubramanyam in "Adishankara and Shri Arunagirinathar," in *Tiruppukaḻ Karuvūlam* (Bangalore: Viḻakkuḻuviṉar, 1988), 6.

7. M. Shanmugham Pillai, "S. Arunagirinathar—His Life and Work," in *Bulletin of the Institute of Traditional Cultures* (Madras: University of Madras, 1975), 150.

8. Ibid., 148.

9. For a full discussion of Satchidananthan Swami's life and contributions, see my *Quiescence and Passion,* 32–34; and Sadhu Parthasarathy, "Life of Sri Vallimalai Satchidananthan," *Indian Express,* November 26, 1970, 10.

10. For fuller discussion, see my *Quiescence and Passion,* 35–36; and *Tiruppukal̲ Karuvūlum,* 11–12.

11. Singer, *Great Tradition,* 228.

12. Ibid., 232.

13. Also cited in Clothey, *Quiescence and Passion,* 12–13; all but the second quotation are from A. S. Krishna and an anonymous music teacher, interviewed in Chembur, Mumbai, in August 1990. The second quotation is from Mrs. Lakshmi Swaminathan, who ascribed the quote to her uncle who helped start Aruṇakiri *bhajan̲s* in New Delhi in 1958.

11. Conclusion

1. Fuglerud, *Life on the Outside,* 90–91.

2. Ibid., 91, citing P. Connerton, *How Societies Remember* (Cambridge: Cambridge University Press, 1991), 2.

3. Ibid., 78.

4. Ibid., 79, citing Val Daniel, "The Semiotics of Suicide in Sri Lanka," in *Semiotics, Self and Society,* ed. B. Lee and G. Urban (Berlin: Mouton de Gruyter, 1989), 78.

5. Chidester, "Colonialism," 433.

6. Roland Robertson, *Globalization: Social Theory and Global Culture* (London: Sage Publications, n.d.), 173.

7. David Chidester, "Colonialism," in *Guide to the Study of Religion,* ed. Will Braun and Russell T. McCutcheon (London and New York: Cassell, 2000), 434–35.

SELECTED BIBLIOGRAPHY

Books

Ackerman, Susan E., and Raymond L. M. Lee. *Heaven in Transition: Non-Muslim Religious Innovation and Ethnic Identity in Malaysia.* Honolulu: University of Hawaii Press, 1988.

———. *Sacred Tensions: Modernity and Religious Transformation in Malaysia.* Columbia: University of South Carolina Press, 1997.

Agarwal, Priya. *Passage from India: Post 1965 Indian Immigrants and Their Children.* Paolo Verdes, Calif.: Yuvati Publications, 1991.

Ahmad, Imitiaz, ed. *Ritual and Religion among Muslims in India.* New Delhi: Manohar Books, 1981.

Ampalavanar, R. *The Indian Minority and Political Change in Malaya, 1945–1957.* Kuala Lumpur: Oxford University Press, 1981.

Appadurai, Arjun. *Worship and Conflict under Colonial Rule: A South Indian Case.* Cambridge: Cambridge University Press, 1980.

Arasaratnam, S. *Indian Festivals in Malaya.* Kuala Lumpur: University of Malaya, 1966.

———. *Indians in Malaysia and Singapore.* Kuala Lumpur and New York: Oxford University Press, 1979.

Assayag, Jackie. *At the Confluence of Two Rivers: Muslims and Hindus in South India.* New Delhi: Manohar Books, 2004.

Barth, Fredrik, ed. *Ethnic Groups and Boundaries: The Social Organization of Culture Difference.* London: George Allen and Unwin, 1969.

Bayly, Susan. *Saints, Goddesses and Kings: Muslims and Christians in South Indian Society, 1700–1900.* Cambridge: Cambridge University Press, 1989.

Bell, Catherine. *Ritual: Perspectives and Dimensions.* New York: Oxford University Press, 1997.

———. *Ritual Theory, Ritual Practice.* New York: Oxford University Press, 1992.

Berreman, Gerald D. *Hindus of the Himalayas: Ethnography and Change.* 2nd ed. Berkeley: University of California Press, 1971.

Bloch, Maurice. *Ritual, History and Power: Selected Papers in Anthropology.* London: Athlone Press, 1989.

Bourguignon, Erika, ed. *Religion, Altered States of Consciousness and Social Change.* Columbus: Ohio State University Press, 1973.

Burghart, Richard, ed. *Hinduism in Great Britain: The Perpetuation of Religion in an Alien Cultural Milieu.* London: Tavistock, 1987.

Chandrasekhar, S., ed. *From India to America: A Brief History of Immigration, Problems of Discrimination, Admission and Assimilation.* La Jolla, Calif.: Population Review Publications, 1982.

Clarke, Colin, Ceri Peach, and Steven Vertovec, eds. *South Asians Overseas: Migrations and Ethnicity.* Cambridge: Cambridge University Press, 1990.

Clothey, Fred W. *Quiescence and Passion: The Vision of Aruṇakiri, Tamil Mystic.* Bethesda, Md.: Austin and Winfield, 1996.

———. *Rhythm and Intent: Ritual Studies from South India.* Madras: Blackie and Son, 1983.

Coedès, George. *The Indianized States of Southeast Asia.* Honolulu: East-West Center Press, 1968.

Collins, Elizabeth Fuller. *Pierced by Murugan's Lance: Ritual, Power and Moral Redemption among Malaysian Hindus.* DeKalb: Northern Illinois University Press, 1997.

Coward, Howard, John R. Hinnells, and Raymond B. Williams, eds. *The South Asian Religious Diaspora in Britain, Canada and the United States.* Albany: State University of New York Press, 2000.

Daniel, Valentine E. *Fluid Signs: Being a Person the Tamil Way.* Berkeley: University of California Press, 1984.

Daniels, Roger. *History of Indian Immigration to the United States: An Interpretive Essay.* New York: The Asia Society, 1989.

Dasgupta, Sathi S. *On the Trail of an Uncertain Dream: Indian Immigrant Experience in America.* New York: AMS Press, 1989.

Douglas, Mary. *Purity and Danger: An Analysis of Concepts of Pollution.* London: Routledge and Kegan Paul, 1970.

Fenton, John Y. *Transplanting Religious Traditions: Asian Indians in America.* New York: Praeger, 1988.

Fisher, Maxine P. *The Indians of New York City: A Study of Immigrants from India and Pakistan.* Columbia, Mo.: South Asia Books, 1980.

Fuglerud, Øivind. *Life on the Outside: The Tamil Diaspora and Long Distance Nationalism.* London and Sterling, Va.: Pluto Press, 1999.

Hardgrave, Robert L., Jr. *The Nadars of Tamil Nadu: The Political Culture of a Community in Change.* Berkeley: University of California Press, 1969.

Helweg, Arthur W., and Usha M. Helweg. *An Immigrant Success Story: East Indians in America.* Philadelphia: University of Pennsylvania Press, 1990.

Humphrey, Caroline, and James Laidlaw. *The Archetypal Action of Ritual.* Oxford, U.K.: Clarendon Press, 1994.

Irschick, Eugene. *Politics and Social Conflict in South India: The Non-Brahmin Movement and Tamil Separatism, 1916–1929.* Berkeley: University of California Press, 1969.

Jacobsen, Knut A., and Kumar P. Pratap. *South Asians in the Diaspora: Histories and Religious Traditions.* Leiden: Brill, 2004.

Jain, Ravindra K. *Indian Communities Abroad: Themes and Literature.* Delhi: Manohar, 1993.

———. *South Indians on the Plantation Frontier in Malaya.* New Haven, Conn.: Yale University Press, 1970.

Jenson, Jane. *Passage from India: Asian Indian Immigrants in North America.* New Haven, Conn.: Yale University Press, 1988.

Kitano, Harry H. L., and Roger Daniels. *Asian Americans: Emerging Minorities.* Englewood Cliffs, N.J.: Prentice Hall, 1988.

Kolm, Richard. *The Change of Cultural Identity: An Analysis of Factors Conditioning the Cultural Integration of Immigrants.* New York: Arno Press, 1980.

Kondapi, C. *Indians Overseas, 1838–1949.* Madras: Oxford University Press, 1951.

Kurian, George, and Ram P. Srivastava, eds. *Overseas Indians: A Study in Adaptation.* Dehli: Vikas, 1983.

Lewis, I. M. *Ecstatic Religion: An Anthropological Study of Spirit Possession and Shamanism.* 2nd ed. London and New York: Penguin, 1989.

Madan, T. N., ed. *Religion in India.* Delhi: Oxford University Press, 1991.

Manogaran, C., and B. Pfaffenberger, eds. *The Sri Lankan Tamils: Ethnicity and Identity.* Boulder, San Francisco, and Oxford, U.K.: Westview Press, 1994.

Melendy, Howard Brett. *Asians in America: Filipinos, Koreans and East Indians.* Boston: Twayne Publishers, 1977.

Muzaffar, Chandra. *Islamic Resurgence in Malaysia.* Petaling Jaya, Malay.: Penerbit Fajar Bakti Sdn. Bhd., 1987.

Pandey, Raj Bali. *Hindu Saṁskāras.* Delhi: Motilal Banarsidass, 1987.

Petievich, Carla, ed. *The Expanding Landscape: South Asians and the Diaspora.* New Delhi: Manohar Books, 1999.

Rajakrishnan, R. *Caste Consciousness among Indian Tamils in Malaysia.* Petaling Jaya, Malay.: Pelanduk, 1984.

Ramasamy, R. *Sojourners to Citizens: Sri Lanka Tamils in Malaysia, 1885–1965.* Kuala Lumpur: Sri Veera Trading, 1988.

Rayaprol, Aparna. *Negotiating Identities: Women in the Indian Diaspora.* Delhi: Oxford University Press, 1997.

Robertson, Roland. *Religion and Global Order.* New York: Paragon House, 1991.

Rudner, David West. *Caste and Capitalism in Colonial India: The Nattukottai Chettiars.* Berkeley: University of California Press, 1994.

Rukmani, T. S., ed. and trans. *Hindu Diaspora, Global Pespectives.* Montreal: Concordia University, 1999.

Ryan, N. J. *The Making of Modern Malaysia: A History from Earliest Times to 1966.* Kuala Lumpur: Oxford University Press, 1967.

Sandhu, K. S. *Indians in Malaya: Some Aspects of Their Immigration and Settlement, 1786–1957.* London: Cambridge University Press, 1969.

Sandhu, K. S., and A. Mani, eds. *Indian Communities in Southeast Asia.* Singapore: Times Academic Press, 1993.

Saran, Parmatma. *The Asian Indian Experience in the United States.* Cambridge, Mass.: Schenkman Publishing, 1985.

Saran, Parmatma, and Edwin Eames, eds. *The New Ethnics: Asian Indians in the United States.* New York: Praeger Publishers, 1980.

Schimmel, Annemarie. *Mystical Dimensions of Islam.* Leiden: Brill, 1980.

Sharma, Kalpana. *Rediscovering Dharavi.* New Delhi: Penguin Books, 2002.

Siddique, S., and N. Purushotam. *Singapore's Little India: Past, Present and Future.* Singapore: Institute for Southeast Asian Studies, 1990.

Singer, Milton. *When a Great Tradition Modernizes: An Anthropological Approach to Indian Civilization.* New York: Frederick A. Praeger, 1972.

Singh, I. J. Bahadur, ed. *The Other India: The Overseas Indians and Their Relationship with India.* New Delhi: Arnold-Heinemann, 1979.

Singh, Jane, ed. *South Asians in North America: An Annotated and Selected Bibliography.* Berkeley: CSSEAS Publications, 1988.

Smith, Jonathan Z. *To Take Place: Toward Theory in Ritual.* Chicago: University of Chicago Press, 1992.

Stein, Burton. *Peasant State and Society in Medieval South India.* Delhi: Oxford University Press, 1980.

———, ed. *South Indian Temples.* New Delhi: Vilkas Publishing House PVT, 1978.

Sucked Oranges: The Indian Poor in Malaysia. Kuala Lumpur: Institute for Social Analysis, 1989.

Templeman, Dennis. *The Northern Nadars of Tamil Nadu: An Indian Caste in the Process of Change.* Delhi: Oxford University Press, 1996.

Thomas, Chris D. *Diaspora Indians: Church Growth among Indians in West Malaysia.* Penang: Malaysia Indian Evangelist Council, 1978.

Thomas, W. M. *Hinduism Invades America.* New York: Beacon Press, 1930.

Thurston, Edgar. *Castes and Tribes of Southern India.* 7 vols. Madras: Government Press, 1909; New Delhi: Asian Educational Services, 1993.

Tinker, Hugh. *The Banyan Tree: Overseas Emigrants from India, Pakistan and Bangladesh.* Oxford: Oxford University Press, 1977.

Turner, Victor. *Ritual Process: Structure and Anti-structure.* New York: Aldine, 1997.

Van der Veer, Peter. *Religious Nationalism: Hindus and Muslims in India.* Berkeley: University of California Press, 1994.

———, ed. *Nation and Migration: The Politics of Space in the South Asian Diaspora.* Philadelphia: University of Pennsylvania Press, 1995.

Von der Mehden, Fred R., ed. *The Ethnic Groups of Houston.* Houston: Rice University Studies, 1984.

Waghorne, Joanne P. *Diaspora of the Gods: Modern Hindu Temples in an Urban Middle Class World.* New York: Oxford University Press, 2004.

Wales, H. G. Q. *The Malay Peninsula in Hindu Times.* London: Bernard Quaritch, 1976.

———. *Prehistory and Religion in Southeast Asia.* London: Bernard Quaritch, 1957.

Waters, O. W. *The Fall of Srivijaya.* Kuala Lumpur: Oxford University Press, 1970.

Weber, Max. *The Sociology of Religion.* Boston: Beacon Press, 1963.

Welbon, Guy R., and Glenn E. Yocum, eds. *Religious Festivals in South India and Sri Lanka.* New Delhi: Manohar Books, 1982.

Wheatley, Paul. *The Golden Khersonese: Studies in the Historical Geography of the Malay Peninsula before A.D. 1500.* Westport, Conn.: Greenwood Press, 1973.

Wiebe, Paul, and S. Mariappen. *Indian Malaysians: The View from the Plantations.* Delhi: Manohar, 1978.

Williams, Raymond. *Religions of Immigrants from India and Pakistan: New Threads in the American Tapestry.* Cambridge: Cambridge University Press, 1988.

———, ed. *A Sacred Thread: Modern Transmission of Hindu Traditions in India and Abroad.* Chambersburg, Pa.: Anima Press, 1992.

Williams, Ron G., and James W. Boyd. *Ritual Art and Knowledge.* Columbia: University of South Carolina Press, 1993.

Xenos, Peter, Herbert Barrings, and Michael J. Levin. *Asian Indians in the United States: A 1980 Census Profile.* Honolulu: East-West Center Press, 1989.

Younger, Paul. *Playing Host to Deity: Festival Religion in the South Indian Tradition.* New York: Oxford University Press, 2002.

Zachariah, K. C. *Migrants in Greater Bombay.* Bombay: Asia Publishing House, 1968.

Theses, Dissertations, and Papers

Babb, Lawrence A. "Thai Pusam in Singapore: Religious Individualism in a Hierarchical Culture." Working Paper 49, Department of Sociology, University of Singapore at Chapmen.

Belle, Carl Vadivella. "Thai Pusam in Malaysia: A Hindu Festival Misunderstood?" Ph.D. diss., Deakin University, 2004.

Bhutani, Shalini Dev. "A Study of Asian Indian Women in the United States: The Reconceptualization of Self." Ph.D. diss., University of Pennsylvania, 1994.

Joshi, Khyati. "Patterns and Paths: Ethnic Identity Development in Second Generation Indian Americans." Ph.D. diss., University of Massachusetts, 2001.

LaBrack, Bruce. "The East Indian Experience in America." Unpublished manuscript, 1975.

Macchiawalla, Tasqeen. "A Sense of Belonging: A Study at the Muslim Community Center of Greater Pittsburgh." Master's thesis, University of Pittsburgh, 1990.

Mody, Niloufer. "The Development of Ego Identity and Ethnic Identity in Asian Indian Adolescents Living in America." Ph.D. diss., California School of Professional Psychology at Fresno, 1994.

Pettys, Gregory Lee. "Asian Indians in the United States: An Analysis of Identity Formation and Retention." Ph.D. diss., University of Illinois at Champaign-Urbana, 1994.

Rajoo, R. "Politics, Ethnicity and Strategies of Adaptation in an Urban Indian Squatting Settlement in Peninsular Malaysia." Ph.D. diss., University of Malaya at Kuala Lumpur, 1985.

Sinha, Vineeta. "Hinduism in Singapore: A Sociological and Ethnographic Perspective." Master's thesis, Singapore National University, 1987.

Underwood, Kelsey Clark. "Negotiating Tamil Identity in India and the United States." Ph.D. diss., University of California at Berkeley, 1986.

Articles

Berreman, Gerald D. "Bizarre Behavior: Social Identity and Social Interaction in Urban India." In *Ethnic Identity: Cultural Continuities and Change,* edited by George De Vos and Lola Romanucci-Ross. Palo Alto, Calif.: Mayfield Publishing, 1975.

Chidester, David. "Colonialism." In *Guide to the Study of Religion,* edited by Will Braun and Russell T. McCutcheon, 423–37. London and New York: Cassell, 2000.

Clothey, Fred W. "Toward a Comprehensive Interpretation of Ritual." *Journal of Ritual Studies* 2 (Summer 1988): 147–61.

D'Aquili, Eugene G., and Andrew B. Newberg. "Liminality, Trance and Unitary States in Ritual and Meditation." *Studia Liturgica* 23, no. 1 (1993): 2–34.

Fanselow, Frank S. "Muslim Society in Tamil Nadu (India): An Historical Perspective." *Journal of the Institute of Muslim Minority Affairs* 10, no. 1 (1989): 264–89.

Fuller, C. J., and Penny Logan. "The Navarāttiri Festival in Madurai." *Bulletin of the School of Oriental and African Studies* 48, part 1 (1985): 79–105.

Geertz, Clifford. "Religion as a Cultural System." In *Reader in Comparative Religion: An Anthropological Approach,* edited by William A. Lessa and Evon Z. Vogt, 78–88. 4th ed. New York: Harper and Row, 1979.

Knott, Kim. "Hindu Temple Rituals in Britain: The Reinterpretation of Tradition." In *Hinduism in Great Britain: The Perpetuation of Religion in an Alien Cultural Milieu,* edited by Richard Burghart, 157–79. London: Tavistock Publications, 1987.

Lee, Raymond. "Thaipusam in Malaysia: Ecstasy and Identity in a Tamil Hindu Festival." *Contributions to Indian Sociology* 23, no. 2 (1989): 317–37.

Mani, A. "Aspects of Identity and Change among Tamil Muslims in Singapore." *Journal of the Institute of Muslim Minority Affairs* 13, no. 2 (1992): 337–57.

Mathur, S. S. "Indian Families in U.S.A. and the Problem of Rearing Children." In *Indians Overseas: A Research Publication, Seminar Papers,* edited by Syed Ashfaq, 38–43. Bhopal, India: Jai Bharat Publishing House, 1984.

McGilvray, Dennis B. "Arabs, Moors, and Muslims: Sri Lankan Muslim Ethnicity in Regional Perspective." *Contributions to Indian Sociology* 32, no. 2 (1999): 433–83.

Miller, Barbara D. "Precepts and Practices: Researching Identity Formation and Indian Hindu Adolescents in the United States." In *Cultural Practices as Contexts for Development: New Directions for Child Development,* edited by Jacqueline J. Goodenow et al., 71–85. San Francisco: Jossey-Bass, 1995.

Naidoo, Josephine C. "Contemporary South Asian Women in the Canadian Mosaic." *International Journal of Women's Studies* 8, no. 4 (1985): 338–50.

Platvoet, Jan. "Ritual as Confrontation: The Ayodhya Conflict." In *Pluralism and Identity: Studies in Ritual Behavior,* edited by Jan Platvoet and K. van der Toorn, 185–226. Leiden: Brill, 1995.

Rahim, M. Abdul. "The *Dargah* of Nagore and the Culture of the Tamil Muslims." In *The Bulletin of the Institute of Traditional Cultures,* 93–111. Madras: University of Madras Press, 1973.

Waghorne, Joanne Punzo. "The Diaspora of the Gods: Hindu Temples in the New World System, 1640–1800." *Journal of Asian Studies* 58, no. 3 (August 1999): 648–86.

Ward, Colleen. "Thaipusam in Malaysia: A Psycho-Anthropological Analysis of Ritual Trance, Ceremonial Possession and Self-Mortification Practices." *Ethos* 12 (1984): 307–34.

INDEX

ABOUT THE AUTHOR

FRED W. CLOTHEY, professor emeritus of religious studies, has taught at the University of Pittsburgh for more than thirty years and also served as chair of its Department of Religious Studies. A founder of the *Journal of Ritual Studies,* he has produced and directed six documentary films on ritual and has written or edited seven books, including *Rhythm and Intent: Ritual Studies from South India* and *The Many Faces of Murukan.* Clothey has been a visiting professor at Charles University in Prague, the University of Hyderabad, and West Virginia University. He is the recipient of four Fulbright grants and four fellowships of the American Institute of Indian Studies. Clothey resides in Pittsburgh.